Communications in Computer and Information Science   1829

Rationale

The CCIS series is devoted to the publication of proceedings of computer science conferences. Its aim is to efficiently disseminate original research results in informatics in printed and electronic form. While the focus is on publication of peer-reviewed full papers presenting mature work, inclusion of reviewed short papers reporting on work in progress is welcome, too. Besides globally relevant meetings with internationally representative program committees guaranteeing a strict peer-reviewing and paper selection process, conferences run by societies or of high regional or national relevance are also considered for publication.

Topics

The topical scope of CCIS spans the entire spectrum of informatics ranging from foundational topics in the theory of computing to information and communications science and technology and a broad variety of interdisciplinary application fields.

Information for Volume Editors and Authors

Publication in CCIS is free of charge. No royalties are paid, however, we offer registered conference participants temporary free access to the online version of the conference proceedings on SpringerLink (http://link.springer.com) by means of an http referrer from the conference website and/or a number of complimentary printed copies, as specified in the official acceptance email of the event.

CCIS proceedings can be published in time for distribution at conferences or as post-proceedings, and delivered in the form of printed books and/or electronically as USBs and/or e-content licenses for accessing proceedings at SpringerLink. Furthermore, CCIS proceedings are included in the CCIS electronic book series hosted in the SpringerLink digital library at http://link.springer.com/bookseries/7899. Conferences publishing in CCIS are allowed to use Online Conference Service (OCS) for managing the whole proceedings lifecycle (from submission and reviewing to preparing for publication) free of charge.

Publication process

The language of publication is exclusively English. Authors publishing in CCIS have to sign the Springer CCIS copyright transfer form, however, they are free to use their material published in CCIS for substantially changed, more elaborate subsequent publications elsewhere. For the preparation of the camera-ready papers/files, authors have to strictly adhere to the Springer CCIS Authors' Instructions and are strongly encouraged to use the CCIS LaTeX style files or templates.

Abstracting/Indexing

CCIS is abstracted/indexed in DBLP, Google Scholar, EI-Compendex, Mathematical Reviews, SCImago, Scopus. CCIS volumes are also submitted for the inclusion in ISI Proceedings.

How to start

To start the evaluation of your proposal for inclusion in the CCIS series, please send an e-mail to ccis@springer.com.

Hermann Kaindl · Mike Mannion ·
Leszek A. Maciaszek
Editors

Evaluation of Novel Approaches to Software Engineering

17th International Conference, ENASE 2022
Virtual Event, April 25–26, 2022
Revised Selected Papers

 Springer

Editors
Hermann Kaindl
TU Wien
Vienna, Austria

Mike Mannion
Glasgow Caledonian University
Glasgow, UK

Leszek A. Maciaszek
Wroclaw University of Economics
Wroclaw, Poland

ISSN 1865-0929   ISSN 1865-0937 (electronic)
Communications in Computer and Information Science
ISBN 978-3-031-36596-6   ISBN 978-3-031-36597-3 (eBook)
https://doi.org/10.1007/978-3-031-36597-3

This Springer imprint is published by the registered company Springer Nature Switzerland AG
The registered company address is: Gewerbestrasse 11, 6330 Cham, Switzerland

Preface

The present book includes extended and revised versions of a set of selected papers from the 17th International Conference on Evaluation of Novel Approaches to Software Engineering (ENASE 2022), which was exceptionally held as an online event, due to COVID-19, from 25–26 April.

ENASE 2022 received 109 paper submissions from 35 countries, of which 14% were included in this book.

The papers were selected by the event chairs and their selection is based on a number of criteria that include the classifications and comments provided by the program committee members, the session chairs' assessment and also the program chairs' global view of all papers included in the technical program. The authors of selected papers were then invited to submit a revised and extended version of their papers having at least 30% innovative material.

The mission of ENASE (Evaluation of Novel Approaches to Software Engineering) is to be a prime international forum to discuss and publish research findings and IT industry experiences with relation to novel approaches to software engineering. The conference acknowledges evolution in systems and software thinking due to contemporary shifts of the computing paradigm to e-services, cloud computing, mobile connectivity, business processes, and societal participation. By publishing the latest research on novel approaches to software engineering and by evaluating them against systems and software quality criteria, ENASE conferences advance knowledge and research in software engineering, including and emphasizing service-oriented, business-process driven, and ubiquitous mobile computing. ENASE aims at identifying the most promising trends and proposing new directions for consideration by researchers and practitioners involved in large-scale systems and software development, integration, deployment, delivery, maintenance, and evolution.

The papers selected to be included in this book contribute to the understanding of relevant trends of current research on Evaluation of Novel Approaches to Software Engineering, including: Software Project Management, Collaborative Software Engineering, Sustainable Software Development, Secure Software Systems Modelling, Data Lake Management, Software Metrics, Software and Service Maintenance and Evolution, User-Centred Software Engineering, and Software Execution Modelling.

We would like to thank all the authors for their contributions and also the reviewers who have helped to ensure the quality of this publication.

April 2022

Hermann Kaindl
Mike Mannion
Leszek Maciaszek

Organization

Conference Chair

Leszek Maciaszek — Macquarie University, Australia and Wroclaw University of Economics and Business, Poland

Program Co-chairs

Hermann Kaindl — TU Wien, University for Continuing Education Krems, Wiener Neustadt / Vienna University of Economics and Business, Austria

Mike Mannion — Glasgow Caledonian University, UK

Program Committee

Wasif Afzal	MDH, Sweden
Faheem Ahmed	Thompson Rivers University, Canada
Mehmet Aksit	University of Twente, The Netherlands
Issa Atoum	World Islamic Sciences and Education University, Jordan
Marco Autili	University of L'Aquila, Italy
Ellen Barbosa	University of São Paulo, Brazil
Iuliana Bocicor	Babes-Bolyai University, Romania
Ahmet Cakir	Ergonomic Institute for Social and Occupational Sciences Research, Germany
Anis Charfi	Carnegie Mellon University, Qatar
Dickson K. W. Chiu	University of Hong Kong, China
Guglielmo De Angelis	IASI-CNR, Italy
Fatma Dhaou	Faculty of Sciences of Tunis, Tunisia
Vladimir Estivill	Universitat Pompeu Fabra, Spain
Anna Rita Fasolino	Federico II University of Naples, Italy
Massimo Ficco	University of Salerno, Italy
Tarik Fissaa	INPT, Morocco
Stéphane Galland	Université de Technologie de Belfort Montbéliard, France
José Garcia-Alonso	Universidad de Extremadura, Spain

José-María Gutiérrez-Martínez	Universidad de Alcalá, Spain
Hatim Hafiddi	INPT, Morocco
Ralph Hoch	TU Wien, Austria
Akos Horvath	IncQuery Labs, Hungary
Geylani Kardas	Ege University, Turkey
Osama Khaled	American University in Cairo, Egypt
Siau-cheng Khoo	National University of Singapore, Singapore
Diana Kirk	University of Auckland, New Zealand
Piotr Kosiuczenko	Military University of Technology, Poland
Horst Lichter	RWTH Aachen University, Germany
Jorge López	Airbus, France
Ivan Lukovic	University of Belgrade, Serbia
Lech Madeyski	Wroclaw University of Science and Technology, Poland
Nazim Madhavji	University of Western Ontario, Canada
Tomi Männistö	University of Helsinki, Finland
Patricia Martin-Rodilla	University of A Coruña, Spain
Francesco Mercaldo	National Research Council of Italy (CNR), Italy
Arthur-Jozsef Molnar	Babes-Bolyai University, Romania
Ines Mouakher	Faculty of Sciences of Tunis, University of Tunis El Manar, Tunisia
Malcolm Munro	Durham University, UK
Janis Osis	Riga Technical University, Latvia
Mourad Oussalah	University of Nantes, France
Ricardo Pérez-Castillo	University of Castilla-La Mancha, Spain
Dana Petcu	West University of Timişoara, Romania
Kai Petersen	Blekinge Institute of Technology, Sweden
Deepika Prakash	NIIT University, India
Adam Przybylek	Gdansk University of Technology, Poland
Elke Pulvermüller	Osnabrück University, Germany
Ricardo Rabelo	Federal University of Santa Catarina, Brazil
Lukasz Radlinski	West Pomeranian University of Technology in Szczecin, Poland
Filippo Ricca	University of Genoa, Italy
Philippe Roose	University of Pau, France
Otto-von-Guericke	University Magdeburg, Germany
Gwen Salaün	Grenoble INP, Inria, France
Rainer Schmidt	Munich University of Applied Sciences, Germany
Camelia Serban	Babes-Bolyai University, Romania
Richa Sharma	Lock Haven University, USA
Josep Silva	Universitat Politècnica de València, Spain
Riccardo Sisto	Polytechnic University of Turin, Italy

Ioana Sora	Politehnica University of Timisoara, Romania
Andreas Speck	Christian-Albrechts-University Kiel, Germany
Maria Spichkova	RMIT University, Australia
Witold Staniszkis	Intelligent Document Engineering, Poland
Jakub Swacha	University of Szczecin, Poland
Gary Tan	Penn State University, USA
Stephanie Teufel	University of Fribourg, Switzerland
Francesco Tiezzi	University of Camerino, Italy
Hanh Nhi Tran	University of Toulouse, France
Christos Troussas	University of West Attica, Greece
Andreea Vescan	Babes-Bolyai University, Romania
Bernhard Westfechtel	University of Bayreuth, Germany
Martin Wirsing	Ludwig-Maximilians-Universität München, Germany
Igor Wojnicki	AGH University of Science and Technology, Poland
Sebastian Wrede	Bielefeld University, Germany
Dinghao Wu	Penn State University, USA
Jifeng Xuan	Wuhan University, China
Nina Yevtushenko	Ivannikov Institute for System Programming of the Russian Academy of Sciences, Russian Federation

Additional Reviewers

Natalia Kushik	Télécom SudParis, France
Erick Petersen	Télécom SudParis, Institut Polytechnique de Paris, France
Naveen Prakash	ICLC, India
Johannes Schröpfer	University of Bayreuth, Germany
Quang Trung Ta	National University of Singapore, Singapore
Fanlong Zhang	Guangdong University of Technology, China

Invited Speakers

Davor Svetinovic	Vienna University of Economics and Business, Austria
Brian Fitzgerald	University of Limerick, Ireland
Birgit Penzenstadler	Chalmers University of Technology, Sweden

Contents

Systems and Software Quality

Theory and Practice of Systems and Applications Development

An Approach-Based on Allen's Interval Algebra to Provision Resources for Disrupted Business Processes

Zakaria Maamar[1]([✉]) [ID], Fadwa Yahya[2] [ID], and Lassaad Ben Ammar[2] [ID]

[1] Zayed University, Dubai, UAE
zakaria.maamar@zu.ac.ae
[2] Prince Sattam Bin Abdulaziz University, Al kharj, Kingdom of Saudi Arabia
{ff.yahya,l.benammarg}@psau.edu.sa

Abstract. This paper presents an approach that provisions resources to a set of business processes' tasks for consumption at run-time. However, it happens that these tasks are disrupted by other urgent tasks that require immediate resource provisioning. Besides resources' consumption properties like limited and shareable, and tasks' transactional properties like pivot and retriable, disruptions make tasks suspend their ongoing execution, so they release their resources to the disrupting tasks that now need to be executed. These resources were initially assigned to what is now referred to as disrupted tasks. To consider the intrinsic characteristics of the consumption properties, transactional properties, and disruptions when resources are provisioned to disrupted/disrupting tasks, the approach adopts Allen's interval algebra to ensure a free-of-conflict consumption of resources. A system demonstrating the technical doability of the approach based on a case study about loan applications and a real dataset is presented in the paper, as well.

Keywords: Allen's interval algebra · Business process · Disruption · Resource

1 Introduction

Commonly called organizations' *know-how*, a Business Process (BP) *"is a set of activities that are performed in coordination in an organizational and technical environment. These activities jointly realize a business goal"* [18]. A BP has a process model that is a chronology of tasks (or activities) specified using a dedicated language like Business Process Model and Notation (BPMN) [13] and then, executed on top of a Business Process Management System (BPMS). Prior to executing a BP's tasks, its owner could have a say on the expected outcomes. For instance, one owner could insist that some tasks must succeed regardless of technical obstacles while the rest of tasks could either fail or be undone despite the successful execution. All these options from which a BP's owner can select are framed using pivot, retriable, and compensatable transactional properties [10].

In addition to defining who does what, where, when, and why, a process model is also concerned with resources like personnel and equipment that its respective BP's

ⓒ The Author(s), under exclusive license to Springer Nature Switzerland AG 2023
H. Kaindl et al. (Eds.): ENASE 2022, CCIS 1829, pp. 3–19, 2023.
https://doi.org/10.1007/978-3-031-36597-3_1

tasks will "consume/need" at run-time. Contrarily to what some assume about resource abundance, we argue the opposite. Some resources are limited (e.g., 2 h to complete a transaction), limited-but-extensible (e.g., 2-week validity for an access permit that can be renewed for another week), and not-shareable (e.g., a delivery truck is booked between 8am and 9am). We capture resources' characteristics using unlimited, limited, limited-but-extensible, shareable, and non-shareable consumption properties [11].

In a previous work [12], we looked from a temporal perspective into the impact of resources' consumption properties on tasks' transactional properties by addressing concerns like how could a limited resource accommodate a retriable task knowing that this resource could become unavailable after a certain number of necessary execution retrials of this task, and how could a limited-but-extensible resource accommodate a compensatable task knowing that extending this resource would be required to support the undoing of the task. In a nutshell, we blended time with consumption properties resulting into the definition of resource's availability-time interval. Then, we blended time with transactional properties resulting into the definition of task's consumption-time interval. Finally, we resorted to Allen's interval algebra, [2], to identify relations (e.g., equals and overlaps) between availability-time interval and consumption-time interval. Based on these relations, we recommended to BP engineers and resource owners what to do when for instance, a task's consumption-time interval overlaps with a resource's availability-time interval, a task's consumption-time interval is during a resource's availability-time interval, a task's consumption-time interval and a resource's availability-time interval start at the same time, etc. Despite the benefits of our recommendations, they fell short of handling disruptions that could impact the effective consumption of resources by tasks at run-time. Ad-hoc events like urgent system upgrade to counter a cyber-attack and urgent demand to execute a last-minute task, disrupt the ongoing consumption of resources. Gartner relates digital disruption to organizations adopting new Information and Communication Technologies (ICTs) as "*an effect that changes the fundamental expectations and behaviors in a culture, market, industry or process that is caused by, or expressed through, digital capabilities, channels or assets*"[1]. Typically, disruption means suspending an ongoing task's execution, initiating the disrupting task's execution, and resuming the suspended task's execution without missing deadlines, for example. How to handle ad-hoc events with minimal impact on under-consumed resources and how to get under-consumed resources ready for such events since some are not always available and not even ready to accommodate these changes? These are examples of questions that we address in this paper by extending the work we report in [12] on task/resource time-based coordinated consumption.

On top of our initial contributions namely, (*i*) temporal analysis of consumption and transactional properties, (*ii*) illustration of how resources' availability times are adjusted to accommodate tasks' transactional properties, (*iii*) identification of Allen's time relations between consumption-time and availability-time intervals, and (*iv*) development of a system allowing to reason over the identified Allen's time relations, the new contributions include (*v*) identification of disruption types, (*vi*) temporal analysis of disruption impact on consumption-time and availability-time intervals, and (*vii*) extension of the system handling disruptions during the on-going consumption of resources. The rest of

---

[1] https://www.gartner.com/en/information-technology/glossary/digital-disruption.

this paper is organized as follows. Section 2 discusses disruption in the context of BPs. Section 3 defines some concepts deemed necessary for understanding the coordination approach for resource consumption. Prior to detailing this approach in Sect. 5, a case study is presented in Sect. 4. Implementation details and experiments are reported in Sect. 6. Finally, concluding remarks and future work are presented in Sect. 7.

2   Disruption in the Business-Process Literature

In [12], our related-work exercise focused on resource allocation to BPs' tasks with some approaches and techniques reported in [1, 4, 16] and [19]. In this part of the paper, we present some related works on the impact of disruptions on BP continuity as well as resource consumption.

In [3], Ayoub and Elgammal propose a social BPM monitoring framework to discover, diagnose, and react to customer relationship management BP's disruptions defined as any event that undermines a customer's satisfaction in the delivery and/or completion of a specific service that a provider offers. The framework proposes preventive/corrective actions to avoid/minimize the consequences of disruptions using data mining and machine learning techniques.

In [6], Fernández el al. present a framework to model and simulate the supply process monitoring, so that disruptive events are detected and predicted. These events produce negative effects and hence, affected schedules should be fixed, for example. The authors developed a Web service that organizations could use to develop discrete event-based simulation models of monitoring processes so these organizations can evaluate their readiness to detect and anticipate disruptive events.

In [14], Paul et al. discuss disruption types like equipment breakdown and raw material shortage that could impact supply chain BPs. To address these disruption, 3 strategies are put forward allowing to mitigate disruption risks before they actually occur, to implement recovery actions after disruptions occurred, and to accept the disruption risks without any action when the previous strategies outweigh their potential advantages.

In [15], Petzold et al. show that the development of disruptive technologies and their integration into BPs characterize disruptiveness. They conceptualize the disruptive innovation introduced by entrants and considered as a threat by incumbents as being shaped by the continued interplay of the entrants' actions, the incumbents' (re-)actions, and the events within the external environment. Petzold et al. conclude that these actions and events shape the entrant's path.

In [17], Thorisson et al. mitigate potential sources of risks that could disrupt vessel scheduling BPs in maritime ports. To mitigate disruptions, the authors extended a graphical process modelling language called Integrated Definition (IDEF) with new elements namely, source of risks (e.g., higher container volume) and potential of disruption (e.g., service cancellation and slow down of operation). In IDEF, BP tasks like berth allocation are described with 4 elements: *input* referring to artefacts (e.g., service contracts) that an activity transforms into *output* (e.g., schedule), *control* referring to conditions (e.g., service requirements) to satisfy to produce correct output, and *mechanism* referring to means (e.g., optimization and simulation) used to perform an activity.

Although the works above offer a glimpse of the large body of research on disruptions and BPs, they all acknowledge the impact that disruptions could have on BPs.

Some works like [3] and [17] suggest recovery and mitigation strategies at run-time, while others like [8] and [15] discuss how to benefit from these disruptions. Our work is different; we establish a coordinated approach between disrupted and disrupting tasks of BPs, so that resource provisioning and thus, consumption is ensured to both. The approach taps into Allen's interval algebra to suggest the actions to take in response to both disruptions and time intervals that frame this consumption.

3 Definitions

This section presents 3 concepts deemed necessary for defining the coordination approach for resource provisioning to BPs. These concepts are consumption properties of resources, transactional properties of tasks, and Allen's interval algebra. Some diagrams are included for illustration purposes.

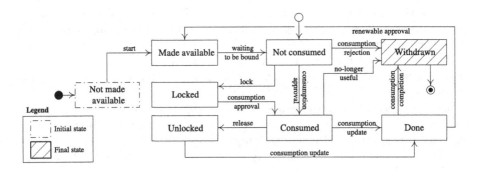

Fig. 1. Representation of a resource's multiple consumption cycles ([11]).

Consumption Properties of Resources. In compliance with our previous work on social coordination of BPs [11], the consumption properties of a resource ($\mathcal{R}$) could be unlimited (u), shareable (s), limited (l), limited-but-extensible (lx), and non-shareable (ns). A resource is limited when its consumption is restricted to an agreed-upon period of time (also quantity but is not considered). A resource is limited-but-extensible when its consumption continues to happen after extending the (initial) agreed-upon period of time. Finally, a resource is non-shareable when its concurrent consumption needs to be coordinated (e.g., one at a time). Unless stated, a resource is by default unlimited and/or shareable. The consumption cycles (cc) of the 5 properties are presented in Fig. 1 but, only, 2 consumption cycles are listed below:

1. Unlimited Property:
   - $\mathcal{R}.cc_{ul}$: not-made-available $\xrightarrow{start}$ made available $\xrightarrow{waiting-to-be-bound}$ not-consumed $\xrightarrow{consumption-approval}$ consumed $\xrightarrow{no-longer-useful}$ withdrawn.
2. Limited Property:

- $\mathcal{R}.cc_{l_1}$: not-made-available $\xrightarrow{start}$ made available $\xrightarrow{waiting-to-be-bound}$ not-consumed $\xrightarrow{consumption-approval}$ consumed $\xrightarrow{consumption-update}$ done $\xrightarrow{consumption-completion}$ withdrawn. The transition from done to withdrawn shields a resource from any new or additional tentative of consumption by consumers after completing a consumption cycle.

- $\mathcal{R}.cc_{l_2}$: not-made-available $\xrightarrow{start}$ made available $\xrightarrow{waiting-to-be-bound}$ not-consumed $\xrightarrow{consumption\ rejection}$ withdrawn. The transition from not-consumed to withdrawn shields a resource from any new or additional tentative of consumption by consumers in response to temporal constraints like expiry date.

Transactional Properties of Tasks. Many definitions of transactional properties of a BP's tasks are reported in the literature for instance, [7] and [10]. A task ($\mathcal{T}$) is pivot (p) when the outcomes of its successful execution remain unchanged forever and cannot be semantically undone. Should this execution fail, then it will not be retried. A task is compensatable (c) when the outcomes of its successful execution can be semantically undone. Like with pivot, should this execution fail, then it will not be retried. Finally, a task is retriable (r) when its successful execution is guaranteed to happen after multiple activations bound to a threshold ($\mathcal{TH}$). It happens that a task is both compensatable and retriable. The transactional cycles (tc) of the 3 properties are presented in Fig. 2 and listed below:

1. Pivot property:
   - $\mathcal{T}.tc_p^1$: not-activated $\xrightarrow{start}$ activated $\xrightarrow{commitment}$ done.
   - $\mathcal{T}.tc_p^2$: not-activated $\xrightarrow{start}$ activated $\xrightarrow{failure}$ failed.
2. Retriable property:
   - $\mathcal{T}.tc_r^1$: not-activated $\xrightarrow{start}$ activated $0[\xrightarrow{failure}$ failed $\xrightarrow{retrial}$ activated]$* \xrightarrow{commitment}$ done.
3. Compensatable property:
   - $\mathcal{T}.tc_c^1$: not-activated $\xrightarrow{start}$ activated $\xrightarrow{commitment}$ done.
   - $\mathcal{T}.tc_c^2$: not-activated $\xrightarrow{start}$ activated $\xrightarrow{failure}$ failed.
   - $\mathcal{T}.tc_c^3$: not-activated $\xrightarrow{start}$ activated $\xrightarrow{commitment}$ done $\xrightarrow{compensation}$ compensated.

Allen's Interval Algebra. Table 1 presents some potential relations (in fact, there exist 13) between time intervals, i.e., pairs of endpoints, allowing to support multiple forms of temporal reasoning in terms of what to do when 2 time intervals start/end together, when a time interval falls into another time interval, etc. [2]. In Allen's interval algebra, each relation is labelled as either distinctive, exhaustive, or qualitative. Typical applications of this algebra include planning and scheduling, natural language processing, temporal databases, workflows, etc. [9].

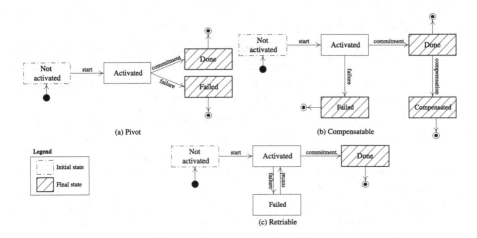

Fig. 2. Representation of a task's transactional cycles.

Table 1. Representation of Allen's time-interval relations.

x before y	x equals y	x meets y
x overlaps y	x during y	x starts y
	x finishes y	

4   Case Study: A Disrupted Loan Application

To illustrate how time-based coordination of tasks consuming resources could be disrupted, we adapt the real case-study of loan-application BP used in the context of BPI challenge 2017 [5].

As per Fig. 3, the process model of the loan-application BP begins when a customer submits online a loan application that a credit staff checks for completeness. Should any document be missing, the staff would contact the customer prior to processing the application further. Otherwise, the staff would do some extra works like assessing the customer's eligibility based on the requested amount, income, and history. Should the

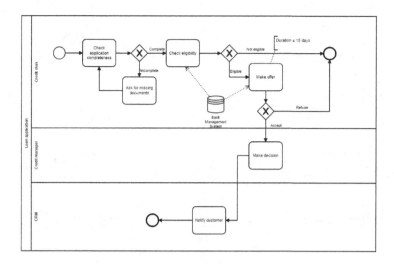

Fig. 3. BPMN-based loan application process-model.

customer be eligible, the staff would make an offer to the customer who needs to either accept or reject to according to a deadline. After the deadline and in the absence of a response, the application would be automatically cancelled. Otherwise, the staff would finalize the paperwork by seeking the manager's acceptance/rejection decision. Finally, the customer is notified of the decision concluding the whole application.

The process model above sheds light on different temporal constraints that disruptions could turn into unsatisfied. For instance, the credit staff could be tasked to prioritize some high-profile customers' applications at the expense of ongoing applications that would temporarily be put on hold. And, the central bank's Web site could be subject to an immediate upgrade forcing the bank to upgrade its online services as well. Would deadlines set by the bank still be met when the suspended applications are resumed? Making room to handle disruptions could deplete resources' availability times despite the confirmed task-resource coordination.

5   Coordination of Tasks Consuming Resources

This section details our approach for time-based coordination of disrupting/disrupted tasks consuming resources (Fig. 4). The approach goes through 3 stages though the first two happen concurrently. In the first stage, the approach blends time with consumption properties defining the availability-time interval of a resource (Sect. 5.1). In the second stage, the approach blends time with transactional properties defining the consumption-time interval of a task (Sect. 5.2). Finally, the approach examines the overlap between availability-time interval and consumption-time interval according to Allen's interval algebra and in the presence of disturbing tasks (Sect. 5.3). This overlap identifies the coordination that should take place when disrupted tasks make room to disrupting tasks to consume resources. The approach also mines processes by analysing logs to guide this coordination.

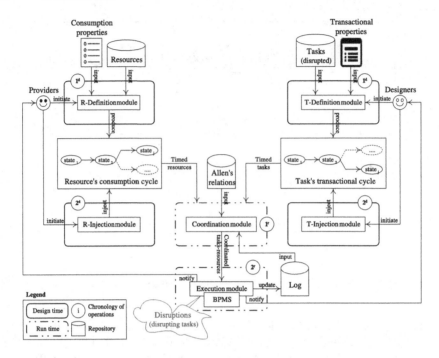

Fig. 4. Coordination of disrupting/disrupted tasks during resource provisioning.

5.1 Blending Time with Consumption Properties

To decide when a task ($\mathcal{T}_i$) would consume ($con_{i\{j=1...\}}$, one-to-many times) a resource ($\mathcal{R}_k$), we proceed as follows. First, we associate the effective consumption with a time interval, $\mathcal{T}_i^{\mathcal{R}_k}[x_{con_{ij}}, y_{con_{ij}}]$, that will be set at run-time (Sect. 5.3). Second, we associate unlimited, limited, limited-but-extensible properties with 3 intervals setting a resource's availability time, $\mathcal{R}_k[b, e[, \mathcal{R}_k[b, e], \mathcal{R}_k[b, e\ 0[+\delta]*]$, where b, e, δ, $0[...]*$, and $\mathcal{R}_k(b|e)$ correspond to begin-time, end-time, extra-time[2], zero-to-many times, and lower|upper values of a resource's availability-time interval. Third, we associate shareable and non-shareable properties with tolerating the concurrent consumption ($con_{in}, con_{jn'}, \ldots$) of a resource by separate tasks ($\mathcal{T}_i, \mathcal{T}_j, \ldots$) during the availability time of this resource, e.g., $((\mathcal{T}_i^{\mathcal{R}_k}[b_{con_{in}}, e_{con_{in}}] \subseteq \mathcal{R}_k[b, e]) \wedge (\mathcal{T}_j^{\mathcal{R}_k}[b_{con_{jn'}}, e_{con_{jn'}}] \subseteq \mathcal{R}_k[b, e]) \wedge \ldots)$ where $i, j \in 1..N$, N is the number of tasks, and $n, n' \in \mathbb{N}^*$. Finally, we ensure that an unlimited resource accommodates any task's multiple consumption requests. In Table 2 that refers to 3 tasks, $\mathcal{T}_{1,2,3}$, and their different resource consumption such as $\mathcal{T}_1$'s con_{11} and $\mathcal{T}_3$'s con_{31-34}, we illustrate the impact of limited and limited-but-extensible properties on a resource's availability-time interval.

1. Limited property means that a resource's availability time, $\mathcal{R}_k[b, e]$, that is set at design-time remains the same at run-time despite the additional resource consumption coming from the same tasks (after their first consumption). A task requesting

---

[2] Requests for extra-time could be repeated, if deemed necessary, but not indefinitely.

Table 2. Representation of a consumed resource's availability-time intervals ([12]).

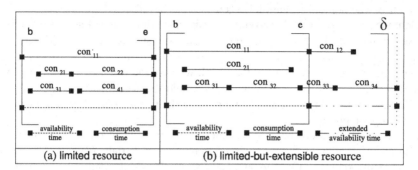

(a) limited resource	(b) limited-but-extensible resource

to consume a limited resource is confirmed *iff* the task's first consumption-time falls into the resource's availability time (e.g., $\mathcal{T}_2^{\mathcal{R}_k}[b_{con_{21}}, e_{con_{21}}] \subset \mathcal{R}_k[b,e]$ in Table 2 (a) where $b_{con_{21}} > b$ and $e_{con_{21}} < e$) and, then, any extra consumption times must fall into the resource's same availability time (e.g., $\mathcal{T}_2^{\mathcal{R}_k}[b_{con_{22}}, e_{con_{22}}] \subseteq r_k[b,e]$ in Table 2(a) where $b_{con_{22}} = e_{con_{21}}$ and $e_{con_{22}} = e$).

2. Limited-but-extensible property means that a resource's availability time, $\mathcal{R}_k[b,e]$, that is set at design-time can be adjusted at run-time, $\mathcal{R}_k[b,e \ 0[+\delta]*]$, so that additional resource consumption coming from the same tasks (after their first consumption) are accommodated. A task requesting to use a limited-but-extensible resource is confirmed *iff* the task's first consumption-time falls into the resource's availability time (e.g., $\mathcal{T}_3^{\mathcal{R}_k}[b_{con_{31}}, e_{con_{31}}] \subset \mathcal{R}_k[b,e]$ in Table 2(b) where $b_{con_{31}} > b$ and $e_{con_{31}} < e$) and, then, any extra consumption times still fall into either the resource's same availability time (e.g., $\mathcal{T}_3^{\mathcal{R}_k}[b_{con_{32}}, e_{con_{32}}] \subset \mathcal{R}_k[b,e]$ in Table 2(b) where $b_{con_{32}} = e_{con_{31}}$ and $e_{con_{32}} < e$) or the resource's extended availability time (e.g., $\mathcal{T}_3^{\mathcal{R}_k}[b_{con_{33}}, e_{con_{33}}] \subset \mathcal{R}_k[e, e+\delta]$ in Table 2(b) where $b_{con_{33}} = e_{con_{32}}$ and $e_{con_{33}} < e+\delta$).

In the 2 cases above, we assume that any additional resource consumption happens immediately after the end of the previous resource consumption, i.e., $b_{con_{ij}} = e_{con_{ij+1}}$. Another option is to have a gap (γ) between the 2 consumption, i.e., $b_{con_{ij}} = e_{con_{ij+1}} + \gamma$, but this is not considered further and does not impact the whole coordination approach.

5.2 Blending Time with Transactional Properties

In Sect. 5.1, $\mathcal{T}_i^{\mathcal{R}_k}[x_{con_{ij}}, y_{con_{ij}}]$ is a task's effective consumption-time interval with regard to a resource. This interval will be defined based on a task's expected consumption-time interval, $\mathcal{T}_i[et, lt]$, where et, lt, and $\mathcal{T}_i(et|lt)$ correspond to earliest time, latest time, and lower|upper values of a task's expected consumption-time interval, respectively. While the expected consumption time is set at design-time, the effective consumption time is set at run-time as per Sect. 5.3 and will happen anytime between the earliest time and latest time. We discuss below how we foresee the impact of a task's transactional properties on a resource's availability-time intervals.

1. Pivot property: a resource's availability-time interval accommodates the execution of a task whether this execution leads to success or failure (Fig. 2).
2. Compensatable property: a resource's availability-time interval accommodates the execution of a task whether this execution leads to success or failure (Fig. 2). Prior to undoing the execution outcomes after success (assuming an undoing decision has been made), there will be a need to check whether the resource's remaining availability time accommodates the undoing. Should the accommodation be not possible, extra availability time would be requested subject to checking the resource's consumption property.
3. Retriable property: a resource's availability-time interval accommodates the execution of a task along with an agreed-upon number of retrials, if deemed necessary, that are all expected to lead to success (Fig. 2). Should this number of retrials still lead to failure, extra availability time would be requested subject to both checking the resource's consumption property and ensuring that the extra number of retrials (that are expected to lead to success) do not go over a threshold ($\mathcal{TH}$).

5.3 Connecting Disrupting/Disrupted Tasks and Resources Together

When working out the effective consumption-time of a resource by a task, $\mathcal{T}_i^{\mathcal{R}_k}[b_{con_{in}}, e_{con_{in}}]$ where n is the nth consumption as per Table 2, we resorted to Allen's interval algebra to identify potential overlaps between the task's expected consumption-time interval and resource's availability-time interval. During the nth consumption, a task labelled as disrupting, $d\mathcal{T}_j$, takes over resource $\mathcal{R}_k$ that task $\mathcal{T}_i$ is currently consuming in accordance with its effective consumption-time interval. Task $\mathcal{T}_i$ has now become disrupted. To accommodate the takeover according to the disrupting task's one-time confirmed consumption-time interval, $d\mathcal{T}_j^{\mathcal{R}_k}[cb_{con_{j1}}, ce_{con_{j1}}]$ where cb and ce stand for confirmed begin-time and confirmed end-time, respectively, the ongoing consumption of the resource by the disrupted task is suspended, $\mathcal{T}_i^{\mathcal{R}_k}[b_{con_{in}}, cb_{con_{j1}}]$, along with satisfying Constraint C_1:$(e_{con_{in}} > cb_{con_{j1}})$. C_1 ensures that there is always some time left for the disrupting task to consume the resource, i.e., $d\mathcal{T}_j^{\mathcal{R}_k}[cb_{con_{j1}}, ce_{con_{j1}}] \subset \mathcal{R}_k[cb_{con_{j1}}, e_{con_{in}}]$. Cases like $d\mathcal{T}_j^{\mathcal{R}_k}[cb_{con_{j1}}, ce_{con_{j1}}] ==$ $\mathcal{R}_k[cb_{con_{j1}}, \mathcal{R}_k(e)]$ and $d\mathcal{T}_j^{\mathcal{R}_k}[cb_{con_{j1}}, ce_{con_{j1}}] \not\subseteq \mathcal{R}_k[cb_{con_{j1}}, \mathcal{R}_k(e)|e_{con_{in}}]$ are dropped from the discussion. When the disrupting task $d\mathcal{T}_j$'s execution ends, we ensure that there is still time left for the disrupted task $\mathcal{T}_i$ to resume the consumption of resource $\mathcal{R}_k$, which means satisfying C_2:$(e_{con_{in}} > ce_{con_{j1}})$. Figure 5 illustrates how disrupted and disrupting tasks take turns to consume resources.

Prior to analysing relations between consumption-time interval and availability-time interval, we recall that a disrupting task's begin- and end-times for consuming a resource are confirmed. However, this is not the case with a disrupted task that has expected and effective begin- and end-times for consuming a resource.

Consumption-time Interval *equals* Availability-time Interval. Since the expected consumption-time interval and availability-time interval are the same, we suggest hereafter different options about task/resource coordinated consumption depending on the resource's consumption property, the disrupted task's transactional property, and the fact that the disrupting task's execution always happens and succeeds:

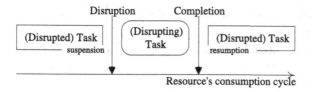

Fig. 5. Disrupted and disrupting tasks taking turns during resource consumption.

1. limited: the effective consumption-time interval of any n^{th} consumption, $T_i^{R_k}[b_{con_{in}}, e_{con_{in}}]$, falls into the availability-time interval in a way that $b_{con_{in}} \geq R_k(b)$ and $e_{con_{in}} \leq R_k(e)$.

   – pivot: T_i execution happens during $T_i^{R_k}[b_{con_{in}}, cb_{con_{j1}}] \cup [ce_{con_{j1}}, e_{con_{in}}]$ while dT_j execution happens during $dT_j^{R_k}[cb_{con_{j1}}, ce_{con_{j1}}]$.

   – compensatable: 2 cases exist depending on when the disruption would happen: during T_i execution with no-confirmed compensation or after T_i execution with confirmed compensation.

     • Case 1: T_i execution happens during $T_i^{R_k}[b_{con_{in}}, cb_{con_{j1}}] \cup [ce_{con_{j1}}, e_{con_{in}}]$ while dT_j execution happens during $dT_j^{R_k}[cb_{con_{j1}}, ce_{con_{j1}}]$. Should T_i need to be compensated, then satisfying C_3:($R_k(e) > e_{con_{in}}$) would allow to accommodate the compensation, $T_i^{R_k}[b_{con_{i(n+1)}}, e_{con_{i(n+1)}}]$ and $b_{con_{i(n+1)}} = e_{con_{in}}$. Should C_3 turn out unsatisfied, then the compensation would be canceled. Despite the cancellation, T_i execution remains compliant with the definition of compensatable property (i.e., done is a final state).

     • Case 2: T_i execution happens during $T_i^{R_k}[b_{con_{in}}, e_{con_{in}}]$ along with satisfying C_4:($e_{con_{in}} < R_k(e)$). Since dT_i execution should happen, then the remaining availability time, $R_k(e) - e_{con_{in}}$, should accommodate this execution as per its confirmed consumption-time interval, $dT_j^{R_k}[cb_{con_{j1}}, ce_{con_{j1}}]$. Regarding T_i compensation, this would depend on satisfying C_5:($R_k(e) > ce_{con_{j1}}$) whose analysis would be similar to verifying the satisfaction of C_3.

   – retriable: regarding the first execution of the disrupted task T_i and as long as C_6:($R_k(e) > e_{con_{i(n-1)}}$ where $1 < n < TH$) is satisfied to accommodate this task's extra retrials, then T_i execution happens during $T_i^{R_k}[b_{con_{in}}, cb_{con_{j1}}] \cup [ce_{con_{j1}}, e_{con_{in}}]$ while dT_j execution happens during $dT_j^{R_k}[cb_{con_{j1}}, ce_{con_{j1}}]$. Should C_6 turn out unsatisfied, then the retrials would be stopped making T_i execution uncompliant with the definition of retriable property (i.e., failed is not a final state).

2. limited-but-extensible: the effective consumption-time interval of any n^{th} consumption, $T_i^{R_k}[b_{con_{in}}, e_{con_{in}}]$, falls into the availability-time interval in a way that $b_{con_{in}} \geq R_k(b)$ and $e_{con_{in}} \leq R_k(e)$ with the option of having $R_k(e)$ extended $(+\delta)$.

- pivot: $\mathcal{T}_i$ execution happens during $\mathcal{T}_i^{\mathcal{R}_k}[b_{con_{in}}, cb_{con_{j1}}] \cup [ce_{con_{j1}}, e_{con_{in}}]$ while $d\mathcal{T}_j$ execution happens during $d\mathcal{T}_j^{\mathcal{R}_k}[cb_{con_{j1}}, ce_{con_{j1}}]$.
- compensatable: 2 cases exist depending on when the disruption would happen: during $\mathcal{T}_i$ execution with no-confirmed compensation or after $\mathcal{T}_i$ execution with confirmed compensation.
    - Case 1: $\mathcal{T}_i$ execution happens during $\mathcal{T}_i^{\mathcal{R}_k}[b_{con_{in}}, cb_{con_{j1}}] \cup [ce_{con_{j1}}, e_{con_{in}}]$ while $d\mathcal{T}_j$ execution happens during $d\mathcal{T}_j^{\mathcal{R}_k}[cb_{con_{j1}}, ce_{con_{j1}}]$. Should $\mathcal{T}_i$ need to be compensated, then satisfying C_3:($\mathcal{R}_k(e) > e_{con_{in}}$) would allow to accommodate the compensation, $\mathcal{T}_i^{\mathcal{R}_k}[b_{con_{i(n+1)}}, e_{con_{i(n+1)}}]$ and $b_{con_{i(n+1)}} = e_{con_{in}}$. Should C_3 turn out unsatisfied, then the resource's availability time would be extended, $\mathcal{R}_k(e) + \delta$, in a way that $\mathcal{T}_i^{\mathcal{R}_k}[b_{con_{i(n+1)}}, e_{con_{i(n+1)}}] \subseteq \mathcal{R}_k[e_{con_{in}}, e + \delta]$, $b_{con_{i(n+1)}} = e_{con_{in}}$, and $e_{con_{i(n+1)}} \leq \mathcal{R}_k(e) + \delta$. Whether the extension happens or not, $\mathcal{T}_i$ execution remains compliant with the definition of compensatable property (i.e., both done and canceled are final states).
    - Case 2: $\mathcal{T}_i$ execution happens during $\mathcal{T}_i^{\mathcal{R}_k}[b_{con_{in}}, e_{con_{in}}]$ along with satisfying C_4:($e_{con_{in}} < \mathcal{R}_k(e)$). Since $d\mathcal{T}_i$ execution should happen, then the remaining availability time, $\mathcal{R}_k(e) - e_{con_{in}}$, should accommodate this execution as per its confirmed consumption-time interval, $d\mathcal{T}_j^{\mathcal{R}_k}[cb_{con_{j1}}, ce_{con_{j1}}]$. Regarding $\mathcal{T}_i$ compensation, this would depend on satisfying C_5:($\mathcal{R}_k(e) > ce_{con_{j1}}$) whose analysis would be similar to verifying the satisfaction of C_3.
- retriable: regarding the first execution of the disrupted task $\mathcal{T}_i$ and as long as C_6:($\mathcal{R}_k(e) > e_{con_{i(n-1)}}$ where $1 < n < \mathcal{T}\mathcal{H}$) is satisfied to accommodate this task's extra retrials, then $\mathcal{T}_i$ execution happens during $\mathcal{T}_i^{\mathcal{R}_k}[b_{con_{in}}, cb_{con_{j1}}] \cup [ce_{con_{j1}}, e_{con_{in}}]$ while $d\mathcal{T}_j$ execution happens during $d\mathcal{T}_j^{\mathcal{R}_k}[cb_{con_{j1}}, ce_{con_{j1}}]$. Should C_6 turn out unsatisfied, then the resource's availability time would be extended a certain number of times, $\mathcal{R}_k(e) + 1[\delta]*$, in a way that $(\mathcal{T}_i^{\mathcal{R}_k}[b_{con_{in}}, cb_{con_{j1}}] \cup [ce_{con_{j1}}, e_{con_{in}}]) \subseteq \mathcal{R}_k[e_{con_{i(n-1)}}, e + 1[\delta]*]$, $b_{con_{in}} = e_{con_{i(n-1)}}$, and $e_{con_{in}} \leq \mathcal{R}_k(e) + \delta$. Thanks to the extension, $\mathcal{T}_i$ execution remains compliant with the definition of retriable property (i.e., done is a final state).

Consumption-time Interval *overlaps* Availability-time Interval. Because of the overlap between the expected consumption-time interval and availability-time interval, 2 mandatory adjustments need to happen. The first adjustment concerns the lower value of the disrupted task's expected consumption-time interval, so that it matches the lower value of the resource's availability-time interval, i.e., $\mathcal{T}_i = [\mathcal{R}_k(b), lt]$. And, the second adjustment concerns the upper value of the resource's availability-time interval, so that it matches the upper time of the task's expected consumption-time interval, i.e., $\mathcal{R}_k = [b, \mathcal{T}(lt)]$. After these 2 adjustments, the analysis of "consumption-time interval overlaps availability-time interval" is similar to "consumption-time interval equals availability-time interval". The task's expected consumption-time interval and resource's availability-time interval are equals.

Availability-time Interval *overlaps* Consumption-time Interval. Contrarily to "consumption-time interval overlaps availability-time interval" where 2 mandatory adjustments were required, "availability-time interval overlaps consumption-time interval" would require 1 mandatory adjustment that concerns the lower value of the resource's availability-time interval, so that it matches the lower value of the task's expected consumption-time interval, i.e., $\mathcal{R}_k = [\mathcal{T}(et), e]$. We suggest hereafter different options about task/resource coordinated consumption depending on the resource's consumption property, the disrupted task's transactional property, and the fact that the disrupting task's execution always happens and succeeds:

1. limited: the effective consumption-time interval of any n^{th} consumption, $\mathcal{T}_i^{\mathcal{R}_k}[b_{con_{in}}, e_{con_{in}}]$, falls into the adjusted availability-time interval in a way that $b_{con_{in}} \geq \mathcal{R}_k(b)$ and $e_{con_{in}} \leq \mathcal{R}_k(e)$. In fact, the disrupted task $\mathcal{T}_i$'s expected consumption-time interval is trimmed before in a way that its upper-value matches this adjusted availability-time interval's upper-value; i.e., $lt - \mathcal{R}(e)$ makes the disrupted task waste some time from its expected availability-time interval. After this trimming, the analysis of "availability-time interval overlaps consumption-time interval" is similar to "consumption-time interval equals availability-time interval". The task's expected consumption-time interval and resource's adjusted availability-time interval are equals.

2. limited-but-extensible: taping into a resource's extension capability, the upper value of the availability-time interval is automatically adjusted without waiting for a task's extension requests offering a complete coverage of this task's expected consumption-time interval. The resource's adjusted availability-time interval becomes $\mathcal{R}_k = [\mathcal{T}(et), \mathcal{R}_k(e) + \delta)]$ where $\mathcal{R}_k(e) + \delta = \mathcal{T}(lt)$. As a result, the effective consumption-time interval of any n^{th} consumption, $\mathcal{T}_i^{\mathcal{R}_k}[b_{con_{in}}, e_{con_{in}}]$, falls into the adjusted availability-time interval in a way that $b_{con_{in}} \geq \mathcal{R}_k(b)$ and $e_{con_{in}} \leq \mathcal{R}_k(e)$. This also results into a similar analysis of "availability-time interval overlaps consumption-time interval" to "consumption-time interval equals availability-time interval". The task's expected consumption-time interval and resource's extended availability-time interval are equals.

Rest of Eligible Time-relations. By analogy with equals and overlaps time-relations between consumption-time interval and availability-time interval discussed above, the rest of eligible time-relations namely, during, starts, and finishes will be subject to the same analysis as equals and overlaps, i.e., these 2 intervals' respective lower- and upper-values will be adjusted resulting into equals intervals.

6   Implementation

To demonstrate the feasibility of provisioning resources to disrupted and disrupting tasks, we developed an in-house testbed that consists of several Python programs along with using BPI-Challenge-2017's real dataset [5] referring to a credit application system's execution traces. It is available in eXtensible Event Stream (XES).

6.1 Dataset Preprocessing

This includes how to transform the BPI-Challenge-2017's dataset into a useful and efficient format as per the following steps:

- Data transformation from XES into pandas DataFrame[3] format permits to use pandas library's predefined routines, which we applied to the next preprocessing steps. DataFrame is suitable for manipulating data and building prediction models.
- Data reduction scales down the size of the dataset to make it manageable. We applied reduction to extract disrupted tasks and their corresponding disrupting tasks from the original dataset.
- Feature selection identifies relevant features to describe the necessary data. Indeed, the initial dataset includes some features that are either redundant or irrelevant. We dropped them from the dataset without incurring any loss of relevant information. For instance, *FirstWithdrawalAmount*, *case:ApplicationType*, and *CreditScore* features were dropped, while *org:resource*, *concept:name*, and *time:timestamp* features were kept.
- Feature creation generates new features that capture the most important data in a dataset compared to the original dataset. This time we use extraction- and construction-feature techniques while in the previous work [12] we focused on resource's availability time-interval and consumption-time interval of each resource by the tasks. We added new features related to the disrupting tasks and execution status of the disrupted tasks. The disrupting tasks are executed after the suspension of under-execution tasks using the same resource. The execution status of a disrupted task is extracted from *lifecycle:transition* feature and refers to the final status of the task after resumption.

6.2 Resource Consumption by Disrupted/Disrupting Tasks

To coordinate the consumption of a resource by both disrupted and disrupting tasks, we resorted to process mining. It is well used to improve future BP executions based on past experiences reported in event logs. Process mining usually adopt machine learning techniques (e.g., Decision Tree (DT), KNN, and SVM) to automate activities (such as process discovery, data visualization, and process monitoring). We opted for DT due to its easiness, efficiency, and limited data preprocessing before building a prediction model. We created our prediction model for coordinating the consumption of resources by both disrupted and disrupting tasks following 2 stages, offline and online.

- During the offline stage, we used Sklearn[4] that is an open-source Python library. We started by specifying the prediction model's parameters namely, attribute selection criterion (Entropy or Gini index) and maximum depth of the tree. In terms of inputs, the elaboration of a prediction model requires a training dataset and a test dataset that are derived from the preprocessed dataset. Furthermore, the target of the prediction model must be defined. This latter is about recommending the actions to take when

---

[3] https://pandas.pydata.org/docs/reference/api/pandas.DataFrame.html.

[4] https://scikit-learn.org/stable/index.html.

the consumption of a resource is suspended by a disrupting task (e.g., adjusting the resource-availability time). Last but not least, the set of variables that may affect the recommendations such as resource's availability-time, disrupted and disrupting tasks with their consumption-time.

- During the online stage and after building the prediction model, we evaluated the accuracy of our prediction model to measure its quality regarding unseen examples that are not used for training the model. For evaluation purposes, a set of new instances are considered with the aim to determine the action to perform when an under-execution task is suspended by another task. Such actions are recommended thanks to the already built prediction model.

6.3 Result Discussions

To appreciate our DT-based prediction model's recommendations, we also adopted the k-Nearest Neighbors (KNN) as another technique for developing prediction models. As for the DT prediction model, the experiments showed encouraging results. In this context, we used *precision, recall,* and *accuracy* as performance measures (Eqs. 1, 2, and 3).

$$Precision = \frac{TruePositiveObservations}{TotalPositiveObservations} \tag{1}$$

$$Recall = \frac{TruePositiveObservations}{(TruePositiveObservations + FalseNegativeObservations)} \tag{2}$$

$$Accuracy = \frac{(TruePositiveObservations + TrueNegativeObservations)}{TotalObservations} \tag{3}$$

First, we computed *precision, recall,* and *accuracy* after applying the DT prediction model to the test dataset as per the offline stage. We obtained acceptable values as per Table 3. Then, we computed the same ratios after applying our prediction model on a set of simulated instances. The obtained results also prove the performance of our DT prediction model (Table 3). Furthermore, we opted for a further validation of our prediction model by using KNN prediction model to compare the results obtained using both techniques (DT and KNN). Similarly to the DT prediction model, we used our preprocessed dataset to build the KNN prediction model and, then, we applied it to the simulated instances. The results are shown in Table 3. These results are in line with those of the DT and prove its performance.

Table 3. Experiments' results.

	DT prediction model		KNN prediction model	
	Test dataset	Simulation	Test dataset	Simulation
Precision	80	66	67	62
Recall	87	60	71	55
Accuracy	83	60	77	53

7 Conclusion

This paper discussed the provisioning of resources to business processes' tasks referred to as either disrupted or disrupting. While tasks are under-execution, multiple events like urgent requests to process immediately could disrupt these tasks making them release their resources for the benefit of the disrupting tasks. To avoid conflicts on resources and ensure the execution resumption of the disrupted tasks, we examined the provisioning of resources using Allen's interval relations such as equals, overlaps, starts, and finishes. During this provisioning we also considered the types of disruptions and both the consumption properties of resources and the transactional properties of tasks. To demonstrate resource provisioning to disrupted and disrupting tasks, a Python-based in-house testbed was developed and deployed along with using BPI Challenge 2017 as a real dataset. In term of future work we would like to examine the scalability of the system when a large number of disrupted and disrupting tasks co-exist and hence, compete on the same resources. Resource unavailability due to some specific consumption properties like limited could refrain their provisioning to tasks that are already disrupted.

References

1. Alessandro, S., Davide, A., Elisabetta, B., Riccardo, D., Valeria, M.: A data-driven methodology for supporting resource planning of health services. Socio-Econ. Plan. Sci. **70**, 100744 (2020)
2. Allen, J.: Maintaining knowledge about temporal intervals. Commun. ACM **26**(11), 832–843 (1983)
3. Ayoub, A., Elgammal, A.: Utilizing twitter data for identifying and resolving run-time business process disruptions. In: Proceedings of OTM Confederated International Conferences "On the Move to Meaningful Internet Systems" (OTM 2018), Valletta, Malta (2018)
4. Delcoucq, L., Lecron, F., Fortemps, P., van der Aalst, W.M.: Resource-centric process mining: clustering using local process models. In: Proceedings of the 35th Annual ACM Symposium on Applied Computing (SAC 2020) (2020)
5. van Dongen, B.: BPI Challenge 2017 (2017). https://data.4tu.nl/articles/dataset/BPI_Challenge_2017/12696884
6. Fernández, E., Bogado, V., Salomone, E., Chiotti, O.: Framework for modelling and simulating the supply process monitoring to detect and predict disruptive events. Comput. Ind. **80**, 31–42 (2016)
7. Frank, L., Ulslev Pedersen, R.: Integrated distributed/mobile logistics management. Trans. Large-Scale Data- Knowl.-Center. Syst. **5**, 206–221 (2012)
8. Gilbert, C., Bower, J.L.: Disruptive change: when trying harder is part of the problem. Harvard Bus. Rev. **80**, 94–101 (2002)
9. Janhunen, T., Sioutis, M.: Allen's Interval Algebra makes the Difference. CoRR abs/1909.01128 (2019)
10. Little, M.: Transactions and web services. Commun. ACM **46**(10), 49–54 (2003)
11. Maamar, Z., Faci, N., Sakr, S., Boukhebouze, M., Barnawi, A.: Network-based social coordination of business processes. Inf. Syst. **58**, 56–74 (2016)
12. Maamar, Z., Yahya, F., Ben Ammar, L.: On the use of allen's interval algebra in the coordination of resource consumption by transactional business processes. In: Proceedings of the 17th International Conference on Evaluation of Novel Approaches to Software Engineering (ENASE 2022) (2022)

13. Object Management Group (OMG): Business Process Model and Notation. https://www.omg.org/spec/BPMN/2.0.2
14. Paul, S., Sarker, R., Essam, D.: Managing risk and disruption in production-inventory and supply chain systems: a review. J. Ind. Manag. Optim. **12** (2016)
15. Petzold, N., Landinez, L., Baaken, T.: Disruptive innovation from a process view: a systematic literature review. Innov. Organ. Behav. eJ. **28**, 157–174 (2019)
16. Rania Ben, H., Kallel, K., Gaaloul, W., Maamar, Z., Jmaiel, M.: Toward a correct and optimal time-aware cloud resource allocation to business processes. Fut. Gener. Comput. Syst. **112**, 751–766 (2020)
17. Thorisson, H., Alsultan, M., Hendrickson, D., Polmateer, T., Lambert, J.: Addressing schedule disruptions in business processes of advanced logistics systems. Syst. Eng. **22**, 66–79 (2019)
18. Weske, M.: Business process management architectures. In: Business Process Management. Springer, Heidelberg (2019). https://doi.org/10.1007/978-3-540-73522-9_7
19. Zhao, W., Pu, S., Jiang, D.: A human resource allocation method for business processes using team faultlines. Appl. Intell. **50**(9), 2887–2900 (2020)

BPMN4FRSS: An BPMN Extension to Support Risk-Based Development of Forensic-Ready Software Systems

Lukas Daubner[1]($\boxtimes$) , Raimundas Matulevičius[2] , Barbora Buhnova[1] ,
and Tomas Pitner[1]

[1] Faculty of Informatics, Masaryk University, Botanická 68a, 60200 Brno, Czechia
{daubner,buhnova,tomp}@mail.muni.cz
[2] Institute of Computer Science, University of Tartu, Narva mnt 18, 51009 Tartu, Estonia
raimundas.matulevicius@ut.ee

Abstract. The importance of systems secure-by-design is well recognised. However, incidents or disputes requiring thorough investigation might occur even in highly secure systems. Forensic-ready software systems aim to ease the investigations by including requirements for reliable, admissible, and on-point data - potential evidence. Yet, the software engineering techniques for such systems have numerous open challenges. One of them, representation and reasoning, is tackled in this chapter by defining the syntax and semantics of modelling language BPMN for Forensic-Ready Software Systems (BPMN4FRSS). In addition to representing the requirements and specific controls, a semantic mapping to forensic-ready risk management is defined to support risk-oriented design. This approach of designing forensic-ready software systems, supported by BPMN4FRSS models, is then demonstrated.

Keywords: Forensic readiness · Forensic-ready software systems ·
Modelling · BPMN · Software design · Risk management · Security

1 Introduction

Building secure software systems are becoming the norm in today's world. Hence, the need for methods to build systems secure-by-design is acknowledged and pursued in research [23]. However, even in highly secure systems, the threat of a security incident cannot be ruled out entirely [11]. When such an incident occurs, it is prudent to investigate it to trace its origin, uncover possible culprits, and identify the exploited vulnerability.

Digital forensics methods [10] are utilised to conduct a sound investigation [31] of such an incident. Their purpose is to ensure that the results are reliable, independently

This research was supported by ERDF "CyberSecurity, CyberCrime and Critical Information Infrastructures Center of Excellence" (No. CZ.02.1.01/0.0/0.0/16_019/0000822).

H. Kaindl et al. (Eds.): ENASE 2022, CCIS 1829, pp. 20–43, 2023.
https://doi.org/10.1007/978-3-031-36597-3_2

verifiable, and built on solid evidence. This (digital) evidence is based on digital arte-facts, which must be handled in a way that preserves their original meaning to be use-able in legal proceedings [39]. Such conditions make the investigation time-consuming, laborious, and thus costly. Moreover, its success is not guaranteed.

Prior to the incident, proactive measures labelled as forensic readiness [60] can be employed to minimise the cost of the investigation and maximise the value of potential evidence. These are commonly organisation-wide measures focused on general investi-gation preparedness [12,26,52]. Moreover, the notion of engineering systems forensic-by-design started to surface, producing the name forensic-ready software systems [44]. Such systems should ensure sound production, handling of digital evidence and general support for the investigation.

The challenge in software systems is not only the amount of produced digital arte-facts (e.g., logs [59]) but their quality, completeness, documentation, and contribution to a successful investigation [14]. Failing to meet such properties, investigators must pro-cess the artefacts ad-hoc, which is costly [33]. Evidence might be ruled inadmissible if based on unreliable data [10] or admitted, but corrupted data might lead to a miscar-riage of justice [28]. However, the lack of a mature software engineering approach for forensic-ready software systems makes their design and development difficult.

To fill this gap, we proposed a risk-based design approach [17]. The ideas stem from the closeness to cybersecurity [26] and, in extension, security engineering, where risk management is a key factor [37]. Coincidentally, risk management is considered a vital part of implementing forensic readiness [52] but lacks detailed specification in the context of forensic-ready systems [1,25]. Furthermore, a systematic software engineering approach requires representation in models to capture the requirements and evaluate the design alternatives, which is also a pillar of a risk-based design where the models support assessment. Moreover, models can serve as a basis for verification [15]. These factors are essential for a comprehensive approach to developing forensic-ready software systems.

We tackle the software engineering challenge of representing and reasoning about forensic-ready systems formulated by Pasquale et al. [44]. Concretely, we introduce a modelling language, an extension to Business Process Model and Notation (BPMN) [43], called BPMN for Forensic-Ready Software Systems (BPMN4FRSS). It is focused on capturing and reasoning over the forensic-ready controls (i.e., implementation of requirements), revolving around potential digital evidence, including its source, storage, and mutual corroboration with others. With it, we aim to support the design of well-focused and sound forensic-ready software systems with integrated risk management support.

This chapter is an extension to [18], which introduced syntax and basic semantics of BPMN4FRSS to cover the controls coming from the high-level requirements by [44]. Here, we study the role of risk management in the design of forensic-ready software systems and propose the alignment with the BPMN4FRSS to support risk assessment. This capability is then demonstrated in the running scenario consisting of risk assess-ment and treatment supported by BPMN4FRSS models.

Therefore, we expand the original research question *"How to model the forensic-ready software systems to support the risk management decisions?"* with the following contributions:

C1: Integrating Forensic-ready Risk Management Concepts into BPMN4FRSS Models. Within the context of the modelling language, this means introducing a semantic mapping to the forensic-ready risk management concepts. Such definition reduces ambiguity and enables seamless support for the decisions.

C2: Enabling Joint Representation of Security and Forensic-Ready Risk Management Concepts in BPMN4FRSS Models. Forensic readiness tends to overlap with cybersecurity. For example, the risks are often the same. Therefore, BPMN4FRSS models must allow compatibility with security risk-focused BPMN notation.

C3: Supporting Model-Based Assessment of Forensic Readiness Treatments. The creation of models must have a greater purpose than just simple documentation. As such, the models themselves must serve as a foundation for assessing forensic readiness treatments.

This chapter is structured as follows: After the introduction, Sect. 2 explores related work. Section 3 discusses the essential aspects of the risk-oriented design and establishes the semantic domain. Then, Sect. 4 explains the syntax and semantics of the BPMN4FRSS, followed by Sect. 5 demonstrating its use on an example. Section 6 discusses the results, followed by the concluding Sect. 7.

2 Related Work

Forensic readiness is traditionally employed as primarily organisational measures [12,26,52]. Nevertheless, the need to supplement them with technical measures is well recognised as well [21]. Forensic-ready software systems are a specific class of such measures. The research in the area deals with the availability (i.e., existence) of potential evidence through logging instrumentation [49], or deployment of forensic agents [30,34]. Specific focus is put on the self-adaptive capabilities of the systems [2,45,46].

Considerable variation in practice regarding the forensic readiness requirement has been reported [24]. While several frameworks exist in the literature, they tend to remain only conceptual [1,7,21,25]. However, there also exist more methodological approaches, utilising a catalogue of forensic readiness requirements (constraints) [55] or utilising a risk management approach [12]. In fact, risk management is widely discussed in the context of forensic-ready systems [17]. However, the concrete utilisation is often left ambiguous [1,25].

Approaches focusing on modelling and representation of forensic-ready software systems are sparse, especially in comparison with the cybersecurity domain [8,23]. UML diagrams were utilised for this purpose, describing code-level incident scenarios using sequence diagrams [49] and high-level models of cloud services with forensic constraints using activity diagrams [55]. Furthermore, a custom, domain-specific modelling notation is described for incident investigation in cyber-physical systems, which includes their topology [3].

This chapter, in particular, builds on the idea of a risk-oriented design approach [17]. It utilised the Security risk-oriented BPMN [4], describing system assets, security risks, and treatments. The BPMN models were enhanced by an ad-hoc extension representing evidence sources. A proper definition of the BPMN extension for forensic-ready systems (BPMN4FRSS) [16] was then published, focusing on representing forensic readiness controls. However, the proper alignment with risk management and related security concepts was not defined, leaving space for semantical ambiguity.

Several other modelling approaches are overlapping with the forensic readiness domain. For example, a notation for modelling security requirements, including non-repudiation and attack detection [13,51]. As for BPMN-based notation, the mentioned Security risk-oriented BPMN [4] aims at supporting security risk management. SecBPMN is expressing security annotations on BPMN models supplemented by SecBPMN-Q for security policies [53]. Similarly, an extension defining annotations to a BPMN model allows for transformations into security policies and composition with pre-existing fragments [41]. A privacy-focused BPMN extension adds privacy-enhancing technologies into BPMN model [47] aiming at data leakage analysis, supported by extensive tooling [48].

3   Risk-Oriented Forensic-Ready Design

This section covers the essential aspects of the risk-oriented design for forensic-ready software systems outlined in [17]. Primarily, it discusses the forensic-ready risk management concepts and the overlaps with security risk management. This helps to establish the semantic domain of BPMN4FRSS concerning risk management. Therefore, it is an essential step in integrating forensic-ready risk management concepts (**C1**) and enabling joint representation with security risk management (**C2**) in BPMN4FRSS.

3.1   Forensic-Ready Risk Management

The importance of risk management is recognised for establishing forensic readiness in the organisation, as well as for engineering forensic-ready systems. For example, risk management practices are a key component in conceptual forensic-by-design frameworks for cyber-physical systems in medical [25] and cloud [1] domains. Often, risk management is utilised to identify and assess scenarios where there is a need for digital evidence [52]. Such scenarios are typically based on the need to investigate security incidents (i.e., the occurrence of security risks), utilising the outputs from security risk management. However, it is suggested that the scenarios should go beyond security and consider the need for digital evidence involving business risks [52]. Similar to security risk management, another purpose of defining risks in a forensic-ready context is to allow an assessment for a good return on investment.

Information Systems Security Risk Management (ISSRM) provides a definition of a domain model drawn from concepts of various security risk management standards and methods [20]. It was successfully used as a foundation of model-based security risk management [38]. Forensic-ready engineering was inspired by the ISSRM, and an idea of a risk-oriented design approach for forensic-ready software systems we proposed [17]. We then investigated the concepts in the forensic readiness domain, creating an extended Forensic-Ready ISSRM (FR-ISSRM) [16]. The domain model is depicted in Fig. 1. In this chapter, the concepts of FR-ISSRM will be utilised to align the BPMN4FRSS modelling language to forensic readiness concepts. Following is a brief summary of the new forensic readiness concepts.

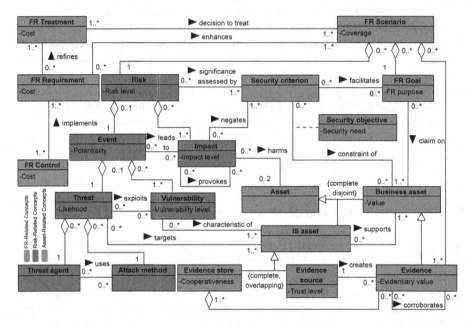

Fig. 1. Domain Model of FR-ISSRM [16] (without Risk Treatment-Related concepts).

Forensic Readiness-Related Concepts are defined by the FR-ISSRM extension. Importantly, they do not override any ISSRM definition to remain compatible with ISSRM-aligned methods. Here, *Evidence* is defined as a specialised *Business asset* representing information potentially important in forensic investigation and can be corroborated by others. Each *Evidence* is created by an *Evidence source* and subsequently stored in *Evidence storage*, both possibly overlapping specialisations of *IS asset*. The purpose of implementing forensic readiness is expressed by the *Forensic readiness goal*, which is a claim towards a *Business asset* which can be supported or refuted using evidence. Then, the *Forensic readiness scenario* describes how exactly is the *Forensic readiness goal* addressed, using *Evidence*, covering a specific *Risk*.

Treatment in forensic readiness means enhancing the *Forensic readiness scenario*, not the *Risk* itself. Here, the *Forensic readiness treatment* is the course of action to meet the *FR Goal* of the *FR Scenario*. Decisions to enhance the *FR Scenario* lead to the formulation of *Forensic readiness requirements*, i.e., conditions to be satisfied to meet the *FR Goal*. In contrast to security risk management, the *Risk* is not directly modified. Nevertheless, the *FR Scenario* can be enhanced by implementing *Security requirements* which would impact the *Risk* in a standard ISSRM manner. Lastly, *Forensic readiness control* is a concrete implementation of the *FR Requirements*.

3.2   Forensic-Ready Requirements

With the introduction of the concept of forensic-ready software systems, a set of initial, high-level requirements for such systems were formulated [44]. These include the *Availability* of the evidence, when needed, and its *Non-Repudiation*. These can be understood as the requirement categories or factors [22] of forensic-ready software systems, which serve as a foundation for requirements engineering tasks, including elicitation and validation [58].

Risk management is a method that can be used to support the requirements elicitation. This approach is used in security engineering, where security risk management is a key activity supporting the elicitation of security requirements, providing inputs for their evaluation, comparison and prioritisation [37]. A concrete example of such utilisation is the SQUARE method [40]. Similarly, forensic-ready risk management provides input for deciding how to cover forensic readiness goals at an acceptable level and the cost-effectiveness of implementing the controls.

3.3   Model-Based Approach

In order to systematically support risk management decisions in software engineering, the usage of models was proposed [6,61]. Within the security engineering field, many modelling languages exist that capture security phenomena in the early stages of software development like Misuse Cases [57] or Mal-Activities [56]. However, they were not designed to represent a risk. Thus, they are limited in leveraging the outputs from risk management [20]. The ISSRM bridges this gap and provides a foundation for model-based risk management [38]. As a result, risk-oriented modelling languages supporting security risk management were formulated [4]. A similar approach has been proposed for forensic-readiness engineering, where the idea of a risk-oriented design approach [17] is supported by modelling language for capturing the controls [18].

Following the idea, this chapter takes BPMN4FRSS modelling language [18], created to capture the forensic-ready controls in the form of a scenario. Particularly, it focuses on potential evidence, its relationships and its lifecycle within the modelled software system. However, to fully integrate with the forensic-ready risk management, an alignment with the FR-ISSRM domain model is needed in addition to the definition of language itself.

The integration allows for a systematic, model-based approach to engineering forensic-ready software systems. It has the following advantages: (1) Enables a formalised analysis and comparison between alternative treatments within the system in question. (2) Supports model-based verification of potential evidence [14]. (3) Highlights the distinction between the forensic readiness goal, requirements, and controls, i.e., problem, solution, and implementation. (4) Allows the documentation and tracing of system evolution which supplements the continuous nature of security risk management [32].

4   BPMN Extension for Forensic-Ready Software Systems

This section describes the syntax and semantics of BPMN4FRSS, an extension of BPMN 2.0 [43] language. The extension design follows the methodology of related

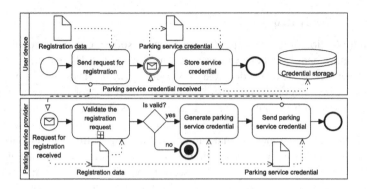

Fig. 2. Example of BPMN diagram [18].

BPMN extensions [4,47]. Specifically for the semantics, we define a semantical mapping [27] of the syntax to the forensic readiness-related concepts of the FR-ISSRM domain model. The semantics of other concepts covered by standard ISSRM is adopted from Security risk-oriented BPMN [4,37].

The language was based on BPMN for three main reasons. (1) The process models capture a dynamic behaviour that can emphasise the relationship between pieces of potential evidence and their lifecycle. It also supports the scenario-based approach toward forensic readiness [52]. (2) A high level of abstraction of the process model contributes to platform independence. It also means the inherent fuzziness of the language. (3) There exists a BPMN-based language that supports security risk management and covers concepts from standard ISSRM [4]. BPMN4FRSS complements the language in the same manner as FR-ISSRM complements ISSRM [16]. However, the downside of BPMN is difficulty in expressing forensic readiness in a broader context, e.g., architecture.

4.1 Business Process Model and Notation

BPMN is a business process modelling language standardised by Object Management Group [37]. While syntactically similar to the flow charts, it has a rich semantic model [19,43], supporting the model execution [54]. Figure 2 contains an example BPMN diagram with basic BPMN constructs used in this chapter.

The diagram contains two *Pools* (User device and Service provider), each containing a process consisting of *Flow Objects* connected by *Sequence Flows* within a single pool and *Message Flows* between the pools. The most prominent *Flow Object* is *Task* (e.g., Send request for registration), representing an atomic activity. Analogously, a *Sub-Process* (e.g., Validate the registration request) represents a composite activity.

Another *Flow Object* is an *Event* (a circle), which has multiple specialised types based on location and trigger condition. A *Start Event* denotes the start of a process, with a variant *Message Start Event* requiring an incoming message as a trigger condition. Similarly, an *End Event* marks the end of the process. *Intermediate Events* are positioned in the middle of the process, with a variant *Message Intermediate Event* requiring an incoming message for process continuation. Lastly, a *Gateway* (a diamond) represents a control point (e.g., branching).

Data exchanged between events and tasks are represented with a *Data Object* (e.g., Registration data), which has its lifecycle tied to the process instance. In contrast, persistent storage is denoted by a *Data Store* (Credential storage). Associations of those constructs are called *Data Associations*.

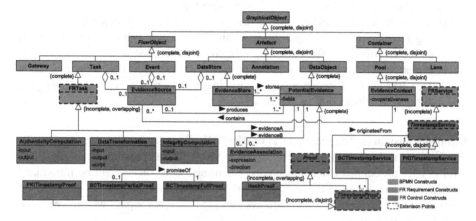

Fig. 3. Abstract Syntax of BPMN4FRSS (revised version of [18]).

4.2 Abstract Syntax

The abstract syntax is a fundamental building block of a modelling language. It captures all concepts of the language and its relationships, which also includes structural semantics [50]. In BPMN4FRSS, the forensic readiness-specific concepts based on FR-ISSRM are aligned with the BPMN abstract syntax [43]. Figure 3 depicts the abstract syntax of BPMN4FRSS extension.

In BPMN4FRSS, the constructs can be divided into two successive levels: requirements and controls. The former contains constructs based on FR-ISSRM [16] concepts (e.g., Potential Evidence, Evidence Source) and constructs representing the forensic readiness requirements as abstract enhancements to the system. The latter represent specific controls, i.e., implementation of requirements, describing a concrete technology utilised in a forensic-ready system. As such, BPMN4FRSS is inherently incomplete in expressing all the controls. Therefore, explicit extension points for the inclusion of new constructs.

Based on the feedback on the original definition of BPMN4FRSS [18] we opted for minor changes to the abstract syntax. We simplified the names of some constructs (e.g., Potential Evidence Type to Potential Evidence). However, the most significant change is making FR Service and FR Task non-abstract, which correctly represents the difference between FR-ISSRM requirements and controls.

Requirement Constructs The core syntactic construct is *Evidence Source*, signifying a point of origin in a process. It can be applied on either BPMN *Task*, *Event*, or *Data Store* and cannot be shared. The BPMN *Pool* which contains the Evidence Source, must also be specified as a *Evidence Context*, providing contextual information about the evidence. Each *Evidence Source* can produce one or more *Potential Evidence* as a specific

BPMN *Data Object*. These instances of *Potential Evidence* can be associated with each other by an *Evidence Association*, describing a relationship specified by an expression (e.g., equality of some fields) and optionally timing by direction (i.e., A precedes B). Lastly, *Evidence Store*, a specialised BPMN *Data Store*, denotes persistent storage for *Potential Evidence*, which can be stored in multiple places.

Diverging from FR-ISSRM concepts, the last two requirement constructs focus on modelling forensic readiness capabilities within the process. The first is an *FR Task*, a specialised BPMN *Task*, for modelling a highly-abstract atomic activity relevant to forensic readiness (e.g., creating a proof of integrity). The second is a *FR Service*, a specialised BPMN *Pool*, representing a participating external service which plays a role in forensic readiness (e.g., a notary service).

Control Constructs The second level of BPMN4FRSS constructs focuses on describing concrete technologies analogous to FR-ISSRM Forensic readiness control. This level is built on defined extension points, where new constructs could be introduced into the language. It allows the inclusion of richer information needed for model-based verification of forensic-ready software systems [15]. In this chapter, we present some realistic representatives.

Examples of more specific but still high-level *FR Tasks* are *Authenticity Computation* and *Integrity Computation* constructs. Such activities create proofs of authenticity or integrity which can overlap. Outputs of those *FR Tasks* are new pieces of *Potential Evidence* providing assurances of another *Potential Evidence* (represented by *Evidence Association*). These specific pieces of *Potential Evidence* are organised under an abstract *Proof*, which can be further specified based on the used technology for better extensibility. For example, *Hash Proof* can result from an *Integrity Computation*, given it computes a cryptographic hash of *Potential Evidence* to prove its integrity. Another specialised *FR Task* is *Data Transformation*, allowing for its documentation and validation to assert the impact on the meaning of potential evidence.

Specialised *FR Service* constructs can also define a specialised *Proofs*. An example of specific technology is blockchain timestamping service, represented by *BC Timestamp Service* with its resulting *BC Timestamp Partial Proof* and *BC Timestamp Full Proof*. Concrete instantiations of the *BC Timestamp Service* are ChainPoint [36], and OpenTimestamps [62]. They both first generate an *BC Timestamp Partial Proof* as a temporal (weak) receipt and *BC Timestamp Full Proof* once it is committed to the blockchain. In another example, OriginStamp [29] can generate *BC Timestamp Full Proof* immediately, if required, so *BC Timestamp Partial Proof* is optional.

4.3 Concrete Syntax

The BPMN4FRSS abstract syntax is realised by introducing new visual elements and stereotypes for existing BPMN constructs. Additionally, details of the stereotypes are specified using the non-visual attributes. This concept of stereotypes and parameters originates from UML profiles [5]. For the sake of clarity, we opt to use green colour to highlight the constructs. However, it is not strictly required. Table 1 contains the basic elements of the concrete syntax, i.e., visual constructs and their mapping to the abstract syntax. Precisely, it is a mapping of each abstract syntactical construct on either visual element, stereotype, or parameter. The mapping to non-visual constructs is motivated by balancing the visual expressiveness and readability of the diagram.

Table 1. Concrete syntax of BPMN4FRSS.

Forensic Readiness Requirement Constructs		
Abstract Syntax	**Concrete Syntax**	**Parameters**
Evidence Source	Q	
Potential Evidence	«Evidence»	Data Fields, Lifecycle Process
Produces	·········>	
Evidence Association	------>	Expression
Evidence Context	«EvidenceContext»	Cooperativeness
Evidence Store	«EvidenceStore»	Stored Potential Evidence
FR Task	«FRTask»	
FR Service	«FRService»	
Forensic Readiness Control Constructs		
Abstract Syntax	**Concrete Syntax**	**Parameters**
Hash Proof	«HashProof»	
PKI Timestamp Proof	«PKITimestampProof»	Originates From
BC Timestamp Partial Proof	«BCTimestampPartialProof»	Originates From
BC Timestamp Full Proof	«BCTimestampFullProof»	Originates From
Promise Of	<<promiseOf>>	
PKI Timestamp Service	«PKITimestampService»	
BC Timestamp Service	«BCTimestampService»	
Authenticity Computation	«AuthenticityComp»	Input, Output
Integrity Computation	«IntegrityComp»	Input, Output
Data Transformation	«DataTransformation»	Input, Output, Script

Requirement Constructs of BPMN4FRSS, in essence, add the potential evidence, its origin, context, and storage to the standard BPMN model. Figure 4 displays a simple process diagram, where Business data and Audit log are considered vital for a future investigation, thus marked as potential evidence. Concretely, Business data is an integral part of the plain process, while the Audit log is added for its role in forensic readiness to support the former. Their relationship is captured by the *Evidence Association*, which is visible in the evidence view (see Sect. 4.5). Both are organised under a *Pool*, marked as *Evidence Context*, which parameter *Cooperativeness* informs about the supposed availability of the potential evidence during an investigation. Lastly, the Business data is persistently stored in *Data Store*, marking it accordingly.

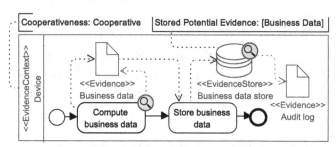

Fig. 4. Example: Concrete syntax of BPMN4FRSS requirement constructs [18].

FR Task-based Control Constructs deal with representing actions using specific technologies with a BPMN *Task*. The *FR Task* stereotype is replaced by a set of more specific ones (due to the overlap). Figure 5 contains a process model, where a digest (i.e., hash) was computed for Business data to prove its integrity. Here, the hashing is modelled as the *Integrity Computation*, taking *Data Object* as input and producing a *Hash Proof*, specialised evidence (*Proof*), as an output. Notably, as *Proof* itself is abstract, it must be represented by specialised stereotypes. Other stereotypes rooted in *FR Task* can be defined for mode concrete techniques, e.g., keyed hashing with a key as additional input. The analogous approach applies to the specialisations of the abstract *Proof*.

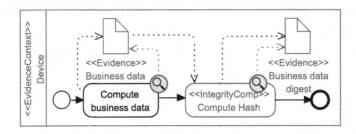

Fig. 5. Example: Concrete syntax of BPMN4FRSS task-based control constructs [18].

FR Service-based Control Constructs also use the stereotypes in a similar manner, applied to a BPMN *Pool*. They emphasise the externality of the service to the system under the scope. Figure 6 depicts a process model of utilising a blockchain-based timestamping service to prove the integrity and authenticity of Business data, verifiable by a third party. To that end, a signed digest is sent to the *BC Timestamp Service*, receiving a *BC Timestamp Partial Proof* as a reply. Once is the signed digest committed to the blockchain, *BC Timestamp Full Proof* is received. The *PKI Timestamp Service* would be modelled analogously but with a single *PKI Timestamp Proof*. However, the syntactical rules themselves do not enforce a correct usage in BPMN (e.g., swapping of proofs is syntactically correct). For this reason, semantic rules also need to be specified for the control constructs.

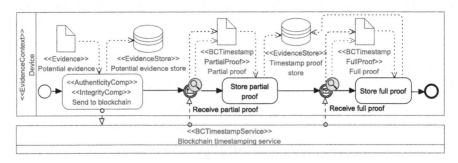

Fig. 6. Example: Concrete syntax of BPMN4FRSS service-based control constructs [18].

4.4   Semantics

Some portions of BPMN4FRSS semantics were discussed jointly with syntax, as it inherently forces some semantical rules [50]. While such an informal description suffices for a basic description of a forensic-ready software system, there is a danger of misinterpretation. Furthermore, the support for forensic-ready risk management is limited as correct assessment requires a precise definition of how the FR-ISSRM concepts are represented. In other words, a definition of semantical mapping [27] between FR-ISSRM concepts and BPMN4FRSS concrete syntax.

A semantical mapping of ISSRM concepts and (extended) BPMN has already been defined in the Security risk-oriented BPMN [4] language. Besides adding new visual elements and characteristics, it primarily describes an approach for creating BPMN models usable for security risk management which is a question of pragmatics [50]. Importantly, it does not override the semantics of BPMN. Therefore, the mapping is expanded to accommodate the FR-ISSRM concepts with the help of the BPMN4FRSS language. This expanded semantic mapping of BPMN4FRSS into the FR-ISSRM domain is summarised in Table 2.

Table 2. Semantic mapping between FR-ISSRM domain model and BPMN4FRSS constructs.

FR-ISSRM Concept	Concrete Syntax	Note
Evidence	<<Evidence>>	Stereotyped Data Object
Evidence source		Evidence Source attached to Task, Data Store, or Event
Evidence store	<<EvidenceStore>>	Stereotyped Data Store
Creates	<<Evidence>>	Produces association between Evidence Source and Potential Evidence
Corroborates	<<Evidence>> <<Evidence>>	Evidence Association with direction from Potential Evidence to Potential Evidence
Forensic readiness goal	Annotation	Annotation
Claim on	Annotation <<Evidence>>	Annotation associated with Task or Data Object
Facilitates	-	-
Forensic readiness scenario		Process or its fragment
Forensic readiness treatment	-	-
Decision to treat	-	-
Forensic readiness requirement + *Enhances*	<<FRTask>> <<FRService>>	Process or its fragment containing requirement constructs
Refines	-	-
Forensic readiness control	<<BCTimestampService>> <<IntegrityComp>>	Process or its fragment containing requirement constructs and control constructs
Implements	-	-

Table 3. BPMN4FRSS semantical rules.

Data Objects and *Data Stores* with the same name in a single model namespace are considered the same object for all intents and purposes.
Non-cooperative *Evidence Context* cannot contain *Evidence Sources* nor *Evidence Stores*.
Hash Proof must be an output of an *Integrity Computation Task*.
PKI Timestamp Proof must be an output of *Event or Task*, which has *Message Flow* directed to it from a *PKI Timestamp Service Pool*.
BC Timestamp Partial Proof must be an output of *Event or Task*, which has *Message Flow* directed to it from a *BC Timestamp Service Pool*.
BC Timestamp Full Proof must be an output of *Event or Task*, which has *Message Flow* directed to it from a *BC Timestamp Service Pool*.
BC Timestamp Full Proof which is *promise of* BC *Timestamp Partial Proof*, must both *originate from* the same *BC Timestamp Service Pool*.

FR-ISSRM further defines Evidence source, specialised IS Asset, as a point of origin of Evidence. It is mapped to a new visual element, *Evidence Source*, attached to a *Task*, *Event*, or *Data Store*. Not only this mapping tells which IS asset is the origin, but in the BPMN context, it also describes its position and timing within a process. From the other side of the spectrum, Evidence store, an IS asset which persistently stores *Potential Evidence*, is mapped on the stereotyped *Data Store* as it represents persistent storage.

Both Evidence source and Evidence store are context-sensitive. FR-ISSRM describes this sensitivity by a notion of cooperativity of the Evidence source and storage, denoting how accessible the potential evidence is before and during the investigation. In BPMN4FRSS, the context is expressed by a stereotyped *Pool* with a cooperativeness attribute, as it is a native container for BPMN processes. The cooperativeness can be (1) Non-Cooperative: potential evidence is inaccessible (e.g., personal device), (2) Cooperative: potential evidence is accessible, and (3) Semi-Cooperative: potential evidence accessibility is specific and further specified.

One of the objectives of utilising BPMN4FRSS is to create models of Forensic readiness scenarios. Therefore, the FR-ISSRM forensic readiness scenario maps the combination of *Pools* and *Graphical Objects* they contain. According to FR-ISSRM, the combination must include *Risk*, *Potential Evidence*, and a *Graphical Object* annotated with *Forensic Readiness Goal*. Then, the Forensic readiness goal is mapped by an *Annotation* on a *Graphical Object* representing a Business asset, signifying the claim on the Business asset.

The last concepts to cover are the treatments. In other words, it allows the modelling of Forensic readiness requirements and controls, capturing different stages of development and evolution. Forensic readiness requirement is mapped to a combination of *Flow Objects* and FRSS4BPMN requirement concepts. Then, the Forensic readiness controls extend this mapping to include FRSS4BPMN control concepts, which describe the technical details. This paper explicitly defines a trusted timestamping service based on PKI [63] and blockchain [62].

Semantical rules were discussed as a tool, enforcing the correctness of the BPMN4FRSS models. They pose several restrictions on the use of BPMN4FRSS, which is especially important for representing controls. Therefore, extensions should also provide new rules in addition to syntactic constructs. Table 3 provides an overview of the rules.

4.5   Model Views

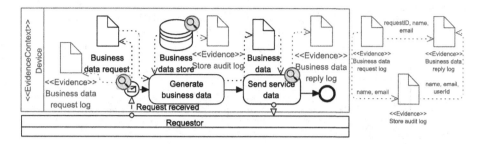

Fig. 7. Scenario View (left) and Evidence View (right) [18].

Visualisation of all BPMN4FRSS constructs, specifically *Evidence Associations*, can result in an overly complicated diagram. A trivial solution is abstaining from visualising chosen constructs and representing them in purely textual form. However, we opted to provide two concurrent views on a model, a well-known approach in software architecture modelling [35]. The views focus on (1) scenarios and (2) evidence relationships.

Furthermore, we adopt the model view approach, allowing a combination of several models into a single goal-oriented view [9]. It is used to model separate and reusable processes of potential evidence lifecycle to supplement the main process model.

Scenario View is a default view visualising the BPMN process diagram enhanced by the BPMN4FRSS constructs. The emphasis is put on a clear display of forensic readiness scenario, omitting any associations between *Potential Evidence*. An example is depicted in Fig. 7 (left).

Evidence View is a specialised view visualising relationships between *Potential Evidence*. Specifically, it consists of annotated *Evidence Associations* with optional direction representing timing. An example is depicted in Fig. 7 (right). The labels on each *Evidence Association* depicts expression parameter. For brevity, the shared data fields are displayed, and more complex functions are enclosed in curly brackets.

Lifecycle Process is a separate process, capturing the lifecycle of potential evidence. It also covers its processing and strengthening (e.g., integrity and availability proofs). While it can be expressed as a part of the main process, the separation aims for reusability and readability. The process can be shared among multiple *Potential Evidence* and cascaded if remaining acyclic (i.e., new *Potential Evidence* in a Lifecycle Process can have its own). Currently, we restrict the lifecycle process to the *Potential Evidence*, which is unhandled in its creation process. Figure 6 is an example of a lifecycle process.

5   BPMN4FRSS Example in Risk-Oriented Design

To demonstrate the utilisation of BPMN4FRSS and validate our contribution, we apply it to an Automated Valet Parking (AVP) scenario [42]. We utilised this scenario to demonstrate the preliminary idea of risk-oriented design for forensic-ready software systems [17] and the representation of forensic readiness controls [16]. We expanded on the results with explicit semantic mapping to the FR-ISSRM domain model, which

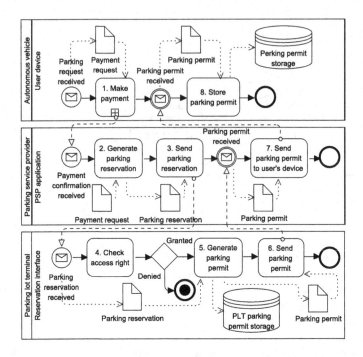

Fig. 8. Excerpt from Automated Valet Parking case: Issuing a parking ticket [18].

Table 4. Automated Valet Parking case initial assets and risks.

Business Assets	Parking reservation, Parking permit
IS Assets	PSP application, Parking lot terminal, PLT parking permit storage
Risk (R1)	A malicious insider injects a parking permit into the PLT parking permit storage due to their capability to access it, leading to a loss of Parking permit integrity.
Risk (R2)	An attacker fabricates a fake Parking reservation and sends it to the Parking lot terminal due to access control tampering, leading to the loss of Parking permit integrity.
Risk (R3)	A dishonest customer repudiates a Parking permit to demand a reimbursement, leading to a loss of Parking permit integrity.
FR Goal	Prove valid creation of a Parking permit.
Evidence	Parking reservation, Parking permit
Evidence Sources	Parking service provider application, Parking lot terminal
Evidence Stores	PLT parking permit storage

allows model-based support for the forensic-ready risk management process. Additionally, the mapping allows for the creation of models with different levels of abstraction, capturing requirements or specific controls, and cooperation with Security risk-oriented BPMN [4].

5.1 Default Case

Figure 8 is an excerpt from the BPMN model describing a case of issuing a parking ticket. This part of the models the process from the payment made on an Autonomous Vehicle (AV) to generating a parking permit by Parking Lot Terminal (PLT), all facilitated by Parking Service Provider (PSP), which sends the parking permit back to the AV – the user device.

The default case contains numerous vulnerabilities and a lack of sufficient forensic-ready properties [17]. This makes attacks from malicious parties both possible and hard to detect. We employed the ISSRM risk management process [37] to identify Assets, Risks, and possible Security requirements, followed by initial steps of FR-ISSRM to define Forensic readiness goal. Table 4 contains a summary of the relevant outputs, and Fig. 9 contains a diagram of a model with a joint representation of risks and initial evidence. The risk-related concepts are modelled by Security risk-oriented BPMN [4] and forensic readiness concepts by BPMN4FRSS.

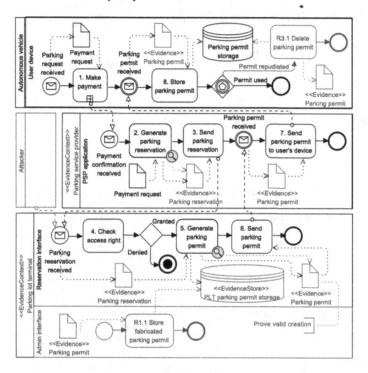

Fig. 9. Risks and initial evidence.

Concerning the forensic readiness goal, the main issue is that the Parking permit is not corroborated by independent evidence and might be easily fabricated (R1, R2). While the Parking reservation can be used for corroboration, its permanent storage is not defined and also fabricated on the PLT level. Furthermore, the ease of fabrication makes defence against repudiation by a customer (R3) highly unreliable. Forensic readiness requirements aim to make the risk occurrence provably detectable and traceable.

5.2 Forensic-Ready Case

Based on the identified Risks and defined Forensic readiness goals, the FR-ISSRM process formulates Forensic readiness scenarios, which are iteratively enhanced with Forensic readiness requirements to ensure the satisfaction of the Goals. Then, the Requirements are specified and implemented as Forensic readiness controls, summarised in

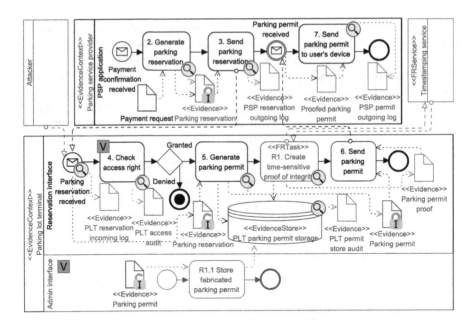

Fig. 10. Forensic readiness requirements (scenario view).

Table 5. Automated Valet Parking case forensic readiness requirements and controls.

Requirement	Control	Risk
Insertions into the PLT parking permit storage shall be recorded	PLT parking permit storage generates a PLT access audit record	R1
Requests on Reservation interface shall be recorded on both sides	PSP generates a PSP reservation outgoing log record, and PLT generates a PLT reservation incoming log record	R1, R2
Access attempts to PLT shall be recorded	PLT generates PLT access audit record	R1, R2
Parking permit creation shall be verifiable by 3rd party	Hashed and signed Parking permit is sent to OpenTimestamp service for timestamped proof	R3
Responses to AV shall be recorded	PSP generates PSP permit outgoing log	R3

Table 5. The Scenarios are jointly represented using BPMN4FRSS models on the requirement level in Fig. 10 and the control level in Fig. 11. Additionally, the evidence view corresponds to the control-level model in Fig. 12. The AV is not displayed on the diagrams as its *Evidence Context* is non-cooperative, and no potential evidence can be relied upon.

One of the model's purposes is to evaluate the satisfaction of the Forensic readiness goal. In this chapter, we perform a manual evaluation and reasoning based on the information from models. It consists of elicitation of the potential evidence covering the parts of the process related to the Risk. Additionally, the pieces of potential evidence are correlated with others, increasing their value, quantified by the number of copies and related potential evidence. This idea translates into the preliminary model-based metrics we proposed for Forensic readiness scenarios [16]. The Risks are addressed as follows:

R1: The actions of a malicious insider injecting a parking permit into the PLT parking permit storage are recorded as PLT permit storage audit records. Moreover, evidence

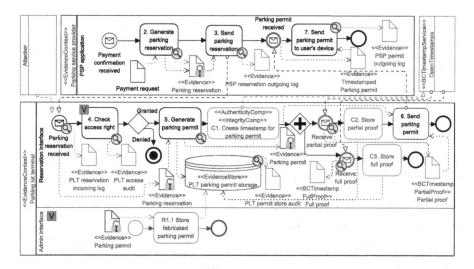

Fig. 11. Forensic readiness controls (scenario view).

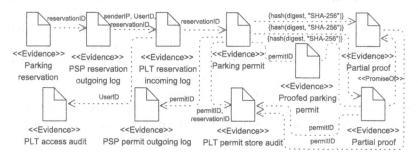

Fig. 12. Forensic readiness controls (evidence view).

associations show the related pieces of evidence which would be missing and therefore pointing to the injection. For example, PLT reservation incoming log, as the association is transitive.

R2: From the PLT perspective, a fabricated parking reservation is indistinguishable. However, the fabrication can be detected by reconstructing the evidence links. For example, a PSP reservation outgoing log will be missing. Alternatively or additionally, PSP can store issued parking reservations and copies of corresponding permits, enabling a comparison between the stores.

R3: The main issue of proving the reputation of the parking permit is the inability to access the user's device due to the privacy and user's unwillingness (i.e., non-cooperating device). Therefore, supporting evidence must be established to prove the creation and transmission of the parking permit. Specifically, the blockchain-based timestamping service OpenTimestamps was introduced, which creates proofs of the parking permit verifiable by 3rd party.

Notably, the models do not capture the persistent storage of the most potential evidence (e.g., logs), which is essential in evaluating the evidentiary value. For example, local and remote storage has a vastly different impact on both value and costs. The life-cycle process should be modelled to represent how the potential evidence is stored. For the purpose of this example, simple storage to the local filesystem is assumed.

6   Discussion

Modelling forensic-ready software systems is a critical enabler towards systematic reasoning over such systems. BPMN4FRSS facilitates capturing the specific requirements and later the specific controls relating to a particular scenario. Aligned with forensic-ready risk management, BPMN4FRSS supports the assessment by providing a foundation for evaluating treatment options.

In our example, we mainly focus on requirements and controls on PLT, which is only one of the options. Alternatively, duplicate storage for parking reservations and permits on PSP would preserve evidence resistant to PLT tampering. BPMN4FRSS aligned with risk management allows for exploration and comparison of these alternatives using models.

As apparent from the models, the forensic readiness controls do not reduce the risk directly. However, it could be argued that it acts as a deterrence [52]. Still, it is a viable precaution in cases where security controls might not adequately cover business risks (R3) or risks from insider threats (R1). In this regard, forensic readiness controls complement the security measures by providing means to detect and trace the occurrence of a risk. This interplay with security is further apparent by the overlap with traditional security controls (e.g., hashing, signatures, trusted timestamping).

6.1   Meeting the Research Goal

As stated, the primary goal of BPMN4FRSS is the support forensic-ready risk management decisions in the design of forensic-ready software systems. Arguably, BPMN4FRSS addressed the set contributions in the following way:

C1: Integrating Forensic-Ready Risk Management Concepts into BPMN4-FRSS Models. We aligned the BPMN4FRSS constructs with the FR-ISSRM domain model and validated it by demonstrating a particular case. This semantical mapping to the FR-ISSRM domain significantly reduces the ambiguity of BPMN4FRSS models and allows for their clear interpretation. Compared to the initial version, a concrete outcome of this mapping is a division of requirement and control constructs. As a result, the BPMN4FRSS models can be used in various stages of the design process. Furthermore, it enables the instantiation of FR-ISSRM as a BPMN4FRSS model.

C2: Enabling Joint Representation of Security and Forensic-Ready Risk Management Concepts in BPMN4FRSS Models. We utilised the idea of FR-ISSRM being an extension of ISSRM and focused the BPMN4FRSS only on the novel features without overriding existing semantics. Effectively, this enables the seamless extension of BPMN-based notation which is aligned with ISSRM, separating the concerns between the two. The example case validates this claim, as the models use both Security risk-oriented BPMN and BPMN4FRSS, each focused on their specific part.

C3: Supporting Model-Based Assessment of Forensic Readiness Treatments. The presented semantic mapping is a crucial foundation for systematic risk assessment. It reduces the redundancy and ambiguity of the modelled constructs, correctly placing them within the FR-ISSRM approach with a clear interpretation. While in the example case, we conducted only an informal assessment of the treatments, the semantics is meant to support FR-ISSRM metrics defined in our previous work [16].

6.2 Future Direction

While the BPMN4FRSS is an essential contribution to the challenge of representing and reasoning over forensic-ready software systems [44], it is just a piece of the jigsaw. This section briefly discusses further research directions supported by BPMN4FRSS.

Model-Based Assessment is one of the key reasons why BPMN4FRSS was formulated and aligned with FR-ISSRM. However, future directions should focus on automating the risk assessment based on BPMN4FRSS models. A possible way includes computation of model metrics [16], potentially supplemented by user inputs (e.g., likelihoods of the risks). Examples of such are computing coverage of given risk by potential evidence or trustability score of potential evidence based on its copies and relations. As a result, the assessment should provide a more precise comparison of alternatives and facilitate a better return on investment.

Model-Based Assurance refers to techniques of using BPMN4FRSS models for verification of the forensic-ready software systems. Models can be analysed by themselves for an indicator of bad design or used as a reference in analysing runtime artefacts (e.g., correct generation of potential evidence) [14, 15] The semantical rules discussed in Sect. 4.4 are an example of a technique for design-time assurance.

Tool Support is another open challenge for forensic-ready software systems [44], as well as an important component for broader adoption of BPMN4FRSS. Such a tool should enable the effective creation, validation, and analysis of BPMN4FRSS models. Currently, we are developing such a tool to facilitate further research in BPMN4FRSS and analysis of the models.

7   Conclusion

In this chapter, we presented the BPMN4FRSS modelling language, an extension of BPMN to represent forensic-ready software systems. The language defines syntactical constructs for expressing the specific requirements of forensic-ready software systems and concrete controls which implement them. Importantly, we also defined semantical mapping of the language to the FR-ISSRM domain model, establishing the language semantics. This way, the BPMN4FRSS models can be utilised to support forensic-ready risk management in the systematic design of forensic-ready software systems, which we demonstrated in an example. Consequently, our result contributes to the evolving state-of-the-art forensic-ready software systems development and is an enabler for further evolution.

References

1. Ab Rahman, N.H., Glisson, W.B., Yang, Y., Choo, K.K.R.: Forensic-by-design framework for cyber-physical cloud systems. IEEE Cloud Comput. **3**(1), 50–59 (2016). https://doi.org/10.1109/MCC.2016.5

2. Alrajeh, D., Pasquale, L., Nuseibeh, B.: On evidence preservation requirements for forensic-ready systems. In: Proceedings of the 2017 11th Joint Meeting on Foundations of Software Engineering, ESEC/FSE 2017, pp. 559–569. ACM (2017). https://doi.org/10.1145/3106237.3106308

3. Alrimawi, F., Pasquale, L., Nuseibeh, B.: Software engineering challenges for investigating cyber-physical incidents. In: 2017 IEEE/ACM 3rd International Workshop on Software Engineering for Smart Cyber-Physical Systems (SEsCPS), pp. 34–40 (2017). https://doi.org/10.1109/SEsCPS.2017.9

4. Altuhhova, O., Matulevičius, R., Ahmed, N.: An extension of business process model and notation for security risk management. Int. J. Inf. Syst. Model. Des. **4**, 93–113 (2013). https://doi.org/10.4018/ijismd.2013100105

5. Arlow, J., Neustadt, I.: UML 2 and The Unified Process: Practical Object-Oriented Analysis and Design. Pearson Education, Boston (2005)

6. Asnar, Y., Giorgini, P.: Modelling risk and identifying countermeasure in organizations. In: Lopez, J. (ed.) CRITIS 2006. LNCS, vol. 4347, pp. 55–66. Springer, Heidelberg (2006). https://doi.org/10.1007/11962977_5

7. Baror, S.O., Venter, H.S., Adeyemi, R.: A natural human language framework for digital forensic readiness in the public cloud. Aust. J. Forensic Sci. **53**(5), 566–591 (2021)

8. Van den Berghe, A., Scandariato, R., Yskout, K., Joosen, W.: Design notations for secure software: a systematic literature review. Softw. Syst. Model. **16**(3), 809–831 (2017)

9. Bruneliere, H., Burger, E., Cabot, J., Wimmer, M.: A feature-based survey of model view approaches. Softw. Syst. Model. **18**(3), 1931–1952 (2019)

10. Casey, E.: Digital Evidence and Computer Crime, 3rd edn. Academic Press, New York (2011)

11. Casey, E., Nikkel, B.: Forensic analysis as iterative learning. In: Keupp, M.M. (ed.) The Security of Critical Infrastructures. ISORMS, vol. 288, pp. 177–192. Springer, Cham (2020). https://doi.org/10.1007/978-3-030-41826-7_11

12. CESG: Good Practice Guide No. 18: Forensic Readiness. Guideline, National Technical Authority for Information Assurance, United Kingdom (2015)

13. Chergui, M.E.A., Benslimane, S.M.: A valid BPMN extension for supporting security requirements based on cyber security ontology. In: Abdelwahed, E.H., Bellatreche, L., Golfarelli, M., Méry, D., Ordonez, C. (eds.) MEDI 2018. LNCS, vol. 11163, pp. 219–232. Springer, Cham (2018). https://doi.org/10.1007/978-3-030-00856-7_14

14. Daubner, L., Macak, M., Buhnova, B., Pitner, T.: Towards verifiable evidence generation in forensic-ready systems. In: 2020 IEEE International Conference on Big Data (Big Data), pp. 2264–2269 (2020)

15. Daubner, L., Macak, M., Buhnova, B., Pitner, T.: Verification of forensic readiness in software development: a roadmap. In: Proceedings of the 35th Annual ACM Symposium on Applied Computing, SAC 2020, pp. 1658–1661. ACM (2020). https://doi.org/10.1145/3341105.3374094

16. Daubner, L., Macak, M., Matulevicius, R., Buhnova, B., Maksovic, S., Pitner, T.: Addressing insider attacks via forensic-ready risk management. J. Inf. Secur. Appl. **73**, 103433 (2023). https://doi.org/10.1016/j.jisa.2023.103433

17. Daubner, L., Matulevičius, R.: Risk-oriented design approach for forensic-ready software systems. In: The 16th International Conference on Availability, Reliability and Security. ACM (2021). https://doi.org/10.1145/3465481.3470052

18. Daubner, L., Matulevičius, R., Buhnova, B., Pitner, T.: Business process model and notation for forensic-ready software systems. In: Proceedings of the 17th International Conference on Evaluation of Novel Approaches to Software Engineering, ENASE 2022, Online Streaming, 25–26 April 2022, pp. 95–106. SCITEPRESS (2022). https://doi.org/10.5220/0011041000003176

19. Dijkman, R.M., Dumas, M., Ouyang, C.: Semantics and analysis of business process models in BPMN. Inf. Softw. Technol. **50**(12), 1281–1294 (2008)

20. Dubois, É., Heymans, P., Mayer, N., Matulevičius, R.: A systematic approach to define the domain of information system security risk management, pp. 289–306. Springer, Heidelberg (2010). https://doi.org/10.1007/978-3-642-12544-7_16

21. Elyas, M., Ahmad, A., Maynard, S.B., Lonie, A.: Digital forensic readiness: expert perspectives on a theoretical framework. Comput. Secur. **52**, 70–89 (2015). https://doi.org/10.1016/j.cose.2015.04.003

22. Firesmith, D.: Using quality models to engineer quality requirements. J. Object Technol. **2**(5), 67–75 (2003)

23. Geismann, J., Bodden, E.: A systematic literature review of model-driven security engineering for cyber-physical systems. J. Syst. Softw. **169**, 110697 (2020). https://doi.org/10.1016/j.jss.2020.110697

24. Grispos, G., García-Galán, J., Pasquale, L., Nuseibeh, B.: Are you ready? towards the engineering of forensic-ready systems. In: 2017 11th International Conference on Research Challenges in Information Science (RCIS), pp. 328–333 (2017). https://doi.org/10.1109/RCIS.2017.7956555

25. Grispos, G., Glisson, W.B., Choo, K.K.R.: Medical cyber-physical systems development: a forensics-driven approach. In: 2017 IEEE/ACM International Conference on Connected Health: Applications, Systems and Engineering Technologies (CHASE), pp. 108–113 (2017)

26. Grobler, C.P., Louwrens, C.P.: Digital forensic readiness as a component of information security best practice. In: Venter, H., Eloff, M., Labuschagne, L., Eloff, J., von Solms, R. (eds.) SEC 2007. IIFIP, vol. 232, pp. 13–24. Springer, Boston, MA (2007). https://doi.org/10.1007/978-0-387-72367-9_2

27. Harel, D., Rumpe, B.: Meaningful modeling: what's the semantics of "semantics"? Computer **37**(10), 64–72 (2004). https://doi.org/10.1109/MC.2004.172

28. Henley, J.: Denmark frees 32 inmates over flaws in phone geolocation evidence. The Guardian (2019). https://www.theguardian.com/world/2019/sep/12/denmark-frees-32-inmates-over-flawed-geolocation-revelations

29. Hepp, T., Schoenhals, A., Gondek, C., Gipp, B.: Originstamp: a blockchain-backed system for decentralized trusted timestamping. it - Inf. Technol. **60**(5–6), 273–281 (2018)

30. Iqbal, A., Ekstedt, M., Alobaidli, H.: Digital forensic readiness in critical infrastructures: a case of substation automation in the power sector. In: Matoušek, P., Schmiedecker, M. (eds.) ICDF2C 2017. LNICST, vol. 216, pp. 117–129. Springer, Cham (2018). https://doi.org/10.1007/978-3-319-73697-6_9

31. ISO/IEC: Information technology - Security techniques - Incident investigation principles and processes. Standard, International Organization for Standardization, Switzerland (2015)

32. ISO/IEC: Information technology - Security techniques - Information security risk management. Standard, International Organization for Standardization, Switzerland (2018)

33. Kävrestad, J.: Fundamentals of Digital Forensics. Springer, Heidelberg (2018). https://doi.org/10.1007/978-3-030-38954-3

34. Kebande, V.R., Venter, H.S.: On digital forensic readiness in the cloud using a distributed agent-based solution: issues and challenges. Aust. J. Forensic Sci. **50**(2), 209–238 (2018)

35. Kruchten, P.: The 4+1 view model of architecture. IEEE Softw. **12**(6), 42–50 (1995). https://doi.org/10.1109/52.469759

36. Liang, X., Shetty, S., Tosh, D., Kamhoua, C., Kwiat, K., Njilla, L.: Provchain: a blockchain-based data provenance architecture in cloud environment with enhanced privacy and availability. In: 2017 17th IEEE/ACM International Symposium on Cluster, Cloud and Grid Computing (CCGRID), pp. 468–477 (2017). https://doi.org/10.1109/CCGRID.2017.8

37. Matulevičius, R.: Fundamentals of Secure System Modelling. Springer, Heidelberg (2017). https://doi.org/10.1007/978-3-319-61717-6

38. Mayer, N.: Model-based Management of Information System Security Risk. Theses, University of Namur (2009). https://tel.archives-ouvertes.fr/tel-00402996

39. McKemmish, R.: When is digital evidence forensically sound? In: Ray, I., Shenoi, S. (eds.) DigitalForensics 2008. ITIFIP, vol. 285, pp. 3–15. Springer, Boston, MA (2008). https://doi.org/10.1007/978-0-387-84927-0_1

40. Mead, N.R., Stehney, T.: Security quality requirements engineering (square) methodology. In: Proceedings of the 2005 Workshop on Software Engineering for Secure Systems-Building Trustworthy Applications, SESS 2005, pp. 1–7. Association for Computing Machinery, New York (2005). https://doi.org/10.1145/1083200.1083214

41. Mülle, J., Stackelberg, S.v., Böhm, K.: A security language for bpmn process models. Technical Report 9, Karlsruher Institut für Technologie (2011)

42. Nwaokolo, A.O.: A Comparison of Privacy Enhancing Technologies in Internet of Vehicle Systems. Master's thesis, University of Tartu (2020)

43. OMG: Business process model and notation (2010). https://www.omg.org/spec/BPMN/2.0/

44. Pasquale, L., Alrajeh, D., Peersman, C., Tun, T., Nuseibeh, B., Rashid, A.: Towards forensic-ready software systems. In: Proceedings of the 40th International Conference on Software Engineering: New Ideas and Emerging Results, ICSE-NIER 2018, pp. 9–12. ACM (2018)

45. Pasquale, L., Hanvey, S., Mcgloin, M., Nuseibeh, B.: Adaptive evidence collection in the cloud using attack scenarios. Comput. Secur. **59**, 236–254 (2016). https://doi.org/10.1016/j.cose.2016.03.001

46. Pasquale, L., Yu, Y., Salehie, M., Cavallaro, L., Tun, T.T., Nuseibeh, B.: Requirements-driven adaptive digital forensics. In: 2013 21st IEEE International Requirements Engineering Conference (RE), pp. 340–341 (2013). https://doi.org/10.1109/RE.2013.6636745

47. Pullonen, P., Matulevičius, R., Bogdanov, D.: PE-BPMN: privacy-enhanced business process model and notation. In: Carmona, J., Engels, G., Kumar, A. (eds.) BPM 2017. LNCS, vol. 10445, pp. 40–56. Springer, Cham (2017). https://doi.org/10.1007/978-3-319-65000-5_3

48. Pullonen, P., Tom, J., Matulevičius, R., Toots, A.: Privacy-enhanced bpmn: enabling data privacy analysis in business processes models. Softw. Syst. Model. **18**(6), 3235–3264 (2019)

49. Rivera-Ortiz, F., Pasquale, L.: Automated modelling of security incidents to represent logging requirements in software systems. In: Proceedings of the 15th International Conference on Availability, Reliability and Security. ACM (2020)

50. Rodrigues da Silva, A.: Model-driven engineering: A survey supported by the unified conceptual model. Comput. Lang. Syst. Struct. **43**, 139–155 (2015). https://doi.org/10.1016/j.cl.2015.06.001

51. Rodríguez, A., Fernández-Medina, E., Piattini, M.: A bpmn extension for the modeling of security requirements in business processes. IEICE - Trans. Inf. Syst. **E90-D**(4), 745–752 (2007)

52. Rowlingson, R.: A ten step process for forensic readiness. Int. J. Digital Evid. **2**, 1–28 (2004)

53. Salnitri, M., Dalpiaz, F., Giorgini, P.: Modeling and verifying security policies in business processes. In: Bider, I., et al. (eds.) BPMDS/EMMSAD -2014. LNBIP, vol. 175, pp. 200–214. Springer, Heidelberg (2014). https://doi.org/10.1007/978-3-662-43745-2_14

54. Silver, B.: BPMN Method and Style, with BPMN Implementer's Guide: a structured approach for business process modeling and implementation using BPMN 2.0. Cody-Cassidy Press Aptos, CA, USA (2011)

55. Simou, S., Kalloniatis, C., Gritzalis, S., Katos, V.: A framework for designing cloud forensic-enabled services (CFeS). Requir. Eng. **24**(3), 403–430 (2018). https://doi.org/10.1007/s00766-018-0289-y

56. Sindre, G.: Mal-activity diagrams for capturing attacks on business processes. In: Sawyer, P., Paech, B., Heymans, P. (eds.) REFSQ 2007. LNCS, vol. 4542, pp. 355–366. Springer, Heidelberg (2007). https://doi.org/10.1007/978-3-540-73031-6_27

57. Sindre, G., Opdahl, A.L.: Eliciting security requirements with misuse cases. Requir. Eng. **10**(1), 34–44 (2005). https://doi.org/10.1007/s00766-004-0194-4

58. Sommerville, I.: Software Engineering, 9th edn. Pearson, Boston (2011)

59. Studiawan, H., Sohel, F., Payne, C.: A survey on forensic investigation of operating system logs. Digital Invest. **29**, 1–20 (2019). https://doi.org/10.1016/j.diin.2019.02.005

60. Tan, J.: Forensic readiness. Technical report, @stake, Inc. (2001)

61. Vraalsen, F., Mahler, T., Lund, M., Hogganvik, I., Braber, F., Stølen, K.: Assessing enterprise risk level: the CORAS approach, pp. 311–333 (2007). https://doi.org/10.4018/978-1-59904-090-5.ch018

62. Weilbach, W.T., Motara, Y.M.: Applying distributed ledger technology to digital evidence integrity. SAIEE Afr. Res. J. **110**(2), 77–93 (2019). https://doi.org/10.23919/SAIEE.2019.8732798

63. Ćosić, J., Bača, M.: (im)proving chain of custody and digital evidence integrity with time stamp. In: The 33rd International Convention MIPRO, pp. 1226–1230 (2010)

Evaluating Probabilistic Topic Models for Bug Triaging Tasks

Daniel Atzberger$^{(\boxtimes)}$, Jonathan Schneider, Willy Scheibel, Matthias Trapp,
and Jürgen Döllner

Hasso Plattner Institute, Digital Engineering Faculty, University of Potsdam, Potsdam, Germany
`daniel.atzberger@hpi.uni-potsdam.de`

Abstract. During the software development process, occurring problems are collected and managed as bug reports using bug tracking systems. Usually, a bug report is specified by a title, a more detailed description, and additional categorical information, e.g., the affected component or the reporter. It is the task of the triage owner to assign open bug reports to developers with the required skills to fix them. However, the bug assignment task is time-consuming, especially in large software projects with many involved developers. This observation motivates using (semi-)automatic algorithms for assigning bugs to developers. Various approaches have been developed that rely on a machine learning model trained on historical bug reports. Thereby, the modeling of the textual components is mainly done using topic models, mainly Latent Dirichlet Allocation (LDA). Although different variants, inference techniques, and libraries for LDA exist and various hyperparameters can be specified, most works treat topic models as a black box without exploring them in detail. In this work, we extend a study of Atzberger and Schneider et al. on the use of the Author-Topic Model (ATM) for bug triaging tasks. We demonstrate the influence of the underlying topic model, the used library and inference techniques, and the hyperparameters on the bug triaging results. The results of our conducted experiments on a dataset from the *Mozilla Firefox* project provide guidelines for applying LDA for bug triaging tasks effectively.

Keywords: Bug triaging · Topic models · Latent dirichlet allocation · Inference techniques

1 Introduction

The complexity of modern software development processes requires the systematic coordination of the communication and work steps of the involved stakeholders. For example, changes to the source code are managed within a version control system, tasks are coordinated in issue tracking systems, or occurring errors are documented in bug tracking systems. Therefore, throughout the entire development process, data is generated and archived in the various repositories. The *Mining Software Repositories*

The first two authors contributed equally to this work. This work is mainly based on a former publication of the two main authors and their co-authors and the master thesis of the second author.

H. Kaindl et al. (Eds.): ENASE 2022, CCIS 1829, pp. 44–69, 2023.
https://doi.org/10.1007/978-3-031-36597-3_3

research field is now concerned with gaining insights from this data, e.g., by applying algorithms from the machine learning domain. One issue that is often addressed in related work is the aim to increase efficiency during the software development process is the (semi-)automatic assignment of open bug reports to suitable developers. This is especially of interest in large distributed development teams, where the triage owner may not be informed about the specific skills of each developer. Here and in the following, we always refer to bug reports, though the assignment of issue reports or change requests are treated equally in our considerations. Precisely, we refer to the problem defined as follows: "Given a new bug report, identify a ranked list of developers whose expertise qualifies them to fix the bug" [27].

Various approaches for automatic bug triaging have been proposed utilizing different data sources, e.g., source code [11,13,14,17,31], question-and-answer platforms [26], or solely historical bugs [6]. Thereby the textual components of the bug reports are usually modeled using LDA [6]. LDA is a probabilistic topic model proposed by Blei et al., often used to capture a intrinsic semantic structure of a collection of documents [5]. Given a set of documents, a so-called corpus, LDA detects patterns of co-occurring words and derives topics as multinomial distributions over the vocabulary. An underlying human-understandable concept of a topic can then often be derived from its most probable words, thus supporting explainability to the user. Furthermore, the semantic structure of a document is modeled as a distribution over the extracted topics, thus allowing a mathematical treatment of the documents. When applying topic models, different specifications can be made by the user:

Variant of LDA. The baseline LDA model can be extended by meta-information about the documents, e.g., the ATM, which incorporates knowledge about the authorship of the documents [25], or Labeled LDA for documents associated with discrete categories [23].

Inference Technique. Since exact inference for LDA is intractable, an approximation algorithm has to be taken into account when training LDA, e.g., Collapsed Gibbs Sampling (CGS) [9] or Variational Bayes (VB) [5].

Implementation. Different software libraries implement different inference algorithms and also differ in their default settings.

Hyperparameters. Besides the number of topics, the Dirichlet priors for the document-topic distribution and the topic-term distribution can be specified by the user.

Though the application of LDA incorporates many specifications by the user, in most related work, the model is treated as a black box without fully exploring the effect of the parameters [6].

Atzberger and Schneider et al. proposed three novel bug triaging algorithms that rely on the ATM, a variant of LDA, and compared them against an approach proposed by Xie et al. [2]. In their work, the authors evaluated the effect of the inference technique, as well as the Dirichlet prior and the number of topics as hyperparameters of the underlying LDA model. We extend their work by additionally comparing the effect of an online training method with the batch training algorithm and detailing the effect of the used topic modeling library. We further discuss statements made by Xie et al. about a hyperparameter in their proposed approach. Our results are derived from experiments on a large dataset of bug reports from the *Mozilla Firefox* project. As a result of our work, we formulate different guidelines for applying LDA effectively for the bug triaging task, which can be seen as a starting point for other software engineering tasks that rely on topic models.

The remainder of this work is structured as follows: Section 2 presents existing bug triaging approaches utilizing probabilistic topic models. The techniques of Xie et al. and Atzberger and Schneider et al. are explained in Sect. 3, together with an introduction to LDA and the ATM. Our experimental setup for conducting our study is shown in Sect. 4. The results of our experiments are presented in Sect. 5 and their implications are discussed in Sect. 6. We conclude this work and point out directions for future work in Sect. 7.

2   Related Work

In this section, we present existing approaches for assigning bug reports to developers. We focus our presentation of related work on approaches that rely on LDA for modeling the textual components of a bug report as this is the focus of our work and therefore ignore approaches utilizing information from the version control system [11,13,14,17, 31], or question-and-answer platforms [26]. An overview of the approaches that we consider is shown in Table 1.

Xie et al. were the first who applied LDA for the bug triaging task [39]. Their approach Developer Recommendation based on Topic Models (DRETOM) comprises three parts. First, an LDA model is trained on a corpus of historical bug reports with known resolvers. Then, for an incoming bug report, for each developer, a score is computed that is meant to capture their familiarity with the dominant topic of the bug report. In the last step, the developers are ranked according to their scores. In a later work, Atzberger and Schneider et al. built up on the idea of Xie et al. and proposed three algorithms based on the ATM. An advantage of the ATM is its interpretability, as each developer can be modeled as a distribution over the topics. This sort of explainability is particularly interesting for its use in real-world settings [1,45]. The modifications Developer Recommendation based on the Author-Topic Model (DRATOM) and Developer Recommendation based on the Author-Topic Model and Bayes Formula (DRATOMBayes) replace the LDA core with the ATM. Their third approach Developer Recommendation based on Author Similarity (DRASIM) exploits the fact that the ATM can describe bug reports and developers in a joint feature space and thus allows them to draw associations direct from the model itself.

The approach presented by Xia et al. takes a bug report's title and description as textual components, the product and component affected by the bug, and the developers who participated in resolving the bug into account [38]. For an incoming bug report, similar historical bug reports are detected based on an abstraction based on the terms occurring in the bug textual components, its topic distribution derived from LDA, and both the categorical features component and product. The developers are then associated with an affinity score. Similarly, a second affinity score is derived from comparing the new bug report with developers by considering their past activities. Combining the two affinity scores results in a list of potential developers.

Table 1. Comparison of related work that used probabilistic topic models.

All approaches (in chronological order) used the natural language title and description for topic modeling (LDA). Further attributes are used to improve the predictions of ground truth developers with regard to the chosen evaluation scheme and metrics covered in Sect. 4. We also examined the work in relation to the following aspects: (Q1) Mentioned inference technique, (Q2) Optimized number of topics K, and (Q4) Optimized Dirichlet priors (α, β). Depending on whether it is true or not, we use ✓ or ✗, respectively. ✍ denotes that the authors claimed but did not report this optimization and ? that the publication did not report the parameters at all.

Authors	Topic Model	Q1	Q2	Q3	Q4	Further used Features	Ground Truth	Evaluation Scheme	Evaluation Metric
Xie et al. [39]	LDA	✗	✗	✗	✗		assignee, commenters	fixed train/test split	Precision@k, Recall@k, F_1
Xia et al. [38]	LDA	✗	✗	✗	✗	product, component	assignee, commenters	10-fold time-split	Precision@k, Recall@k, F_1
Naguib et al. [20]	LDA	✓	?	?	?	component	assignee, reviewer, resolver	fixed train/test split	Accuracy@k
Zhang et al. [43]	LDA	✗	✍	✗	✗	& comments, & assignments	assignee, commenters	fixed train/test split	Precision@k, Recall@k, F_1, MRR
Yang et al. [40]	LDA	✗	✗	✗	✗	product, component, priority, severity, & comments, & commits, & assignments, & attachments	assignee	fixed train/test split	Precision@k, Recall@k, F_1, MRR
Zhang et al. [44]	LDA	✓	✗	✍	✗	commenters, submitters	commenters	8-fold time-split	Recall@k
Nguyen et al. [22]	LDA	✗	?	✗	?	fixer, time to repair, severity	commenters	fixed train/test split	Median absolute error for time to repair
Zhang et al. [42]	LDA	✗	✗	✓	✗	product, component, priority, & comments, & fixed bugs, & reopened bugs	assignee, commenters	10-fold time-split	Precision@k, Recall@k, F_1, MRR
Xia et al. [37]	MTM	✓	✓	✓	✗	product, component	assignee	10-fold time-split	Accuracy@k

Naguib et al. presented an approach for bug triaging based on LDA and the affected system component [20]. In their approach, each developer's activity profile is computed based on past activities as an assignee, reviewer, or resolver of a bug. Given the topic distribution of a new bug, the developers are then ranked according to their activity profiles.

Zhang et al. proposed an algorithm utilizing the textual components of a bug and the developers' social network [43]. First, an LDA model is trained, which allows for comparing a new bug report with a historical data basis. A developer's expertise in a topic is modeled from past bug reports' activities. Besides actual assignments, also comments are taken into account. Furthermore, a metric is derived that represents the role of a developer in the social network by relating a potential candidate to the most active reporter. The combination of both metrics leads to a ranking for a new bug based on its semantic composition.

The approach of Yang et al. also trains an LDA model on a corpus of historical bug reports [40]. Their approach detects similar bug reports for a new incoming bug report by considering its topics, product, component, severity, and priority. Then, from those similar bug reports, their approach extracts potential candidates. Based on the number of assignments, attachments, commits, and comments, the candidates are ranked according to their potential to fix the bug.

Zhang et al. presented BUTTER, another approach based on training an LDA model on a corpus of historical bug reports [44]. For each developer, a score in a topic is derived from a heterogeneous network consisting of submitters, developers, and bugs using the RankClass model. Combining the topic distribution from the RankClass model with the topic distribution derived from the LDA model, a candidate list of developers for a new bug is computed.

Nguyen et al. translated the task of assigning a bug report to the task of predicting the resolution time for fixing a bug report [22]. By assuming a log-normal regression model for the defect resolution time, their approach predicts a bug report's resolution time based on its topic distribution along with the bug fixer and the severity level [22]. Also in their approach, the topic distribution of a bug is inferred from a previously trained LDA model. The bug report is then assigned to the developer, who is most likely the fastest to fix the bug.

Similar to Xia et al. [38], the approach presented by Zhang et al. detects the K-nearest neighbors for a new bug report based on its textual components, product and component, and its topic distribution [42]. From the K most similar bug reports, the developers are then ranked according to their activities as assignees and commenters. The approach allows for the choice of 18 hyperparameters, of which only the number of topics concerns the underlying LDA model, the remaining hyperparameters of the LDA model remain on the default settings.

This is an example of a general trend whereby the algorithm for developer recommendations is becoming more complex, but the underlying topic models remain unchanged. Researchers usually treat topic models as black boxes without fully exploring their underlying assumptions and hyperparameter values [6]. The approaches presented so far used LDA without considering the impact of all of its hyperparameters or the used inference technique.

A significant exception is the work by Xia et al., who extend the basic topic modeling algorithm LDA and propose the Multi-feature Topic Model (MTM) [37]. The MTM includes a bug report's feature combination, e.g., its product and component, as an additionally observed variable and models the topic distributions for each feature combination. They recommend the developers based on the affinity scores of a developer towards a topic and the feature combination. Although they systematically evaluated the number of topics and iterations required for Gibbs sampling, they omit the influence of the Dirichlet priors, which remain at the tool's default settings.

All presented works use Gibbs sampling as the inference technique for LDA, although most do not mention it, only the used topic modeling tool. Therefore, it is likely that this choice was made unconsciously, especially since the authors often explicitly emphasize using the default hyperparameters for LDA. Only two of the previous works reported the influence of the most critical hyperparameter – the number of topics – on the quality of the developer recommendations [37,42]. Others set this value arbitrarily [22,38,39], kept the number of topics at the default value of the used implementation [40,43], or did not report this value [20].

Although much of the work compares directly with the basic DRETOM approach by Xie et al. , comparability of study results is limited due to different definitions of ground truth developers, evaluation setups, evaluation metrics, varying projects selected for evaluation, and chosen preprocessing techniques. Among those works that reimplement DRETOM [40,42–44], none of them describe how DRETOM's trade-off parameter θ was chosen. In contrast, these approaches introduce their own hyperparameters to weigh various influencing factors. The impact of their hyperparameters on the quality of developer recommendations is considered and optimized for, but not those of the methods compared with, let alone the hyperparameters of LDA. Therefore, in our work, we put particular emphasis on the influence of the hyperparameters of LDA and the ATM as well as the used inference techniques on the hyperparameters of the proposed approaches.

A detailed overview of how topic models are used for software engineering tasks, in general, is presented by Chen et al. [6]. In this systematic literature study, the authors show that only a small number of related work fully uses the possibilities of tuning the hyperparameters of a topic model or its implementation. Our work follows their suggestion of reimplementing existing approaches and taking various preprocessing steps and hyperparameter tuning into account.

3   Assigning Bug Reports Using LDA

In this section, we present four approaches proposed by Xie et al. and Atzberger and Schneider et al. for assigning bug reports to developers. Both works rely solely on analyzing bug reports' textual components using probabilistic topic models. We, therefore, present details about the preprocessing steps, the underlying structure of the topic model, and its hyperparameters before detailing the ranking schemes in the different bug triaging approaches.

Table 2. Three extracted topics with the highest probability from the exemplary bug report. The example is taken from Atzberger et al. [2].

Topic # 1	Topic # 2	Topic # 3
private	preferences	bar
browsing	pref*	url
mode	options	location
clear	dialog	autocomplete
cookies	default	text
history	set	address
window	prefs	results
data	option	type
cookie	preference	enter
cache	change	result

3.1 Preprocessing

We combine each bug report's title and more detailed description to form a document. The resulting corpus $\mathcal{D} = \{d_1, \ldots, d_M\}$ consists of documents that contain the textual components of the given bug reports. In our considerations, we ignore the discussions attached to a historical bug report as they are not available at the time when a bug report is assigned. In order to remove words that carry no meaning, we need to undertake the corpus $\mathcal{D}$ several preprocessing steps. The work of Atzberger and Schneider et al., follows the best practices studies by Schofield et al. [28–30], specifically:

1. Removal of URL, hex code, stack trace information, timestamps, line numbers, tokens starting with numerics, tokens consisting of only one character and punctuation,
2. Lower casing the entire document,
3. Removal of all words from the English *NLTK Stopwords Corpus*[1]
4. Removal of words with a frequency less than 5 as well as a maximum word occurrence of no more than 20% across all bug reports.

In contrast to Xie et al., we intentionally do not apply stemming. Topic model inference often groups words sharing morphological roots in the same topics, making stemming redundant and potentially damaging to the resulting model [29]. After preprocessing, we store each document as a Bag-of-Words (BOW), i.e., we neglect the ordering of the terms within a document and only keep their frequencies. The entire corpus $\mathcal{D}$ is written as a document-term matrix, whose rows are the BOW vectors of the documents.

3.2 Latent Dirichlet Allocation and Its Variants

Starting from the document-term matrix, whose rows contain the term frequencies of the corresponding preprocessed documents, LDA detects clusters within the vocabulary by observing patterns of co-occurring words [5]. These clusters $\varphi_1, \ldots, \varphi_K$ are called

---

[1] http://www.nltk.org/nltk_data/.

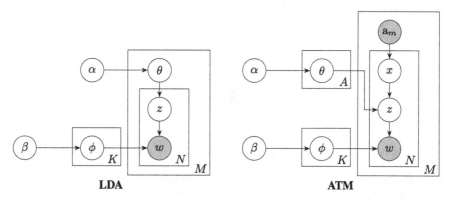

LDA   **ATM**

Fig. 1. (Left) Graphical model underlying LDA in plate notation, (Right) Graphical model underlying the ATM in plate notation. The shaded circles denote observed variables.

topics and are formally given by multinomial distributions over the vocabulary $\mathcal{V}$. Here K, denotes the number of topics and is a hyperparameter of the model which needs to be set by the user initially. Table 2 shows three exemplary topics extracted from the *Mozilla Firefox* dataset that will be presented in detail in Sect. 4.1. From its ten most probable words, we derive that topic #1 concerns browsing in private mode, topic #2 concerns preference settings, and topic #3 is about the user interface. Besides a description of the topics, LDA results in a document-specific topic distributions $\theta_1, \ldots, \theta_M$ that capture the semantic composition of a document in a vector of size K. LDA assumes a generative process underlying a corpus $\mathcal{D}$, which is given by:

1. For each topic $\varphi_1, \ldots, \varphi_K$ choose a distribution according to the Distribution Dirichlet(β)
2. For each document d in the corpus $\mathcal{D}$
   (a) Choose a document-topic distribution θ according to Dirichlet(α)
   (b) For each term w in d
      i. Choose a topic $z \sim$ Multinomial(θ)
      ii. Choose the word w according to the probability $p(w|z, \beta)$

The generative process as a graphical model is shown in Fig. 1.

Here, α and β denote the Dirichlet priors for the document-topic and topic-term distribution, respectively. The meaning of the parameter $\alpha = (\alpha_1, \ldots, \alpha_K)$, where $0 < \alpha_i$ for all $1 \leq i \leq K$, is best understood when written as the product $\alpha = a_c \cdot m$ of its concentration parameter $a_c \in \mathbb{R}$ and its base measure $m = (m_1, \ldots, m_K)$, whose components sum up to 1. Depending on whether the base measure is uniform, i.e., $m = (1/K, \ldots, 1/K)$, or not, we call the Dirichlet distribution symmetrical or asymmetrical, respectively. In the case of a symmetric prior, small values of a_c, the Dirichlet distribution would favor points in the simplex that are close to one edge, i.e., LDA would try to describe a document with a minimum of topics. The larger the value of a_c, the more likely that LDA is to fit all topics with a non-zero probability for a document. Figure 2 illustrates the effect of the chosen concentration parameter of a symmetric prior.

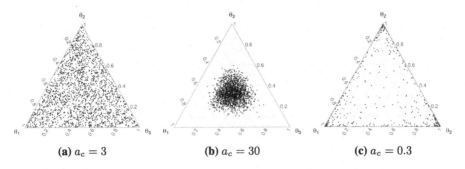

(a) $a_c = 3$ **(b)** $a_c = 30$ **(c)** $a_c = 0.3$

Fig. 2. 2,000 randomly sampled topic distributions θ using varying concentration parameters a_c for symmetrical Dirichlet prior α. We illustrate the distributions for $K = 3$ topics in the three-dimensional topic space $\theta = (\theta_1, \theta_2, \theta_3)$. The base measure $m = (1/3, 1/3, 1/3)$ is uniform for every symmetrical Dirichlet distribution.

A symmetrical prior distribution of topics within documents assumes that all topics have an equal prior probability of being assigned to a document. However, setting a symmetrical α prior ignores that specific topics are more prominent in a corpus and, therefore, would naturally have a higher probability of being assigned to a document. Conversely, some topics that are less common and, thus, not appropriately reflected with a symmetrical prior for the document-topic distributions. In contrast, an asymmetrical β prior over the topic-term distributions is not beneficial [32,35]. The case of an asymmetric Dirichlet prior is shown in Fig. 3.

The goal of fitting such a model is to infer the latent variables from the observed terms. However, since exact inference is intractable, approximation algorithms need to be taken into account [5], e.g.,CGS [9], batch VB [5], and its online version Online Variational Bayes (OVB) [10]. Geigle provides a comparison of these techniques [8].

Different variants of LDA have been developed for the case, where additional meta-information to the documents is available. One such variant is the ATM, proposed by Rosen-Zvi et al. [25]. By observing the authors of a document, it assumes a generative process underlying a corpus, which is given by:

1. For each author $a \in \{a_1, \ldots, a_A\}$:
   (a) Choose a distribution over topics $\theta_a \sim \text{Dirichlet}(\alpha)$,
2. For each topic $\varphi_1, \ldots, \varphi_K$ choose a distribution according to the distribution $\text{Dirichlet}(\beta)$
3. For each document d in the corpus $\mathcal{D}$:
   (a) Given a group of authors, $\mathbf{a}_m \subseteq \{a_1, \ldots, a_A\}$, for document d,
   (b) For the nth word $w_{m,n}$ of the N words to be generated in document m:
      i. Choose an author $x_{m,n} \sim \text{Uniform}(\mathbf{a}_m)$,
      ii. Choose a topic $z_{m,n} \sim \text{Multinomial}(\theta_{x_{m,n}})$,
      iii. Choose a word $w_{m,n} \sim \text{Multinomial}(\varphi_{z_{m,n}})$.

Its generative process is shown in Fig. 1. Rosen-Zvi et al. provided the CGS algorithm for fitting an ATM model, the batch and online VB algorithm were presented by Mortensen [19].

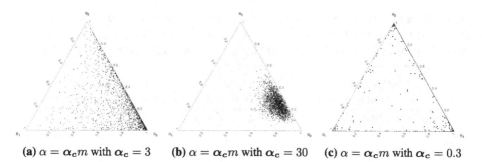

(a) $\alpha = \alpha_c m$ with $\alpha_c = 3$ **(b)** $\alpha = \alpha_c m$ with $\alpha_c = 30$ **(c)** $\alpha = \alpha_c m$ with $\alpha_c = 0.3$

Fig. 3. 2,000 randomly sampled topic distributions θ using varying concentration parameters a_c for an asymmetrical Dirichlet prior α. We illustrate the distributions for $K = 3$ topics in the three-dimensional topic space $\theta = (\theta_1, \theta_2, \theta_3)$. The base measure $m = (1/12, 1/4, 2/3)$ defines the asymmetry where the third topic is most likely independent of the concentration parameter.

3.3 Ranking Developers

DRETOM. After training a LDA model on a corpus of historical bug reports with known resolvers, each bug report is associated with its dominant topic. The aptitude $P(d|b)$ for a developer d to solve a bug report b can be computed using the sum rule of conditional probabilities

$$P(d|b) = \sum_z P(d|z) \cdot P(z|b), \tag{1}$$

where $P(d|z)$ denotes the skill level of the developer d in the respective topic z, and $P(z|b)$ is the probability of the topic in the given bug report. In the considerations of Xie et al. the skill of a developer d in topic z is composed by two parts, which are balanced by a trade-off parameter $\theta \in [0, 1]$:

$$P(d|z) = \theta P(d \to z) + (1 - \theta)P(z \to d), \tag{2}$$

where $P(d \to z)$ is called interest and $P(z \to d)$ is called expertise. Given the number of bug reports $N_{d,z}$ of developer d that belong to topic z, and the number of bugs N_d, where d has contributed, the interest part is computed as

$$P(d \to z) = \frac{N_{d,z}}{N_d}, \tag{3}$$

Given the total number N_z of bug reports that are associated with topic z, the expertise component is computed as

$$P(z \to d) = \frac{N_{d,z}}{N_z}. \tag{4}$$

For an incoming bug report, its topic distribution is inferred using the trained LDA model and the developers are ranked according to their conditional probabilities from Eq. (1).

DRATOM & DRATOMBayes. Atzberger and Schneider et al. proposed two adaptions of DRETOM by utilizing the ATM [2]. Their first modification DRATOM simply replaces the LDA core of DRETOM by the ATM, i.e., only the probability $P(z|b)$ is derived from another model.

Their second modification DRATOMBayes circumvents the choice of the trade-off parameter θ by taking the description of a developer as distribution over topics, learned from the ATM, into account. From the Bayes' formula, we derive

$$P(d|z) = \frac{P(z|d) \cdot P(d)}{P(z)}. \tag{5}$$

The probability $P(d)$ is approximated by the fraction

$$P(d) = \frac{N_d}{N_{total}}, \tag{6}$$

where N_{total} denotes the number of all bug reports in the training corpus. The marginal probability $P(z)$ is approximated from the base measure of the Dirichlet prior α, i.e.,

$$m = (m_1, \ldots, m_K) = (P(z_1), \ldots, P(z_K)). \tag{7}$$

DRASIM. Linstead et al. were the first to apply the ATM for software engineering tasks [15]. Atzberger and Schneider et al. adopted this approach for the case of bug reports, which results in a joint embedding of developers and bug reports in a common feature space. Their approach DRASIM therefore reduces the bug triaging tasks to a Nearest Neighbor (NN) search, i.e., for an incoming bug report the developers are ranked according to a measure $D(b, d)$, where D denotes a chosen similarity measure, e.g., the Jensen-Shannon distance, the cosine similarity, or the Manhattan distance.

4   Experimental Setup

In our experiments, we investigate the effect of the underlying topic model, the inference technique, the topic modeling library used, and the hyperparameters on the results of the presented bug triaging algorithms. In this section, we present details on our experimental setup. The dataset on which the experiments are carried out contains bugs from the *Mozilla Firefox* project for over 15 years. To take into account this long development history, we chose the Longitudinal Evaluation Scheme for quantifying the bug triaging algorithms. To compare different topic modeling libraries, we have chosen the three actively maintained libraries *Gensim*, *MALLET*, and *Vowpal Wabbit*. We present details regarding their implementations at the end of the section.

4.1   Dataset

Xie et al. evaluated their approach on a data set from the *Mozilla Firefox* and the Eclipse projects, which are widely used in related work [3,4,7,16,20,36,37,42,43]. For the *Mozilla Firefox* project, their corpus contains 3005 bug reports, collected between

September 2008 to July 2009, with 96 involved developers. In contrast, we compare the approaches DRETOM, DRATOM, DRATOMBayes, and DRASIM on a dataset published by Mani et al., which contains bug reports of the *Mozilla Firefox* project collected between July 1999 until June 2016 [16]. In contrast to Xie et al., we only train our model on bug reports with an assigned developer, and a status marked as *verified fixed*, *resolved fixed*, or *closed fixed*. The final assignee is considered as ground truth. As our experiments depend on the Author-Topic Model, we ensure that each training set has at least 20 bug reports per developer. In total, our dataset contains 18,269 bug reports with 169 bug resolvers.

4.2 Evaluation Scheme

In our experiments, each bug triaging algorithm is evaluated on ten runs. For this purpose, the bug reports are ordered chronologically and divided into 11 equally sized disjoint subsets. In the k-th run, where $1 \leq k \leq 10$, the k first subsets are used for training, and the $(k + 1)$-th subset is used for testing. This evaluation scheme is known as the longitudinal evaluation scheme and has been shown to increase internal validity [4, 12, 16, 33, 37]. Furthermore, the time allocation considers that the available developers change throughout the project. As Xie et al. only train on bug reports collected within one year, this circumstance is not critical for their work.

Like most related work, Xie et al. evaluate their approach using the metrics Recall@k and Precision@k. Both metrics only consider if the ground-truth assignee is among the top k recommendations but do not consider the actual position. However, a good bug triaging algorithm should place the real assignee at a higher rank, as the triager usually checks the higher positions first. In our experiments, we consider the Mean Reciprocal Rank (MRR)@10 as an evaluation metric, which is affected more by a hit in the first rank. The MRR@10 is given by

$$MRR@10 = \frac{1}{\#bug\ reports} \sum_{i=1}^{\#bug\ reports} (RR@10)_i, \text{ where} \tag{8}$$

$$(RR@10)_i = \begin{cases} \frac{1}{\text{rank}_i}, & \text{if rank}_i \leq 10 \\ 0, & \text{otherwise} \end{cases} \tag{9}$$

and RR denotes the reciprocal rank and rank_i is the rank position of the real assignee for the ith bug report.

4.3 Topic Modeling Implementations

Xie et al. used the LDA implementation provided by the *Stanford Topic Modeling Toolbox (STMT)* [23]. In our work, we use more recently maintained libraries. Among the most widely used topic modeling libraries are *MALLET* [18] for Java, *Gensim* [24] for Python, and *Vowpal Wabbit*[2] for C++. The LDA implementation of the *Gensim* library is based on the VB algorithm proposed by Blei et al. [5] and offers its online version

---

[2] https://hunch.net/?p=309.

presented by Hoffman et al. [10]. In the single-threaded mode, *Gensim* allows the automatic adjustment of both Dirichlet priors. However, in the multi-core version, this feature is not available. For the ATM we refer to *Gensim*'s implementation of the ATM, which applies VB and OVB respectively. The *Vowpal Wabbit* implementation is written in C++ and implements the same OVB as *Gensim*, though it supports neither parallelization nor hyperparameter optimization. It only allows specifying the LDA hyperparameter, i.e., the number of topics and symmetrical Dirichlet priors α and β, as well as the hyperparameters necessary for OVB. In contrast, *MALLET* is the most advanced topic modeling toolkit of those we consider. It implements the simple parallel threaded implementation proposed by Newman et al. [21] with the SparseLDA Gibbs scheme and the data structure introduced by Yao et al. [41]. Based on the work of Wallach, *MALLET* implements several strategies for hyperparameter optimizations of Dirichlet priors [34].

5   Results

In this section, we give details on the conducted experiments and present their results. In their study, the Xie et al. evaluated their proposed approach DRETOM regarding its potential for recommending bug resolvers and the influence of the hyperparameter θ on the bug triaging results. In our first three experiments, we compare different implementations of LDA and inference techniques for replicating the DRETOM approach. With the DRETOM approach, we want to discuss our first research question:

RQ1: *To what extent does the chosen implementation of LDA and inference technique affect results for the bug triaging task?*

In the next step, we compare DRETOM with the three approaches presented by Atzberger and Schneider et al. based on the ATM. Precisely, we want to answer the following research question:

RQ2: *Are the approaches based on the ATM able to outperform DRETOM?*

Both topic models, LDA and the ATM, require to specify the number of topics K and the Dirichlet prior α for the document-topic distribution. In our fifth experiment, we varied the possible hyperparameters to address the following research question:

RQ3: *How far do the choice of hyperparameter, i.e., the number of topics and the Dirichlet prior, affect the approaches for bug triaging tasks?*

Our results further allow us to discuss statements made by Xie et al. on the hyperparameter θ, that will be discussed in the fourth research question:

RQ4: *What is the influence of the hyperparameter θ for the quality of the recommendation results?*

Table 3. DRETOM's default parameter settings for LDA in *Gensim, Vowpal Wabbit* and *MALLET*.

	Gensim	Vowpal Wabbit	MALLET
α	alpha $= 0.01$	--lda_alpha $= 0.01$	--alpha $= 0.2$[a]
β	alpha $= 0.01$	--lda_rho $= 0.01$	--beta $= 0.01$
K	num_topics $= 20$	--lda $= 20$	--num-topics $= 20$
i_{CGS}	n/a	n/a	--num-iterations $= 100$
P	workers $= 6$	n/a	--num-threads $= 6$
Random seed	random_state $= 42$	--random_seed $= 42$	--random-seed $= 42$

[a]*MALLET* expects the concentration parameter, i.e., $0.01 \cdot K = 0.2$, for $K = 20$.

5.1 Naive Replication Study of DRETOM

In the first three experiments, we want to investigate how the chosen LDA implementation and the underlying inference technique affect the results of a bug triaging algorithm. In our first experiment, we therefore replicated the study by Xie et al. and adopt their parameter configurations. We assume symmetric distributions for both Dirichlet priors α and β, each with a concentration parameter of 0.01. The number of latent topics is set to $K = 20$, and the number of iterations in the Gibbs sampling is set to $i_{CGS} = 100$. To reduce computation time, we resort to the parallelized variants in *Gensim* and *MALLET* and set the number of parallel threads to 6. *Vowpal Wabbit* does not allow the use of hardware acceleration. All remaining parameters are set to their default values defined by the library. The parameter values are summarized in Table 3.

Table 4. Impact of underlying inference techniques using default parameters for LDA implementations on MRR@10 obtained on the Mozilla Firefox project with 10-fold cross validation. The mean over the cross validation and standard deviation are reported. The optimal hyperparameter setting for θ is highlighted.

Model	θ	& 1	& 2	& 3	& 4	& 5	& 6	& 7	& 8	& 9	& 10	Average
DRETOM Gensim (parallel)	0.0	**8.5**	**6.8**	9.2	13.0	9.4	4.4	**10.2**	6.9	8.4	6.1	**8.3 ± 2.4**
	0.1	7.6	6.6	8.4	12.5	9.0	**4.4**	9.2	**7.0**	**8.8**	6.2	8.0 ± 2.2
	0.2	7.0	6.0	7.6	11.6	6.3	4.0	7.7	6.2	7.3	5.4	6.9 ± 2.0
	0.3	6.2	5.5	6.7	9.7	5.4	3.9	7.0	5.4	5.7	5.1	6.1 ± 1.5
	0.4	5.8	5.6	5.8	7.5	4.6	3.7	6.1	4.5	4.4	4.4	5.2 ± 1.1
DRETOM Gensim	0.0	**8.4**	**6.6**	9.4	**13.5**	12.7	5.3	10.1	7.0	**9.0**	6.4	8.8 ± 2.7
	0.1	7.7	6.4	9.1	13.3	**13.2**	**5.6**	**10.6**	**7.3**	8.9	**6.5**	**8.9 ± 2.8**
	0.2	6.9	5.5	8.4	12.1	10.8	4.5	9.3	6.3	8.4	6.3	7.8 ± 2.4
	0.3	6.2	5.5	7.3	10.5	8.6	4.3	7.6	4.9	7.2	5.7	6.8 ± 1.9
	0.4	5.8	5.3	6.4	8.9	6.8	3.7	6.2	4.0	6.5	4.9	5.9 ± 1.5
DRETOM MALLET	0.0	**9.0**	9.8	15.0	16.0	14.3	8.5	13.7	8.8	13.1	13.1	12.1 ± 2.8
	0.1	8.8	10.6	**16.5**	**16.7**	**15.1**	**9.8**	**13.9**	**9.7**	**15.0**	**14.8**	**13.1 ± 3.0**
	0.2	8.0	11.1	15.5	16.3	12.9	9.0	10.8	8.6	13.5	14.8	12.0 ± 3.0
	0.3	7.1	**11.6**	13.5	15.6	10.3	7.8	8.4	7.6	12.1	14.1	10.8 ± 3.0
	0.4	6.4	11.0	12.2	13.0	7.8	6.6	6.5	7.0	10.0	13.1	9.4 ± 2.8
DRETOM Vowpal Wabbit	0.0	**9.0**	**7.1**	7.9	14.5	8.4	**5.5**	8.1	**7.0**	**7.7**	**6.9**	**8.2 ± 2.4**
	0.1	8.3	7.1	**8.7**	15.2	**8.5**	4.7	7.1	6.2	7.1	6.5	7.9 ± 2.8
	0.2	8.2	6.3	7.3	**16.8**	7.5	3.2	5.6	4.7	6.0	5.2	7.1 ± 3.7
	0.3	5.7	5.2	4.6	16.0	4.5	2.0	4.2	3.2	5.7	3.1	5.4 ± 3.9
	0.4	6.7	4.5	4.0	8.1	3.2	1.5	3.3	2.5	3.9	2.3	4.0 ± 2.0

We report the results of the first experiments over all ten runs according to the longitudinal evaluation scheme in terms of the MRR@10 in Table 4. As the optimal value for θ never exceeds a value more than 0.3, we only present the results for values $\theta \leq 0.4$.

In nearly every run, the single-threaded variant of *Gensim* (8.9%) is superior to its multi-threaded version (8.3%). On average, the single-threaded variant outperforms the multi-threaded variant by 7.2%. The *MALLET*-based implementation (13.1%) outperforms all other versions in nearly every run. 47,2% gives the average advantage against the single-threaded *Gensim* implementation, 57,8% against the multi-threaded *Gensim* implementation, and 59,8% against the *Vowpal Wabbit* implementation (8.2%). This indicates the supremacy of the CGS against the VB. Furthermore, the trade-off parameter θ seems to influence all implementations strongly. Xie et al. report that the average precision and recall peak at $\theta = 0.6$ for the *Mozilla Firefox* project, which favors the developer's interest slightly more than a developer's expertise. Surprisingly, regardless of the LDA implementation, DRETOM never reaches an optimal value of θ greater than 0.3 in the first experiment of our reproduction study. The developer's expertise is much more critical concerning the bug assignment prediction accuracy measured with the MRR@10 compared to a developer's interest. Across all cross-validation splits, the MRR@10 peaks at $\theta = 0.0$ in 47.5% of the cases, which means that the recommendation is wholly based on a developer's expertise.

5.2   Multi-pass Online Variational Bayes Inference

In the second experiment, we investigated to what extent the inferiority of the VB implementations in the first experiment is because the LDA model has not converged. To determine whether the frequently used default value $i_{CGS} = 100$ is sufficient, we increase the number of Gibbs iterations to $i_{CGS} = 1000$. Furthermore, we increase the number of iterations for *Gensim*'s number of variations to $i_{VB} = 400$. *Vowpal Wabbit* does not offer a parameter to modify this stopping criterion and runs as many iterations as required to reach the convergence threshold δ. Both libraries use the learning parameters κ and τ set to 0.5 and 1.0 to guarantee convergence [10]. To allow a more direct comparison between both libraries implementing OVB we increase the batch size for *Vowpal Wabbit* from 256 to match the default value of *Gensim*, which results in updating the topic-term distributions in the M-step after processing 2,000 documents.

Table 5. Additional LDA learning parameters for *Gensim*, *Vowpal Wabbit* and *MALLET*.

	Gensim	Vowpal Wabbit	MALLET
S	chunksize = 2000	--minibatch = 2000	n/a
κ	decay = 0.5	--power_t = 0.5	n/a
τ_0	offset = 1.0	--initial_t = 1.0	n/a
δ	gamma_threshold = 0.001	--lda_epsilon = 0.001	n/a
passes	passes = 10	--passes = 10	n/a
i_{VB}	iterations = 400	n/a[a]	n/a
i_{CGS}	n/a	n/a	--num-iterations = 1000

[a]*Vowpal Wabbit* does not offer this parameter to stop earlier, i.e., it is implicitly set to ∞.

Table 6. Impact of underlying inference techniques using multi-pass VB on MRR@10 obtained on the Mozilla Firefox project with 10-fold cross validation The mean accuracy over the cross validation and standard deviation are reported. The best hyperparameter setting for θ is highlighted.

Model	θ	& 1	& 2	& 3	& 4	& 5	& 6	& 7	& 8	& 9	& 10	Average
DRETOM *Gensim* (parallel)	0.0	8.6	7.2	11.5	15.2	14.5	8.5	14.2	9.4	10.9	9.1	10.9 ± 2.8
	0.1	8.6	**7.3**	**11.8**	**15.2**	**14.8**	**9.6**	**15.2**	**10.0**	**11.2**	**9.7**	**11.3 ± 2.9**
	0.2	8.3	6.6	10.9	14.5	12.9	8.2	12.8	8.9	9.2	9.1	10.1 ± 2.5
	0.3	8.4	6.3	9.9	13.6	10.8	6.8	9.8	7.5	7.5	8.6	8.9 ± 2.2
	0.4	8.7	6.4	8.1	11.6	8.7	6.1	8.5	6.2	5.9	7.5	7.8 ± 1.8
	0.5	9.0	5.9	7.2	9.6	7.4	5.3	7.1	4.9	4.8	6.8	6.8 ± 1.6
	0.6	9.3	5.9	6.2	8.6	6.2	5.0	6.3	4.3	4.4	6.5	6.3 ± 1.6
	0.7	**9.5**	5.7	5.6	7.3	5.3	4.4	5.8	4.0	4.0	6.2	5.8 ± 1.7
DRETOM *Gensim*	0.0	8.7	7.0	10.2	15.0	11.3	5.8	10.1	7.4	8.8	6.3	9.1 ± 2.8
	0.1	8.7	**7.0**	**10.6**	**15.5**	**12.4**	**6.1**	**10.3**	**7.6**	**9.1**	6.5	**9.4 ± 2.9**
	0.2	8.2	6.7	10.0	14.8	10.7	4.7	9.7	6.6	8.6	**6.6**	8.7 ± 2.8
	0.3	8.4	6.3	8.6	13.3	8.6	3.9	8.5	5.5	7.6	6.3	7.7 ± 2.5
	0.4	8.8	6.4	7.2	11.2	7.1	3.5	7.0	4.5	6.4	5.5	6.8 ± 2.2
	0.5	8.8	6.1	6.5	9.1	5.9	3.0	5.9	3.9	5.1	4.7	5.9 ± 1.9
	0.6	9.2	5.9	5.6	7.4	4.8	2.6	4.7	3.4	4.2	4.1	5.2 ± 2.0
	0.7	**9.4**	6.0	5.1	6.3	4.0	2.3	4.2	3.0	3.7	3.9	4.8 ± 2.0
DRETOM *MALLET*	0.0	**8.9**	9.7	15.3	15.9	14.7	7.8	14.6	10.0	13.4	12.0	12.2 ± 2.9
	0.1	**8.9**	10.4	**16.8**	**16.3**	**16.0**	**8.8**	**15.0**	**10.7**	**14.3**	**13.7**	**13.1 ± 3.1**
	0.2	8.0	11.3	15.5	15.7	13.1	7.3	13.1	9.3	12.6	13.5	11.9 ± 2.9
	0.3	7.4	**11.5**	12.7	14.7	10.5	6.0	10.4	8.1	11.1	13.0	10.5 ± 2.7
	0.4	7.0	11.2	10.9	12.1	8.6	5.0	8.5	7.3	9.5	12.1	9.2 ± 2.4
	0.5	7.0	11.0	9.8	10.2	7.4	4.2	7.6	6.3	8.4	11.3	8.3 ± 2.2
	0.6	6.8	10.5	9.2	9.3	6.1	3.8	6.9	5.8	8.0	10.7	7.7 ± 2.2
	0.7	6.9	9.9	8.8	8.3	5.3	3.4	6.3	5.3	7.6	10.2	7.2 ± 2.2
DRETOM *Vowpal Wabbit*	0.0	**9.0**	6.2	**11.3**	14.4	**8.0**	**6.4**	8.1	7.4	**9.6**	**11.6**	**9.2 ± 2.6**
	0.1	8.2	6.6	10.8	**15.3**	6.8	5.9	**8.9**	**8.8**	8.6	9.2	8.9 ± 2.7
	0.2	5.6	6.5	8.3	14.7	4.1	4.8	6.5	8.4	6.9	7.0	7.3 ± 3.0
	0.3	4.8	6.4	6.3	15.2	2.9	3.3	5.5	6.1	4.8	5.4	6.1 ± 3.4
	0.4	4.7	8.1	5.1	8.3	2.5	2.7	4.7	3.3	3.6	3.9	4.7 ± 2.0
	0.5	5.2	8.5	3.8	6.3	2.0	2.2	1.9	2.2	2.7	3.3	3.8 ± 2.2
	0.6	5.1	8.8	4.1	5.7	1.4	1.5	1.3	1.8	2.5	3.1	3.5 ± 2.4
	0.7	5.1	**9.0**	3.9	5.6	1.0	1.3	1.1	1.6	2.3	2.6	3.4 ± 2.6

In both tools, the parameter `passes` controls how many passes will be used to train the topic models. The remaining parameters for the LDA model are unchanged. Table 5 summarizes the parameters changed to our first experiment. The results of our second experiment are presented in Table 6.

On average, the result of the *MALLET*-based implementation does not improve. This shows that a number of $i_{CGS} = 100$ iterations is sufficient to guarantee the convergence of the LDA model. As expected, all implementations based on VB improved. The gains here are 36.1% on average for the parallelized version of *Gensim* (11.3%), 5.6% for its single-threaded version (9.4%), and 12.2% for *Vowpal Wabbit* (9.2%). On average, however, all are still worse than the CGS-based variant and inferior by at least 15.9%.

5.3   Multi-pass Batch Variational Bayes Inference

Our third experiment investigates how batch VB LDA differs from online VB LDA in their results. The primary motivation for using online VB is to study large data sets that can no longer be processed in a single step. However, using online VB entails three additional hyperparameters (S, τ_0, κ), which need to be optimized for. Moreover, OVB is not able to handle a changing vocabulary. In our case, where we analyze bug reports of more than 15 years, this might be problematic. In addition, we evaluate DRETOM based on the batch variant of *Gensim*. However, since *Vowpal Wabbit* does not allow batch learning, and its online variant is inferior to *Gensim*'s, we neglect this setup.

Table 7. Impact of underlying inference techniques using batch VB on MRR@10 obtained on the Mozilla Firefox project with 10-fold cross validation The mean accuracy over the cross validation and standard deviation are reported. The best hyperparameter setting for θ is highlighted. *Vowpal Wabbit* does not implement batch VB LDA.

Model	θ	&1	&2	&3	&4	&5	&6	&7	&8	&9	&10	Average
DRETOM *Gensim* using online VB LDA	0.0	8.7	7.0	10.2	15.0	11.3	5.8	10.1	7.4	8.8	6.3	9.1 ± 2.8
	0.1	8.7	7.0	10.6	15.5	12.4	6.1	10.3	7.6	9.1	6.5	9.4 ± 2.9
	0.2	8.2	6.7	10.0	14.8	10.7	4.7	9.7	6.6	8.6	6.6	8.7 ± 2.8
	0.3	8.4	6.3	8.6	13.3	8.6	3.9	8.5	5.5	7.6	6.3	7.7 ± 2.5
	0.4	8.8	6.4	7.2	11.2	7.1	3.5	7.0	4.5	6.4	5.5	6.8 ± 2.2
	0.5	8.8	6.1	6.5	9.1	5.9	3.0	5.9	3.9	5.1	4.7	5.9 ± 1.9
	0.6	9.2	5.9	5.6	7.4	4.8	2.6	4.7	3.4	4.2	4.1	5.2 ± 2.0
	0.7	9.4	6.0	5.1	6.3	4.0	2.3	4.2	3.0	3.7	3.9	4.8 ± 2.0
DRETOM *Gensim* using batch VB LDA	0.0	8.7	7.2	10.8	15.1	13.0	7.4	13.8	9.1	10.9	7.4	10.3 ± 2.9
	0.1	8.7	7.0	10.4	15.7	13.6	8.1	14.8	9.9	12.0	7.9	10.8 ± 3.1
	0.2	8.2	6.5	9.2	15.6	11.0	7.7	12.6	8.8	10.2	6.8	9.7 ± 2.8
	0.3	8.4	6.1	7.7	13.6	8.9	6.5	9.6	7.9	9.0	5.9	8.4 ± 2.2
	0.4	8.8	5.9	6.3	11.5	7.8	5.7	8.1	6.6	8.1	5.2	7.4 ± 1.9
	0.5	8.8	5.7	5.4	10.3	6.5	5.2	6.9	6.0	7.0	4.5	6.6 ± 1.8
	0.6	9.2	5.7	4.5	9.2	5.8	4.9	5.9	5.6	6.6	4.1	6.2 ± 1.8
	0.7	9.4	5.6	4.1	8.2	4.9	4.7	5.5	5.3	6.3	4.0	5.8 ± 1.8
DRETOM *Mallet*	0.0	9.0	9.8	15.3	15.9	14.5	7.9	14.7	10.0	13.6	12.0	12.3 ± 2.9
	0.1	8.9	10.4	16.7	16.2	15.8	9.0	15.0	10.8	14.2	13.7	13.1 ± 3.0
	0.2	8.1	11.4	15.6	15.8	13.1	7.4	12.9	9.4	12.6	13.5	12.0 ± 2.9
	0.3	7.4	11.6	12.6	14.8	10.6	6.1	10.4	8.0	11.6	13.0	10.6 ± 2.7
	0.4	6.9	11.3	10.9	12.2	8.6	5.0	8.5	7.2	9.9	12.0	9.3 ± 2.4
	0.5	7.0	10.9	9.9	10.3	7.4	4.2	7.5	6.4	9.0	11.3	8.4 ± 2.3
	0.6	6.8	10.5	9.1	9.3	6.2	3.8	6.9	5.7	8.5	10.8	7.8 ± 2.2
	0.7	6.9	9.9	8.7	8.4	5.4	3.4	6.2	5.4	8.2	10.2	7.2 ± 2.2

We keep the parameters the same as in the first two experiments. The results of this experiment are shown in Table 7.

The results show that the OVB variant (9.4%) performs worse than the batch VB variant (10.8%) in every run. The only exception is the first run, where OVB and batch VB practically match since the number of documents was set to 2000. On average, batch VB performs 14.9% better than its online version. Despite all the optimizations, *MALLET* (13.1%) still outperforms *Gensim*; on average, *MALLET* outperforms *Gensim* by 21.3%. In the following two experiments, we neglect OVB.

5.4 Learning Asymmetrical Dirichlet Priors

In the first three experiments, we investigated the underlying inference technique's influence on the bug triaging algorithm's results using DRETOM as an example. In the remaining two experiments, we compared DRETOM with DRATOM, DRATOMBayes, and DRASIM, all of which are based on the ATM. In particular, we want to investigate the influence of the common hyperparameters α and K. In most existing work, a symmetric Dirichlet prior α is assumed, for which the default value of the respective implementation is mainly used. However, work by Wallach et al. shows that an asymmetric Dirichlet prior in combination with a symmetric beta prior has advantages over the default setting [35]. To evaluate the impact, we set the parameter alpha = 'auto' in the *Gensim* implementation for LDA and the ATM. Starting from the symmetrical standard α prior, we let *MALLET* optimize the hyperparameters every 20 iterations after a burn-in period of 50 iterations following David Mimno's advice[3]. The results of the fourth experiment are reported in Table 8.

---

[3] https://stackoverflow.com/questions/47310137/mallet-hyperparameter-optimization.

Table 8. Impact of an optimized, asymmetric α prior on MRR@10 obtained on the Mozilla Firefox project with 10-fold cross validation. DRATOM, DRATOMBayes and DRASIM use the same trained ATM. The mean accuracy over the cross-validation and standard deviation are reported. The best hyperparameter setting for θ and the best distance metric for DRASIM are highlighted.

Model	θ	& 1	& 2	& 3	& 4	& 5	& 6	& 7	& 8	& 9	& 10	Average
DRETOM *Gensim*	0.0	8.8	**7.4**	10.7	15.2	12.8	7.3	13.5	9.3	11.3	7.3	10.4 ± 2.8
	0.1	8.7	7.3	**10.8**	**16.0**	**13.5**	7.9	**14.5**	**9.9**	**12.1**	**8.0**	**10.9 ± 3.0**
	0.2	8.2	7.3	10.1	15.7	11.0	7.5	12.4	8.9	10.2	7.0	9.8 ± 2.7
	0.3	8.2	6.9	8.9	14.0	8.2	6.4	9.3	7.9	8.8	6.1	8.5 ± 2.2
	0.4	8.6	6.9	7.8	11.4	7.2	5.7	7.9	6.9	7.9	5.2	7.5 ± 1.7
	0.5	8.5	6.7	6.8	9.9	6.5	5.3	6.5	6.4	6.9	4.5	6.8 ± 1.5
	0.6	9.0	6.6	5.7	8.7	5.6	5.1	5.6	5.8	6.5	4.0	6.3 ± 1.5
	0.7	9.0	6.7	5.2	7.8	4.7	4.9	5.1	5.5	6.2	4.0	5.9 ± 1.5
	0.8	8.9	6.7	4.6	7.2	4.1	4.7	4.9	5.3	6.2	3.8	5.6 ± 1.6
	0.9	**9.1**	6.7	4.2	6.7	4.0	4.4	4.6	5.1	5.8	3.7	5.4 ± 1.7
	1.0	8.3	6.7	3.9	6.5	3.7	4.3	4.4	4.8	5.7	3.7	5.2 ± 1.5
DRETOM *MALLET*	0.0	9.1	9.3	14.8	15.9	16.8	9.3	16.9	9.3	13.5	12.0	12.7 ± 3.3
	0.1	9.4	10.0	**16.3**	16.7	**17.7**	**10.1**	**17.9**	**10.8**	**14.3**	13.6	**13.7 ± 3.4**
	0.2	9.4	10.2	14.3	**16.8**	16.0	9.7	17.6	10.6	13.6	**14.4**	13.3 ± 3.1
	0.3	9.8	**10.7**	12.1	16.5	13.3	7.6	14.5	9.2	12.0	14.3	12.0 ± 2.7
	0.4	9.9	10.4	10.6	14.2	8.5	6.3	11.7	8.4	10.7	12.8	10.4 ± 2.3
	0.5	10.7	10.3	9.2	12.0	6.7	5.3	10.0	7.7	9.4	11.9	9.3 ± 2.2
	0.6	11.4	10.1	8.1	10.3	5.7	4.8	8.9	7.2	8.3	11.1	8.6 ± 2.2
	0.7	11.5	9.8	7.1	8.9	4.9	4.4	8.1	6.5	7.7	10.2	7.9 ± 2.3
	0.8	11.5	9.4	6.6	8.3	4.3	4.2	7.3	6.1	7.4	9.6	7.5 ± 2.3
	0.9	**11.5**	9.2	6.2	7.8	3.9	4.1	6.8	5.9	7.1	9.2	7.2 ± 2.4
	1.0	10.6	9.0	5.9	7.0	3.8	3.9	6.5	5.8	6.9	8.8	6.8 ± 2.2
DRATOM	0.0	**11.3**	11.8	**13.6**	**15.8**	17.0	10.9	17.2	11.1	**14.3**	**17.3**	14.0 ± 2.7
	0.1	11.2	12.3	12.9	15.4	18.0	12.0	**17.5**	**11.7**	14.1	17.2	**14.2 ± 2.6**
	0.2	11.0	12.6	12.3	15.6	**18.2**	**12.3**	16.6	11.5	13.7	17.0	14.1 ± 2.6
	0.3	10.9	**12.7**	11.7	15.3	17.9	12.0	14.9	11.6	13.4	16.5	13.7 ± 2.4
	0.4	10.8	12.7	11.1	14.9	17.7	11.6	13.9	11.1	12.7	16.5	13.3 ± 2.4
	0.5	10.6	12.3	9.5	15.0	16.9	10.6	13.2	10.9	13.1	16.0	12.8 ± 2.5
	0.6	10.5	12.2	8.9	14.9	17.2	10.3	11.8	10.3	12.7	16.3	12.5 ± 2.8
	0.7	10.3	11.1	8.2	11.1	16.6	9.7	10.7	10.0	12.4	15.8	11.6 ± 2.7
	0.8	10.0	10.2	7.6	10.0	15.3	9.5	8.8	9.5	10.4	14.5	10.6 ± 2.4
	0.9	10.2	9.9	6.5	9.2	12.9	9.4	8.2	9.1	10.2	13.1	9.9 ± 2.0
	1.0	9.7	8.5	6.2	8.7	13.1	9.2	8.0	8.8	9.6	12.2	9.4 ± 2.0
DRATOMBayes	n/a	**11.2**	**13.9**	12.9	15.0	16.6	10.1	15.3	10.6	12.8	15.0	13.3 ± 2.2
DRASIM	Jensen-Shannon	10.2	7.8	**8.6**	6.1	6.7	3.8	5.6	6.2	5.0	5.3	**6.5 ± 1.9**
	Cosine	10.2	**7.9**	6.8	**6.4**	**6.8**	3.8	5.3	6.2	5.0	5.1	6.3 ± 1.8
	Manhattan	6.0	7.3	7.3	4.6	5.2	3.0	**6.3**	3.0	3.7	3.2	5.0 ± 1.7

Changing the symmetric α prior to an asymmetric one has little effect in either implementation of DRETOM. Concretely, the *Gensim*-based implementation improves by about 0.9% and the *MALLET*-based implementation by about 4.6%. However, the selected topic model seems to have a more significant impact. The results show that DRATOM (14.2%) achieves significantly better results than DRETOM. Specifically, DRATOM outperforms the *Gensim* variant (10.9%) by about 30.3% and the *MALLET* variant (13.7%) by 3.6%. It is worth mentioning here that *MALLET* implements CGS inference, which was superior in earlier experiments. In all three cases, the ideal value for theta changes abruptly. The DRATOMBayes approach (13.3%) overcomes this problem and still outperforms the DRETOM variant based on *Gensim* by about 22.0%. Regardless of the distance metric, DRASIM seems practically unusable, as it is inferior to all three comparison methods.

Table 9. Impact of a varying number of topics K on MRR@10 obtained on the Mozilla Firefox project with 10-fold cross validation. DRATOM, DRATOMBayes and DRASIM use the same trained ATM. The mean accuracy over the cross-validation and standard deviation are reported. The best hyperparameter setting for θ and the best distance metric for DRASIM are highlighted.

Model	Parameter	$K = 20$	$K = 30$	$K = 40$	$K = 50$	$K = 60$
DRETOM *Gensim*	$\theta = 0.0$	10.4 ± 2.8	11.1 ± 2.7	11.6 ± 2.7	11.9 ± 3.2	11.9 ± 2.6
	$\theta = 0.1$	$\mathbf{11.0 \pm 3.0}$	$\mathbf{11.6 \pm 2.9}$	$\mathbf{12.0 \pm 2.8}$	$\mathbf{12.3 \pm 3.4}$	12.2 ± 2.8
	$\theta = 0.2$	10.1 ± 2.7	11.3 ± 2.9	11.8 ± 2.9	12.1 ± 3.5	$\mathbf{12.3 \pm 2.9}$
	$\theta = 0.3$	8.7 ± 2.1	10.3 ± 2.9	11.0 ± 2.7	11.5 ± 3.4	11.7 ± 2.8
	$\theta = 0.4$	7.7 ± 1.6	9.3 ± 2.7	10.0 ± 2.4	10.8 ± 3.1	10.9 ± 2.7
	$\theta = 0.5$	6.9 ± 1.3	8.4 ± 2.5	9.0 ± 2.0	9.7 ± 2.7	10.0 ± 2.3
	$\theta = 0.6$	6.4 ± 1.3	7.6 ± 2.1	8.1 ± 1.7	8.7 ± 2.3	9.1 ± 2.0
	$\theta = 0.7$	6.0 ± 1.4	6.9 ± 1.7	7.4 ± 1.5	8.0 ± 1.9	8.2 ± 1.7
	$\theta = 0.8$	5.7 ± 1.4	6.4 ± 1.6	6.8 ± 1.5	7.3 ± 1.6	7.5 ± 1.4
	$\theta = 0.9$	5.5 ± 1.5	6.1 ± 1.6	6.3 ± 1.6	6.7 ± 1.5	6.9 ± 1.3
	$\theta = 1.0$	5.3 ± 1.4	5.7 ± 1.5	6.0 ± 1.5	6.4 ± 1.5	6.4 ± 1.2
DRETOM *MALLET*	$\theta = 0.0$	12.7 ± 3.3	13.4 ± 3.1	14.3 ± 3.6	15.0 ± 3.9	15.8 ± 3.7
	$\theta = 0.1$	$\mathbf{13.7 \pm 3.4}$	$\mathbf{14.2 \pm 3.1}$	15.1 ± 3.8	15.8 ± 4.1	16.6 ± 3.9
	$\theta = 0.2$	13.2 ± 3.1	14.1 ± 2.7	$\mathbf{15.1 \pm 3.7}$	$\mathbf{15.8 \pm 3.9}$	$\mathbf{16.7 \pm 3.9}$
	$\theta = 0.3$	12.0 ± 2.7	13.1 ± 2.2	14.3 ± 3.4	15.0 ± 3.3	16.4 ± 3.6
	$\theta = 0.4$	10.3 ± 2.3	11.9 ± 2.0	13.0 ± 2.9	14.0 ± 2.5	15.6 ± 3.1
	$\theta = 0.5$	9.3 ± 2.2	10.9 ± 1.7	11.9 ± 2.5	12.8 ± 2.0	14.6 ± 2.6
	$\theta = 0.6$	8.6 ± 2.2	9.9 ± 1.5	10.7 ± 2.2	11.7 ± 1.5	13.5 ± 2.2
	$\theta = 0.7$	7.9 ± 2.3	9.1 ± 1.6	9.8 ± 2.1	10.7 ± 1.3	12.3 ± 1.8
	$\theta = 0.8$	7.5 ± 2.3	8.5 ± 1.9	9.3 ± 2.1	9.9 ± 1.5	11.3 ± 1.9
	$\theta = 0.9$	7.2 ± 2.3	8.2 ± 2.0	8.7 ± 2.1	9.3 ± 1.6	10.5 ± 2.0
	$\theta = 1.0$	6.8 ± 2.2	7.7 ± 2.1	8.2 ± 2.0	8.8 ± 1.6	9.9 ± 2.3
DRATOM	$\theta = 0.0$	14.0 ± 2.7	15.5 ± 3.8	15.8 ± 3.8	15.5 ± 3.8	16.0 ± 3.3
	$\theta = 0.1$	$\mathbf{14.2 \pm 2.6}$	15.8 ± 3.8	16.5 ± 3.8	16.1 ± 3.9	16.6 ± 3.4
	$\theta = 0.2$	14.0 ± 2.5	$\mathbf{15.9 \pm 3.8}$	16.9 ± 3.9	16.5 ± 3.9	17.1 ± 3.4
	$\theta = 0.3$	13.7 ± 2.4	15.8 ± 3.7	$\mathbf{16.9 \pm 3.7}$	16.7 ± 3.8	17.4 ± 3.3
	$\theta = 0.4$	13.2 ± 2.4	15.6 ± 3.6	16.8 ± 3.6	$\mathbf{16.7 \pm 3.6}$	$\mathbf{17.6 \pm 3.2}$
	$\theta = 0.5$	12.8 ± 2.5	15.2 ± 3.3	16.7 ± 3.5	16.7 ± 3.5	17.6 ± 3.2
	$\theta = 0.6$	12.4 ± 2.7	14.9 ± 3.3	16.4 ± 3.4	16.3 ± 3.4	17.5 ± 2.9
	$\theta = 0.7$	11.6 ± 2.7	14.3 ± 3.2	15.7 ± 3.1	16.1 ± 3.2	17.0 ± 2.7
	$\theta = 0.8$	10.6 ± 2.4	13.3 ± 2.4	14.6 ± 2.2	15.5 ± 2.6	16.3 ± 2.1
	$\theta = 0.9$	9.9 ± 2.2	12.2 ± 2.3	13.7 ± 1.9	14.9 ± 2.2	15.5 ± 2.0
	$\theta = 1.0$	9.3 ± 2.0	11.4 ± 2.2	13.0 ± 1.5	14.2 ± 2.2	14.6 ± 1.8
DRATOMBayes	n/a	$\mathbf{13.3 \pm 2.3}$	14.9 ± 2.9	16.0 ± 4.2	15.8 ± 4.2	16.1 ± 3.7
DRASIM	Jensen Shannon	$\mathbf{6.7 \pm 2.0}$	8.6 ± 1.5	10.8 ± 2.6	12.0 ± 2.4	12.7 ± 2.1
	Cosine	6.6 ± 2.0	8.6 ± 1.6	$\mathbf{10.9 \pm 2.7}$	12.0 ± 2.3	12.6 ± 2.0
	Manhattan	5.1 ± 1.9	6.9 ± 1.7	8.5 ± 2.3	10.1 ± 2.5	10.8 ± 2.3

5.5 Increasing the Number of Topics

It remains to investigate the effect of the hyperparameter K. Following Griffiths and Steyvers, Xie et al. fixed the number of topics to 20 [9]. However, the optimal choice of topics is an open research question. Table 9 shows the results for an increasing number of topics. We do not present the results of the individual ten runs here and only give the mean values.

First, it can be observed that in almost all cases, an increase in the number of topics is accompanied by an improvement in the results, except DRATOMBayes, when changing from 40 to 50 topics. In all cases, DRATOM is superior to all other cases. In all other cases, DRATOMBayes is superior to DRETOM based on *Gensim* but does not reach the quality of the *MALLET* variant. The θ-independent variant can outperform the *MALLET* variant only for $K = 30$ and $K = 40$. Also, with an increasing number of topics, DRASIM is inferior, but this approach benefits most from an increase of K.

6 Discussion

In this section, we recapitulate the results of our previous experiments to answer the four research questions stated at the beginning of Sect. 5. This leads to guidelines for applying topic models for bug triaging tasks. We further discuss internal and external threats to validity.

6.1 Main Findings

The first research question concerns the influence of the topic modeling implementation and inference technique for the bug triaging algorithm. In our first experiment, we compared three topic modeling libraries written in different programming languages. The results indicate that the CGS-based implementation *MALLET* is superior to the VB-based implementations *Vowpal Wabbit* and *Gensim*. The difference between the VB-based implementations is neglectable in our experiments. We thus recommend choosing a topic modeling library based on its underlying inference technique rather than its programming language. In our second experiment, we investigated whether the inferior results of the VB-based implementations are due to the non-convergence of the training algorithm and thus increased the number of iterations. It turned out that all VB-based implementations benefit from adjusting the parameter. Therefore, we conclude that the default values in the topic modeling libraries might not be ideal for sufficiently training a topic model. In our third experiment, the batch variant of VB outperforms its online version. We, therefore, recommend the usage of the batch variant if possible and only suggest the use of the online variant for text corpora that are too large to process.

In our fourth and fifth experiments, we compared DRETOM with the three approaches based on the ATM. We referred to *Gensim*'s implementation of the ATM based on VB. Though VB was inferior to CGS in the first three experiments, our approach DRATOM outperformed the DRETOM implementation based on *MALLET*. This effect can be traced back to the underlying topic model. The approach, DRATOMBayes, outperforms the DRETOM variant based on *Gensim* and achieves similar results as the *MALLET* implementation. However, the DRASIM approach is inferior to all algorithms compared in our study.

The last two experiments also investigate the influence of the hyperparameters α and K on the results of the bug triaging algorithms. The asymmetric Dirichlet prior α led to only a slight quality improvement in DRETOM. In contrast, all methods benefited significantly from an increasing number of topics. Overall, we conclude that the hyperparameter K significantly influences the results and should therefore be given special attention.

Xie et al. reported that their approach DRETOM is sensitive to its hyperparameter θ. Based on their experimental results, they formulated statements about its influence on the bug triaging task. As a further result of our study, we revisit four statements about the trade-off parameter θ made by Xie et al. Their first statement reads "The smaller the size of the set of recommended developers is, the larger θ should be." In our experiments, the number of developers is more likely to increase over time, because the training set grows monotonically. However, we do not observe that the parameter θ decreases. Furthermore, the evaluation of a bug triaging technique should be independent of the number of recommended developers [27]. Xie et al. evaluated the effectiveness of their proposed approach DRETOM using Precision@k, Recall@k, and its harmonic mean F_1 score [39]. Although those metrics allow taking multiple ground truth assignees into account, they do not penalize mistakes in the first ranks more than in the following ranks. Therefore, we suspect that the statement depends on the chosen evaluation metric.

The second statement is given by "The shorter the duration of a project's bug repository is, the larger θ should be." Examining this statement independently of the other parameters that affect the optimal value for θ is not easy. We see counterindications with this statement using the hyperparameters for DRETOM used by Xie et al. Because of the evaluation scheme we have chosen, we let the duration, and thus the size of the project's bug repository, grow with each cross-validation fold. Thus, a clear decreasing trend of the optimal θ should be found in the experiments. However, we observe this only very sporadically, e.g., for DRETOM using *Gensim*, but inconsistently between the individual implementations and used inference techniques. Although some experiments suggest such a relationship, a more thorough evaluation would be needed to rule out other influencing factors.

A further statement about θ reads "Prior to putting DRETOM into practice, some trials should be conducted to find out the optimal θ." This recommendation includes the hidden assumption that DRETOM has an optimal value for θ, although this is admittedly dependent on the chosen project. However, our experiments clearly show that the identification of this *optimal* value depends several different factors, including the chosen implementation, the used inference technique and its hyperparameters, the LDA hyperparameters, and most importantly, even if we leave all other factors aside, the point in time during the project.

The last statement is given by "Setting θ in the range from 0.2 to 0.8 is appropriate." Following this recommendation, neither the developer expertise nor the interest of a developer alone is sufficient to make the best possible developer recommendation using DRETOM. However, as long as we do not adjust for the number of topics according to the dataset, on average, across all experiments and all cross-validation folds, the developer expertise has to be weighted much more to make the best possible predictions. During the experiments, the on average optimal value of θ with regard to the MRR@10 is less or equal to 0.1 for DRETOM and DRATOM. Only if we choose an appropriate number of topics, the optimal value of θ is, on average, within the recommended range. Due to the inconsistent and partially conflicting choice of an optimal value for θ, we refer to the more robust DRATOM and DRASIM, which do not require an additional trade-off hyperparameter.

6.2 Threats to Validity

The internal threat to validity mainly consists in the implementation of the studied baseline approach DRETOM. For comparison purposes, we reimplemented the algorithm DRETOM, as there is no implementation publicly available. Although we have implemented the algorithm true to the best of our knowledge, there could be some minor deviations from the original approach.

In our experiments, we were able to access three different LDA libraries. It turned out that *MALLET* generates better results than *Gensim* and *Vowpal Wabbit*. In contrast, we evaluated only a single implementation of ATM. Thus, an accurate comparison is only possible with the LDA of *Gensim*. Based on the results of the first three experiments, we expect that a CGS-based implementation of ATM would yield better results.

The main threat to external validity is the used dataset. Additional research on other projects, such as Chromium or Eclipse, should be consulted to reinforce the generalizability of our conclusions. Furthermore, we assume the final assignee as the ground truth in our experiments. However, bug triaging is a collaborative task involving various stakeholders, e.g., the reporter or other developers participating in the discussion. We see no clear way to generalize to a setting where more than one developer can be seen as ground truth.

7 Conclusions and Future Work

The analysis of software data by machine learning techniques promises to provide insights that will make future development processes more efficient. One concrete task that is particularly important in the maintenance phase of a software project is the automated assignment of pending bugs to suitable developers. Numerous approaches apply topic models, which analyze the textual components of a bug report, and thus allow for a formal treatment of the bug triaging task. Topic models differ among themselves, their underlying inference algorithm, the software libraries used, and the choice of their hyperparameters. To deduce guidelines for the effective use of topic models for bug triaging tasks, we compared four bug triaging algorithms based on LDA and its variant ATM proposed by Xie et al. [39] and Atzberger and Schneider et al. [2]. In our experiments on a dataset taken from the *Mozilla Firefox* project, we evaluated the influence of the chosen topic modeling library and its inference technique, the influence of the topic model itself, the role of the Dirichlet prior α, and the number of topics K.

Our study results show that the topic modeling library should be chosen based on the implemented inference technique rather than its programming language. In our concrete case, the LDA implementation provided by *MALLET* achieved better results than the implementations provided by *Gensim* and *Vowpal Wabbit*. As the approach DRATOM that relies on the ATM was superior to the baseline approach DRETOM, we observe that the choice between LDA and the ATM has a significant effect. In our experiments, the choice of the Dirichlet prior α led to no significant improvement, whereas the number of topics K had a large effect on the bug triaging results. In addition to the specific use case of automated assignment of bug reports, our experiments show that a closer look at the topic models used when examining textual components of software data have the potential to improve the analyses significantly. Instead of considering topic models as black boxes, the used implementations and hyperparameters should be compared and adapted for the individual use case.

One approach for future work is to extend the presented methods by adding categorical attributes of bug reports, for example, by developing novel topic models. Alternatively, it would be conceivable to integrate other repositories, such as coding activities, into the triaging process in addition to ticket management systems. A particular challenge here is the modeling of heterogeneous data sources. To increase the acceptance of the processes in the application, thoughts should also be given to how the results can be made explainable. Although the application of ATM enables a description of developers as a distribution over the topics, concrete conclusions about the data basis have not yet been implemented.

Acknowledgements. This work is part of the "Software-DNA" project, which is funded by the European Regional Development Fund (ERDF or EFRE in German) and the State of Brandenburg (ILB). This work is part of the KMU project "KnowhowAnalyzer" (Förderkennzeichen 01IS20088B), which is funded by the German Ministry for Education and Research (Bundesministerium für Bildung und Forschung).

References

1. Aktas, E.U., Yilmaz, C.: Automated issue assignment: results and insights from an industrial case. Empir. Softw. Eng. **25**(5), 3544–3589 (2020). https://doi.org/10.1007/s10664-020-09846-3
2. Atzberger, D., Schneider, J., Scheibel, W., Limberger, D., Trapp, M., Döllner, J.: Mining developer expertise from bug tracking systems using the author-topic model. In: Proceedings of the 17th International Conference on Evaluation of Novel Approaches to Software Engineering, ENASE 2022, pp. 107–118. INSTICC, SciTePress (2022). https://doi.org/10.5220/0011045100003176
3. Banitaan, S., Alenezi, M.: TRAM: an approach for assigning bug reports using their metadata. In: Proceedings 3rd International Conference on Communications and Information Technology, ICCIT 2013, pp. 215–219. IEEE (2013). https://doi.org/10.1109/ICCITechnology.2013.6579552
4. Bhattacharya, P., Neamtiu, I.: Fine-grained incremental learning and multi-feature tossing graphs to improve bug triaging. In: Proceedings International Conference on Software Maintenance, ICSM 2010, pp. 1–10. IEEE (2010). https://doi.org/10.1109/ICSM.2010.5609736
5. Blei, D., Ng, A., Jordan, M.: Latent Dirichlet allocation. J. Mach. Learn. Res. **3**, 993–1022 (2003)
6. Chen, T.-H., Thomas, S.W., Hassan, A.E.: A survey on the use of topic models when mining software repositories. Empir. Softw. Eng. **21**(5), 1843–1919 (2015). https://doi.org/10.1007/s10664-015-9402-8
7. Dedik, V., Rossi, B.: Automated bug triaging in an industrial context. In: Proceedings 42th Euromicro Conference on Software Engineering and Advanced Applications, SEAA 2016, pp. 363–367. IEEE (2016). https://doi.org/10.1109/SEAA.2016.20
8. Geigle, C.: Inference methods for Latent Dirichlet allocation (course notes in CS 598 CXZ: advanced topics in information retrieval). Technical report, Department of Computer Science, University of Illinois at Urbana-Champaign (2016)
9. Griffiths, T.L., Steyvers, M.: Finding scientific topics. Proc. Nat. Acad. Sci. **101**, 5228–5235 (4 2004). https://doi.org/10.1073/pnas.0307752101

10. Hoffman, M., Bach, F., Blei, D.: Online learning for Latent Dirichlet allocation. In: Advances in Neural Information Processing Systems, NIPS 2010, vol. 23, pp. 856–864. Curran Associates Inc. (2010)

11. Hu, H., Zhang, H., Xuan, J., Sun, W.: Effective bug triage based on historical bug-fix information. In: Proceedings 25th International Symposium on Software Reliability Engineering, ISSRE 2014, pp. 122–132. IEEE (2014). https://doi.org/10.1109/ISSRE.2014.17

12. Jonsson, L., Borg, M., Broman, D., Sandahl, K., Eldh, S., Runeson, P.: Automated bug assignment: ensemble-based machine learning in large scale industrial contexts. Empir. Softw. Eng. **21**(4), 1533–1578 (2015). https://doi.org/10.1007/s10664-015-9401-9

13. Kagdi, H., Gethers, M., Poshyvanyk, D., Hammad, M.: Assigning change requests to software developers. J. Softw. Evol. Process **24**(1), 3–33 (2012). https://doi.org/10.1002/smr.530

14. Khatun, A., Sakib, K.: A bug assignment technique based on bug fixing expertise and source commit recency of developers. In: Proceedings 19th International Conference on Computer and Information Technology, ICCIT 2016, pp. 592–597. IEEE (2016). https://doi.org/10.1109/ICCITECHN.2016.7860265

15. Linstead, E., Rigor, P., Bajracharya, S., Lopes, C., Baldi, P.: Mining eclipse developer contributions via author-topic models. In: Proceedings 4th International Workshop on Mining Software Repositories, MSR 2007, pp. 1–4. IEEE (2007). https://doi.org/10.1109/MSR.2007.20

16. Mani, S., Sankaran, A., Aralikatte, R.: DeepTriage: exploring the effectiveness of deep learning for bug triaging. In: Proceedings India Joint International Conference on Data Science and Management of Data, pp. 171–179. ACM (2019). https://doi.org/10.1145/3297001.3297023

17. Matter, D., Kuhn, A., Nierstrasz, O.: Assigning bug reports using a vocabulary-based expertise model of developers. In: Proceedings 6th International Working Conference on Mining Software Repositories, MSR 2009, pp. 131–140. IEEE (2009). https://doi.org/10.1109/MSR.2009.5069491

18. McCallum, A.K.: MALLET: a machine learning for language toolkit (2002). http://www.cs.umass.edu/%7Emccallum/mallet

19. Mortensen, O.: The author-topic model. Master's thesis, Technical University of Denmark, Department of Applied Mathematics and Computer Science (2017)

20. Naguib, H., Narayan, N., Brügge, B., Helal, D.: Bug report assignee recommendation using activity profiles. In: Proceedings 10th Working Conference on Mining Software Repositories, MSR 2013, pp. 22–30. IEEE (2013). https://doi.org/10.1109/MSR.2013.6623999

21. Newman, D., Asuncion, A., Smyth, P., Welling, M.: Distributed algorithms for topic models. J. Mach. Learn. Res. **10**, 1801–1828 (2009)

22. Nguyen, T.T., Nguyen, A.T., Nguyen, T.N.: Topic-based, time-aware bug assignment. SIGSOFT Softw. Eng. Notes **39**(1), 1–4 (2014). https://doi.org/10.1145/2557833.2560585

23. Ramage, D., Rosen, E., Chuang, J., Manning, C.D., McFarland, D.A.: Topic modeling for the social sciences. In: Proceedings Workshop on Applications for Topic Models: Text and Beyond, pp. 23:1–4 (2009)

24. Řehůřek, R., Sojka, P.: Software framework for topic modelling with large corpora. In: Proceedings Workshop on New Challenges for NLP Frameworks, pp. 45–50. ELRA (2010)

25. Rosen-Zvi, M., Griffiths, T., Steyvers, M., Smyth, P.: The author-topic model for authors and documents. In: Proceedings 20th Conference on Uncertainty in Artificial Intelligence, UAI 2004, pp. 487–494. AUAI Press (2004)

26. Sajedi-Badashian, A., Hindle, A., Stroulia, E.: Crowdsourced bug triaging, ICSME 2015, pp. 506–510. IEEE (2015). https://doi.org/10.1109/ICSM.2015.7332503

27. Sajedi-Badashian, A., Stroulia, E.: Guidelines for evaluating bug-assignment research. J. Softw. Evol. Process **32**(9) (2020). https://doi.org/10.1002/smr.2250

28. Schofield, A., Magnusson, M., Mimno, D.: Pulling out the stops: rethinking stopword removal for topic models. In: Proceedings 15th Conference of the European Chapter of the Association for Computational Linguistics, EACL 2017, pp. 432–436. ACL (2017). https://doi.org/10.18653/v1/E17-2069

29. Schofield, A., Mimno, D.: Comparing apples to apple: the effects of stemmers on topic models. Trans. Assoc. Comput. Linguist. **4**, 287–300 (2016). https://doi.org/10.1162/tacl_a_00099

30. Schofield, A., Thompson, L., Mimno, D.: Quantifying the effects of text duplication on semantic models. In: Proceedings Conference on Empirical Methods in Natural Language Processing, EMNLP 2017, pp. 2737–2747. ACL (2017). https://doi.org/10.18653/v1/D17-1290

31. Shokripour, R., Anvik, J., Kasirun, Z., Zamani, S.: Why so complicated? Simple term filtering and weighting for location-based bug report assignment recommendation. In: Proceedings 10th Working Conference on Mining Software Repositories, MSR 2013, pp. 2–11. IEEE (2013). https://doi.org/10.1109/MSR.2013.6623997

32. Syed, S., Spruit, M.: Exploring symmetrical and asymmetrical Dirichlet priors for latent Dirichlet allocation. Inte. J. Seman. Comput. **12**(3), 399–423 (2018). https://doi.org/10.1142/S1793351X18400184

33. Tamrawi, A., Nguyen, T.T., Al-Kofahi, J.M., Nguyen, T.N.: Fuzzy set and cache-based approach for bug triaging. In: Proceedings 19th SIGSOFT Symposium on Foundations of Software Engineering, FSE/ESEC 2011, pp. 365–375. ACM (2011). https://doi.org/10.1145/2025113.2025163

34. Wallach, H.M.: Structured topic models for language. Ph.D. thesis, Newnham College, University of Cambridge (2008)

35. Wallach, H.M., Mimno, D., McCallum, A.K.: Rethinking LDA: why priors matter. In: Proceedings 22nd International Conference on Neural Information Processing Systems, NIPS 2009, pp. 1973–1981. Curran Associates, Inc. (2009)

36. Wu, W., Zhang, W., Yang, Y., Wang, Q.: DREX: developer recommendation with k-nearest-neighbor search and expertise ranking. In: Proceedings 18th Asia-Pacific Software Engineering Conference, APSEC 2011, pp. 389–396. IEEE (2011). https://doi.org/10.1109/APSEC.2011.15

37. Xia, X., Lo, D., Ding, Y., Al-Kofahi, J.M., Nguyen, T.N., Wang, X.: Improving automated bug triaging with specialized topic model. Trans. Softw. Eng. **43**(3), 272–297 (2016). https://doi.org/10.1109/TSE.2016.2576454

38. Xia, X., Lo, D., Wang, X., Zhou, B.: Accurate developer recommendation for bug resolution. In: Proceedings 20th Working Conference on Reverse Engineering, WCRE 2013, pp. 72–81. IEEE (2013). https://doi.org/10.1109/WCRE.2013.6671282

39. Xie, X., Zhang, W., Yang, Y., Wang, Q.: DRETOM: developer recommendation based on topic models for bug resolution. In: Proceedings 8th International Conference on Predictive Models in Software Engineering, PROMISE 2012, pp. 19–28. ACM (2012). https://doi.org/10.1145/2365324.2365329

40. Yang, G., Zhang, T., Lee, B.: Towards semi-automatic bug triage and severity prediction based on topic model and multi-feature of bug reports. In: Proceedings 38th Annual Computer Software and Applications Conference, COMPSAC 2014, pp. 97–106. IEEE (2014). https://doi.org/10.1109/COMPSAC.2014.16

41. Yao, L., Mimno, D., McCallum, A.K.: Efficient methods for topic model inference on streaming document collections. In: Proceedings SIGKDD International Conference on Knowledge Discovery and Data Mining, pp. 937–945. ACM (2009). https://doi.org/10.1145/1557019.1557121

42. Zhang, T., Chen, J., Yang, G., Lee, B., Luo, X.: Towards more accurate severity prediction and fixer recommendation of software bugs. J. Syst. Softw. **117**, 166–184 (2016). https://doi.org/10.1016/j.jss.2016.02.034
43. Zhang, T., Yang, G., Lee, B., Lua, E.K.: A novel developer ranking algorithm for automatic bug triage using topic model and developer relations. In: Proceedings 21st Asia-Pacific Software Engineering Conference, APSEC 2014, pp. 223–230. IEEE (2014). https://doi.org/10.1109/APSEC.2014.43
44. Zhang, W., Han, G., Wang, Q.: BUTTER: an approach to bug triage with topic modeling and heterogeneous network analysis. In: Proceedings International Conference on Cloud Computing and Big Data, CCBD 2014, pp. 62–69. IEEE (2014). https://doi.org/10.1109/CCBD.2014.14
45. Zou, W., Lo, D., Chen, Z., Xia, X., Feng, Y., Xu, B.: How practitioners perceive automated bug report management techniques. Trans. Softw. Eng. **46**(8), 836–862 (2020). https://doi.org/10.1109/TSE.2018.2870414

Software Project Management Approaches Used in the Context of Agile Development: A Systematic Literature Mapping

Elielton da Costa Carvalho(iD) and Sandro Ronaldo Bezerra Oliveira(✉) (iD)

Graduate Program in Computer Science (PPGCC), Institute of Exact and Natural Sciences
(ICEN), Federal University of Pará (UFPA), Belém, PA, Brazil
`elielton.carvalho@icen.ufpa.br, srbo@ufpa.br`

Abstract. Project management is of significant importance to the success of software development, as experts remind us. However, projects have a high degree
of uncertainty and are complex in nature. This suggests that specific approaches
are needed to manage these threats. Using the right approach can be critical to
the success of a project. Knowing the importance of project management and
how the approaches can be fundamental to help managers, this work sought to
identify in the literature the project management approaches that are used in agile
software development. To achieve the objective, a systematic literature mapping
study was carried out, which made it possible to identify eight distinct categories
of approaches that are used in agile software project management. In addition, it
was possible to identify that the approaches are most commonly applied to manage
the schedule, quality and communication of projects.

Keywords: Software project management · Project management approaches ·
Systematic literature mapping

1 Introduction

Project management dates back to antiquity and remains useful to this day, since from the
time of the construction of the Egyptian pyramids until more recently with the placement
of the International Space Station in orbit the idea of projects is used [1]. Despite the
long period of use of project management, it was only in the 1960s that it came to be seen
as a discipline, mainly because it was widely implemented in the American weapons
and space technology industry [2].

With the challenges imposed by the arrival of the 21st century and, consequently,
with the technological advance, the concepts and implementations of project management reached another level. In the same period, organizations began to realize that
competition increases exponentially over time and that their projects need to be well
managed. Managing what is being developed has become a necessity and no longer a
differential, given that competition forces companies to reinvent themselves so that they
can "survive" in the capitalist market [3].

Now, projects are seen as a powerful means of creating economic value for companies, promoting competitive advantage and generating business benefits. Alignment between project management and business strategy can significantly increase an organization's chances of achieving goals and improving its performance [4]. The author of [3] draws attention to the importance of project management in the development of a correct, organized and controlled planning of organizational resources, in order to meet short-term goals, to fulfill specific goals or even broader objectives.

Demand for better results has increased in recent years due to increasing pressure for faster delivery, cost reduction and scope flexibility. These demands require changes in software development processes and in organizations as a whole, which require significant investments and are complex to evaluate [5]. This demand for more agile processes was the driving force behind the emergence of agile software development, which emerged in the late 1990s to deal with uncertain customer requirements, evolving technology, and ever-changing business environments [6].

There are many characteristics of agile software development that affect decision making, including its iterative and incremental nature, its organic and flexible developer roles, and its emphasis on self-organization [7]. To help project managers and teams make better decisions, there are a number of approaches that offer a wide range of functions in project planning, ongoing monitoring and evaluation of project implementation, and final evaluation when the project is complete [8].

The literature reports a large number of best practices, software tools, guidelines, methodologies and standards (approaches) that guide software development teams. Due to the diversity of approaches, the process of choosing the most suitable for a given project becomes a complex task as new approaches emerge. It is thus observed that the challenges in agile development have been and will continue to be explored, but there is no comprehensive work on what these project management approaches are and how to use them, suggesting the need for further investigation in this area [9].

It is therefore important to research the characteristics of these approaches and map them to minimize decision challenges. Additionally, it is also necessary to investigate how they are used and the lessons learned from their use, in order to identify opportunities for improvement [10]. Finally, it is also important to identify its main strengths and weaknesses based on its application in a real software development context [11].

The objective of this work is to identify primary studies in software engineering that present approaches to support the management of software projects in an agile context. From these studies, we aim to summarize the main strengths and weaknesses of these approaches, and also to identify how these approaches were. To achieve this goal, we performed a systematic literature mapping (SLM) study and selected 65 studies on software project management approaches. In our results, we identified 8 types of distinct approaches, 9 areas that these approaches focus on, as well as 5 project phases they emphasize. It is worth mentioning that this work is an extension of [35], where more data referring to the problems that gave rise to the research, more authors to support the work, as well as more results were included in this work.

In addition to this introductory section, this work is structured as follows: Sect. 2 presents some concepts and definitions about the theme of this work, Sect. 3 presents the work methodology, Sect. 4 presents the research results, Sect. 5 discusses the main results, Sect. 6 brings the main threats to the validity of this work, Sect. 7 presents the works related to this research, and Sect. 8 ends the work presenting the main conclusions.

2   Background

This section describes the theoretical foundation for understanding this work.

2.1   Systematic Literature Mapping

There is a branch of research in software engineering known as Evidence-Based Software Engineering (EBSE). According to [12], the EBSE allows describing the characteristics of a technology in question. Also, according to the authors, in order to reach an adequate stage of evidence, the EBSE uses two types of studies: primary studies and secondary studies, with primary studies aiming to characterize a technology in a specific situation. Meanwhile, secondary studies aim to establish conclusions from primary studies, presenting the summary of common information between them. One of the ways to carry out a secondary study is using an SLM, as pointed out by [13].

According to [14], SLM is an evidence-based technique that uses a well-defined, unbiased and repeatable methodology to identify, analyze and interpret all relevant documents related to a specific research question, subject area or phenomenon of interest. This research method is used by researchers who aim to answer their research questions from studies published by other authors [15].

According to the guidelines formulated by [13, 14, 16], a SLM can be divided into three stages: planning, carrying out the mapping and reporting the mapping. For the authors, there are some reasons that lead researchers to perform a SLM, such as: to provide a summary of existing evidence about a technology, to summarize evidence of the benefits and limitations of a method, to identify gaps in current research, to provide a history of research on a specific area or topic, in addition to allowing the refutation or confirmation of hypotheses.

In a previous work, [13] states that most of the research starts with a review of the literature. However, if this review does not follow a systematic structure, it will have little scientific value. This is due to the fact that a SLM synthesizes existing works in a way that is considered fair. Furthermore, as the author herself states, a SLM is liable to be audited, confirmed or refuted its findings.

2.2   Project Management

Project management as it is known today only emerged in the 1960s, mainly driven by the American defense and aerospace industry [2]. In the following decade, the first software appeared to assist in the planning, control and treatment of projects that increasingly increased the volume of activities to be performed, as is the case of Projacs, Proplan and Artemis [17].

Another important character for the development and diffusion of project management is the Project Management Institute (PMI). PMI is an institute founded in 1969 with the purpose of creating standards of project management practices that can be applied in any activity. The institute was successful, because until today its definitions and norms are followed by thousands of companies that have their goals based on projects. Its main work product is, without a doubt, the Project Management Body of Knowledge (PMBOK), a guide that brings together the best project management practices used and approved over several years. The guide is currently the leading reference for researchers, industry professionals and general project management enthusiasts [18].

The design concept and its applications are given by several authors, guides, norms and standards. [1] defines a project as a temporary effort undertaken to create a unique product, service or result. In turn, project management is defined as the application of knowledge, skills, tools and techniques to project activities in order to fulfill project requirements. Likewise, ISO 21500 conceptualizes a project as a unique set of processes that consists of coordinated and controlled activities with start and end dates. According to [19], the main objective of project management is to provide expected results with quality, planned time, approved costs, in addition to being essential to take care of risks.

2.3 Project Management Approaches

Managing a project, regardless of size, is a challenge for project managers and even the team in general. Dealing with constant communication, documentation (albeit minimal), acquisitions and continuous deliveries, requires a lot of effort, which makes the act of managing practically impossible without the help of some tool. When it comes to project management, teams have an arsenal of software tools, frameworks, guides, methodologies, standards, and roles. These approaches allow each team to choose the one that best fits the objectives and context in which the project is being developed.

Information is a key to the success of an organization, whether internal or external information, both have significant values. Thus, when referring to software that assist in the monitoring and control of projects, there are Project Management Information Systems (PMIS), systems that support managers and teams during the processes that make up the management of a project [20]. The assistance provided by PMIS makes them one of the main information systems of an organization [21].

Some applications stand out for being widely known and used in project activities, such as Jira, Redmine and Trello. According to [22], Trello is the most used application by software project managers, followed by Jira. The authors also verified that some teams develop their own systems or adapt open-source systems to meet their goals, which makes clear the importance of these tools in the daily lives of software development teams.

A survey conducted by the "State of Agile" and published in the 15th Annual State of Agile Report points out which agile methods are most used. It is possible to verify from the research that Scrum is the most commonly used method by respondents, among which 58% use the method autonomously and 75% use it in conjunction with another method. Another method that stands out in the survey is Kanban, which in many cases is used in conjunction with Scrum (10%). However, according to the aforementioned survey, 7% use Kanban individually [23].

First published in 1987, the PMBOK has become a "best seller" among long-term business management. The PMBOK Guide is approved as an American National Standard (ANS) by the American National Standards Institute (ANSI) [24]. The guide is now in its seventh edition and has undergone a major change from the sixth edition to the current one, bringing agile, adaptive and hybrid approaches. In addition, what was previously treated as groups of processes, is now treated as Project Delivery Principles. Finally, the knowledge areas also cease to exist directly and are now called Project Performance Domains [1].

3   Research Methodology

This study aims to identify the approaches used to support the management of software projects in the agile context. We are interested in identifying the type of approach, where it is applied within the project, its main contributions and limitations, as well as the form of evaluation used by its developers.

To formalize the objective of this study, the Goal-Question-Metric (GQM) defined by [25] was used. Therefore, this study aims to:

- Analyze: primary studies, through Systematic Literature Mapping (SLM),
- In order to: identify the approaches used in software project management (SPM) that are reported in the specialized literature,
- Regarding: the definition, use and evaluation of these approaches,
- From the point of view of: researchers, organizations and software project management professionals,
- In context: industrial and academic agile software development.

Thus, we propose the following research questions (RQ):

- RQ1: What is the name and type of approach? – The objective is to identify the type of SPM approach that was used in the work, e.g. method, software tool, technique, etc., as well as the name of the approach,
- RQ2: What are the strengths and limitations of the approach? – The objective is to identify the main points that deal with the advantages and disadvantages of using the identified approach,
- RQ3: How was the approach evaluated? – The objective is to identify the method used to evaluate the use of the approach.

To achieve the objective of this work, an SLM was performed. SML is an evidence-based secondary study method to systematically identify, analyze and interpret all relevant documents related to a specific research question [14]. This method was adopted by the nature of the research questions defined for this work, which seek to identify, classify and analyze the SPM approaches used in the agile context.

We perform the SLM from May/2021 to January/2022. The study was organized into four stages, adapted from [14, 26], as follows:

- Step 1 – Definition of research questions: in this step, three research questions were defined based on the objective of the study,
- Stage 2 – Search: in this stage, based on the research questions, a replicable process was defined to carry out the search for studies in the selected scientific bases,
- Step 3 – Selection of studies: in this step, a replicable process was defined and applied to select only the relevant studies according to the objective of this work,

- Step 4 – Classification of studies and data extraction: in this step, based on the research questions, a strategy was defined to: (i) map the relevant data from the primary studies and (ii) present the results of the work.

Two researchers participated in the planning and execution of the work: an undergraduate student in Computer Science and a professor/researcher with a PhD in Software Engineering.

Regarding the search, this occurred in an automated way through a string formed by a series of keywords and their respective synonyms. These keywords were defined based on the research questions, based on the PICOC (Population, Intervention, Comparison, Outcomes and Context) structure suggested by [14].

However, this work only seeks to identify SPM approaches reported in the literature and is not concerned with making comparisons between them. Therefore, the criterion of "Comparison" was not used. In addition, as the "Intervention" criterion deals with the actions that will be carried out, there was no need to include keywords for it. Thus, the string was formulated with terms related to (i) population, (ii) result and (iii) context. The terms used were:

- Population: project management,
- Result: tool, method, technique, model, technology, practice, standard, guide, work product, methodology, framework, process, principle, theme and profile,
- Context: software and agile.

The search string was applied to the IEEE Xplore and ACM DL databases. We did not search for the EI COMPENDEX and SCOPUS because, according to the results of [36], there was a high redundancy rate of returned studies.

Regarding the selection of studies, inclusion (IC) and exclusion (EC) criteria were applied in order to select only the relevant studies that answered our research questions. The IC and EC are presented below.

- IC: Studies that present some software project management approach applied in the agile context and studies that evaluated the approach used,
- EC: Studies that are not written in English, studies not available for download openly or through the researchers' institutional IP, studies such as workshop reports, posters, presentations, lectures by speakers, books, theses and dissertations.

Each of the studies underwent a selection process consisting of four steps: (i) two researchers read the titles and abstracts of all studies and applied the exclusion criteria, this step was defined as pre-selection, (ii) the same researchers discussed differences in the application of exclusion criteria to reach consensus, (iii) researchers read the title and abstract, and the full text if necessary, of the studies selected in the first step to apply the inclusion criteria, (iv) the researchers discussed differences in the application of exclusion criteria to reach a consensus. The process described resulted in 65 primary studies, identified in this work through the code (PS00 – Primary Study and the sequential number), where their references are available at the link https://zenodo.org/record/587 6282#.YefGov7MLIV.

To collect the necessary data that answer the research questions defined for this work, a researcher was responsible for reading the 65 selected studies. Data analysis aims to classify the studies according to the proposed research questions. Therefore, the SLM result should map and classify studies regarding: the presence of software project management approaches, the project area and phase approach was used, the advantages and disadvantages of its use, and the form of evaluation of the approach.

4 Data Summary and Extraction

This section presents the results of the SLM. Subsection 4.1 presents an overview of the results. Subsections 4.2, 4.3, and 4.4 describe the results for RQ1, RQ2, and RQ3, respectively. In these subsections, primary studies will be referenced and identified by codes and are available at the URL presented in Sect. 3.

4.1 Bibliometric Results

When applying the search string to the selected databases, a total of 2825 studies were returned, of which 1486 returned from the ACM Digital Library and 1339 returned from the IEEE Xplore. After the search, 161 duplicate studies were removed, leaving, therefore, 2664 total studies. After reading the titles and abstracts of each of the studies, 355 studies were selected, 251 from the ACM and 104 from the IEEE. The next step was to read the studies in full and apply the criteria established and described in Sect. 3. Figure 1 shows the number of studies included and excluded after reading the studies in full. Among the 65 selected studies, 40 come from the ACM and 25 from the IEEE.

The SLM looked for studies between the years 2001 and 2021. However, the 65 selected primary studies are distributed between the years 2004 and 2021, as shown in Fig. 2. Still based on Fig. 2, it is possible to notice that, despite a drop in the number of studies after 2008, the trend is for a growth in the number of publications related to the subject of this work, with a sharper peak from 2015. However, it is also noted that the years 2020 and 2021 showed a significant drop in the number of publications. According to [27], there was a reduction in the number of publications in 2020 as many universities and companies had to reduce their research activities, as the laboratories were closed. It should also be taken into account that the number of studies in 2021 is lower as a result of the period of execution of this work.

Regarding the countries that published the most studies in the area, Fig. 3 points out that Brazil, Germany and the United States were the countries that most published works related to the topic of this research, with 11, 9 and 7 studies respectively. On the other hand, countries such as Holland, Japan and Peru had only 1 work published each.

Another data collected from the selected studies is the type of institution from which the main author of the work comes. As can be seen in Fig. 4, the academy is responsible for most of the published studies that are related to the topic, with a total of 54 studies. Meanwhile, the industry published a total of 11 studies related to the topic of this research.

Figure 5 presents the project areas where the identified approaches are used. Based on this figure, it is possible to verify that the focus of the approaches is mainly focused on the areas of schedule (22 studies), quality (19 studies) and communication (17 studies), as is the case of the following primary studies: [PS61], [PS59] and [PS30], respectively.

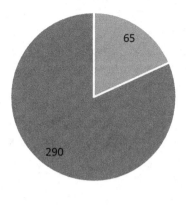

Included   Excluded

Fig. 1. Number of papers included and excluded.

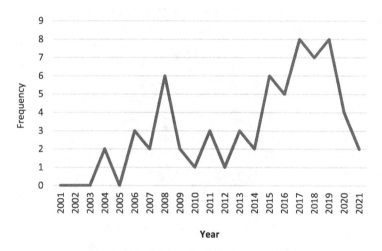

Fig. 2. Distribution of studies by year [35].

Regarding the project phases in which the approaches identified in this work are used, it was possible to notice that the approaches give more emphasis to the project planning phase (36 studies), in addition to the monitoring and control (28 studies) of the same, as can be seen from be exemplified by [PS64] and [PS10], respectively.

It is important to note that some studies focus on more than one phase of the project at the same time, as is the case, for example, of the following studies: [PS07, PS12, PS28, PS54, PS65]. The same goes for the project areas, because, as in the phases, there are studies that are focused on more than one area simultaneously, for example: [PS04, PS34, PS39, PS47, PS57].

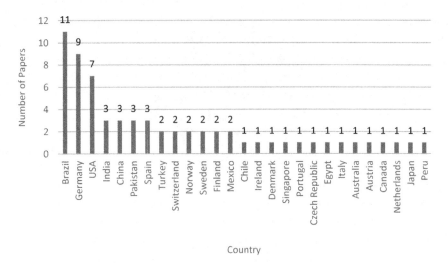

Fig. 3. Distribution of papers by country.

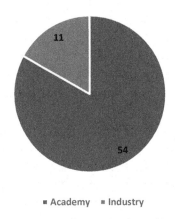

■ Academy   ■ Industry

Fig. 4. Distribution of papers by type of institution.

4.2   RQ1: What is the Name and Type of Approach?

From the selected studies, it was possible to identify eight types of approaches, they are: software, methodology, method, model, tool, technique, framework and practice. Figure 5 illustrates the types of approaches identified, as well as the number of studies that address each of them.

Still based on Fig. 6 it is possible to verify that "software" is the most common type of approach used to support the management of software projects, this approach being identified in 15 studies. Soon after, approaches of the "methodology" type are the ones that stand out the most, developed and / or used in 12 studies. Finally, among the types of approaches that are most used, "method" appears in third place, with this type of approach being identified in 11 primary studies.

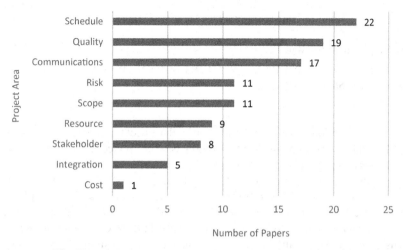

Fig. 5. Project areas where identified approaches are used [35].

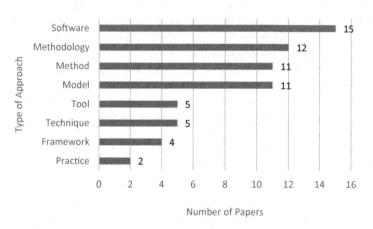

Fig. 6. Types of approaches identified [35].

It is worth noting that "framework" and "practice" approaches are the least used, according to data extracted from primary studies. Such approaches were observed only in four and two studies, respectively.

Software. As mentioned earlier, software is the most common type of approach used to support software project management. Table 1 presents the studies that present this type of approach.

Morgan and Maurer [PS44] report in their study the use of MasePlanner. Mase-Planner is a software aimed at planning communication in the project. It is a software that, according to the authors, supports interactions, facilitating non-verbal communication. MasePlanner provides teams with a digital environment that supports information

Table 1. Studies that present a "Software" approach [35].

Studies that present a "Software" approach
[PS01], [PS02], [PS06], [PS07], [PS10], [PS14], [PS16], [PS21], [PS30], [PS40], [PS43], [PS44], [PS52], [PS61], [PS62]

management in addition to natural interactions. With respect to support for natural interaction, MasePlaner allows planning work products to be created, edited and organized in a similar way to paper planning meetings.

More recently, Alhazmi and Huang [PS01] developed the Sprint Planning Decision Support System (SPESS). This software aims to assist managers in sprint planning. SPESS is primarily based on three factors: developer competence, developer seniority, and task dependency. This software aims to assign the tasks of each Sprint to the developers ensuring that each team member contributes to the maximum of their potential, and the project planning is optimized for the shortest possible time.

The other studies that use software are focused on communication [PS06, PS10, PS30, PS40, PS52], quality [PS02, PS07, PS14, PS16, PS62], schedule [PS07, PS14, PS43, PS61], scope [PS07] and stakeholders [PS21]. It is worth noting that software does not necessarily serve only one area of the project. Begosso et al. [PS07], for example, introduces SimScrumF. This software is a game that focuses on promoting student engagement in the process of learning the concepts of Scrum methodology, widely used to manage software development projects around the world. The game addresses the process of managing the scope defined for the project, aiming to deliver a product with quality, within the pre-established schedule.

Methodology. Behind only software, methodologies were the most used approaches to support project management. Table 2 presents the studies that focus on this type of approach.

Table 2. Studies that present a "Methodology" approach [35].

Studies that present a "Methodology" approach
[PS04], [PS09], [PS12], [PS13], [PS17], [PS20], [PS28], [PS37], [PS39], [PS47], [PS53], [PS54]

Castillo-Barrera et al. [PS13] state that before starting the execution of the project, it is necessary to have previously carried out an analysis and also a synthesis of the information that permeates it. To this end, the authors present BloomSoft, a methodology adapted from Bloom's Taxonomy and used in conjunction with Scrum, which aims to support teams in planning the construction, integration and testing of the software that will be developed in the project.

Not only that, as the authors also point out that the methodology makes it possible to have an agile way of classifying the complexity of user stories based on the verbs identified in them and, concomitantly, to determine from this classification the stage of Software Development for which it belongs. Thus, the development team has the possibility to classify the stories in stages and, with that, make a better planning for each sprint.

Bierwolf et al. [PS09] report the use of DevOps methodology in software project management. DevOps aims to mitigate risks, in particular to achieve a stable, secure and reliable production environment. Through this form of communication and collaboration, all stakeholders manage uncertainties that arise, for example, due to changes in technology or the environment. The work also makes a comparison between the results of using traditional approaches in relation to DevOps approaches. The comparison is mainly related to aspects such as control and mitigation of uncertainties and risks.

There is also a methodology that varies from Scrum and is presented by Baptista [PS04]. uScrum, the methodology described in the aforementioned study, manages uncertainty and the unknown, allowing the team involved in the project to react quickly to changes in the most diverse conditions. uScrum allows the team to effectively prioritize regular work alongside more difficult creative work. The methodology prioritizes tasks in monthly iterations based on their importance, urgency and timeliness and, like Scrum, they are also called sprints.

Method. Another type of approach that stands out are the methods, as this type of approach was identified in 11 of the 65 selected studies and, together with the models, is the third most used to support the management of software projects. Table 3 presents the studies that deal with methods.

Table 3. Studies that present a "Method" approach [35].

Studies that present a "Method" approach
[PS03], [PS05], [PS08], [PS11], [PS15], [PS23], [PS26], [PS31], [PS50], [PS56], [PS64]

Haugen [PS26] describes using Planning Poker. The objective of the study is to verify if the introduction of this method in the estimation of user stories improves the estimation performance compared to the unstructured group estimation. In this process, the customer first explains each user story to the developer group. Developers then discuss the work involved in implementation to the point where everyone feels they have enough information to estimate the effort required. All developers then estimate the user story independently and reveal their estimates simultaneously. Then the developers with the lowest and highest estimates justify their estimates, and the group continues the discussion to decide on a collective estimate, possibly performing one or more additional rounds of individual estimates.

Zhang et al. [PS64] address in their study on Early Software Size Estimation (ESSE), a method that can extract semantic features from natural language requirements automatically and build size estimation models for the project. ESSE performs a semantic analysis of requirements specification documents by extracting information and disseminating activation. Then, characteristics related to complexity are extracted from the semantic analysis results. In addition, ESSE extracts local resources and global resources to do word-level semantic analysis. Then, using these features, size drivers and actual sizes from historical project data, the size estimation model can be established by regression algorithms. Finally, ESSE can estimate the size of a new project using this size estimation model.

The other studies that use some software project management methods are concerned with managing quality [PS05, PS50], schedule [PS11], resources [PS31, PS56], scope [PS03] and project risks [PS23]. In addition, these same studies are focused on the following project phases: planning [PS11, PS23, PS31], execution [PS50] and monitoring and control [PS03, PS05, PS23, PS31, PS56].

Model. In addition to the methods, it was possible to identify, through the selected studies, 11 models that aim to support the management of software projects in the agile context. Table 4 presents the studies that focus on this type of approach.

Table 4. Studies that present a "Model" approach [35].

Studies that present a "Model" approach
[PS22], [PS25], [PS27], [PS29], [PS34], [PS36], [PS46], [PS48], [PS55], [PS58], [PS59]

Godoy et al. [PS22] present a new software development tool based on agile methodologies Scrum and Kanban and adapted to the current trend of the global software environment. The Blueprint model proposes a lightweight project management that is combined with an organization of teams to encourage and facilitate communication between teams in different locations. Blueprint introduces important adaptations to Scrum and Kanban to reduce unwanted bureaucracy and facilitate global software development.

Perkusich et al. [PS48] developed a Probabilistic Model with Baysian Network. As the name suggests, the model is a Bayesian network that represents a software development project managed in essence with the Scrum methodology. Scrum Masters should use it to identify project issues and guide the team to improve the project's chances of success. The model produces data with probability values that represent the current status of key project factors. It should be used to identify problems and prioritize areas for improvement. The prioritization of areas for improvement should be a collaborative activity and the model should be used only as a source of information to guide the discussion.

The other studies that deal with some model focus on project schedule management [PS34, PS36, PS58]. In addition to the studies mentioned, there are those focused on risk management [PS27, PS46], communication [PS25], scope [PS29], stakeholders [PS55] and quality [PS59]. These same studies still focus on different phases of the project, such as: planning [PS25, PS46, PS58, PS59], execution [PS36, PS55] and monitoring and control [PS27, PS29].

Tool. Based on the selected studies, five tools were identified that help the management of software projects. Table 5 presents these studies.

Vivian et al. [PS63] expose in their study a Panel to View Online Teamwork Discussions. The tool is a dashboard that extracts and communicates the distribution of team roles and emotional information from members in real time. The dashboard is made up of a number of elements: team participation and role distribution, team and individual

Table 5. Studies that present a "Tool" approach [35].

Studies that present a "Tool" approach
[PS18], [PS38], [PS42], [PS49], [PS63]

sentiment analysis, and team and individual emotions. It provides real-time analysis of teamwork discussions and visualizes team members' emotions, roles they have taken on, and overall team sentiment during the course of a collaborative project.

Mateescu et al. [PS42] feature a tool called aWall. It is an agile team collaboration tool for large multi-touch wall systems. aWall was designed based on empirical user research using new concepts of interaction and visualization to support and promote the highly collaborative and communicative agile work style. The tool is based on web technology and can be used both in co-located and distributed environments.

According to Mateescu et al. [PS42], the tool can be crucial for agile teams, since the agile process depends on intense interaction, collaboration and constant open communication between team members. The other studies dealing with tools turned their attention to monitoring and controlling the project schedule and to planning the scope. Fehlmann and Kranich [PS18], for example, through a Bayesian Approach Burn-Up Chart, were able to provide estimates of how much additional time is needed to complete the planned work.

Technique. Following what was verified about the tools, from the selected studies, five techniques were also identified that aim to support the management of software projects, as shown in Table 6.

Table 6. Studies that present a "Technical" approach [35].

Studies that present a "Technique" approach
[PS33], [PS35], [PS41], [PS51], [PS60]

Stapel et al. [PS60] present Flow Mapping, a technique of the FLOW Method to plan and guide communication in distributed development projects. To achieve these goals, the technique is centered on the visualization of a FLOW map. A FLOW map is a special FLOW model (that is, visualization of project participants, documents, and information flows) extended by features to improve awareness in distributed teams. According to the authors, when using the Flow Mapping approach, the communication of a distributed project can be planned in one working day.

Kroll et al. [PS35] used a genetic algorithm based assignment technique. The technique was used to assign tasks in a global software development project (GSD). The technique uses a queue-based GSD simulator to evaluate the fitness function. Results based on a multiple case study (applying the technique to data from three real-world projects) show that the approach can be as good or better than the project managers' task assignments.

Framework. Four studies present some frameworks that support the management of software projects in the agile context, as can be seen in Table 7.

Table 7. Studies that present a "Framework" approach [35].

Studies that present a "Framework" approach
[PS19], [PS24], [PS32], [PS45]

Silva and Oliveira [PS19] developed an agile project portfolio management framework. The framework refers to a flexible approach to portfolio management, suggesting faster and more dynamic meetings, focusing mainly on the interaction and commitment of those involved in the process. Some agile practices that can be used in each activity of this framework are: planning portfolio management, identifying new proposals, analyzing candidate projects, composing the project portfolio and monitoring the portfolio.

Guerreiro et al. [PS24] present Eagle, a framework that supports a systematic way to define, measure and visualize the practices of members of software development teams following agile principles. Specifically, the framework provides microservices architecture based on the "Governify" ecosystem to properly manage. The framework provides an ecosystem of tools for organizations to define their best practices to track and track the buy-in of their teams and members in order to know their pitfalls and improve the project over time.

Jain and Suman [PS32] expose in their study on a project management framework for global software development (GSD). The GSD Project Management Framework, as the authors call the approach, assimilates the PMBOK knowledge areas with the knowledge areas necessary for effective GSD management. It would guide the project manager on aspects to consider when running distributed projects. The framework presented covers feasibility and risk management, virtual team management, knowledge management, scope and resource management, performance management, and GSD integration management.

Practice. As shown in Fig. 5, practices were the least identified types of approaches in the selected studies, with a total of two studies addressing only some of them, as shown in Table 8.

Table 8. Studies that present a "Practice" approach [35].

Studies that present a "Practice" approach
[PS57], [PS65]

Schreiber et al. [PS57] discuss a practice called Metrics Driven Research Collaboration (MEDIATION). The practice aims to ensure that all project participants have an ongoing common goal: the success of the project. As per established practice, the project team should focus on the most important requirements and continually verify that the software product conforms to the defined scope and corresponding metrics. The practice further establishes that the status, challenges and progress of the project are always transparent to all team members.

Zhang et al. [PS65] implemented a practice called Fireteam, a practice that focuses on small teams in the software industry. Fireteam is nothing more than a teamwork style. The practice defines two to five members to handle division of labor and coordination issues in traditional development teams. Briefly, the practice aims to reduce project management overheads and improve productivity, through the institutionalization of the practice of small teams throughout the organization, to solve problems arising from human and social aspects, such as friendship, talent, skill and communication.

4.3   RQ2: What Are the Strengths and Limitations of the Approach?

This section provides an overview of the main advantages and disadvantages/limitations of the approaches identified from the selected studies.

Strengths. When a researcher/developer proposes to develop a certain approach, he seeks some means that help him to break specific barriers of the context in which he is inserted. Regarding the approaches that aim to support the management of software projects, identified from the selected studies, it is no different. They all have some advantages and, although they are, in some cases, different from each other, at the end of the day, they all have the same goal: to efficiently support software development teams.

Some approaches, although virtual, try to get as close as possible to the real world [PS38], as is the case with the tool developed by Liskin and Schneider [PS38]. Likewise, the approaches identified always try to reduce the effort required by the team to complete a project task [PS34, PS56, PS58, PS59]. These approaches are considered robust enough to identify problems in the project and correct them in time, avoiding further damage to resources, schedule and, consequently, to the project [PS48].

Also noteworthy are the approaches that provide great ease in planning communications, as is the case of Flow Mapping presented by Stapel et al. [PS60] that allows communication planning in up to one day. In addition, there is an approach that allows the reduction of Sprint time, when working with Scrum, without the project losing quality, even if the reduction is minimal, as reported by Alhazmi and Huang [PS01], and Kroll et al. [PS35].

Limitations. One of the points to consider when talking about any type of approach, whatever the purpose for which it was developed, is its limitations (now called disadvantages). Limitations are inherent in any study, especially when it comes to team-focused approaches. In relation to software project management approaches, there are a series of limitations identified in some selected studies and that end up extending to the others, in some situations.

Initially, it was possible to observe that there is an approach that focuses, among other things, on the constant repair of the project and the work products generated by it. However, the act of constantly fixing defects can bring additional efforts to developers, as reported by Tang [PS34]. There are also approaches that rely entirely on solid and equal commitment from all team members. If the team is not 100% focused and committed, the project naturally tends to fail [PS12, PS28, PS47, PS54], as less engaged employees can perform activities inappropriately, even with the help of some approach, as reported by Godoy et al. [PS22].

Some approaches are not so recommended for planning a small number of tasks, as they were developed to deal with large volumes of data, such as the Sprint Planning Decision Support System (SPESS), developed by Alhazmi and Huang [PS01]. Other approaches do not constantly monitor the project and this limits the team's view of the progress of what is being developed, according to Stapel et al. [PS60].

With regard specifically to software, many plugins that are developed to compose them end up falling into disuse quickly, as is the case of plugins developed for Redmine, reported in the study by Dowling and McGrath [PS16]. For the authors, while there is an active community of developers working on Redmine and creating valuable plugins, this is a double-edged sword. This is because plugins are not always compatible with the latest versions, causing headaches during the update and failures in functionality of features that teams previously used.

4.4   RQ3: How Was the Approach Evaluated?

This section presents the main ways used by the authors of the selected studies to evaluate and validate their approaches. Figure 7 illustrates the number of studies for each type of evaluation.

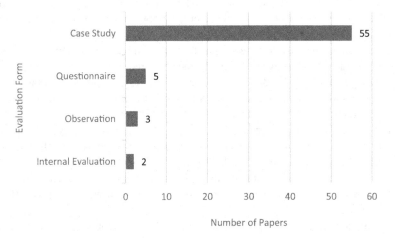

Fig. 7. Number of studies for each type of evaluation.

As can be seen in Fig. 7, the way most used by the authors of the studies to evaluate their approaches was the case study, with a total of 55 studies that used this method. Trapa and Rao [PS61], for example, applied their approach to a project called Cronos, where user stories were broken down into tasks and fed into the software. Each task was assigned to two developers who were responsible for assigning the time estimate for each task they were responsible for. Then, reports were generated with information about the project completion time and the impacts of the additions of new features that came into existence.

Some studies used questionnaires to obtain feedback on the approach developed, five studies more precisely, as illustrated in Fig. 7. Bastarrica et al. [PS05] formulated two research questions to identify the advantages and disadvantages of using their approach. Data collection involved a structured questionnaire that was made available to the CEO and a technical professional from each company. The purpose of the questionnaire was to capture actual and desired practices in relation to project management.

Regarding observational evaluations, we can highlight the study by Mateescu et al. [PS42] who, from the observation of the use of the proposed approach, were able to identify positive points and points for improvement, as well as conclusions about how efficient the proposed approach can be in a project. The authors found that aWall leverages the resolution of web technology and thus surpasses the possibilities of existing desktop tools. They noted that each agile meeting has its main task and specific objective, but also needs a lot of support information and work products.

Figure 7 also shows that two studies carried out internal evaluations, that is, the developers of the approaches themselves evaluated them based on their own metrics, without necessarily making the approaches available to third parties. Bruegge et al. [PS11] evaluated the feasibility and performance of their approach from two classification experiments. The first experiment classified the tasks according to the activity to which they belonged. In the second experiment, the approach was employed to classify the status of tasks, that is, the machine learning engine predicts whether these tasks have already been completed or not.

5   Analysis of Results

This section presents our main conclusions and impressions of the results presented in Sect. 4.

The first item to note refers to the results on which areas and phases of project management the approaches emphasize. As illustrated in Fig. 5, the areas of schedule, quality and communication are the ones that received the most attention from the authors. Something similar can be observed in [22]. The authors identified, through an opinion survey with software project managers, that the areas of programming and communication are the two that most concern these professionals.

Specifically on the schedule, the area most emphasized in the studies, it was possible to observe that the focus in this area is due to the fact that estimating the time and the project schedule are crucial tasks and extremely influence the project results [PS64]. Regarding the phases, it was observed that the authors place greater emphasis on project planning [28]. That's because planning is crucial to the success of a project. Tasks need to be allocated to team members, taking into account task precedence, balancing the workload of team members, and ensuring quality [29].

Regarding the type of approach, it was possible to verify that the software is the most used type of approach to support the management of software projects. Results like this can be considered common, considering that currently several systems that automate processes are becoming increasingly common. Such systems facilitate the work of people in different fields of application [30]. The authors of [31] also state that project management software is widely used, as it includes several useful features that facilitate the work of the team, especially the project manager, features such as task management, real-time monitoring, chatbox, notifications and alerts.

In addition to software, project management methodologies also stood out. During the analysis of the selected studies, it was possible to identify 12 studies dealing with this type of approach. Among these methodologies, one that stands out is Scrum. This methodology was used directly in four studies [PS12, PS28, PS47, PS54] and indirectly, through adaptations, in two studies [PS04, PS07]. One of the reasons for this is that Scrum teams are the most important factors in improving the performance of a project's success. Like any agile development method, Scrum follows a collaborative and guided approach to software development, reflecting the principles of the Agile Manifesto [32].

Something that caught our attention when analyzing the studies was how the approaches focus on team commitment and engagement. However, some approaches impose a process of communication and constant interaction, using these items as a way of evaluating the performance of team members. However, care needs to be taken with this particular issue, as there are approaches that can give the false impression that a collaborator is not helping or is not engaged in the project. This is because this type of approach is based on and draws its conclusions from constant interactions. However, not always someone who helps with the project interact as often, but can contribute more technical information [PS63].

Still on the limitations, it was found that some approaches are not recommended to plan a small number of tasks, as they were developed to deal with large volumes of data. In this case, the ideal is for the organization to invest in tools that constantly monitor it, especially when it comes to a large project [PS01].

Regarding the evaluations of the approaches carried out by the authors, it was possible to perceive a considerable index of studies that used the case study as a form of evaluation, an index that corresponds to 86% of the analyzed studies. This index makes it possible to verify that this type of evaluation can generate more satisfactory and reliable results, since the approach is submitted to a real environment and from its use, data are extracted that allow the planning and conduct of improvements, in addition to the reduction of possible limitations that the approach may present.

Based on the results listed and described in this work, it is possible to state that, although there was a drop in the number of studies in the years 2020 and 2021 (the latter year justified as it was the year of this SLM), there was interest on the part of academia and industry to develop research aimed at managing software projects, especially research that focuses on approaches that aim to facilitate this process.

6 Threats to Validity

This section discusses potential threats to the validity of this study and actions taken to address validity issues. We used the structure proposed in [37].

6.1 Construct Validity

To minimize the risk that the SLM would not bring the studies that answered the research questions, a test was performed with the search string. Four studies were manually selected that proved to meet the research objectives and then it was verified if, when executing the string in the bases, those same studies would return, which in fact happened.

6.2 Internal Validity

During the extraction process, studies were ranked based on our judgment. Studies that depend on the authors' judgment can carry a bias that needs to be mitigated as much as possible. With this in mind, throughout the study analysis process, weekly meetings were held to discuss and reach a consensus on which studies should really be selected.

6.3 External Validity

It is possible that the SLM does not return all relevant studies on approaches that support software project management. To mitigate this risk, we identified and relied on studies similar to this one so that it would not start from scratch.

6.4 Conclusion Validity

To ensure the validity of the conclusion of our study, we present throughout Sect. 4 charts and tables exposing the results generated directly from the data and we discuss the observations and explicit trends. This ensures a high degree of traceability between data and conclusions. In addition, our corpus of studies is available to other researchers. In addition, the SLM process was carried out with the support of a PhD professor who has extensive experience in genre studies, with several publications in software engineering.

7 Related Works

This section presents similar studies that are directly or indirectly related to the investigation of the present study. Despite all efforts, we did not find secondary studies that searched the literature for approaches to support software project management in an agile context. However, there are secondary studies that explore other aspects of software project management.

The authors of [33] performed a systematic literature review with the objective of identifying the challenges faced in the execution of agile projects and how to deal with these challenges. The authors selected a total of 23 studies and from them the challenges were categorized into the PMBOK knowledge areas. This study brings a list of agile challenges and their mapped solutions. The biggest challenge arises from stakeholder management, which includes challenges related to agile adaptation, agile transition and agile transformation.

The authors of [34] performed a systematic literature mapping (SLM) to understand how risk management is being explicitly integrated into agile software development methods. The authors identified 18 studies that achieved their goals and as a result found that the most used agile method to integrate explicit risk management practices is Scrum. In general, the selected studies indicate that the results of integrating risk management with agile methods are positive, encompassing better communication, better product quality, greater risk visibility, cost reduction and better team efficiency.

As can be seen in the studies described above, they are not focused on the same context, nor on the same objective of this SLR. However, we believe that they serve as a basis for our work, as they focus on software project management or part of it, as is the case of [34] that focus only on project risk management. Therefore, this work is unique in that it explicitly deals with software project management approaches in an agile context, focusing not only on one type of approach and not just on one area or phase of the project, but covering it as a whole.

8 Conclusion

Project management has evolved a lot over the years and has gone from being a set of desirable processes to a structured discipline crucial to the survival of companies. When we talk about software, project management becomes even more necessary, given the high volatility of the market and the constant changes in requirements. Managing all the areas that make up a project without the help of some approach becomes an almost impossible task.

Knowing this, this work presented a set of approaches used in software project management, within the agile development context. Through SLM, it was possible to verify that the approaches that most of the works studies on are project management software, such as Jira, for example. In addition, methodologies are common among the identified approaches.

According to the authors who produced the studies selected in this SLM, the approaches seek to reduce the efforts made by professionals when dealing with the numerous uncertainties that surround a project. In addition, the approaches aim to give greater visibility to the status of projects and, thus, the team can work with greater transparency, mainly because we are talking about an agile context.

As future works, we plan to apply a survey to software project managers who work in industry and / or academia to verify if what is being presented in the literature is being used in organizations and later define a catalog of use of these approaches to support project management professionals in the context of agile software development.

Acknowledgements. The authors would like to thank the Coordination for the Improvement of Higher Education Personnel (CAPES) in Brazil for the financial support for the granting of a scholarship for a master's degree.

References

1. Project Management Institute: A Guide to the Project Management Body of Knowledge (PMBOK Guide), 6th edn., Project Management Institute (2021)
2. Martins, J.C.C.: Gerenciando Projetos de Desenvolvimento de Software com PMI, RUP e UML. Brasport (2010)
3. Kerzner, H.: Project Management: A Systems Approach to Planning, Scheduling, and Controlling. Wiley (2017)

4. Gomes, J., Romão, M.: Improving project success: a case study using benefits and project management. Procedia Comput. Sci. **100**, pp. 489–97 (2016). https://doi.org/10.1016/j.procs.2016.09.187
5. Franco, E.F., Hirama, K., Carvalho, M.M.: Applying system dynamics approach in software and information system projects: a mapping study. Inf. Softw. Technol. **93**, 58–73 (2018). https://doi.org/10.1016/j.infsof.2017.08.013
6. Beck, K.: The Agile Manifesto. Agile Alliance. - References - Scientific Research Publishing (2001)
7. Drury-Grogan, M.L., Conboy, K., Acton, T.: Examining decision characteristics & challenges for agile software development. J. Syst. Softw. **131**, 248–65 (2017). https://doi.org/10.1016/j.jss.2017.06.003
8. Kostalova, J., Tetrevova, L., Svedik, J.: Support of project management methods by project management information system. Procedia – Soc. Behav. Sci. **210**, 96–104 (2015). https://doi.org/10.1016/j.sbspro.2015.11.333
9. Shrivastava, S.V., Rathod, U.: A risk management framework for distributed agile projects. Inf. Softw. Technol. **85**, 1–15 (2017). https://doi.org/10.1016/j.infsof.2016.12.005
10. Varajão, J., Colomo-Palacios, R., Silva, H.: ISO 21500:2012 and PMBoK 5 processes in information systems project management. Comput. Stan. Interfaces **50**, 216–222 (2017). https://doi.org/10.1016/j.csi.2016.09.007
11. Radujković, M., Sjekavica, M.: Project management success factors. Procedia Eng. **196**, 607–615 (2017). https://doi.org/10.1016/j.proeng.2017.08.048
12. Soares, M.d.S.: Metodologias Ágeis Extreme Programming e Scrum para o Desenvolvimento de Software. Revista Eletrônica de Sistemas de Informação **3**(1) (2004). https://doi.org/10.21529/resi.2004.0301006
13. Kitchenham, B.: Systematic reviews. In: 10th International Symposium on Software Metrics, Proceedings. IEEE (2004). https://doi.org/10.1109/metric.2004.1357885. Acedido em 19 jul 2022
14. Kitchenham, B., Charters, S.: Guidelines for performing systematic literature reviews in software engineering (2007)
15. Ghapanchi, A.H., Aurum, A.: Antecedents to IT personnel's intentions to leave: a systematic literature review. J. Syst. Softw. **84**(2), 238–49 (2011). https://doi.org/10.1016/j.jss.2010.09.022
16. Biolchini, J.C.de.A., Mian, P.G., Natali, A.C.C., Conte, T.U., Travassos, G.H.: Scientific research ontology to support systematic review in software engineering. Adv. Eng. Inf. **21**(2), 133–151 (2007)
17. Codas, M.M.B.: Gerência de projetos: uma reflexão histórica. Revista de Administração de Empresas **27**(1), 33–37 (1987). https://doi.org/10.1590/s0034-75901987000100004
18. Heldman, K.: Gerência de projetos: guia para o exame oficial do PMI. Gulf Professional Publishing (2006)
19. Banica, L., Hagiu, A., Bagescu, A., Gherghinescu, A.: Designing a website for a recruitment agency with Pmbok methodology. Sci. Bull.-Econ. Sci. **17**(1), 60–67 (2018)
20. Gonçalves, R.Q., von Wangenheim, C.G.: An Instructional unit for teaching project management tools aligned with PMBOK. In: 2016 IEEE 29th International Conference on Software Engineering Education and Training (CSEET). IEEE (2016). https://doi.org/10.1109/cseet.2016.10
21. Taniguchi, A., Onosato, M.: Effect of continuous improvement on the reporting quality of project management information system for project management success. Int. J. Inf. Technol. Comput. Sci. **10**(1), 1–15 (2018). https://doi.org/10.5815/ijitcs.2018.01.01
22. Carvalho, E.da.C., Malcher, P.R.C., Santos, R.P.D.: A survey research on the use of mobile applications in software project management. In: SBQS 2020: 19th Brazilian Symposium on Software Quality. ACM (2020). https://doi.org/10.1145/3439961.3439963

23. Versionone, C.: 15th annual state of agile report. CollabNet (2021)
24. Matos, S., Lopes, E.: Prince2 or PMBOK – a question of choice. Procedia Technol. **9**, 787–94 (2013). https://doi.org/10.1016/j.protcy.2013.12.087
25. Basili, V.R.: Software modeling and measurement: the Goal/Question/Metric paradigm (1992)
26. Petersen, K., Vakkalanka, S., Kuzniarz, L.: Guidelines for conducting systematic mapping studies in software engineering: an update. Inf. Softw. Technol. **64**, 1–18 (2015). https://doi.org/10.1016/j.infsof.2015.03.007
27. Yanow, S.K., Good, M.F.: Nonessential research in the new normal: the impact of COVID-19. Am. J. Trop. Med. Hyg. **102**(6), 1164–1165 (2020). https://doi.org/10.4269/ajtmh.20-0325
28. Zhang, S., Lan, J.: Research on software project schedule management method based on monte Carlo simulation. In: 2020 IEEE 5th Information Technology and Mechatronics Engineering Conference (ITOEC). IEEE (2020). https://doi.org/10.1109/itoec49072.2020.9141570
29. Lin, X., et al.: Health literacy, computer skills and quality of patient-physician communication in Chinese patients with cataract. PLoS One **9**(9), e107615 (2014)
30. Uspenskiy, M.B., Smirnov, S.V., Loginova, A., Shirokova, S.V.: Modelling of complex project management system in the field of information technologies. In: 2019 III International Conference on Control in Technical Systems (CTS). IEEE (2019). https://doi.org/10.1109/cts 48763.2019.8973245
31. Shaikh, T.H., Khan, F.L., Shaikh, N.A., Shah, H.N., Pirani, Z.: Survey of web-based project management system. In: 2018 International Conference on Smart Systems and Inventive Technology (ICSSIT). IEEE (2018), https://doi.org/10.1109/icssit.2018.8748784
32. Michael, D., Dazki, E., Santoso, H., Indrajit, R.E.: Scrum team ownership maturity analysis on achieving goal. In: 2021 Sixth International Conference on Informatics and Computing (ICIC). IEEE (2021). https://doi.org/10.1109/icic54025.2021.9632969
33. Raharjo, T., Purwandari, B.: Agile project management challenges and mapping solutions. In: ICSIM 2020: The 3rd International Conference on Software Engineering and Information Management. ACM (2020). https://doi.org/10.1145/3378936.3378949
34. Vieira, M., Hauck, J.C.R., Matalonga, S.: How explicit risk management is being integrated into agile methods: results from a systematic literature mapping. In: SBQS 2020: 19th Brazilian Symposium on Software Quality. ACM (2020). https://doi.org/10.1145/343 9961.3439976
35. Carvalho, E., Oliveira, S.: The diversity of approaches to support software project management in the agile context: trends, comparisons and gaps. In: 17th International Conference on Evaluation of Novel Approaches to Software Engineering, SCITEPRESS - Science and Technology Publications (2022). https://doi.org/10.5220/0011063500003176
36. Souza, M.R.de.A., Veado, L., Moreira, R.T., Figueiredo, E., Costa, H.: A systematic mapping study on game-related methods for software engineering education. Inf. Softw. Technol. **95**, 201–218 (2018). https://doi.org/10.1016/j.infsof.2017.09.014
37. Wohlin, C., Runeson, P., Höst, M., Ohlsson, M.C., Regnell, B., Wesslén, A.: Experimentation in Software Engineering - An Introduction. Kluwer Academic Press (2000)

Empirical Validation of Entropy-Based Redundancy Metrics as Reliability Indicators Using Fault-Proneness Attribute and Complexity Metrics

Dalila Amara[✉][iD] and Latifa Ben Arfa Rabai[iD]

Université de Tunis, Institut Supérieur De Gestion De Tunis, SMART Lab, Tunis, Tunisia
dalilaa.amara@gmail.com

Abstract. Software reliability is one of the most important software quality attributes. It is generally predicted using different software metrics that measure internal quality attributes like cohesion and complexity. Therefore, continuous focus on software metrics proposed to predict software reliability still required. In this context, an entropy-based suite of four metrics is proposed to monitor this attribute. The different metrics composing this suite are manually computed and only theoretically validated. Hence, we aim to propose an empirical approach to validate them as useful indicators of software reliability. Therefore, we start by assessing these metrics, using a set of programs retrieved from real software projects. The obtained dataset is served to empirically validate them as reliability indicators. Given that software reliability as external attribute, cannot be directly evaluated, we use two main experiments to perform the empirical validation of these metrics. In the first experiment, we study the relationship between the redundancy metrics and measurable attributes of reliability like fault-proneness. In the second one, we study whether the combination of redundancy metrics with existed complexity and size metrics that are validated as significant reliability indicators can ameliorate the performance of the developed fault-proneness prediction model. The validation is carried out using appropriate machine learning techniques. The experiments outcome showed up that, redundancy metrics provide promising results as indicators of software reliability.

Keywords: Software reliability · Software redundancy metrics · Software metrics validation · Fault-proneness · Complexity metrics

1 Introduction

The quality of software systems is usually reflected by different attributes related to process and product entities. These attributes are classified into internal and external categories [1,2]. Internal product factors are related to its structure such as complexity and cohesion. While, external ones are related to its functionality like reliability and maintainability [3].

According to [4], monitoring software quality needs the development of a measurement plan. Software quality measurement aims to describe real world software entities

H. Kaindl et al. (Eds.): ENASE 2022, CCIS 1829, pp. 93–115, 2023.
https://doi.org/10.1007/978-3-031-36597-3_5

(process/product) by assigning a category or a number to their attributes [5,6]. One common way to perform software quality measurement is the use of software metrics providing quantitative measures of internal quality factors. For the external ones, they are usually predicted by means of various metrics of internal attributes [3,4,7–9]. Further, software metrics can be used for developing quality prediction models [3,4,9].

Many software metrics were proposed to evaluate the quality of software products using the properties of the source code. The literature review shows that the well discussed software metrics evaluate internal quality attributes [4,10,11]. For external attributes, their measurement is usually determined by combining various internal characteristics measured by the cited metrics [12,13]. According to [3], internal factors are more concrete to be evaluated. Whereas, external ones are more difficult for two main reasons: (1) they depend on the program behaviour and, (2) they are available at later phases of software development.

Although the literature on metrics' use for reliability assessment and prediction as one of the most important quality attributes, is abundant, less attention has been devoted to the suite of metrics proposed by [14,15]. This suite was defined based on the information theory of software programs and assessed using the entropy measure [16,17]. It aims to quantify the redundancy of the source code in order to monitor its reliability. The major shortcomings of this suite include (1) the proposed metrics are theoretically presented and manually computed for basic arithmetic operations, (2) it is unclear how they can be computed for more complex programs (functions and classes). Using basic programs containing simple operations, we cannot assume that the metrics are related to programs' redundancy, (3) there are no concrete examples or evidence of how these metrics can be linked to reliability and (4) reliability is one of the most important quality attributes on which further studies focusing on its assessment and prediction still required. The presented reasons prevents us to consider the redundancy metrics as a valid and correct suite to monitor software reliability.

Therefore, we aim in this paper to propose an empirical validation approach to study the concrete relationship between these metrics and reliability. Thus, we need first to perform their empirical assessment using more complex software programs (functions/classes) to convincingly show that the proposed metrics are related to program redundancy. To perform the empirical assessment and validation of the redundancy metrics, the data collection phase is required. For that step, Apache Common Mathematics Library was deployed in this research to extract two main elements of data:

- Different classes satisfying the redundancy metrics' assumption (Metrics are computed at method-level). These methods manipulate input and output variables. This means programs with input states represented by the declared variables and output states represented by the modified states of these variables [14] are selected to compute them in order to construct an empirical data set containing the values of these metrics. Further details of the extraction process are available in our previous paper [45]
- The bug information of the selected classes needed to compute the values of the fault-proneness attribute was unavailable. Therefore, a fault injection procedure was used to obtain them and to perform the empirical validation of the redundancy metrics. Thus, in this study, the dataset we used to perform our validation and to train

and evaluate the classification models contains the values of the redundancy metrics for each function and the related fault-proneness (0 or 1) attribute. This experiment was also performed in our previous paper [51]

Compared with our previous paper [51], in this research we added a new experiment to reach the cited objective. Thus, literature review shows also that different software metrics have been validated as reliability indicators like those of complexity defined by [10]. Therefore, we perform another experiment in this research to test whether the redundancy metrics combined with complexity and size metrics can ameliorate the performance of fault-proneness attribute. Machine learning techniques are used to address these issues. The experiments outcome showed up that, redundancy metrics provide promising results as indicators of software reliability.

2   Related Works

In this section, we present the key elements of software reliability and how this attribute can be predicted. Then, we present the basics of redundancy metrics suite. We also provide an overview of software fault prediction using software metrics. Furthermore, we present a brief literature review of most software metrics that are validated as reliability indicators.

2.1   Software Reliability

Software reliability is an important software quality attribute defined as the probability of failure-free operation for a specified period of time in a specified environment. It can be described by other sub-characteristics like maturity, availability, fault tolerance and recoverability [18, 19]. For [48], it is one of high-level quality attributes that cannot be directly observed and measured.

Different models based on direct metrics were proposed to predict it [21, 22]. These models used software metrics (called independent variables) to evaluate measurable reliability attributes (called dependent variable) like defect density, fault-proneness and defect count [12]. Authors in [14] also proposed a suite of four metrics to monitor programs reliability based on their redundancy. Different forms of software redundancy were defined including information redundancy (code redundancy) [16], functional redundancy [23] and time redundancy [24]. The redundancy metrics proposed by [14] assess the information redundancy provided by the different states of the program [16]. These states reflect the uncertainty about the outcome of the program' variables. The terminology related to program states includes [14]:

- Software program state: is the set of values given by its variables which may change by one or more actions (functions) of the program.
- State space: is the set of values taken by the declared program variables.
- Initial state space: is the state of the program represented by its input variables.
- Current state (actual state): represents the different states that the program may be in at any given point in the program.

- Final state space: represents the state of the program that is produced by its outputs for the relevant initial states.
- State redundancy: the extra range of values allowed by a program than it is needed to represent the program states. The state redundancy is represented by the initial and final state redundancy metrics defined above.

The following example illustrates these definitions related to a program g.
int s; /*state space of g*/
s=2; /*initial state of g */
s=s+1; /*internal state 1 of g*/
s=2*s; /* internal state 2 of g*/
s=s % 3; /* internal state 3 of g */
s= s + 12; /* final state of g */

2.2 Software Redundancy Metrics Suite

Redundancy metrics were defined based on Shannon entropy measure of programs code [16]. Four metrics were defined which are initial state redundancy, final state redundancy, functional redundancy and non-injectivity [14].

Initial and Final State Redundancy Metrics. The state redundancy represents the gap between the declared state and the actual state (really used) of a program [14,25]. For instance, the age of an employee is generally declared as an integer variable type. However, only a restrict range i.e. between 0 and 120 is really required. This means that 7 bits are sufficient to store the age variable but the typical 32 bits size of an integer variable is used. The unused bits measure the code redundancy. The program moves from its initial states (σ_1) to its final states (σ_f), then two state redundancy measures namely initial state redundancy (ISR) and final state redundancy (FSR) were defined by:

$$ISR(g) = \frac{H(S) - H(\sigma_1)}{H(S)} \tag{1}$$

$$FSR(g) = \frac{H(S) - H(\sigma_f)}{H(S)} \tag{2}$$

Notation:

- ISR : is the gap between the declared state and the initial state of the program.
- FSR : is the gap between the declared state and the final state of the program

- S : is the program' declared state represented by its all declared variables.

- H(S) : is the state space of the program as the maximum entropy (bits) taken by its declared variables.

- σ_1 : is the initial state of the program g, represented by its input variables.

- $H(\sigma_f)$: is the state space (entropy) of the initial program' state.

- σ_f : is the final state of the program given by its output variables.

- $H(\sigma_f)$: is the entropy of the final program' state.

To compute the state redundancy (SR) metric (ISR and FSR), each data type is mapped to its width in bits. For instance, for Java language, the entropy of variable declarations of basic data types is illustrated in Table 1.

Table 1. Entropy for basic data type [51].

Data type	Entropy
Boolean	1
Byte	8
Char, short	16
Int, float	32
Double, long	64

Table 2 illustrates examples of the different states that can be taken by a program.

Table 2. example of a program (method) g states: [51].

int x, y, z; //the program state is represented by x, y and z variables
x= 21; // initial state of x
y= 90; // initial state of y
z=(x+y)/2; //final state

The declared space of this program is defined by three integer variables; x, y and z, hence, using the metrics definitions, H(S) = 96 bits since 3 integer variables are used. Its initial state is defined by three variables; x, y and z. The input variables x and y require respectively 5 and 7 bits to be stored. The output variable z has a free range (32 bits). Hence $H(\sigma_1)$ = 5+7+32= 44 bits. For the final state, is determined by the state of the variable z (its entropy), $H(\sigma_f)$ =H((21+90)/2)=6 bits, then: ISR= (96-44)/96 =0.54 FSR= (96-6)/96 =0.93.

Functional Redundancy Metric (FR). According to [14,25], the functional redundancy metric is a function from initial states to final states. It reflects how initial states are mapped to final states. For a program (function) g, FR is the ratio of the output data delivered by g prorated to the input data received by g and given by:

$$FR = \frac{H(Y)}{H(X)} \tag{3}$$

Notation.

– X : is a random variable representing the program' input data.

– Y : is a random variable that represents the program' output data.

– H(Y) : is the entropy of the output data delivered by g

– H(X) : is the entropy of input data passed through parameters, global variables, read statements, etc.

In the previous example, H(S) = 96 bits. The Random variable Y is defined by the integer variable z represented by 32 bits. Then, $H(Y) = log_2(2^{32}) = 32bits$. H(X) is the input data received by g and represented by the two integer variables x and y. Then, $H(X) = 2 * log_2(2^{32}) = 64bits$. FR is given by :

$$FR = \frac{32}{64} = 0.5 \tag{4}$$

Non-injectivity (NI). According to [21], a major source of program (function) redundancy is its non-injectivity. An injective function is a function whose value changes whenever its argument does. A function is non-injective when it maps several distinct arguments (initial states σ_1) into the same image (final states σ_f). NI was defined by:

$$NI = \frac{H(\sigma_1|\sigma_f)}{H(\sigma_1)} = \frac{H(\sigma_1) - H(\sigma_f)}{H(\sigma_1)} \tag{5}$$

In the previous example, NI is equal to (44-6)/44=0.86.

2.3   Overview of Software Fault-Proneness Prediction

Fault-proneness consists on classifying modules (functions or classes) as defective or not defective [26]. For [27, 28], software fault prediction (SFP) consists on identifying faulty modules as software parts containing faults. This attribute was usually estimated and predicted using predictive models compromised of software metrics [29]. The early application of these models helps reducing the testing effort [26] as the identified defect-prone parts are tested with more rigor compared to other ones. In addition, effective resource allocation and reduction in cost and development time will be obtained [30].

Different software fault prediction models have been studied since 1990. The development of these models was performed using classification techniques as fault-proneness attribute consists on classifying modules (functions or classes) as defective or not defective. These models play a crucial role in understanding, evaluating and improving the quality of software systems. According to [26], the early application of these models helps to reduce the testing effort as testing activities will be planned. Also, the parts of software system identified as defect-prone will be tested with more rigor in comparison to other system parts [29]. In the same context, [30] noted that the early identification of faulty software parts provides an effective resource allocation and reduces the cost and time of software development. Numerous studies were defined to predict this attribute based on software metrics.

[31] conducted an experiment where different fault prediction models were constructed using CART, NB and J48 algorithms over different projects taken from PROMISE repository. Results showed that the performance provided by NB is better than that is provided by J48.

[32] investigated six different versions of Mozilla Rhino project. The goal of the study was to study the ability of C&K, QMOOD, MOOD suites of metrics in predicting faulty modules. They applied the Univariate and multivariate binary logistic regression to the cited suites. The authors concluded that C&K and QMOOD suites are very useful for fault prediction by contrast to the MOOD.

[33] examined C&K metrics suite for a defect prediction models based on LR, NB, RF algorithms. The data set under study consists on KC1 project taken from NASA data set. The objective was to predict the severity of faults. Authors concluded that the best fault prediction is achieved by most of C&K metrics expected NOC.

[21] conducted a comparative analysis to study the efficiency of RF and NB algorithms in predicting fault-proneness modules. Authors examined C&K metrics suite taken from NASA data sets. Results showed that for large data sets, RF, provides the best prediction, whereas, for small data sets, NB provides best results.

[34] compared the performance of LR, J48, NB, SVM, DT and BN algorithms in predicting faulty classes. They examined 34 releases obtained from 10 open source' PROMISE projects. Authors concluded that SVM and DT perform well in predicting faulty classes.

[35] compared the performance of Bagging, J48, DT, RF and NB classifiers. They constructed different defect prediction models based on C&K and QMOOD metrics. Authors concluded that only Bagging and J48 are the best defect predictors.

[36] have also compared the performance of Machine and Deep Learning models in predicting faults. They have conducted a case study among 33 Java projects and results showed that deep learning provide a more accurate fault detection accuracy.

2.4 Complexity Metrics for Reliability Prediction

As mentioned earlier, external attributes like reliability and maintainability are generally predicted using a combinations of software metrics measuring internal ones like complexity and cohesion [21,22,38,48,49]. A literature mapping study performed by [13] shows that different metrics especially those of [10] show good link with reliability including those of cohesion and coupling. However, they note that complexity measures perform better than measures of other properties. Therefore, in this study we have considered two of the well studied complexity metrics named WMC, LOC and Cyclomatic Complexity [10] to study their relationship with redundancy ones.

3 Empirical Validation Approach of Redundancy Metrics as Reliability Indicators

Software metrics validation aims to ensure that a proposed metric is really useful for measuring a specified quality attribute [32,37,38]. For [39], metrics validation helps to compare the quality of different software components. In addition, it helps to identify the most relevant software metrics providing the required information, and avoid the unnecessary ones causing the lost of metrics' purpose [40]. Different studies focusing on metrics validation approaches have been proposed [10,32,38,41].

These studies show that usually the used validation approach is based on a common process consisting of the following steps:

1. Data set collection: to validate a software metric, the first step to deal with is to collect software metrics from different types of data repositories. Authors in [9,42] showed that most of metrics' validation works have used programs (classes or methods) taken from NASA projects like CM1, JM1, KC1, etc. In this context, authors in [43] showed that from 64 metrics' validation studies performed from 1991 to 2013, NASA projects were the most used (60%) followed by PROMISE repository data sets (15%) and other Open source projects (12%). From these repositories, two main elements are required:
   - The values of the metrics to validate generated from different sources using automated support tools.
   - The values of the related quality attribute: once the values of software metrics to validate are obtained, the values of the quality attribute to consider like defect count and fault-proneness are also required.
2. Data set analysis: this step aims to analyze the relationship between the metrics to validate and the selected quality attribute. It requires different analysis methods:
   - Machine learning techniques were usually applied to identify the relationship between dependent and independent variables.
   - Some validation studies evaluate the proposed metric against existed metrics measuring the same quality attribute.
3. Results evaluation: numerous performance evaluation measures are defined to evaluate the performance of software quality prediction models.

The three steps of the presented validation approach will be investigated in our research in order to perform the validation of redundancy metrics as reliability indicators. Thus, two main experiments will be conducted: the first one consisting on developing a fault-proneness prediction model in order to study the relationship between the fault-proneness attribute as one of reliability measurable attributes and redundancy metrics. While, the second experiment aims to test whether the existed size and complexity metrics which are validated in literature as adequate indicators of software reliability, can ameliorate the performance of the developed fault-proneness prediction model resulted from the first experiment.

3.1 Data Set Collection

This step consists on gathering data related to software metrics and the related quality attribute measured by these metrics. As we are interested in validating redundancy metrics as reliability indicators, the attribute to consider is software reliability. As mentioned earlier, this attribute can not be directly measured and usually reflected by other measurable attributes like fault-proneness.

The development of fault prediction models starts by data set collection phase that requires two main elements; software metrics and software faults. Data related to these elements can include data from similar software projects or existed software metrics and historical fault data-sets of previous projects [44]. In this paper, the fault-proneness attribute indicating whether a module is fault-free (0) or fault-prone (1) will be considered to perform our validation work. As explained in our previous work [45], as redundancy metrics are computed from the programs states manipulated by its variables, software classes containing functions of input/output types were selected. This means programs (functions) with input states represented by the declared variables and output states represented by modified states of these variables.

We have focused on Apache Commons Math library http://commons.apache.org/ [46] to selected different classes from which the metrics were computed. To select the needed repository, we have considered Apache Commons products library which respects all our requirements and hypothesis. Then, from the selected repository, we have considered a set 43 classes (see [45]) containing functions manipulating variables in the input and the output state. A description of each class and its related function is available at [2]. As this library contains only the source code and the associated unit tests, we have used fault injection procedure to obtain the fault-proneness values.

One of the well-known fault injection techniques is mutation testing which consists on automatically seeding into each class' code a number of faults (or mutations). The fault injection procedure is used to obtain fault data set. This prevents us to compute fault-proneness values at the class-level as all of the classes contain faults. Therefore, we ought to compute this attribute at the function-level. The redundancy metrics will be also computed at this level leading to increase the size of our data set.

Added to these elements, as indicated in the validation approach, some validation studies evaluate the metrics to validate against existed metrics measuring the same quality attribute. Therefore, we aim to perform study the relationship between the redundancy metrics and other exited complexity metrics that are validated as reliability indicators. These complexity metrics will be extracted based on the same functions from which we generate the redundancy metrics. Details of the redundancy metrics, fault-proneness and complexity metrics computing process are described in the subsequent sub-sections.

Redundancy Metrics Collection. We have computed the redundancy metrics at the function-level of each class as all classes will contain faults. The process we used to compute these metrics consists of the following steps:

- For each class, we have considered each function separately to generate the different metrics.
- For each function, we have focused on its input and output variables. Then, we have computed the metrics for random inputs using their equations (1) to (4).
- The output of this process is an Excel file in which the four redundancy metrics values of the different functions of each class were saved. These steps were performed using the Eclipse development environment (version: Neon.3 Release (4.6.3)). Details of metrics computing are available in [45].

Fault Proneness Data Set Collection. Software fault-proneness attribute is a direct reflection of software reliability since as noted by [9], more trusted software consists of less fault-prone units. Software fault prediction (SFP) consists on classifying modules (functions or classes) as defective or not defective by identifying the faulty modules as software parts containing faults [26,27,44]. According to [29], this attribute can be estimated and predicted using prediction models based on software metrics. Fault injection procedure is performed based on automated mutation tools like MuJava, MuEclipse, PiTest and much more [47]. In our research work, PiTest is used within Maven environment. To inject faults, we have adopted the following steps:

- All possible faults which are active by default in PiTest are injected into the source code of the selected classes These faults include the replacement of binary arithmetic operations by another ones (+ by -, - by +, * by /, / by *), etc.
- PiTest runs, and related reports are generated. They indicate for each function, the type and the location of the injected fault.
- PiTest reports are analyzed to identify for each function whether it is fault-free or not. Thus, we have determined the value of fault-proneness attribute (1 or 0) as follows:
  - If all injected faults are detected (killed), then the function is not defective (killed) and the value 0 (fault-free) is assigned to fault-proneness attribute of this function. An example of non-defective function is depicted in Fig. 1 [51].

```
474    public static int lcm(int a, int b) throws MathArithmeticException {
475 2     if (a == 0 || b == 0){
476 1         return 0;
477     }
478 1     int lcm = FastMath.abs(ArithmeticUtils.mulAndCheck(a / gcd(a, b), b));
479 1     if (lcm == Integer.MIN_VALUE) {
480         throw new MathArithmeticException(LocalizedFormats.LCM_OVERFLOW_32_BITS,
481                                             a, b);
482     1. lcm : replaced return of integer sized value with (x == 0 ? 1 : 0) → KILLED
483 1
484     }
```

Fig. 1. Non-Defective method (all injected faults are detected) [51].

  - If at least one of the injected faults is masked (survived), then this function is considered as defective and the value 1 is assigned to the attribute fault-proneness for this function. An example of defective function is depicted in Fig. 2 [51].

The final obtained data set contains for each method the values of the redundancy metrics and the associated fault proneness attribute indicating whether this function contains faults (1) or not (0).

Complexity Metrics Data Set Collection. As mentioned earlier, various metrics have been validated as appropriate software reliability indicators. Among these metrics, size and complexity are the most important as discussed in [13]. To collect these metrics

```
public static double erf(double x) {
   if (FastMath.abs(x) > 40) {
       return x > 0 ? 1 : -1;
   }
   final double ret = Gamma.regularizedGammaP(0.5, x * x, 1.0e-15, 10000);
   return x < 0 ? -ret : ret;
   }
}
```

```
1. erf : changed conditional boundary → SURVIVED
2. erf : removed negation → KILLED
3. erf : negated conditional → KILLED
4. erf : replaced return of double value with -(x + 1) for
org/apache/commons/math3/special/Erf::erf → KILLED
```

Fig. 2. Defective method (There is at least one masked fault from those injected) [51].

from our constructed dataset selected from the common math classes, we have used the Metrics[1] tool within the Eclipse environment. This tool provides for each class, the well-discussed software metrics like those of size, coupling, cohesion and complexity. These steps will be explained in details in the following sub-sections. Thus, in this phase, we obtain a dataset composed for each class, of the values of redundancy metrics and complexity metrics (LOC, WMC and Cyclomatic Complexity). The objective is to test whether combining these metrics with redundancy ones can ameliorate the performance of predicting fault-proneness attribute.

4   Data Set Analysis

In this section, we have performed two main experiments to study the effectiveness of redundancy metrics in predicting fault-proneness attribute.

4.1   Experiment 1: Study the Relationship Between Redundancy Metrics and Fault-proneness Attribute

In this experiment, we study the relationship between the redundancy metrics and fault-proneness attribute. The presented fault prediction studies highlighted the usefulness and the effectiveness of classification techniques in fault-proneness prediction. Thus, to validate the redundancy metrics as reliability indicators using fault-proneness attribute, we have designed the following hypotheses:

- H1 (Alternative Hypothesis): redundancy metrics are significant indicators of software fault-proneness attribute.
- H2 (Null Hypothesis): there is no significant relationship between the redundancy metrics and fault-proneness attribute. Through these hypothesis, we aim to verify if a relationship between the different metrics and fault proneness attribute exists in order to confirm their utility in monitoring software reliability.

---

[1] http://metrics.sourceforge.net/.

Therefore, we proceeded as follows:

– we have performed the data exploration and correlation analysis. Data exploration is an important step required before the application of classification techniques to analyze the data set. Thus, we visualize in Fig. 3 [51], the percentage of fault-prone (1) and no-fault prone (0) functions. Figure 3 shows that 43% of functions in the selected classes are defective and 57% are fault-free.

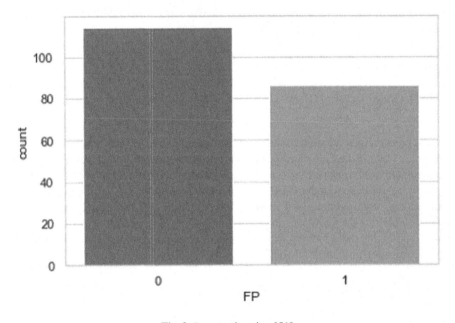

Fig. 3. Data exploration [51].

– We have used the correlation matrix to identify the correlation between the independent variables; ISR, FSR, FR and NI. The objective is to consider metrics which are not inter-correlated in order to achieve better model accuracy. Results are illustrated in Fig. 4 [51].

Figure 4 shows a strong correlation between ISR and FSR as their correlation coefficient is strong and equal to 0.93. FSR and NI have also significant correlation as their correlation coefficient is 0.63. Therefore, FSR will be omitted in our prediction. ISR and FSR metrics are strongly correlated as the FSR metric is computed using the value of H(sf) which in turn depends on the value of H(s1) used to compute ISR metric (See equations (1) and (2)). Therefore any changes in ISR values will lead to changes in FSR and NI ones which explain their correlation.

The development of fault prediction models requires the use of software prediction techniques. To select which technique to use, we have to focus first on the response variable we aim to predict. In this paper, the output to predict is fault-proneness classifying modules (functions or classes) as fault-prone or fault-free. Therefore, classification techniques are useful to predict this attribute using the redundancy metrics. Different classification techniques were defined including Decision Trees (DT), Support Vector Machine (SVM), Naive Bayes (NB), Logistic Regression (LR), Random Forest (RF) and much others [26,43,44].

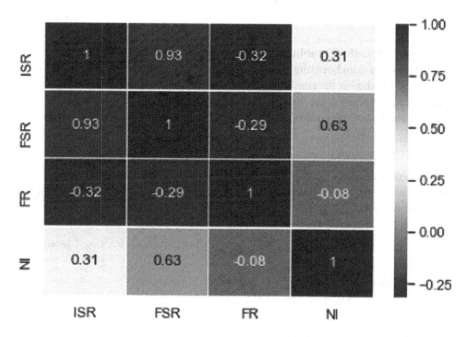

Fig. 4. Pearson correlation coefficients between the independent variables [51].

As mentioned earlier, several studies are proposed to predict the fault-proneness attribute based on these techniques. The objective is to validate different software metrics or to compare the performance of these techniques. Most of these studies showed up the effectiveness of the classification techniques in predicting fault-proneness attribute. However, we have stated that different criteria like the size of the used data set [21], the level of metrics' computing [50] provide a variation in the performance of these techniques. As our main objective is to study the usefulness of the redundancy metrics in reflecting fault-proneness attribute and not to compare the classification techniques, we have started by applying some of them to reach this issue. To build the classification models, we have proceeded as follows:

1. To start with, data exploration phase is performed as explained above. In addition, required Python packages are imported.
2. Next, data set analysis and models building are performed. In this step, we have studied the correlation between the independent variables (redundancy metrics) to consider only metrics that are not inter-correlated as explained above. Also, data is divided into two parts; train data (80%) and test data (20%). In addition, the different cited classification techniques are used to build prediction models based on the train data.

3. Finally, the prediction is performed on the test data and evaluated based on different performance evaluation measures. The presented steps are performed based on appropriate modules and scripts available in the Python language and used to build the different considered classification techniques in order to test the stated hypothesis.

Experiment 2: Test the Combination of Redundancy Metrics with Size and Complexity Metrics in Ameliorating Fault-proneness Prediction. This experiment consists on studying whether the combination of redundancy metrics with existed complexity and size metrics which are validated as effective indicators of software reliability, can ameliorate the performance of fault-proneness prediction model obtained in the first experiment.

- We have considered the same set of 200 functions used in the first experiment.
- Next, as explained above, we have used an eclipse plugin called Metrics providing for each class, the well-discussed software metrics like those of size, coupling, cohesion and complexity as it is illustrated in Fig. 5).

Metric	Total	Mean	Std. Dev.	Maxim...
> Number of Parameters (avg/max per method)		1,5	0,671	2
> Number of Static Attributes (avg/max per type	2	2	0	2
> Specialization Index (avg/max per type)		0	0	0
Number of Classes	1			
> Number of Attributes (avg/max per type)	0	0	0	0
> Number of Static Methods (avg/max per type)	9	9	0	9
Number of Interfaces	0			
Total Lines of Code	202			
> Weighted methods per Class (avg/max per typ	59	59	0	59
> Number of Methods (avg/max per type)	1	1	0	1
> Depth of Inheritance Tree (avg/max per type)		1	0	1
> McCabe Cyclomatic Complexity (avg/max per		5,9	4,549	15
> Nested Block Depth (avg/max per method)		2,2	1,077	5
> Lack of Cohesion of Methods (avg/max per typ		0	0	0

Fig. 5. Complexity and size metrics extraction using Metrics plugin.

- We obtain a dataset that contains for each of the selected function, the values of complexity ones (WMC and CyclomaticComplexity) and size metrics.
- We have used the same classification techniques we have used in the first experiment to test whether the performance of the fault-proneness prediction model developed in the first experiment will be ameliorated.

5 Results

5.1 Results of Experiment 1

In this section, we present the results of predicting faulty and non faulty modules using the classification techniques in order to answer the specified question; "Is there a significant correlation between the redundancy metrics and the fault-proneness attribute?". Then, we compare their performance based on different performance evaluation measures.

Various measures were defined to evaluate the performance of the classification techniques [9]. A binary classifier uses data instances in the test data to predict either they are positive or negative. Then, four possible outcomes are obtained: True positive (TP), False positive (FP), True negative (TN), and False negative (FN). These four outcomes are presented in a confusion matrix from which different measures were derived:

- Precision: indicates how many classes are actually defect-prone from those returned by a model. The best value of this measure is 1. The high value of precision indicates fewer FP (correct elements which are classified incorrectly as defect-prone elements). This measure is defined by : Precision = TP / TP+FP
- Recall: indicates how many of the defect-prone classes are returned actually by a model. The best value of this measure is 1. High value of recall measure indicates lower number of FN (defective classes non indicated by the model). It is defined by: Recall = TP / TP+FN
- Accuracy: indicates the rate of correct classification. It is presented as ratio of the number of correctly predicted modules to the total number of modules and defined by: Accuracy = TP+TN / TP+TN +FP+FN
- Area under the curve (AUC) : is a curve with two dimensions; x-axis is represented by FP and y-axis is represented by TP.

Results. The presented evaluation measures are used to evaluate the performance of the different used classification techniques. Results are illustrated in Tables 3 to 7 [51].

Table 3. Results of DT prediction model [51].

(a) Performance measure

	Precision	Recall	F1-score
0	0.83	0.87	0.70
1	0.81	0.76	0.79
Accuracy			0.82

(b) Confusion matrix

	1	0
1	20	3
0	4	13

Table 4. Results of LR prediction model [51].

(a) Performance measure

	Precision	Recall	F1-score
0	0.61	0.83	0.70
1	0.56	0.29	0.38
Accuracy			0.60

(b) Confusion matrix

	1	0
1	19	4
0	12	5

Tables 3 to 7 illustrate the different evaluation measures obtained for the selected classification techniques. Thus, for each technique, we have summarized the classification report providing us with the values of the presented performance evaluation measures and we have presented the confusion matrix from which these measures are computed. As shown in these tables, the support measure for the different techniques indicates that the data tested for 1 (fault-prone functions) is 17 and for 0 (fault-free functions) is 23. For these values, we have stated that:

Table 5. Results of NB prediction model [51].

(a) Performance measure

	Precision	Recall	F1-score
0	0.63	0.83	0.72
1	0.60	0.35	0.44
Accuracy			0.82

(b) Confusion matrix

	1	0
1	19	4
0	11	6

Table 6. Results of SVM prediction model [51].

(a) Performance measure

	Precision	Recall	F1-score
0	0.70	0.83	0.76
1	0.69	0.53	0.60
Accuracy			0.70

(b) Confusion matrix

	1	0
1	19	4
0	8	9

Table 7. Results of RF prediction model [51].

(a) Performance measure

	Precision	Recall	F1-score
0	0.80	0.87	0.83
1	0.80	0.71	0.77
Accuracy			0.80

(b) Confusion matrix

	1	0
1	20	3
0	4	13

– The precision measure shows that DT and RF perform well in predicting fault-prone modules with values of respectively 0.81 and 0.80. NB and SVM perform moderately with a precision values of respectively 0.60 and 0.69. Precision shows also that LR is the least effective model for fault-proneness prediction with precision value of 0.56.
– In terms of recall and F-measure, LR and NB classifiers had low comparable performance and these measures range from 0.29 to 0.44. SVM has a moderate F-measure and recall rate that ranges from 0.53 to 0.60. DT and RF have the highest recall and F-measure rate that ranges from 0.71 to 0.79.
– Accuracy shows that LR and NB are the least effective models for fault-proneness prediction as their accuracy rates are respectively of 0.60 and 0.62. For SVM classifier, it has a moderate accuracy rate that is 0.7. DT and RF have the highest accuracy rates that are respectively of 0.82 and 0.81.
– Confusion matrix shows that for LR, there were 23 points in the first class (label 0) and 17 in the second one (1). From these 17 points, we have stated that:
  • LR and NB present comparative results and succeed in identifying respectively 5 and 6 of those correctly in label 1, but 12 and 11 were respectively marked as label 0.
  • For SVM, from the 17 points, it succeed in identifying 9 of those correctly in label 1, whilst, 8 points were marked as label 0.
  • Concerning DT, we have stated that from the 17 points, the model succeed in identifying 13 of those correctly in label 1 and only 4 points were marked as label 0. The same results were given by the RF classifier.

We summarize in Table 8, the accuracy rate of the different techniques. Taking accuracy as the most used models' evaluation measure, results in Table 8. show that DT is the most appropriate technique followed by RF succeeded in measuring fault-proneness attribute based on redundancy metrics.

Table 8. Accuracy rate for the selected classifiers (Experiment 1) [51].

Classifier	Accuracy rate
Logistic Regression	60%
Naive Bayes	62%
Support Vector Machine	70%
Decision Tree	82%
Random Forest	80%

5.2 Results of Experiment 2

As mentioned, in the second experiment, the objective is to combine the size and complexity metrics cited above with the redundancy metrics and test their effect on fault proneness attributes. We have used the same classification techniques identified in the

Table 9. Accuracy rate for the selected classifiers (Experiment 2).

Classifier	Accuracy rate
Logistic Regression	57%
Naive Bayes	62%
Support Vector Machine	70%
Decision Tree	87%
Random Forest	82%

first experiment. Results presenting accuracy rate of the different techniques are illustrated in Table 9 As shown in Table 9, we have identified that the accuracy rate for most of the used classifiers is more important than that identified in the first experiment. Thus, we can note that using different source code attributes as information redundancy, complexity and size can be useful in predicting fault-proneness of functions.

6   Discussion, Threats to Validity and Comparison Width Related Works

This section summarizes the results and presents the identified threats to validity. Also, a comparison with the related works is presented.

6.1   Overall Discussion of Results and Threats to Validity

We have experimented with different popular classifiers the usefulness of the redundancy metrics as reliability indicators using fault-proneness attribute. A set of 200 functions selected from Commons-math Apache project is used. Considering accuracy as the evaluating parameter, results show that the fault proneness attribute can be predicted using the redundancy metrics with a good accuracy rate of 0.82. This leads us to accept the stated H1 hypothesis indicating that the redundancy metrics are useful indicators of fault proneness attribute and reject the null hypothesis of no relationship between these two variables. Therefore, these results can be used as first guidance to predict faulty modules based on the redundancy metrics.

Considering complexity and size attributes of the source code with information redundancy measured by redundancy metrics showed that predicting fault-proneness based on classification techniques can be ameliorated compared with predicting it only based on redundancy metrics.

We have obtained promising results proposing validated ISR and NI redundancy metrics as significant reliability indicators for the both considered defect density and fault-proneness attributes. However, we have noted several threads to validity:

– First, the proposed redundancy metrics are semantic as they depend on the program functionality; each program (function or class) has its state represented by the manipulated variables. Hence, each time the used variables in the program input state change, the output state will change, and the values of the redundancy metrics will change too. Therefore, the proposed computing process described in the previous work is not fully automated and it is implemented separately for each program.

– Second, as more we use larger training data sets and optimizing model parameters, better we improve the model prediction performance [26], our data set can be extended to enhance the performance of the proposed prediction model.
– Comparing the redundancy metrics with other existed metrics validated as fault-proneness indicators can enhance their performance as significant quality indicators.
– Performing other experiments using the same dataset and the same classification techniques by taking into account different metrics that include internal attributes such as complexity and cohesion measured by C&K metrics [10] and compare results with entropy metrics.

6.2   Comparison Between Our Proposed Approach and Related Works

In [25], authors have proposed an empirical validation of the redundancy metrics using the rate of mutants as quality attribute. We compare our work with their work in Table 10. Only ISR and FR are considered in our experimentation because we have identified a strong correlation between ISR and FSR as shown in Fig. 4 which leads us to omit the FSR metric. Concerning the FR metric, we have included it in our experimentation, but we have stated that it hasn't any change on the results contrary to ISR and NI.

As shown in Table 10, little works are proposed to empirically validate the redundancy metrics as reliability predictors. The presented comparison shows that:

Table 10. Some differences and similarities between the related works and our work.

Criteria	[25]	Our work
Suite of metrics (Independent variables)	ISR, FSR, FR and NI	ISR, FSR, FR and NI
Quality attribute (Dependent variable)	Survival rate of mutants	Fault-proneness
Data repository	Apache Common Mathematics Library	Apache Common Mathematics Library
Size of the used data set	- 19 functions	- 200 functions for fault-proneness attribute
Quality attribute collection procedure	Fault injection procedure based on PiTest tool is used then PiTest reports are analyzed to obtain the values of the considered attribute	Fault injection procedure based on PiTest tool is used then PiTest reports are analyzed to obtain the values of the considered attribute
Statistical techniques	- Correlation analysis between the independent variables is not performed. - Linear multivariate regression technique is used	- Correlation analysis between the independent variables is performed. - Different classification techniques are used
Results	All redundancy metrics are identified as significant indicators of the survival rate of mutants.	Only ISR and NI are identified as significant indicators of defect density and fault-proneness attributes

- The same validation approach was used. In both cases, data set is first collected, then, data analysis, models building and performance evaluation steps are performed. In addition, the work described in [25] is comparable to our work as the same data repository is used to compute the metrics.
- Authors in [25] showed that all of the redundancy metrics are significant predictors of the survival rate of mutants and software reliability. However, in our validation work, only ISR and NI metrics appeared to be adequate in predicting software reliability using defect density and fault-proneness attributes. The lack of correlation tests between the independent variables in their study and the difference in selecting reliability quality attributes can explain these different results. On another hand, the nature of the considered fault-proneness quality attribute as dependent variable lead us to use various classification techniques.

7   Conclusion and Perspectives

In this paper we have proposed an empirical validation of four redundancy semantic metrics as indicators of software reliability. These metrics named respectively Initial state redundancy, final state redundancy, non-injectivity, and functional redundancy metrics were proposed to assess the source code' redundancy as the excess of bits declared and not used to store the program variables. Therefore, w have used two main experiments to reach this objective. The first one uses the fault proneness attribute as a direct reflection of software reliability and study the effectiveness of redundancy metrics in predicting it. The second one combines redundancy metrics with existed complexity and size metrics to test their performance in ameliorating the prediction of fault-proneness attribute.

The empirical validation is based on a set of 200 Java functions taken from the Commons Math Library, from which we have computed all related redundancy metrics' values, and the fault-proneness attribute as a direct reliability indicator. Five classification techniques (LR, SVM, DT, RF, and NB) are then used in the first experiment to study whether these metrics are useful as indicators of fault-proneness attribute. For the second experiment, we have studied the performance of combining the redundancy metrics with existed complexity and size metrics in ameliorating the accuracy level of predicting faulty modules by the development prediction model of the first experiment.

As a future work, we aim to study the effectiveness of software product source code metrics like complexity, cohesion, coupling in predicting software defects based on machine learning and deep-learning techniques. The objective is to identify the most relevant metrics in predicting defective modules in one side and the most important techniques in this prediction in the other one.

References

1. Boehm Barry, W., Brown John R., Lipow, Mlity: Quantitative evaluation of software quality. In: Proceedings of the 2nd International Conference On Software Engineering, pp. 592–605 (1976)

2. Iso, ISO: iec/ieee international standard-systems and software engineering-vocabulary. In: ISO/IEC/IEEE 24765 (2017)
3. Fenton, N., Bieman, J.: Software metrics: a rigorous and practical approach. CRC Press (2014)
4. Arvanitou, E., Ampatzoglou, A., Chatzigeorgiou, A., Galster M., Avgeriou, P.: A mapping study on design-time quality attributes and metrics. In: Journal of Systems and Software, pp. 52–77. Elsevier (2017)
5. Fenton, N.: Software measurement: A necessary scientific basis. In: IEEE Transactions on Software Engineering, pp. 199–206. Elsevier (1994)
6. Gómez, O., Oktaba, H., Piattini, M., García, F.: A systematic review measurement in software engineering: state-of-the-art in measures. In: Filipe, J., Shishkov, B., Helfert, M. (eds.) ICSOFT 2006. CCIS, vol. 10, pp. 165–176. Springer, Heidelberg (2008). https://doi.org/10.1007/978-3-540-70621-2_14
7. Lyu Michael, R.: Handbook of software reliability engineering. In: IEEE Computer Society Press CA, pp. 165–176. IEEE (1996)
8. Nuñez-Varela, S., Pérez G., Héctor, G., Martínez P., Francisco E., Soubervielle-Montalvo, C.: Source code metrics: A systematic mapping study. In: Journal of Systems and Software, pp. 164–197. Elsevier (2017)
9. Reddivari, S., Raman, J.: Software Quality Prediction: An Investigation Based on Machine Learning. In: 2019 IEEE 20th International Conference on Information Reuse and Integration for Data Science (IRI), pp. 115–122. IEEE (2019)
10. Chidamber S.R., Kemerer, C.F.: A metrics suite for object oriented design. In: IEEE Transactions on software engineering, pp. 476–493. IEEE (1994)
11. Li, W.: Another metric suite for object-oriented programming. In: Journal of Systems and Software, pp. 155–162. Elsevier (1998)
12. Briand, L.C., Wüst, J.: Empirical studies of quality models in object-oriented systems. In: Advances in Computers, pp. 97–166. Elsevier (2002)
13. Jabangwe, R., Börstler, J., Šmite, D., Wohlin, C.: Empirical evidence on the link between object-oriented measures and external quality attributes: a systematic literature review. Empirical Softw. Eng. 20(3), 640–693 (2014). https://doi.org/10.1007/s10664-013-9291-7
14. Mili, A., Jaoua, A., Frias, M., Helali, R.G.M.: Semantic metrics for software products. Innov. Syst. Softw. Eng. 10(3), 203–217 (2014). https://doi.org/10.1007/s11334-014-0233-3
15. Mili, A., Tchier, F.: Software testing: Concepts and operations. In: John Wiley & Sons. (2015)
16. Shannon, C.E.: A mathematical theory of communication. In: ACM SIGMOBILE Mobile Computing and Communications Review, pp. 3–55. Springer (2001)
17. Singh, V.B., Chaturvedi, K.K.: Semantic metrics for software products. In: International Conference on Computational Science and Its Applications, pp. 408–426. Springer (2013)
18. Singh, V.B., Chaturvedi, K.K.: Software reliability modeling based on ISO/IEC SQuaRE. In: Information and Software Technology, pp. 18–29. Elsevier (2016)
19. Amara, D., Rabai, L.B.A.: Towards a new framework of software reliability measurement based on software metrics. In: Procedia Computer Science, pp. 725–730. Elsevier (2017)
20. Bansiya, J., Davis, C.G.: A hierarchical model for object-oriented design quality assessment. In: IEEE Transactions on software Engineering, pp. 4–17. IEEE, (2002)
21. Catal, C., Diri, B.: A systematic review of software fault prediction studies. In: Expert Systems with Applications, pp. 7346–7354. Elsevier (2009)
22. Radjenović, D., Heričko, M., Torkar, R., Živkovič, A.: Software fault prediction metrics: A systematic literature review. In: Information and Software Technology, pp. 1397–1418. Elsevier (2013)

23. Asghari, S.A., Marvasti, M.B., Rahmani, A.M.: Enhancing transient fault tolerance in embedded systems through an OS task level redundancy approach. In: Future Generation Computer Systems, pp. 58–65. Elsevier (2018)

24. Dubrova, E.: Fault-tolerant design. Springer (2013). https://doi.org/10.1007/978-1-4614-2113-9

25. Ayad, A., Marsit, I., Mohamed Omri, N., Loh, J.M., Mili, A.: Using semantic metrics to predict mutation equivalence. In: van Sinderen, M., Maciaszek, L.A. (eds.) ICSOFT 2018. CCIS, vol. 1077, pp. 3–27. Springer, Cham (2019). https://doi.org/10.1007/978-3-030-29157-0_1

26. Singh, A., Bhatia, R., Singhrova, A.: Taxonomy of machine learning algorithms in software fault prediction using object oriented metrics. In: Procedia Computer Science, pp. 993–1001. Elsevier (2018)

27. Rathore, S.S., Kumar, S.: An empirical study of some software fault prediction techniques for the number of faults prediction. Soft Comput. **21**(24), 7417–7434 (2016). https://doi.org/10.1007/s00500-016-2284-x

28. Kumar, L., Misra, S., Rath, S.Ku.: An empirical analysis of the effectiveness of software metrics and fault prediction model for identifying faulty classes. In: Computer Standards & Interfaces, pp. 1–32. Elsevier (2017)

29. Gondra, I.: Applying machine learning to software fault-proneness prediction. In: Journal of Systems and Software, pp. 186–195. Elsevier (2008)

30. Ayad, A., Marsit, I., Mohamed Omri, N., Loh, J.M., Mili, A.: Using semantic metrics to predict mutation equivalence. In: van Sinderen, M., Maciaszek, L.A. (eds.) ICSOFT 2018. CCIS, vol. 1077, pp. 3–27. Springer, Cham (2019). https://doi.org/10.1007/978-3-030-29157-0_1

31. Menzies, T., DiStefano, J., Orrego, A., Chapman, R.: Assessing predictors of software defects. In: Proceedings of the Workshop Predictive Software Models (2004)

32. Olague, H.M. Etzkorn, L.H., Gholston, S., Quattlebaum, S.: Empirical validation of three software metrics suites to predict fault-proneness of object-oriented classes developed using highly iterative or agile software development processes. In: IEEE Transactions on software Engineering, pp. 402–419. IEEE (2007)

33. Zhou, Y., Xu, B., Leung, H.: On the ability of complexity metrics to predict fault-prone classes in object-oriented systems. In: Journal of Systems and Software, pp. 660–674. Elsevier (2010)

34. He, P., Li, B., Liu, X., Chen, J., Ma, Y.: An empirical study on software defect prediction with a simplified metric set. In: Information and Software Technology, pp. 170–190. Elsevier (2015)

35. Kaur, A., Kaur, I.: An empirical evaluation of classification algorithms for fault prediction in open source projects. In: Journal of King Saud University-Computer and Information Sciences, pp. 2–17. Elsevier (2018)

36. Lomio, F., Moreschini, S., Lenarduzzi, V.: Fault Prediction based on Software Metrics and SonarQube Rules. Machine or Deep Learning?. In: arXiv preprint arXiv:2103.11321 Elsevier (2021)

37. Kitchenham, B., Pfleeger, S.L., Fenton, N.: Towards a framework for software measurement validation. In: IEEE Transactions on Software Engineering, pp. 929–944, IEEE (1995)

38. Basili, V.R., Briand, L.C., Melo, W.L.: A validation of object-oriented design metrics as quality indicators. In: IEEE Transactions on Software Engineering, pp. 751–761, IEEE (1996)

39. Schneidewind, N.F.: Methodology for validating software metrics. In: IEEE Transactions on Software Engineering, pp. 410–422, IEEE (1992)

40. Arvanitou, E.Maria., Ampatzoglou, A., Chatzigeorgiou, A., Avgeriou, P.: Software metrics fluctuation: a property for assisting the metric selection process. In: Information and Software Technology, pp. 110–124, Elsevier (2016)

41. Kumar, L.N., Debendra, K., Rath, S.Ku.: Validating the effectiveness of object-oriented metrics for predicting maintainability. In: Procedia Computer Science, pp. 798–806, Elsevier (2015)

42. Verma, D.K., Kumar, S.: Prediction of Defect Density for Open Source Software using Repository Metrics. In: J. Web Eng, pp. 294–311 (2017)

43. Malhotra, R.: A systematic review of machine learning techniques for software fault prediction. In: Applied Soft Computing, pp. 504–518, Elsevier (2015)

44. Turabieh, H., Mafarja, M., Li, X.: Iterated feature selection algorithms with layered recurrent neural network for software fault prediction. In: Expert Systems with Applications, pp. 27–42, Elsevier (2019)

45. Amara, D., Fatnassi, E., Rabai, L.: An Empirical Assessment and Validation of Redundancy Metrics Using Defect Density as Reliability Indicator. In: Scientific Programming, Hindawi (2021)

46. Rathore, S.S., Kumar, S.: Software fault prediction based on the dynamic selection of learning technique: findings from the eclipse project study. Appl. Intell. **51**(12), 8945–8960 (2021). https://doi.org/10.1007/s10489-021-02346-x

47. Delahaye, M., Du Bousquet, L.: A comparison of mutation analysis tools for java. In: 13th International Conference on Quality Software, pp. 187–195, IEEE (2013)

48. Bansiya, J., Davis, C.G.: A hierarchical model for object-oriented design quality assessment. In: IEEE Transactions on Software Engineering, pp. 4–17, IEEE (2002)

49. Gall, CS., et al.: Semantic software metrics computed from natural language design specifications. In: IET Software, pp. 17–26, IET (2008)

50. Koru, A.G., Liu, H.: Building effective defect-prediction models in practice. In: IEEE Software, pp. 23–29, IEEE (2005)

51. Amara, D., Rabai, L.B.A.: Classification Techniques Use to Empirically Validate Redundancy Metrics as Reliability Indicators based on Fault-proneness Attribute. In: ENASE, pp. 209–220, ENASE, (2022)

Dynamic Link Network Emulation
and Validation of Execution Datasets

Erick Petersen[1,2(✉)], Jorge López[1], Natalia Kushik[2], Maxime Labonne[1],
Claude Poletti[1], and Djamal Zeghlache[2]

[1] Airbus, Issy-Les-Moulineaux, France
{erick.petersen,jorge.lopez-c,maxime.labonne,
claude.poletti}@airbus.com
[2] Télécom SudParis, Institut Polytechnique de Paris, Palaiseau, France
{erick_petersen,natalia.kushik,
djamal.zeghlache}@telecom-sudparis.eu

Abstract. We present a network emulator for *dynamic link networks*, i.e., networks whose parameter values vary; for example, satellite communication networks where bandwidth capacity varies. We describe the design of the emulator, which allows *replicating* any network system, through the use of state-of-the-art virtualization technologies. This paper is also devoted to the verification of the datasets produced by monitoring the network emulation. We propose a model-based design for a dynamic link network emulator and discuss how to extract data for network parameters such as bandwidth, delay, etc. These data can be verified to ensure a number of desired properties. The main goal is to try to guarantee that the emulator behaves as the real physical system. We rely on model checking strategies for the dataset validation, in particular, we utilize a Satisfiability Module Theories (SMT) solver. The properties to check can include one or several network parameter values and can contain dependencies between various network instances. Experimental results showcase the pertinence of our emulator and proposed approach.

Keywords: Model-based Design · Dynamic link Networks · Emulator · Many-sorted First Order Logic · Satisfiability Modulo Theories

1 Introduction

As the demand for interactive services, multimedia and network capabilities grows in modern networks, novel software and/or hardware components should be incorporated [6]. As a consequence, the evaluation and validation process of these newly developed solutions is critical to determine whether they perform well, are reliable (and robust) before their final deployment in a real network [1]. However, thorough testing or qualifying [29] the produced software under a wide variety of network characteristics and conditions is a challenging task [9].

Currently, many of these tests are done through operational, controlled, and small-scale networks (physical testbeds) or alternatively software-based testbeds. Ideally, if available, such tests are performed on the original system in order to replicate the

H. Kaindl et al. (Eds.): ENASE 2022, CCIS 1829, pp. 116–138, 2023.
https://doi.org/10.1007/978-3-031-36597-3_6

conditions in which a service or protocol will be used at the highest level of fidelity [12]. Unfortunately, while system modeling is not needed, such testbeds are not always desirable or pertinent due to several reasons [33]. For example, there are difficulties in creating various network topologies, generating different traffic scenarios, and testing the implementations under specific conditions (network load or weather conditions that may affect the radio-physical links in specific network technologies such as wireless or satellite communications).

A very well-known alternative method is the use of network simulators [15]. Through network simulation, researchers can mimic the basic functions of network devices and study specific network-related issues on a single computer or high-end server. However, the adequacy of simulated systems is always in question due to the model abstraction and simplification. At the same time, not simulation but emulation for the related networks can also be a solution [17]. Network emulation provides the necessary mechanisms to reproduce the behavior of real networks at low infrastructure costs compared to physical testbeds. Emulation is also capable of achieving better realism than simulations since it allows interacting with interfaces, protocol stacks, and operating systems. Moreover, it is possible to perform continuous testing on the final implementation without having to make any changes in the solution once it is deployed in a real network. However, the emulation of dynamic link networks, i.e., networks whose link parameters change, complicates the emulation architecture. For example, certain radio-frequency links have different up/down bandwidth capacity [9], large delays (due to distant transmitters), and the links' capacities may change due to external interference, propagation conditions (weather), traffic variations (due to the shared medium), or others. Therefore, it is extremely important to have methods that allow controlling key parts of the emulation over time, such as the generation of traffic or the modification of the link property values (capacity, delay). These are required in order to build a proper emulation environment of interest which is the main focus of this work. To cope with such requirements, we herein propose a dynamic link network emulation and traffic generation which combines the functional realism and scalability of virtualization and link emulation to create virtual networks that are fast, customizable and portable.

At the same time, the tool needs to ensure the emulation of dynamic link networks exactly as expected and requested by an end user. There are a number of ways to provide such kind of assurance. On the one hand, the emulator can be permanently monitored and the captured data can be analyzed online to check if they satisfy the necessary properties. We investigated this approach previously and the interested Reader can find more details in [24]. With such an online approach, verifying complex properties can be problematic, as the verification time must be reasonable. On the other hand, it is also possible to analyze the monitored data offline. If the generated dataset does not hold expected properties, the emulator should be updated accordingly. The latter strategy is applied in the paper.

We therefore present a design and architecture of the solution that meets dynamic link emulation needs by the effective use of software technologies, such as virtualization (containers and virtual machines) and Linux kernel capabilities. Furthermore, our dynamic link network emulator provides a fast and user-friendly workflow, from the installation to the configuration of scenarios by using a formal model of the network.

We note that the emulator architecture was first presented in [25]. In this paper, we extend the previous results through the validation of the data generated by the emulator in question. For the latter, we rely on the methodology we proposed in [20]. This paper thus extends the two conference papers presented in ENASE'2022 and IC3K'2021, respectively. The main contributions of the current extension are the following: i) monitoring and data extraction within the dynamic link network emulator; ii) creation of a large list of interesting network properties that should be verified, and finally iii) experimental results on the dynamic link dataset verification.

The structure of the paper is as follows. Section 2 describes existing network emulators and simulators and their capabilities. Section 3 details the background and concepts upon which this work is based on. Section 4 presents the dynamic link emulator under design. Section 5 describes the monitoring and data collection possibilities of the emulator, which is further used in the experimental study. The dataset verification approach is presented in Sect. 6 while the experimental results are summarized in Sect. 7. Section 8 concludes the paper.

2   Related Work

Several works have been devoted to the simulation and emulation of different network types, to perform experiments on novel or existing protocols and algorithms. Below, we briefly summarise some relevant existing solutions.

Ns-3 [11] is a widely used network simulator. Ns-3 simulates network devices by compiling and linking C++ modules while providing data monitoring, collection, and processing capabilities through the Data Collection Framework (DCF). Thus, it simulates the behavior of components in a user-level executable program. However, real-world network devices are highly complex (functionally speaking) or cannot be compiled and linked together with Ns-3 to form a single executable program. Therefore, Ns-3 cannot run real-world network devices but only specific ones developed for it.

Emulab [31] is a network testbed with a minimum degree of virtualization, aiming to provide application transparency and to exploit the hierarchy found in real computer networks for studying networked and distributed systems. Its architecture uses FreeBSD jail namespaces [13] to emulate virtual topologies. Monitoring and data collection can be achieved by running software on each node using a combination of .ns scripts (python for the latest version) and the Emulab web interface. Similarly, Mininet [18] enables rapid testbeds by using several virtualization features, such as virtual ethernet pairs and processes in Linux container network namespaces. It emulates hosts, switches and controllers, which are simple shell processes that are given their network namespace and links between them. Python is used to implement all the essential functions for the monitoring and data collection process. However, both still present some limitations, including the lack of support for dynamic features such as link emulation, resource management and traffic generation.

EstiNet [35] is based on network simulation/emulation integration for different kinds of networks. Unlike previous simulators, EstiNet allows not only monitoring but also configuration and data collection through a GUI. It also supports wireless channel modeling. However, since EstiNet is a commercial solution, it cannot be easily extended. Moreover, its features are limited and depend on the EstiNet developers. Thus, the performance fidelity and the expansion to new features are reduced. OpenNet [4] also merges simulation and emulation network capabilities by connecting Mininet and Ns-3. As a result, monitoring and data collection can also be achieved through the implementation of python functions within each node. However, it also inherits the limitations of Ns-3 and Mininet. Additionally, its main focus is software-defined wireless local area networks (SDWLAN).

More recently, the introduction of lightweight virtualization technologies (e.g., containers) has led to some few container-based emulation tools [8,27,30]. SDN Owl [30] is a network emulation tool to create simple SDN testbeds using few computers with Linux OSs. SDN Owl utilizes Ansible to send a set of scripts to configure each virtual component properly and can also be used to set up monitoring and data collection tasks. However, it fails to provide scalability and isolation since experiments with different types of network topologies or resource allocation are not shown. vSDNEmul [8] and ContainerNet [27] are network emulators based on Docker container virtualization, allowing autonomous and flexible creation of independent network elements, resulting in more realistic emulations. Similar to other container-based tools, data collection and monitoring tasks can be performed using the statistics collected by Docker or through services implemented in any programming language that collects the information within each container. However, these emulators can only create SDN networks. Furthermore, the network descriptions remain rather informal and do not facilitate the emulator's verification to guarantee that it properly replicates the desired network.

A feature comparison is shown in Table 1. We therefore are not aware of any work that meets all the required features to properly emulate dynamic link networks in order

Table 1. Comparison of Software-based Network Testbeds.

NAME	OS	LN	GUI	EM	SC	PO	DL	AT	FD	MD	DV
Ns-3 [11]	✓	C++/Python	x	x	+++	x	✓	x	x	✓	x
Mininet [14]	✓	Python	✓	✓	+	✓	x	x	x	✓	x
Containernet [27]	✓	Python	✓	✓	++	✓	x	x	x	✓	x
OMNet++ [34]	x	C++	✓	x	+++	x	✓	x	x	✓	x
Emulab [31]	✓	C	✓	✓	+	✓	x	x	x	✓	x
OpenNet [4]	✓	C++	✓	x	+++	x	✓	x	x	✓	x
vSDNEmul [8]	✓	Python	x	✓	++	✓	x	x	x	x	x
EstiNet [35]	x	-	✓	✓	++	✓	✓	-	-	✓	x
SDN Owl [30]	✓	Python	x	✓	++	✓	x	x	x	✓	x
NetEM [10]	✓	-	x	✓	-	x	✓	x	x	x	x

Abbreviations: OS, Open Source; LN, Language; GUI, Graphical User Interface; EM, Emulation Support; SC, Scalability; PO, Portability; DL, Dynamic Links; AT, Automatic Traffic Generation; FD, Formal Description; MD, Monitoring and Data collection; DV, Dataset Verification to qualify novel engineered solutions. Moreover, none provided a formal approach to verify that the extracted dataset (collected data from the emulator) holds the expected properties to ensure that the produced network behaves exactly as requested by an end user.

3   Background

3.1   Dynamic Link Networks

Examples of networks range from different types of connections or collaboration between individuals (social networks [28]), products (distribution networks [7]), computers (internet [22]) to software networks [19] where edges may represent function calls. In this work, we focus on computer networks, i.e., a set of interconnected computing devices that can exchange data and share resources with each other through links.

Computer networks [26] tend to be classified into many different types in terms of size, distance, structure, connection type or even their function. Local Area Networks (LAN) are perhaps one of the most frequently used and straightforward examples (under normal operation) of what we refer to as a *static network*, i.e., a computer network with static link parameters. A LAN consists of an interconnected group of computer devices, through a common communication path, within a single limited area. In this scenario, network adapters are typically configured (by default) to automatically negotiate the maximum transfer speed with the device they are connected to. Usually, for LAN links, those values are 1Gbps, 100 Mbps or 10 Mbps for up/down connections (full/half duplex modes), i.e., the whole LAN network operates at those constant values.

Unlike those networks, we focus on what we refer to as *dynamic link networks*, i.e., a computer network where the link parameters may change at different time instances. One example of such networks is a satellite communication network [16]. For instance, Geostationary Orbit (GEO) satellite communication systems usually have a high end-to-end latency (at normal operation) of at least 250 ms. Depending on several internal or external factors, it may vary as high as 400 ms, which has a great impact on the speed of their communication links. Additionally, medium conditions may directly have an impact on the bandwidth capacity of the link. However, we consider that the network topology does not change (as for example in ad-hoc networks) in *dynamic link networks*.

Modeling Dynamic Link Networks. We view a *static* network as a computer network where each link has a set of parameters that do not change, for example bandwidth (capacity) or delay. Differently from static networks, the parameters of the links may change in dynamic link networks; such change can be the consequence of the physical medium (e.g., in wireless / radio frequency networks) or due to logical changes (e.g., rate limiting the capacity of a given link). Therefore, static networks can be modeled as (directed) weighted graphs $(V, E, p_1, \ldots, p_k)$, where V is a set of nodes, $E \subseteq V \times V$ is a set of directed edges, and p_i is a link parameter function $p_i : E \to \mathbb{N}$, for $i \in \{1, \ldots, k\}$; without loss of generality we assume that the parameter functions map to non-negative integers (denoted by $\mathbb{N}$) or related values can be encoded with them. Similarly, dynamic link networks can be modeled as such graphs, however, p_i

maps an edge to a non-empty set of integer values, i.e., $p_i : E \rightarrow 2^{\mathbb{N}} \setminus \emptyset$, where $2^{\mathbb{N}}$ denotes the power-set of $\mathbb{N}$, and represents all the possible values p_i can have. As an example, consider the dynamic link network depicted in Fig. 1, and its model $\mathcal{N} = (V, E, p_1(e), p_2(e))$, where:

$V = \{1, 2, 3, 4\}$

$E = \{(1, 2), (2, 1), (1, 3), (3, 1), (1, 4),$
$\qquad (4, 1), (2, 4), (4, 2), (3, 4), (4, 3)\}$

$p_1(e) = b((s, d)) = \begin{cases} \{4, 5, 6\}, & \text{if } d = 2 \\ \{2, 3, 4\}, & \text{otherwise} \end{cases}$

$p_2(e) = d((s, d)) = \begin{cases} \{1, 2, 3\}, & \text{if } d = 2 \\ \{9, 10, 1\}, & \text{otherwise} \end{cases}$

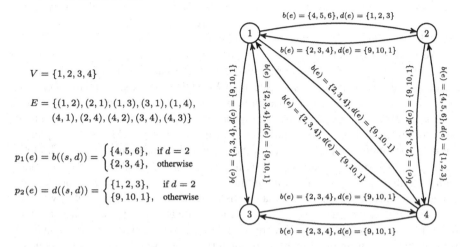

Fig. 1. Example dynamic network [25].

Semantically, this model represents a dynamic link network in which the link's available bandwidth can vary according to the function b (for *bandwidth*), and the link's delay can vary according to the function d (for *delay*). Note that a dynamic link network snapshot, at a given time instance, is a static network, and thus, both terms can be used interchangeably.

3.2 Satisfiability Modulo Theories Based Verification

In this subsection, we briefly describe some basic notions of SMT [3] (mostly the syntax) and how it can be used for formal verification.

SMT Model, Syntax, and Semantics. A *signature* is a tuple $\Sigma = (S, C, F, P)$, where S is a non-empty and finite set of sorts, C is a countable set of constant symbols whose sorts belong to S, F and P are countable sets of function and predicate symbols correspondingly whose arities are constructed using sorts that belong to S. Predicates and functions have an associated arity in the form $\sigma_1 \times \sigma_2 \times \ldots \times \sigma_n \rightarrow \sigma$, where $n \geq 1$ and $\sigma_1, \sigma_2, \ldots, \sigma_n, \sigma \in S$.

A Σ-*term* of sort σ is either each variable x of sort (type) σ, where $\sigma \in S$, or each constant c of sort (type) σ, where $\sigma \in S$; and $f \in F$ with arity $\sigma_1 \times \sigma_2 \times \ldots \times \sigma_n \rightarrow \sigma$, is a term of sort σ, thus, for $f(t_1, \ldots, t_n)$, t_i (for $i \in \{1, \ldots, n\}$) is a Σ-term of sort σ_i.

A Σ-*atom* (Σ-atomic formula) is an expression in the form $s = t$ or $p(t_1, t_2, \ldots, t_n)$, where $=$ denotes the equality symbol, s and t are Σ-terms of the same sort, $t_1, t_2, \ldots, t_n$ are Σ-terms of sort $\sigma_1, \sigma_2, \ldots, \sigma_n \in S$, respectively, and p is a predicate of arity $\sigma_1 \times \sigma_2 \times \ldots \times \sigma_n$.

A Σ-*formula* is one of the following: (i) a Σ-atom; (ii) if ϕ is a Σ-formula, $\neg\phi$ is a Σ-formula, where $\neg$ denotes negation; (iii) if both ϕ, ψ are Σ-formulas, then, $\phi \wedge \psi$ and $\phi \vee \psi$ are Σ-formulas (likewise, the short notations $\phi \rightarrow \psi$ and $\phi \leftrightarrow \psi$ for $\neg\phi \vee \psi$ and $(\phi \wedge \psi) \vee (\neg\phi \wedge \neg\psi)$); finally, (iv) if ϕ is a Σ-formula and x is a variable of sort σ, then, $\exists x \in \sigma \; \phi$ ($x \in \sigma$ is used to indicate that x has the sort σ) is a Σ-formula (likewise, the short notation $\forall x \in \sigma \; \phi$ for $\neg\exists x \in \sigma \; \neg\phi$), where $\exists$ denotes the existential quantifier and $\forall$ denotes the universal quantifier, as usual.

We leave out the formal semantics of MSFOL formulas, their interpretations and satisfiability as we feel it can unnecessarily load the paper with unused formalism. However, we briefly discuss some aspects of MSFOL formula satisfiability. For some signatures, there exist decision procedures, which help to determine if a given formula is satisfiable. For example, consider the signature with a single sort $\mathbb{R}$, all rational number constants, functions $+, -, *$ and the predicate symbol $\leq$; SMT will interpret the constants, symbols and predicates as in the usual real ($\mathbb{R}$) arithmetic sense. The satisfiability of Σ-formulas for this theory (real arithmetic) is decidable, even for formulas with quantifiers [3,21], i.e., for some infinite domain theories, there exist procedures[1] to decide if a given quantified formula is satisfiable. Therefore, the satisfiability for formulas as $\exists n \in \mathbb{R} \; \forall x \in \mathbb{R} \; x + n = x$ can be automatically determined (via a computer program implementing the decision procedure, i.e., an SMT solver). If a formula is satisfiable, there exists an interpretation (or model) for the formula, i.e., a set of concrete values for the variables, predicates and functions of the formula that makes this formula evaluate to TRUE.

Throughout this paper, we use the previously described syntax for the properties of interest (formulas). Note that for the experimental part, we use the z3 solver [5]. This solver uses the SMT-LIB language, which possesses a syntax that is very close to the described formalism (we do not detail it in this paper, however, the interested Reader may refer to [2]). For example, the formula $\exists n \in \mathbb{R} \; \forall x \in \mathbb{R} \; x + n = x$ can be expressed in SMT-LIB as follows:

```
(exists ( (n Real) ) (forall ( (x Real) ) (= (x + n) x) ) )
```

Listing 3. Example SMT-LIB code.

4   Dynamic Link Network Emulator

We hereafter present the first contribution of the work, namely, the emulation platform design and architecture. It is based on well-known state-of-the-art technologies, such as virtualization (VMs and containers) and Linux kernel features (namespaces or cgroups). When combined efficiently, these technologies provide excellent capabilities for emulating a diverse set of network topologies alongside dynamic links and interconnected network devices. The emulation platform architecture [25], shown in Fig. 2, consists of several independent, flexible and configurable components. We describe each of these components in detail in the following paragraphs.

---

[1] Often such procedures seek to "eliminate" the quantifiers and obtain an equivalent quantifier-free formula.

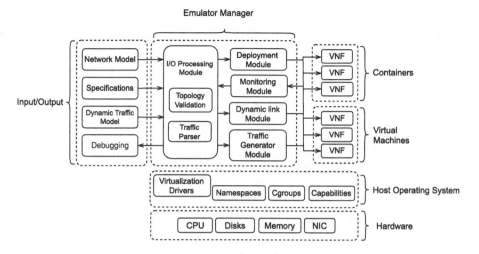

Fig. 2. Emulation Platform Architecture [25].

The **Emulator Manager** is the main component and the central processing unit. It has a single instance per physical machine and is composed of several independent modules in charge of the management, deployment and verification of the emulator components for a given network description (input for the emulation). In addition, it is responsible for providing, within the same physical host, the containers or virtual machines required for each emulated device as well as their own emulated network specifications.

The **Input/Output Processing Module** fulfills several tasks. First, since our emulation platform relies on state-of-the-art virtualization (or container-based) solutions, it is in charge of creating and maintaining a network model that is later used by other modules to implement the necessary infrastructure elements for each emulation. To achieve this, we utilize a formal network description (specification) in terms of first-order logic formulas verified throughout the emulation by an SMT solver. The interested Reader can find more details in [24]. Indeed, the network topology can be verified using model checking strategies before its actual implementation, as well as at run-time, to ensure that certain properties of interest hold for the static network instances. Finally, the module is also in charge of parsing and verifying the file to generate dynamic traffic scenarios between the components of an emulated network as well as the debugging output of the platform. An example of a network description is given in Listing 4 [25] (for the network in Fig. 1).

```
( declare −datatypes ( ) ( ( Edge ( mk−edge ( src Int ) ( dst Int ) ) ) ) )
( declare −fun bandwidth ( Edge ) Int )
( declare −fun delay ( Edge ) Int )
;; Node storage omitted on purpose to reduce the space ,
;; see edge storage
( declare −const edges ( Array Int Edge ) )
( declare −const edges_size Int )
( assert (= ( store edges 1 ( mk−edge 1 2 ) ) edges ) )
;; Edge storage omitted on purpose to reduce the space ,
```

```
;; see first and last edge
( assert (= ( store edges 10 (mk-edge 4 2)) edges ))
( assert (= edges_size 10))
( assert
  ( forall ((x Int ))
    (=>
      ( and (> x 0) (<= x edges_size ))
      ( and
        (=> (= ( dst ( select edges x )) 2)
          ;; ite not used on purpose
            ( and
                (>= ( bandwidth ( select edges x )) 4)
                (<= ( bandwidth ( select edges x )) 6)
                (>= ( delay ( select edges x )) 1)
                (<= ( delay ( select edges x )) 2)
            )
        )
        (=> ( not (= ( dst ( select edges x )) 2))
            ( and
                (>= ( bandwidth ( select edges x )) 2)
                (<= ( bandwidth ( select edges x )) 4)
                (>= ( delay ( select edges x )) 9)
                (<= ( delay ( select edges x )) 10)
            )
) ) ) ) ) ;; closing parentheses
```

Listing 4. Example of a Network Model description (SMT-LIB) [25].

The **Deployment Module** is in charge of converting the previously generated network model into running instances of emulated network devices. In order to achieve this, the module makes use of the Pod Manager tool (podman) for the management and support of containers and libvirt for different virtualization technologies such as KVM, VMware, LXC, and virtualbox. The first step takes the input specification and creates the required nodes with their corresponding images and properties. Each emulated node is deployed by means of a VM or a container attached to its own namespace and acts according to the software or service running inside of it (as requested by the input specification). For example, if it is desired to run a virtual switch as a container, the Deployment Module creates the proper container and executes the corresponding Virtual Network Function (VNF) via a container image (e.g., Open vSwitch). Therefore, each node has an independent view of the system resources such as process IDs, user names, file systems and network interfaces while still running on the same hardware. It can also hold several individual (virtual) network interfaces, along with its associated data, including ARP caches, routing tables and independent TCP/IP stack functions. This gives excellent flexibility and capabilities to the emulator: it can execute any real software, just as real physical systems.

In the last step, the module creates the links between the nodes to complete the emulation topology. The links are emulated with Linux virtual networking devices; TUN/TAP devices are used to provide packet reception and transmission for user space processes (applications or services) running inside each node. They can be seen as simple Point-to-Point or Ethernet devices, which, instead of receiving (and transmitting, correspondingly) packets from a physical medium, read (and write, correspondingly) them from a user space process. veth (virtual Ethernet) devices are used for combining the network facilities of the Linux kernel to connect different virtual networking components together. veth are built as pairs of connected virtual Ethernet interfaces and can be thought of as a virtual "patch" cable. Thus, packets transmitted on one device in the pair are immediately received on the other device. When either device is down, the link state of the pair is down too.

The **Dynamic Link Module** is in charge of establishing and modifying the dynamic properties of the links (between the nodes) during the emulation's execution time. An asymmetric link between two nodes, as shown in Fig. 3 [25], is emulated by a set of nesting queues; in the simplest case - two queues.

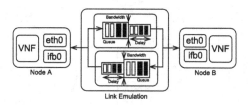

Fig. 3. Asymmetric Link emulation model [25].

In the first step, packets are queued or dropped depending on the size of the first queue. This queue is drained at a rate corresponding to the link's bandwidth. Once outside, packets are staged in a delay line for a specific time (propagation delay of the link) in the second queue and then finally injected into the network stack. This module uses the Linux Advanced traffic control tc, to control and set these properties by using filtering rules (classes) to map data (at the data link or the network layer) to queuing disciplines (qdisc) in an egress network interface. Note that since tc can be used only on egress, traffic Intermediate Functional Block devices (IFB) are created to allow queuing disciplines on the incoming traffic and thus use the same technique.

The **Traffic Generation Module** is in charge of converting the dynamic description of the traffic (see an example of it in Listing 2) into a timed sequence of network packets. This sequence is then introduced into the deployed nodes during the emulation. For the generation of network packets, the module uses nmap at each node, particularly nping, allowing to generate traffic with headers from different protocols. This is achieved using virsh commands using libvirt for virtual machines or by passing execute commands through the podman tool (for containers). It is important to note that nping can be replaced with any other software to generate traffic. Additionally, multiple instances of the same or different traffic generators can be executed inside each emulated node. Finally, the **Monitoring Module** retrieves and collects information from the nodes and their links (see Sect. 5 for more details). This information is used, for example, to verify that the emulation process is executed correctly (see Sect. 7).

5   Monitoring and Dataset Extraction

Monitoring is always an important element in the management of any type of network. Indeed, it can be used for planning, resource provisioning, anomaly detection, or simply to ensure their proper operation. In contrast to real networks, monitoring in simulated/emulated environments is generally only used to assess the performance of solutions under test. However, it does not consider the monitoring of the network emulator tool itself, which may also present problems. For example, bugs in the emulation framework or few available resources could lead to results that may diverge from a real scenario. With this objective, we implement a monitoring module, see Fig. 4, which not only retrieves and collects information from each emulated node and its links but, also extracts a dataset to perform further verification or to be used by other modules, e.g., a learning module.

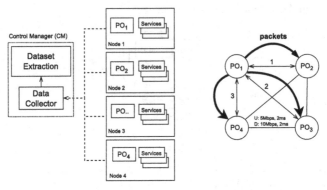

Fig. 4. Monitoring module and dataset extraction.

The Monitoring module, Fig. 4, is organized by a control manager (CM) and several Points of Observation (POs) installed inside each emulated node to inspect its traffic and link dynamics. Each PO is responsible for generating and listening packet events, reporting those events to the CM and collecting its own parameters. The control manager (CM) has a global view of the emulated network and is responsible for coordinating the POs, collecting, computing and keeping the relevant parameters and data structures for the dataset extraction in memory. For example, in order to monitor and extract parameters on links 1, 2 and 3 points of Observation PO_1, PO_2,PO_3,PO_4 are installed in each node. Then, PO_1 initiates packet events towards each neighboring PO (bold arrows), computes and reports to the CM its local measurements. Finally, the CM collects and stores that information and extracts the desired dataset.

Multiple link parameters are measured and added to our dataset, particularly delays, bandwidth and packet loss. Delays are measured using packet exchanges between the source and destination POs, see Fig. 5; this measurement is done using the ping tool. For a single measure, a request packet is sent from a source to the destination node that answers with a response packet. This packet is identified by modifying the header type field. Particularly, the ICMP protocol uses the headers 8 (for request) and 0 (for reply). The reception of the response packet ensures that the communication was successful at the destination. It also allows us to extract parameters of interest, such as the round trip time (RTT) delay, i.e., the time it takes for a packet to reach its destination from a source and then reach back from destination to source. In addition, other delay types can be measured, including: (a) Transmission delay: the time taken to transmit a packet from source to the transmission medium; (b) Propagation delay: the time taken by the packet to reach the destination through the medium; (c) Queueing delay: the time a packet waits in queue, also called buffer time, before being processed by destination; (d) Processing delay: the time taken to process a packet (i.e., packet forward time); (e) Latency: the sum of all possible delays a packet can encounter during data transmission.

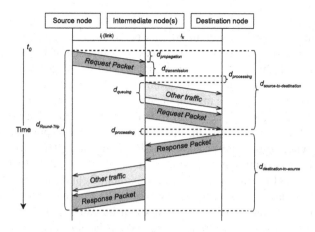

Fig. 5. Delay measure.

Packet loss is computed by sending a specific number of packets and measuring the percentage of those packets that fail to reach their destination. Bandwidth is estimated by continuously sending, over a TCP connection, data packets of known size to a specific destination node. Bandwidth capacity is the maximum amount of transmittable data over a communication channel for a specified amount of time. To estimate this value, it is necessary to know the number of bytes (data packets) sent through the channel and divide it by the time it took to receive them without any loss. For that purpose, few packets are transmitted initially. Over time, the number of transmitted packets is increased until a transmission error occurs. The main idea is to send as much data as possible until an error occurs to obtain the transmission time; bandwidth and packet loss are measured using the iperf tool. Other parameters such as the link source node, link destination node, total number of nodes and the network density (the proportion of possible links in the network that are actually present) are also included; these parameters are calculated (taken from the network description) by our native software.

Table 2. Dataset example.

SRC	DST	BND	PL	MRTT	ARTT	XRTT	DRTT	TN	DEN	LB
1	2	0.00	0	1.67	22.30	107.29	39.62	4	0.83	0
1	2	0.00	10	1.67	28.52	125.89	50.09	4	0.83	0
1	2	0.00	0	1.69	1.75	1.96	0.09	4	0.83	0
2	3	0	0	1.68	3.93	22.95	6.34	4	0.83	0
2	3	0.95	0	1.65	1.71	1.80	0.04	4	0.83	0
2	3	0.94	10	1.68	1.71	1.73	0.01	4	0.83	0
2	3	0.95	10	1.67	19.20	158.71	49.32	4	0.83	0

Abbreviations: BND, Bandwidth; PL, Packet loss; MRTT, Min RTT; ARTT, Avg RTT; XRTT, Max RTT; DRTT, Mdev RTT; TN, Number of nodes; DEN, Network Density; LB, Label

An example of a dataset is given in Table 2. It is composed of rows (measures, at a specific time instance) and columns (the parameters or features measured). For instance, let us consider the first link measure. It is composed of 10 parameters or features (columns) with different values. It is important to note that between rows, the difference in time is one second. It is the minimum value that allows the proper time to execute the probes and obtain the measurements. In each row, the first 2 columns represent the link; first, the source node (SRC) with a value of 1, and second, the destination node (DST) with a value of 2. Then, the following columns represent the measured parameters assigned to this link: Bandwidth (BND) equal to 0.00 Mbps; Packet loss (PL) equal to 0.00%; Minimum Round trip time (MRTT) equal to 1.67 ms; Average Round trip time (ARTT) equal to 22.30 ms; Maximum Round trip time (XRTT) equal to 107.29 ms; Standard deviation round trip time (DRTT) equal to 39.62 ms; network total number of nodes equal to 4, and network density equal to 0.83. Lastly, a label is assigned to 0, without loss of generality. Note that this label is required to be present in our dataset as explained in the next section.

6 Dataset Verification Using STM Solvers

6.1 Structured Datasets

We consider that a *structured dataset* contains *examples* and their *expected outputs*. In our work, we assume that the expected outputs are always present. Thus, a dataset that does not require them (for example, for unsupervised machine learning where there are no expected outputs) has the same expected output for all training examples. Further, we consider only structured datasets.

The inputs are called *features* or *parameters*. A *feature vector*, denoted as $\mathbf{X}$, is an n-tuple of the different inputs, $x_1, x_2, \ldots, x_n$. The expected output for a given feature vector is called a *label*, denoted simply as y, and the possible set of outputs is respectively denoted as Y. The set of examples, called a *dataset*, consists of pairs of a feature vector and a label; each pair is called a *training example*, denoted as $(\mathbf{X}, y)$. For convenience, we represent the dataset as a matrix $D_{m \times n}$ and a vector O_m where D contains the feature vectors and O contains the expected outputs for a dataset of cardinality m. The vector representing the i-th row (training vector) is denoted as D_i, and its associated expected output as O_i. Likewise, the j-th feature (column vector) is denoted as D_j^T (D^T denotes the transpose of the matrix D). Finally, the j-th parameter of the i-th training example is denoted by the matrix element $d_{i,j}$.

6.2 Verifying Properties over Datasets

Note that the definition of the matrix D does not specify the type of each feature in the dataset. In general, there is no theoretical limitation over the type of these features. Nonetheless, for practical reasons, we consider that all features are real-valued. The main reason is that, otherwise, additional information would be required for each feature. Moreover, in practice, well-known libraries work with real-valued features. As usual, for those features which are not *naturally* real, an encoding must be found (for example, one hot encoding for categorical features, etc.). Thus, we consider that $d_{i,j}, o_i \in \mathbb{R} \ \forall i \in \{1, \ldots, m\}, j \in \{1, \ldots, n\}$. If a dataset is not *labeled*, then $\forall i, k \in \{1, \ldots, m\} \ o_i = o_k$.

Encoding a Dataset as a MSFOL Formula. Having a convenient formal description for a dataset eases the encoding of this dataset as a MSFOL formula. To encode the data as a formula, we make use of the theory of arrays[2]. We denote that an object a is of sort array with indices of type (sort) $\mathcal{T}1$ and holding objects of type $\mathcal{T}2$ as $a \in \mathbb{A}_{\mathcal{T}1, \mathcal{T}2}$. Indeed, a dataset can be encoded using Algorithm 1 [20]; the algorithm creates a formula that is satisfiable by an interpretation of arrays representing the dataset.

Algorithm 1. Dataset encoding [20].

Input   : A dataset $D_{M \times N}$ (with N features and M training examples), and its expected output vector O_M

Output: A MSFOL formula representation of the dataset, ϕ

Step 0: Set $\phi \leftarrow$ TRUE, set $labels \leftarrow$ ARRAY(), and set $L \leftarrow 0$;

Step 1: Set $\phi \leftarrow \phi \wedge (m, n, l \in \mathbb{Z}) \wedge (m = M) \wedge (n = N)$;

Step 2: Set $\phi \leftarrow \phi \wedge (\mathcal{D} \in \mathbb{A}_{\mathbb{Z}, \mathbb{A}_{\mathbb{Z}, \mathbb{R}}}) \wedge (\mathcal{O} \in \mathbb{A}_{\mathbb{Z}, \mathbb{R}}) \wedge (\mathcal{L} \in \mathbb{A}_{\mathbb{Z}, \mathbb{R}})$;

Step 3: for $i \leftarrow 0; i < M; i \leftarrow i + 1$ **do**

> Set $add \leftarrow$ TRUE;
>
> **for** $j \leftarrow 0; i < N; j \leftarrow j + 1$ **do**
> > Set $\phi \leftarrow \phi \wedge (\mathcal{D}[i][j] = d_{i,j})$;
>
> Set $\phi \leftarrow \phi \wedge (\mathcal{O}[i] = o_i)$;
>
> **for** $k \leftarrow 0; k < L; k \leftarrow k + 1$ **do**
> > **if** $labels[k] = o_i$ **then**
> > > Set $add \leftarrow$ FALSE;
>
> **if** add **then**
> > Set $labels[L] \leftarrow o_i$;
> > Set $\phi \leftarrow \phi \wedge (\mathcal{L}[L] = o_i)$;
> > Set $L \leftarrow L + 1$;

Step 4: Set $\phi \leftarrow \phi \wedge (l = L)$ and **return** ϕ

6.3   Formal Verification of Datasets

A dataset can be formally defined as an MSFOL formula ϕ_{ds} which holds the following properties: ϕ_{ds} is a conjunction of *five* main parts, that is, i) the assertion that an integer variable m is of the size of the number of training examples, a variable n is of the size of the features and a variable l is of the size of the distinct labels, ii) the assertion that $\mathcal{D}$ is a two-dimensional (integer indexed) real-valued array (of size $m \times n$) and $\mathcal{O}, \mathcal{L}$ are integer indexed real-valued arrays (of size m, and l, respectively), iii) $\mathcal{D}[i][j]$ contains the j-th feature value for the i-th training example, iv) $\mathcal{O}[i]$ contains the expected output for the i-th training example, and v) $\mathcal{L}[i]$ contains the i-th (distinct) label.

---

[2] The theory of arrays considers basic read and write axioms [32].

We assume that we want to verify k properties over the dataset and, furthermore, that these properties are also expressed in MSFOL. Indeed, MSFOL allows to express many properties of interest (we showcase its expressiveness in Sect. 6.4). Therefore, we assume that we are given $\pi_1, \ldots, \pi_k$ MSFOL formulas to verify. These properties involve the variables in ϕ_{ds}. Additionally, we assume that these formulas should all *hold* independently over the dataset, and their conjunction is *satisfiable*. This fact imposes a restriction that $\pi_x \wedge \pi_y$ is satisfiable, for $x, y \in \{1, \ldots, k\}$; we call this set of properties the *dataset specification* σ. This means that two properties should not *contradict* each other. For example, it cannot be required that the dataset has more than 30 training examples and at the same time that it must have at most 20 $((\pi_1 \leftrightarrow (m > 30)) \wedge (\pi_2 \leftrightarrow (m \leq 20)))$. Further, the fact that the conjunction of properties must be satisfiable means that there is an interpretation that makes this formula (the conjunction) evaluate to TRUE, i.e., there exists a dataset that can satisfy this specification. Otherwise, the verification of any dataset is useless as no dataset can hold such set of properties.

The Formal Dataset Verification Problem can be reduced to the following: given a dataset formula ϕ_{ds} (created using Algorithm 1 from D and O) and a dataset specification $\sigma = \bigwedge_{l=1}^{k} \pi_l$, is $\phi_{ds} \wedge \sigma$ satisfiable? If the conjunction of these formulas is satisfiable then each of the properties must hold for the dataset, and we say that the dataset *holds* the properties $\pi_1, \ldots, \pi_k$ or that the dataset *conforms* to the specification σ. Perhaps this is quite an abstract view of the problem. For that reason, in the following subsection we provide concrete examples that should help the Reader to understand better.

6.4 Example Dataset and Properties

Let us consider a very small dataset as shown in Table 2. We assume that the dataset D is presented in the first part of the table and the last column O keeps the expected outputs/labels. After applying Algorithm 1 to D and O, the output (ϕ_{ds}) is:

$(m, n, l \in \mathbb{Z}) \wedge (m = 7) \wedge (n = 2) \wedge (\mathcal{D} \in \mathbb{A}_{\mathbb{Z},\mathbb{A}_{\mathbb{Z},\mathbb{R}}}) \wedge (\mathcal{O} \in \mathbb{A}_{\mathbb{Z},\mathbb{R}}) \wedge (\mathcal{L} \in \mathbb{A}_{\mathbb{Z},\mathbb{R}}) \wedge$
$(\mathcal{D}[0][0] = 1) \wedge (\mathcal{D}[0][1] = 2) \wedge (\mathcal{D}[0][2] = 0.00) \wedge (\mathcal{D}[0][3] = 0) \wedge (\mathcal{D}[0][4] = 1.666) \wedge$
$(\mathcal{D}[0][5] = 22.297) \wedge (\mathcal{D}[0][6] = 107.294) \wedge (\mathcal{D}[0][7] = 39.622) \wedge (\mathcal{D}[0][8] = 4) \wedge$
$(\mathcal{D}[0][9] = 0.83) \wedge (\mathcal{O}[0] = 0) \wedge (\mathcal{L}[0] = 0)$
$(\mathcal{D}[1][0] = 1) \wedge (\mathcal{D}[1][1] = 2) \wedge (\mathcal{D}[1][2] = 0.00) \wedge (\mathcal{D}[1][3] = 10) \wedge (\mathcal{D}[1][4] = 1.672) \wedge$
$(\mathcal{D}[1][5] = 28.520) \wedge (\mathcal{D}[1][6] = 125.892) \wedge (\mathcal{D}[1][7] = 50.092) \wedge (\mathcal{D}[1][8] = 4) \wedge$
$(\mathcal{D}[1][9] = 0.83)$
$(\mathcal{D}[2][0] = 1) \wedge (\mathcal{D}[2][1] = 2) \wedge (\mathcal{D}[2][2] = 0.00) \wedge (\mathcal{D}[2][3] = 0) \wedge (\mathcal{D}[2][4] = 1.687) \wedge$
$(\mathcal{D}[2][5] = 1.753) \wedge (\mathcal{D}[2][6] = 1.964) \wedge (\mathcal{D}[2][7] = 0.090) \wedge (\mathcal{D}[2][8] = 4) \wedge$
$(\mathcal{D}[2][9] = 0.83)$
$(\mathcal{D}[3][0] = 2) \wedge (\mathcal{D}[3][1] = 3) \wedge (\mathcal{D}[3][2] = 0) \wedge (\mathcal{D}[3][3] = 0) \wedge (\mathcal{D}[3][4] = 1.684) \wedge$

$(\mathcal{D}[3][5] = 3.927) \wedge (\mathcal{D}[3][6] = 22.946) \wedge (\mathcal{D}[3][7] = 6.343) \wedge (\mathcal{D}[3][8] = 4) \wedge$
$(\mathcal{D}[3][9] = 0.83)$
$(\mathcal{D}[4][0] = 2) \wedge (\mathcal{D}[4][1] = 3) \wedge (\mathcal{D}[4][2] = 0.95) \wedge (\mathcal{D}[4][3] = 0) \wedge (\mathcal{D}[4][4] = 1.653) \wedge$
$(\mathcal{D}[4][5] = 1.708) \wedge (\mathcal{D}[4][6] = 1.801) \wedge (\mathcal{D}[4][7] = 0.037) \wedge (\mathcal{D}[4][8] = 4) \wedge$
$(\mathcal{D}[4][9] = 0.83)$
$(\mathcal{D}[5][0] = 2) \wedge (\mathcal{D}[5][1] = 3) \wedge (\mathcal{D}[5][2] = 0.94) \wedge (\mathcal{D}[5][3] = 10) \wedge (\mathcal{D}[5][4] = 1.676) \wedge$
$(\mathcal{D}[5][5] = 1.707) \wedge (\mathcal{D}[5][6] = 1.727) \wedge (\mathcal{D}[5][7] = 0.014) \wedge (\mathcal{D}[5][8] = 4) \wedge$
$(\mathcal{D}[5][9] = 0.83)$
$(\mathcal{D}[6][0] = 2) \wedge (\mathcal{D}[6][1] = 3) \wedge (\mathcal{D}[6][2] = 0.95) \wedge (\mathcal{D}[6][3] = 10) \wedge (\mathcal{D}[6][4] = 1.665) \wedge$
$(\mathcal{D}[6][5] = 19.204) \wedge (\mathcal{D}[6][6] = 158.710) \wedge (\mathcal{D}[6][7] = 49.322) \wedge (\mathcal{D}[6][8] = 4) \wedge$
$(\mathcal{D}[6][9] = 0.83) \wedge (l = 1)$

We now showcase some very simple properties together with the formal verification process. Suppose that the specification consists of a single property: "the dataset must contain at least 100 training examples." This property can be expressed in MSFOL simply as $\pi_{\#} \leftrightarrow (m \geq 100)$. Notice how $\phi_{ds} \wedge \pi_{\#}$ is not satisfiable as there does not exist an interpretation that makes it evaluate to TRUE; particularly, if m is greater than 99, then the clause (in ϕ_{ds}) $m = 7$ cannot evaluate to TRUE and since this is a conjunction, $\phi_{ds} \wedge \pi_{\#}$ evaluates to FALSE. Similarly, if m is 7, then the $\pi_{\#}$ makes the conjunction evaluate to FALSE. Thus, we say that the dataset does not hold the property $\pi_{\#}$.

A slightly more complex property to verify is: "the dataset must be min-max normalized," which can be expressed in MSFOL as $\pi_{\pm} \leftrightarrow \nexists (i, j \in \mathbb{Z})((i \geq 0) \wedge (i < n) \wedge (j \geq 0) \wedge (j < m) \wedge ((\mathcal{D}[i][j] < min) \vee (\mathcal{D}[i][j] > max)))$. Certainly, min and max are defined constants (e.g., -1 and 1) and either these variables must be defined or the value must be replaced; for $min = 0$ and $max = 1000$, ϕ_{ds} holds the property $\pi_{\pm}$ (as $\phi_{ds} \wedge \pi_{\pm}$ is satisfiable).

We have showcased the flexibility of the proposed approach with somewhat standard properties to check. Nonetheless, it is interesting to point out that the approach is generic and domain-specific properties coming from expert knowledge can also be used. This is the primary motivation for the dataset verification in our work. As previously stated, we focus on guaranteeing that the behavior of the emulator fulfills the requirements of the physical system; the goal is to reduce the behavioral differences between the emulator and the real system. In general, as the properties to check can be added or removed arbitrarily, checking a given set of those for a particular dataset is possible.

7 Experimental Results

This section discusses an experimental evaluation of our emulator and dataset verification approach. The main objectives of this experimental evaluation are: i) to check the execution of the emulator w.r.t. a set of real physical properties; ii) to check the performance of the proposed approach (in terms of execution time and used space). For this reason, datasets of different sizes were extracted from our emulator; these datasets were verified over a large set of properties with various degrees of dependencies between data. Our dataset verification tool [20] makes use of the z3 theorem prover. In order to replicate our experiments, z3 versions 4.8.11 until 4.11.0 should be avoided, as they contain an incompatibility issue. At the time of this writing, we recommend version 4.8.10. However, future versions (after 4.8.11) should contain a bug fix as per our issue report (issue 6304 on z3's GitHub repository).

Experimental Setup. All experiments were executed on an Ubuntu 22.04LTS, running on an AMD Ryzen 1900X (8-core/16-thread) @ 3.8 GHz, and 64 GB of RAM. An extracted dataset was used by executing our emulator with the topology shown in 1. The data collection time was 20 min. As the monitoring interval is one second, this yields a dataset with 1200 training examples. The properties of interest are divided into three different groups. Group#1 – contains properties that verify features within one training example (line, row) but without dependencies between features. For example, the delay in all measures must not exceed a certain threshold. This verification can be done over a training example or all of them but, it is usually interesting to make it for all. Group#2 – contains properties that verify some dependencies between the network features within one training example. For instance, if in a training example, the source is s and the destination is d, then the delay of this link must not exceed a given constant. Finally, Group#3 – contains properties that reflect dependencies between training examples. For example, for a given link (a, b) the bandwidth must be greater than that on an adjacent link (b, c). The verified properties are written in the SMT-LIB language and are available in our repository [23].

Experimental Results. In the following figures and tables, we show the grouped properties and the performance results. Figures 6a and 6b, show the execution time and maximal required space (respectively) for properties shown in Table 3. Correspondingly, Figs. 7a and 7b, show the execution time and maximal required space (respectively) for properties shown in Table 4. Likewise, Figs. 8a and 8b, show the execution time and maximal required space (respectively) for properties shown in Table 5.

The time taken to verify increases with each group. This is expected and natural as the more complex properties take longer to be checked. However, note that oftentimes properties that are natural to verify for the domain of computer networks mostly fall under the groups #1 and #2. Furthermore, our offline approach is pertinent as verifying properties takes a comparable amount of time w.r.t. the emulation execution time (especially for properties with small execution time results). This is promising, especially for highly sensitive emulations whose correct functioning must be guaranteed and/or certified. The memory consumption of the verification process is confirmed to be polynomial w.r.t. to the dataset size. Finally, the verification yields a satisfiable verdict over our emulation in 86.66% of the verified properties (that is 130 out of 150 properties satisfied).

Table 3. Group#1 network properties.

Description	Formula
The delay (average round trip time) belongs to the range [min,max] (min and max are given constants, e.g., 0 and 300), for all measures (training examples) in the dataset	$\pi_1 = \nexists i \, ((i \geq 0) \wedge (i < m - 1) \wedge ((\mathcal{D}[i][AVG\_RTT] < min) \vee (\mathcal{D}[i][AVG\_RTT] > max)))$
The bandwidth capacity belongs to the range [min,max] (e.g., 0 and 50), for all measures (training examples) in the dataset	$\pi_2 = \nexists i \, ((i \geq 0) \wedge (i < m - 1) \wedge ((\mathcal{D}[i][BANDWIDTH] < min) \vee (\mathcal{D}[i][BANDWIDTH] > max)))$
The average packet loss of all measures (training examples) in the dataset must not exceed a given constant M (for example, 0.3)	$\pi_3 = (\frac{1}{m} \sum_{i=0}^{m-1} \mathcal{D}[i][PACKET\_LOSS]) \leq M$
The minimum bandwidth capacity of all measures (training examples) in the dataset must be greater or equal to a given constant μ (for example, 10)	$\pi_4 = \mathbf{min}\{\mathcal{D}[i][BANDWIDTH] \| i \in \{1, \ldots, m - 1\}\} \geq \mu$ (for readability we do not include the implementation of functions denoted in bold as **min**, however, the interested Reader may refer to our repository [23] to check the code implementations)
The maximum delay of all measures (training examples) in the dataset must not exceed a given constant $\mathcal{M}$ (for example, 300)	$\pi_5 = \mathbf{max}\{\mathcal{D}[i][BANDWIDTH] \| i \in \{1, \ldots, m - 1\}\} \leq \mathcal{M}$

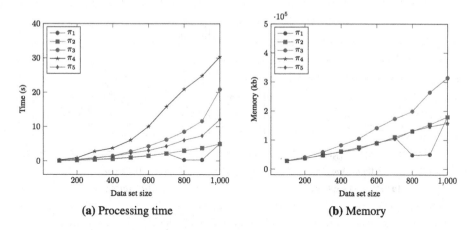

(a) Processing time   (b) Memory

Fig. 6. Results for properties of group #1.

The violated properties are properties related to bandwidth, the reason is that our emulator allows a dynamic change in bandwidth. Thus, the measures that are taken when the bandwidth changes report a capacity of 0mbps (as sending data report a failure). This is a technical limitation and the expected behavior. The failed properties verified that the bandwidth should always be above a given constant (10mbps in our experiments). This showcases the utility of our tool as it helps reveal important details of emulated solutions.

Table 4. Group#2 network properties.

Description	Formula
For all measures (training examples) in the dataset, the delay (average round trip time) belongs to the range [min,max] (min and max are given constants, e.g., 0 and 200) if the source node is s and the destination node is d, for a given particular link (s, d)	$\rho_1 = \nexists i \, (((i \geq 0) \wedge (i < m) \wedge (\mathcal{D}[i][SRC] = s) \wedge (\mathcal{D}[i][DST] = d) \wedge ((\mathcal{D}[i][AVG\_RTT] < min) \vee (\mathcal{D}[i][AVG\_RTT] > max)))$
For all measures (training examples) in the dataset, the bandwidth capacity belongs to the range [min,max] (min and max are given constants, e.g., 10 and 20), if the source node is s and the destination node is d, for a given particular link (s, d)	$\rho_2 = \nexists i \, (((i \geq 0) \wedge (i < m) \wedge (\mathcal{D}[i][SRC] = s) \wedge (\mathcal{D}[i][DST] = d) \wedge ((\mathcal{D}[i][BANDWIDTH] < min) \vee (\mathcal{D}[i][BANDWIDTH] > max)))$
For all measures (training examples) in the dataset, the packet lost belongs to the range [min,max] (min and max are given constants. e.g., 0 and 0.5) if the source node is s and the destination node is d, for a given particular link (s, d)	$\rho_3 = \nexists i \, (((i \geq 0) \wedge (i < m) \wedge (\mathcal{D}[i][SRC] = s) \wedge (\mathcal{D}[i][DST] = d) \wedge ((\mathcal{D}[i][PACKET\_LOST] < min) \vee (\mathcal{D}[i][PACKET\_LOST] > max)))$
For all measures (training examples) in the dataset, the bandwidth capacity must be greater or equal than a given constant B, if the source node is s and the destination node is d, i.e., for a given particular link (s, d)	$\rho_4 = \forall i \, (((i \geq 0) \wedge (i < m) \wedge (\mathcal{D}[i][SRC] = s) \wedge (\mathcal{D}[i][DST] = d)) \implies (\mathcal{D}[i][BANDWIDTH] \geq B))$
For all measures (training examples) in the dataset, the packet loss must not exceed a given constant L if the source node is s and the destination node is d, for a given particular link (s, d)	$\rho_5 = \forall i \, (((i \geq 0) \wedge (i < m) \wedge (\mathcal{D}[i][SRC] = s) \wedge (\mathcal{D}[i][DST] = d)) \implies (\mathcal{D}[i][PACKET\_LOSS] \leq L))$

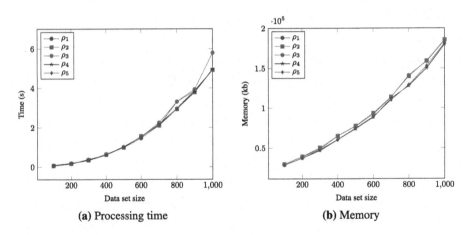

(a) Processing time   (b) Memory

Fig. 7. Results for properties of group #2.

Table 5. Group#3 network properties.

Description	Formula
For a given (valid) path $(a \rightarrow b \rightarrow c)$ the average delay does not differ more than C time units from its return path $(c \rightarrow b \rightarrow a)$	$\phi_1 = \lvert \frac{1}{m}((\mathbf{cond\_sum}(AVG\_RTT, a, b) + \mathbf{cond\_sum}(AVG\_RTT, b, c)) - (\mathbf{cond\_sum}(AVG\_RTT, c, b) + \mathbf{cond\_sum}(AVG\_RTT, b, a)))\rvert \leq C$, where $\mathbf{cond\_sum}(f, s, c) = \sum\{\mathcal{D}[i][f] \mid i \in \{1, \ldots, m-1\} \wedge \mathcal{D}[i][SRC] = s \wedge \mathcal{D}[i][DST] = d\}$
For a given (valid) path $(a \rightarrow b \rightarrow c)$ the average packet loss does not differ more than C units from its return path $(c \rightarrow b \rightarrow a)$	$\phi_2 = \lvert \frac{1}{m}((\mathbf{cond\_sum}(PACKET\_LOSS, a, b) + \mathbf{cond\_sum}(PACKET\_LOSS, b, c)) - (\mathbf{cond\_sum}(PACKET\_LOSS, c, b) + \mathbf{cond\_sum}(PACKET\_LOSS, b, a)))\rvert \leq C$
For a given (valid) path $(a \rightarrow b \rightarrow c)$ the minimum outgoing (upload) bandwidth does not exceed more than C times the minimum incoming bandwidth (download, return path) $(c \rightarrow b \rightarrow a)$	$\phi_3 = \min\{\mathbf{cond\_min}(BANDWIDTH, a, b), \mathbf{cond\_min}(BANDWIDTH, b, c)) \leq C * \min\{\mathbf{cond\_min}(BANDWIDTH, c, b), \mathbf{cond\_min}(BANDWIDTH, b, a)\}$, where $\mathbf{cond\_min}(f, s, c) = \min\{\mathcal{D}[i][f] \mid i \in \{1, \ldots, m-1\} \wedge \mathcal{D}[i][SRC] = s \wedge \mathcal{D}[i][DST] = d\}$
For a given (valid) path $(a \rightarrow b \rightarrow c)$ the minimum outgoing (upload) bandwidth-delay product (the bandwidth-delay product is a common data communications metric used to measure the maximum amount of data that can be transmitted and not yet received at any time instance) does not exceed more than C times the minimum incoming bandwidth-delay product (download, return path) $(c \rightarrow b \rightarrow b)$	$\phi_4 = \min\{\mathbf{cond\_min\_prod}(a, b), \mathbf{cond\_min\_prod}(b, c)) \leq C * \min\{\mathbf{cond\_min\_prod}(c, b), \mathbf{cond\_min\_prod}(b, a)\}$, where where $\mathbf{cond\_min\_prod}(s, c) = \min\{\mathcal{D}[i][BANDWIDTH] * \mathcal{D}[i][AVG\_RTT] \mid i \in \{1, \ldots, m-1\} \wedge \mathcal{D}[i][SRC] = s \wedge \mathcal{D}[i][DST] = d\}$
For all measures in the dataset, for a given link $((s, d))$ the delay (average round trip time) does not differ more than C time units from its return link $((d, s))$, for each observation in the dataset	$\phi_5 = \forall i, j(((i \geq 0) \wedge (i < m) \wedge (j \geq 0) \wedge (j < m) \wedge (\mathcal{D}[i][SRC] = s) \wedge (\mathcal{D}[i][DST] = d) \wedge (\mathcal{D}[i][SRC] = \mathcal{D}[j][DST]) \wedge (\mathcal{D}[i][DST] = \mathcal{D}[j][SRC])) \implies (\lvert \mathcal{D}[i][AVG\_RTT] - \mathcal{D}[j][AVG\_RTT] \rvert \leq C))$

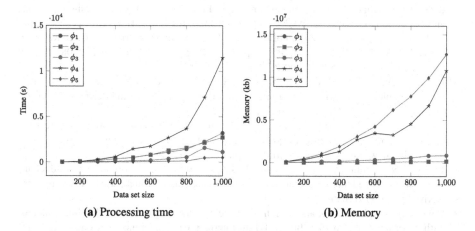

(a) Processing time   **(b)** Memory

Fig. 8. Results for properties of group #3.

8 Conclusion

In this paper, we have showcased the design and architecture for a dynamic link network emulator. Moreover, we have presented an approach for verifying that the emulation execution respects certain properties of interest; this is useful to reduce the difference between the behavior of the emulated and the real system. It is important to note that the emulator is flexible and can run any existing software; additionally, it can dynamically change the link parameter values.

In its current state, the tool proposes a solid framework for the emulation of dynamic link networks. However, certain aspects can be improved and new features can be incorporated. For instance, it is desirable to reduce the monitoring time, to better guarantee that the emulator always holds the properties of interest. Nonetheless, it is technologically difficult to address this issue, which is an interesting avenue for future work. Furthermore, we plan to incorporate more features into the architecture so that it becomes more controllable and realistic. For example, we consider incorporating link state scenarios to qualify the solutions under different conditions (degraded links, weather conditions, etc.). Additionally, enhancing the verification strategies may allow performing the verification in larger time lapses or closer to runtime monitoring.

References

1. Alsmadi, I., Zarrad, A., Yassine, A.: Mutation testing to validate networks protocols. In: 2020 IEEE International Systems Conference (SysCon), pp. 1–8. IEEE, Montreal, QC, Canada (2020). https://doi.org/10.1109/SysCon47679.2020.9275875
2. Barrett, C., Stump, A., Tinelli, C.: The satisfiability modulo theories library (smt-lib). SMT-LIB.org (2010)
3. Barrett, C., Tinelli, C.: Satisfiability modulo theories. In: Handbook of Model Checking, pp. 305–343. Springer, Cham (2018). https://doi.org/10.1007/978-3-319-10575-8_11
4. Chan, M.C., Chen, C., Huang, J.X., Kuo, T., Yen, L.H., Tseng, C.C.: Opennet: A simulator for software-defined wireless local area network. In: 2014 IEEE Wireless Communications and Networking Conference (WCNC), pp. 3332–3336. IEEE (2014)
5. de Moura, L., Bjørner, N.: Z3: an efficient SMT solver. In: Ramakrishnan, C.R., Rehof, J. (eds.) TACAS 2008. LNCS, vol. 4963, pp. 337–340. Springer, Heidelberg (2008). https://doi.org/10.1007/978-3-540-78800-3_24
6. Deng, B., Jiang, C., Yao, H., Guo, S., Zhao, S.: The next generation heterogeneous satellite communication networks: integration of resource management and deep reinforcement learning. IEEE Wirel. Commun. **27**(2), 105–111 (2019)
7. Fambri, G., Diaz-Londono, C., Mazza, A., Badami, M., Sihvonen, T., Weiss, R.: Techno-economic analysis of power-to-gas plants in a gas and electricity distribution network system with high renewable energy penetration. Appl. Energy **312**, 118743 (2022)
8. Farias, F.N., Junior, A.d.O., da Costa, L.B., Pinheiro, B.A., Abelém, A.J.: vsdnemul: A software-defined network emulator based on container virtualization. arXiv preprint arXiv:1908.10980 (2019)
9. Gandhi, S., Singh, R.K., et al.: Design and development of dynamic satellite link emulator with experimental validation. In: 2021 12th International Conference on Computing Communication and Networking Technologies (ICCCNT), pp. 1–6. IEEE (2021)
10. Hemminger, S., et al.: Network emulation with netem. In: Linux conf au, pp. 18–23 (2005)

11. Henderson, T.R., Lacage, M., Riley, G.F., Dowell, C., Kopena, J.: Network simulations with the ns-3 simulator. SIGCOMM Demonstrat. **14**(14), 527 (2008)

12. Horneber, J., Hergenröder, A.: A survey on testbeds and experimentation environments for wireless sensor networks. IEEE Commun. Surveys Tutorials **16**(4), 1820–1838 (2014). https://doi.org/10.1109/COMST.2014.2320051

13. Kamp, P.H., Watson, R.N.: Jails: Confining the omnipotent root. In: Proceedings of the 2nd International SANE Conference. vol. 43, p. 116 (2000)

14. Kaur, K., Singh, J., Ghumman, N.S.: Mininet as software defined networking testing platform. In: International Conference on Communication, Computing & Systems (ICCCS), pp. 139–42 (2014)

15. Khan, A.R., Bilal, S.M., Othman, M.: A performance comparison of open source network simulators for wireless networks. In: 2012 IEEE International Conference on Control System, Computing and Engineering, pp. 34–38. IEEE, Penang, Malaysia (2012). https://doi.org/10.1109/ICCSCE.2012.6487111

16. Kodheli, O., et al.: Satellite communications in the new space era: a survey and future challenges. IEEE Commun. Surv. Tutorials **23**(1), 70–109 (2020)

17. Lai, J., Tian, J., Jiang, D., Sun, J., Zhang, K.: Network emulation as a service (neaas): towards a cloud-based network emulation platform. In: Song, H., Jiang, D. (eds.) Simulation Tools and Techniques, pp. 508–517. Springer International Publishing, Cham (2019)

18. Lantz, B., Heller, B., McKeown, N.: A network in a laptop: rapid prototyping for software-defined networks. In: Proceedings of the 9th ACM SIGCOMM Workshop on Hot Topics in Networks. pp. 1–6. ACM (2010)

19. Liu, Y., Lu, H., Li, X., Zhang, Y., Xi, L., Zhao, D.: Dynamic service function chain orchestration for nfv/mec-enabled iot networks: A deep reinforcement learning approach. IEEE Internet Things J. **8**(9), 7450–7465 (2021). https://doi.org/10.1109/JIOT.2020.3038793

20. López, J., Labonne, M., Poletti, C.: Toward formal data set verification for building effective machine learning models. In: Cucchiara, R., Fred, A.L.N., Filipe, J. (eds.) Proceedings of the 13th International Joint Conference on Knowledge Discovery, Knowledge Engineering and Knowledge Management, IC3K 2021, Volume 1: KDIR, Online Streaming, October 25–27, 2021. pp. 249–256. SCITEPRESS (2021). https://doi.org/10.5220/0010676500003064

21. Manna, Z., Zarba, C.G.: Combining decision procedures. In: Aichernig, B.K., Maibaum, T. (eds.) Formal Methods at the Crossroads. From Panacea to Foundational Support. LNCS, vol. 2757, pp. 381–422. Springer, Heidelberg (2003). https://doi.org/10.1007/978-3-540-40007-3_24

22. Nurlan, Z., Zhukabayeva, T., Othman, M., Adamova, A., Zhakiyev, N.: Wireless sensor network as a mesh: vision and challenges. IEEE Access **10**, 46–67 (2022). https://doi.org/10.1109/ACCESS.2021.3137341

23. Petersen, E., López, J., Kushik, N., Labonne, M., Poletti, C., Zeghlache, D.: Dlemudataverif: Dynamic link network emulation and validation of execution data sets. https://gitlab.ailab.airbus.com/erick.petersen/DLEmuDataVerif.gi (2022)

24. Petersen, E., López, J., Kushik, N., Poletti, C., Zeghlache, D.: On using smt-solvers for modeling and verifying dynamic network emulators: (work in progress). In: 19th IEEE International Symposium on Network Computing and Applications, NCA 2020, Cambridge, MA, USA, November 24–27, 2020. pp. 1–3. IEEE (2020). https://doi.org/10.1109/NCA51143.2020.9306731

25. Petersen, E., López, J., Kushik, N., Poletti, C., Zeghlache, D.: Dynamic link network emulation: A model-based design. In: Kaindl, H., Mannion, M., Maciaszek, L.A. (eds.) Proceedings of the 17th International Conference on Evaluation of Novel Approaches to Software Engineering, ENASE 2022, Online Streaming, April 25–26, 2022. pp. 536–543. SCITEPRESS (2022). https://doi.org/10.5220/0011091100003176

26. Peterson, L.L., Davie, B.S.: Computer networks: a systems approach. Elsevier (2007)
27. Peuster, M., Kampmeyer, J., Karl, H.: Containernet 2.0: A rapid prototyping platform for hybrid service function chains. In: 2018 4th IEEE Conference on Network Softwarization and Workshops (NetSoft), pp. 335–337. IEEE (2018)
28. Rese, A., Görmar, L., Herbig, A.: Social networks in coworking spaces and individual coworker's creativity. RMS **16**(2), 391–428 (2022)
29. Shan, Q.: Testing methods of computer software. In: 2020 International Conference on Data Processing Techniques and Applications for Cyber-Physical Systems, pp. 231–237. Springer (2021)
30. Srisawai, S., Uthayopas, P.: Rapid building of software-based SDN testbed using SDN owl. In: 2018 22nd International Computer Science and Engineering Conference (ICSEC), pp. 1–4. IEEE (2018)
31. Stoller, M.H.R.R.L., Duerig, J., Guruprasad, S., Stack, T., Webb, K., Lepreau, J.: Large-scale virtualization in the emulab network testbed. In: USENIX Annual Technical Conference, Boston, MA (2008)
32. Stump, A., Barrett, C.W., Dill, D.L., Levitt, J.: A decision procedure for an extensional theory of arrays. In: Proceedings 16th Annual IEEE Symposium on Logic in Computer Science, pp. 29–37. IEEE (2001)
33. Sun, Z., Chai, W.K.: Satellite emulator for ip networking based on linux. In: 21st International Communications Satellite Systems Conference and Exhibit, p. 2393 (2003)
34. Varga, A.: Discrete event simulation system. In: Proceedings of the European Simulation Multiconference (ESM'2001), pp. 1–7 (2001)
35. Wang, S.Y., Chou, C.L., Yang, C.M.: Estinet openflow network simulator and emulator. IEEE Commun. Mag. **51**(9), 110–117 (2013)

Predicting Bug-Fixing Time Using the Latent Dirichlet Allocation Model with Covariates

Pasquale Ardimento[(⊠)] and Nicola Boffoli

Department of Informatics, University of Bari Aldo Moro, Via Orabona 4, Bari, Italy
{pasquale.ardimento,nicola.boffoli}@uniba.it

Abstract. The expected bug-fixing resolution time is one of the most important factors in bug triage, as an accurate prediction of bug-fixing times of newly submitted bugs helps to support both resource allocation and the triage process. Our approach treats the problem of bug-fix time estimation as a text categorization problem. To address this problem, we used Latent Dirichlet Allocation (LDA) model, a hierarchical statistical model based on what are called topics. Formally, a topic is a probability distribution over terms in a vocabulary. Such topic models provide useful descriptive statistics for a collection, which facilitates tasks like classification. Here we build a classification model on latent Dirichlet allocation (LDA). In LDA, we treat the topic proportions for a bug report as a draw from a Dirichlet distribution. We obtain the words in the bug report by repeatedly choosing a topic assignment from those proportions, then drawing a word from the corresponding topic. In supervised latent Dirichlet allocation (SLDA), we add to LDA a response variable associated with each document. Finally, we consider the supervised latent Dirichlet allocation with covariates (SLDAX) model, a generalization of SLDA, that incorporates manifest variables and latent topics as predictors of an outcome. We evaluated the proposed approach on a large dataset, composed of data gathered from defect tracking systems of five well-known open-source systems. Results show that SLDAX provides a better recall than those provided by topic models LDA-based.

Keywords: SLDAX · SLDA · Latent topics · Bug-fixing · Repository mining · Software maintenance · Text categorization

1 Introduction

Heraclitus, the Greek philosopher, said "Change is the only constant in life". Decades of experience in software systems development lead to the conclusion that for the software is the same. Changes are unavoidable in the course of the development life cycle. They can occur for different reasons, sometimes they are required for fixing a bug, that is an expected or anomalous behavior of software during its execution.

A bug triage process consists in evaluating, prioritizing, and assigning the resolution of defects. The estimated time for fixing a bug represents a relevant issue in the assignment activity. Depending on the estimated time, the bug triager could allocate a larger or smaller number of programmers, more or less experienced programmers, and, in general, leads to a better allocation of both resources and time. Usually, software projects

H. Kaindl et al. (Eds.): ENASE 2022, CCIS 1829, pp. 139–152, 2023.
https://doi.org/10.1007/978-3-031-36597-3_7

use bug tracking systems (BTS) to store and manage bug reports. A bug report contains a large amount of text information that can help software developers and maintainers understand bugs well and complete bug fixing. Many open-source software projects use BTS. Day by day, the number of bug reports submitted to BTS increases and, at the same time, the knowledge stored by BTS [1,4,29]. For Mozilla, in September 2022, the total number of bug reports was just under 1.8 million. In recent years, lots of work utilized information retrieval technology to explore these massive bug repositories to help developers understand, localize and fix bugs [15,19,21]. Almost all the predictive models proposed for automatizing the prediction of bug-fixing time rely on traditional machine learning techniques. These models extract all text information by bug report attributes, discarding only those that are empty or contain numerical values. Once a bug report is open (not re-open), it is categorized into a discretized time to resolution, based on the learned prediction model.

This study extends the one proposed in [3] whose underpinning idea is to treat the problem of bug-fixing time estimation as a text categorization problem. To address this problem we used a topic model technique named standard unsupervised Latent Dirichlet Allocation (LDA). In LDA each word in a document is generated from a Multinomial distribution conditioned on its own topic, which is a probability distribution over a fixed vocabulary representing a particular latent semantic theme [6]. Once hyperparameters of the model are learned, posterior topic proportion estimates can be interpreted as a low dimensional summarization of the textual bug reporting. It is also considered a supervised Latent Dirichlet Allocation (SLDA) generative model [9], which adds the discriminative signal into the standard generative model of LDA. The response variable is an unordered binary target variable, denoting time to resolution discretized into FAST (negative class) and SLOW (positive class) class labels.

The extensions provided in this work are mainly two:

- taking into account a new statistical model, named supervised latent Dirichlet allocation with covariates (SLDAX), to classify the prediction time. SLDAX jointly incorporates a latent variable measurement model of text and a structural regression model to allow the latent topics and other manifest variables to serve as predictors of an outcome.
- replication of the experiment on the previously analyzed system [3] plus the addition of 4 new systems.

The empirical results show that SLDAX improves recall. Due to the imbalance between the number of positive and negative cases and the importance assumed by the SLOW class for the prediction task, this measure is more useful than simply measuring the accuracy of classifiers.

The rest of the paper is structured as follows. Section 2 discusses the main related works of the bug-fixing time prediction problem. Section 3 describes the proposed prediction model and its main phases. Section 4 presents the empirical study and the results obtained, while Sect. 5 discusses the main threats to the validity of the proposed model. Finally, Sect. 6 draws the conclusions and sketches the future work.

2   Related Work

The issue of bug fixing time has been covered in several academic works. In [2], a machine learning-based semi-automatic method for reducing triaging time was described. The foundation of this approach is understanding the kinds of reported bugs that developers can resolve. A list with a minimal number of developers who can solve the bug is presented as the output once the model receives the reported bug. In the Eclipse and Firefox projects, they respectively received precision of up to 75% and 64%. Their approach categorizes the text of the "Summary" and "Description" fields, and the result lists the developers who can repair the bug. Information retrieval techniques are used to produce the features, and Naive Bayes (NB), Support Vector Machine (SVM), and C4.5 algorithms are used to complete the classification.

Kim in [16] offers an analysis on how to determine how much time is required to fix a bug. In this study, the authors determined when bugs are introduced and when they are corrected in the ArgoUML and PostgreSQL projects. In their technique, Panjer et al. in [25] defined seven groups for bug fix-time and discretized the fix-time data using an equal frequency binning procedure. The binary classification was performed using the 0-R, 1-R, C4.5 DT, NB, and LR algorithms, and the highest precision of 34% was attained.

Using both immutable data, like "Reporter," and fields that can change over time, like "Severity," a binary prediction model built on a Decision Tree algorithm was given in [14]. Six systems from each of the three open-source projects Eclipse, Mozilla, and Gnome were used to test the suggested model. Results collected demonstrate an Eclipse performance of 0.65 precision and 0.62 recall. They add that the addition of bug report data from up to one month post submission promises to enhance prediction models.

Using a specific selection of bug report fields, authors in [18] employed the Random Forest technique to forecast the amount of time needed to solve bugs in Mozilla and Eclipse projects. They achieved a classification accuracy of 65%. They also conducted a sensitivity analysis for the characteristics of both projects and discovered that, while the severity feature is more significant in Eclipse, the time and location of the bug report are more significant in the Mozilla Project for forecasting the bug repair. In contrast, priority is less significant in both initiatives.

In [33], a Markov-based model to forecast how many bugs will be fixed over the course of three months was presented. The Monte Carlo Algorithm was used to extrapolate from previous bug reports how long it would take to solve the bug. Additionally, a KNN-based classification model with an F-measure of 72.45 percent was suggested.

Representation of a Bidirectional Encoder from Transformers (BERT) was employed to forecast a bug's repair time as slow and quickly by [5]. No matter when using BERT, a self-attention mechanism for bidirectional learning a word's usage in context within a phrase, which is one of the primary advantages over the earlier recommended remedies before being deemed mature and able to make a meaningful contribution to the bug-fixing prediction problem, this technique has to be further applied and explored.

Based on data gathered from a bug tracking system, the authors in [27] apply a convolutional neural network (CNN) to categorize bug reports into those with short and lengthy fixing timeframes. To depict the word sequence that the CNN model utilizes for the prediction, they extract the features linked to the bug-fixing time using a

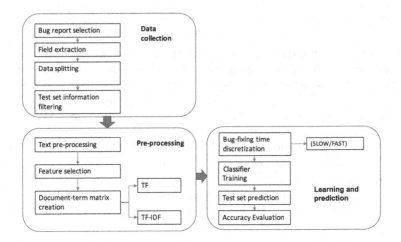

Fig. 1. Proposed Prediction Model [3].

gradient-based visualization approach. An experiment showed that this strategy has a 75–80% accuracy rate in classifying more than 36,000 bug reports from Bugzilla by short and lengthy fixing timeframes.

In [11], the authors increase the temporal information of bug fixing activities as sample features to enhance the discriminability of the data set samples (lowering the inconsistency of the samples in the data set). To capture both sequence interaction features and long-distance-dependent features, a double-sequence input LSTM model (LSTM-DA) is created. The studies' findings indicate that the suggested model, when compared to the HMM model in all dimensions, may increase the F-measure and accuracy indicators by roughly 10%.

3 Proposed Model

No changes have been made to the structure of the proposed prediction model presented in [3]. Figure 1 shows three sequential phases (the same figure appears in [3]): Data Collection, Pre-processing, Learning and evaluation of bug-fixing time Prediction.

3.1 Data Collection

The Data Collection activity consists in gathering the bug reports from any BTS as the proposed model is BTS independent. The first step consists of selecting only those bug reports that have already been fixed, by one or more programmers, and successfully verified, by one or more testers. These bugs are the only ones useful to, first, train the classifier and, then, to predict the newly unseen bug reports. After selecting this subset, for each bug in it, only the attributes sensible for both tasks were extracted, while residual attributes were discarded. In particular, the attributes containing only numeric or empty values in most cases were discarded. Since the bug-fixing time is rarely publicly available in a BTS, it also happens in Bugzilla installations, it was calculated as the number of days elapsed between the date where bug attribute Status was set to RESOLVED and the date on which the bug report was assigned for the first time. This measure, called Days Resolution, represents the bug-fixing time, from here on out. Since the Days Resolution measure does not represent the effective time spent to fix a bug it could affect the outcomes of this research. After completing data gathering and attribute extraction, the dataset was split into a training, test, and validation dataset using a fixed split percentage. This operation takes place after extraction attributes because all post-submission information has to filter out from both test and validation sets. Test and validation instances simulate newly opened and previously unseen bugs and, therefore, attributes that were not available before the bug was assigned must be removed from the information set. To this aim, it is necessary to retrieve the changes history of a bug. The history permits to know when and who assigned a value to the attributes. All the attributes whose values are not filled by the bug reporter are discarded. Severity and priority attributes represent an exception because their values can be filled by the bug reporter and, then, changed. For these attributes, only the initial value, if present, filled by the bug reporter is considered and not discarded. Finally, the model discretizes the bug-fixing times into two classes, conventionally labeled as SLOW and FAST. The SLOW label indicates a discretized bug-fixing time above some fixed threshold in the right-tail of the empirical bug-fixing time distribution. It is assumed that SLOW indicates the positive class, thus SLOW being the target class of the prediction model. Therefore, increasing the number of true positives for the positive class cause an overestimation of bug-fixing times. This situation is preferred to underestimation because it involves a less dangerous error.

3.2 Pre-processing

Unstructured data usually contains a lot of irrelevant information which should be removed before actually passing on the data for training and analysis. This stage involves many steps, we followed the most common used in the literature on text classification and Natural Language Processing [20], and they are listed on the follow.

- Lowercase: all collected data is transformed into an uniform case, i.e. lowercase
- Punctuation Removal: all the punctuation is removed because the words embedding models do not support them.
- Tokenization: a way of alienating bits of text into smaller units which are referred to as tokens. In our case, we tokenized the text into bigrams (sequences of two adjacent words) and stored candidate bigrams whose frequency of occurrence in the text is ≥ 3.
- Stop Word Removal: all the words that do not add much value to the semantics of the content were removed obtaining the following benefits:
  1. size of the dataset decreased after the removal of stop words which also leads to reduced training time.
  2. elimination of these inessentials boosted the performance as the space is narrowed down.
- Stemming: It aims at removing the commoner morphological and inflexional endings from words in English. We used the Porter stemming algorithm.

3.3   Topic Modeling

Basically, topic modeling is an unsupervised machine learning strategy which has the ability of checking a set of documents, identifying words and uncover the patterns within them and consequently cluster word bunches and comparative expressions that best characterize a set of corpus. In short, topic modeling algorithms generate collections of phrases and words that they think are related, allowing the reader to understand what those relationships mean, while classifying topics.

In this work, the LDA model is employed as it works well because it expresses competing sparsity between the topic distribution of bug reports and the word distribution of topics. Inherently, LDA is a probabilistic approach to topic modelling. In other words, it is a Bayesian hierarchical probability generation model for collecting discrete data which works based on the assumption of compatibility between words and topics in the document. It models the corpus as a discrete distribution of the entire subject, and later subjects are displayed as the discrete distribution of the entire term in the document. It is an advance over the other models that also uses competing sparsity because the balance is resolved at the level of documents.

3.4   Baseline LDA Model Using Bag of Words (BoW)

LDA is an excellent technique for covertly distributing topics in a large corpus which have the ability to identify subtopics for technical domains made up of multiple patents, where each patent is represented in an array of subject distributions. Here, a document is considered to be a mixture of subjects, where subjects are probability distributions for a set of terms where each document is considered a probability distribution over the set of topics.

The LDA model is created by simply specifying the corpus the dictionary mapping, and number of topics to be used in the model. BoW is basically a corpus containing the word id and its frequency in each bug report. The BoW model is high-dimensional, as it represents a document with one dimension per word. Specifically, it was first considered a multivariate Bernoulli (MB) model with smoothing Laplace parameter λ, applied to the binary term-document incidence matrix [20]. For each word in V and independently of each other (Naive Bayes assumption) the MB model learns the probabilities $\pi_{t_y} = P(e_t = \frac{1}{y})$ that the word represented by $e_t = (1, 2, ..., |V|)$ will occur at least once in any position in any one of the documents of class y (i.e. $y \equiv \frac{SLOW}{FAST}$, with $SLOW \equiv 1$).

3.5   Hyper Parameter Tuning

This activity aims at finding the best version of a model by running multiple tasks, which test a set of hyper parameters on the dataset. The influence of the LDA model's alpha and beta hyper parameters on the features of the baseline model is discussed in the following section.

Alpha is a parameter that controls the pre-distribution of the weights of topics in each bug report, while beta is the parameter for the pre-distribution of the weights of words in each topic. High alpha means every document is likely to contain a mixture of most of the topics and not just any single topic specifically, whereas low alpha means a bug report is more likely to be represented by just a few of the topics [27]. High beta means each topic is likely to contain a mixture of most of the words, not just any word specifically whereas low beta means the topic may contain a mixture of just a few words.

3.6 Unsupervised Latent Dirichlet Allocation (LDA)

The most important thing to know about a document is the underlying semantic themes rather than words. Latent Dirichlet Allocation (LDA) is a generative model of a textual corpus D, that has the potential to discover topics during the training phase [6, 10]. Formally, a topic is the probability distribution over the elements of V. For each document we have K underlying semantic themes (topics), $B_{1:K} = (B_1, ..., Bk)$, where each $B_K (K = 1, ..., K)$ is a $| V |$-dimensional vector of probabilities over the elements of V. We also have a vector of K-dimensional vectors $Z_{d_{1:N_d}} = (z_{d,1}, ..., z_{d,N_d})$ of topic assignments, where $Z_{d,n}$ is the topic assignment for the nth word (n=1,...,N_d) in document d. The indicator z of the k-th topic is represented as a K-dimensional unit-basis vector such that $z^k = 1$ and $z^j = 0$ for $j \neq k$. Similarly, words in a document $W_{d_{1:N_d}} = (w_{d,1}, ..., w_{d,N_d})$ are represented using superscripts to denote components, that is the th word in $|V|$ is represented as a unit-basis vector w in RV, such that $\omega^\nu = 1$ and $\omega^\nu = 0$ for $\upsilon \neq \nu$. LDA can be summarized as the following generative procedure (independently over d and n):

$$\theta_d \sim Dirichlet_K(\alpha) \text{ for d} \in D \tag{1}$$

$$z_{d,n}|\theta_d \sim Multinomial_k(\theta_d)$$
$$\text{for D} \in D \text{ and } n \in \{1, ..., N_d\} \tag{2}$$

$$\omega_{d,n}|z_{d,n},\beta_{1,K} \sim Multinomial|\nu|(\beta_{z_{d,n}})$$
$$\text{for } d \in D \text{ and } n \in \{1, ..., N_d\} \tag{3}$$

where $B_{z_{d,n}} \equiv B_j$ if $z_{d,n}^j = 1$. Parameters α and $\beta_{1:k}$ are treated as unknown hyper-parameters to be estimated, rather than random variables. In this way, documents are seen as a realization of a stochastic process, which is then reversed by standard machine learning techniques that return maximum-a-posteriori estimates of model parameters for each document (bug) d, given the value of hyper parameters α and β. Posterior estimates of per-document topic proportions θ_d can be interpreted as a low-dimensional summarization of the document. As LDA is an unsupervised algorithm, we used a linear classifier trained with an SVM with soft margins to learn bug-fixing time class y, using posterior θ_d estimates as a reduced feature vector.

Unfortunately, exact inference in the LDA model is NP-hard for a large number of topics [28], and posterior distribution of latent variables $p(Z_{1:D}, \theta_{1:D}|\omega_{1:D}, \alpha, \beta_{1:K})$ has not a closed-form (here, per-word topic assignments $z_{d:1:N_d}$ are collected into the $z_{1:D}$ vector as d varies over 1,...,D, with D = $|D|$, and the same definition applies to $\theta_{1:D}$ and $\omega_{1:D}$). In fact, the marginal likelihood is intractable and cannot be evaluated exactly in a reasonable time for all possible per-word topic assignments $z_{d,n}$. Consequently, we used a mean-field variational Bayes algorithm (VB) for approximate posterior inference [7]. Because the number of topics K is in general not known, models with several different numbers of topics were fitted and the optimal number was determined in a data-driven way by minimizing the geometric mean per-word likelihood (perplexity) on test documents [30]. Since the topic assignments for one document are independent of the topic assignments for all other documents, each test document can be evaluated separately. Once the hyper parameters α and $\beta_{1:k}$ are learned and K has been set, inference can be performed to compute a posterior θ_d vector for each test document (as well as for each document in the validation set), to obtain the reduced representation in topic space, which is subsequently used to predict bug bug-fixing time y_d in a supervised fashion.

3.7 Supervised LDA

Supervised Latent Dirichlet Allocation (SLDA) adds the discriminative signal into the standard generative model of LDA. For each document d, response label y_d ($y_{d=}$SLOW/FAST, with SLOW $\equiv$ 1) is sampled conditionally on the topic assignments:

$$y_d | Z_{d;1:Nd}, \eta \sim Bernoulli(\frac{exp(\eta^\tau \overline{z}_d)}{1 + exp(\eta^\tau \overline{z}_d)}) \tag{4}$$

where $\overline{z}_d = \frac{1}{N_d} \sum_{n=1}^{N_d} z_{d,n}$ is the vector of empirical topic frequencies in document d. Parameters α; $\beta_{1,K}$ and η are treated as unknown hyper parameters to be estimated, rather than random variables. Documents are generated under full word exchangeability, and then topics are used to explain the response. Other specifications are indeed possible, for example y_d can be regressed as a nonlinear function of topic proportions θ_d, but [8] claim that the predictive performance degrades as a consequence of the fact the topic probabilistic mass does not directly predict discretized bug-fix times.

Also in this case posterior inference of latent model variables is not feasible, as the conditional posterior distribution $p(Z_{1:D}, \theta_{1:D}|\omega_{1:D}, \alpha, \beta_{1:K})$ has not a closed-form. Consequently, a variational Bayes (VB) parameter under a mean-field approximation was used. The best number of topics K was optimized through the test set (further details are in Sect. 4).

3.8 Supervised LDA with Covariates

SLDA utility could be limited for bug reports because it does not incorporate any other predictor besides the topics. Since bug reports should be studied in conjunction with other manifest variables, such as, for example, the programmers involved in fixing a bug, a more useful approach could be represented by that two-stage approaches despite their drawbacks. SLDA is a one-stage approach, but it can only model the relationship between the text responses and a single outcome (in our case, time to fixing the bug). For example, in our context, we model relationships between time to fixing a bug, and the programmers who fixed the bugs. SLDA is a one-stage approach, but it can only model the relationship between the text responses and a single outcome (e.g., bug-fixing time). On the other hand, it could estimate a LDA model for the text and then use the topic proportion estimates with the other measures to model time to fixing the bug, but this is a two-stage approach with potentially poor performance, as demonstrated in [32]. To address this limitation, we used the supervised latent Dirichlet allocation with covariates (SLDAX) model [32], a generalization of SLDA, that incorporates manifest variables and latent topics as predictors of an outcome. We used a freely available R package [31] that implements the necessary algorithms to approximate the posterior distribution and, then, for estimating and summarizing SLDAX and related models. As final remark, we note that the SLDAX model used is aligned with SLDA: the empirical topic proportions and an additional set of manifest variables jointly predict a manifest outcome.

4   Experiment and Results

The dataset used for this study covers most of the history of defect tracking systems of five open source projects: LiveCode [17], Novell [24], NetBeans [23], Eclipse [13], Mozilla [22]. The choice fell on these systems because they are characterized by different domains for application and size, are publicly available on the Web, and have a number of bugs, considering all the statud of a bug, greater than twenty thousand. Table 1, shows the projects involved in the experimentation and for each one of them the total number of textual bug reports having both Status field assigned to VERIFIED and Resolution field assigned to FIXED. Next, some textual reports were discarded because of corrupted and unrecoverable records, or missing XML report, or dimension being too large (the resulting number is column labeled Bug reports cleaned). Finally, the last column reports the time period under observation for each period.

Table 1. Systems details.

System name	Bug Reports	Bug reports cleaned	Observation period
LiveCode	9147	8498	June 2003 to November 2016
Novell	32143	27988	October 2000 to November 2016
NetBeans	42636	42627	June 1999 to October 2016
Eclipse	45021	45019	October 2001 to November 2016
Mozilla	120490	119992	September 1994 to November 2016

Data were automatically collected using software routines written in PHP/JavaScript/Ajax. Raw textual reports were pre-processed and analyzed using the R 4.2.1 software system [26]. The application of LDA and SLDA is done through *lda* library, which is a R package used for implements latent Dirichlet allocation (LDA), related models such as, for example, SLDA and providing utilities functions for reading/writing data typically used in topic models, as well as tools for examining posterior distributions are also included. Inference for both LDA and SLDA is implemented via a fast collapsed Gibbs sampler written in C. The application of SLDAX, instead, is done through *psychtm* library, which is a R package ables to estimate the SLDAX topic model. For each project, five thousand bugs were randomly drawn and randomly divided into training, test and validation subsets, using a 70:20:10 split ratio. Bug-fixing time was categorized into FAST and SLOW labels according to the third quartile, $q_{0.75}$, of the empirical distribution of bug resolution times in the training set. Accuracy, precision and recall were used to assess the performance of bug-fixing time prediction models. Accuracy indicates the proportion of correctly predicted bugs:

$$Accuracy = \frac{TP + TN}{TP + FP + TN + FN} \tag{5}$$

where TP (True Positive) denotes the number of bugs correctly predicted as SLOW; FP (False Positive) denotes the number of bugs incorrectly predicted as SLOW, TN (True Negative) denotes the number of bugs reports correctly predicted as FAST, FN (False Negative) denotes the numbers of bugs incorrectly predicted as FAST.

Precision, instead, indicates the proportion of correctly predicted SLOW bugs:

$$Precision = \frac{TP}{TP + FP} \tag{6}$$

Recall denotes the proportion of true positives of all SLOW bugs:

$$Recall = \frac{TP}{TP + FN} \tag{7}$$

The trained set was used to train the classification models, reported in the list below. Then the specific free parameters of each model were assessed over the test set and, finally, performances measures were recalculated over the validation set using the best accuracy values obtained from the test set. For all models used the K parameter varies in $\{2, 5, 10, 15, 20, 25, 30, 35, 40, 50\}$. Table 2 presents the results obtained, it shows that all models considered achieve unstable results for accuracy. The accuracy ranges

Table 2. Results of best configurations for accuracy.

Project	Test set - Best accuracy	Algorithm	Param.	Acc.	Prec.	Recall
LiveCode	0.55	LDA	$C=0.01$	0.57	0	0
	0.61	SLDA	$K=2$	0.62	0.16	0.12
	0.79	SLDAX	$K=2$	0.56	0.35	0.89
Novell	0.61	LDA	$C=0.01$	0.65	0	0
	0.51	SLDA	$K=2$	0.48	0.26	0.62
	0.40	SLDAX	$K=2$	0.36	0.25	0.83
NetBeans	0.61	LDA	$C=0.01$	0.60	0	0
	0.64	SLDA	$K=3$	0.63	1	0.17
	0.30	SLDAX	$K=3$	0.33	0.18	0.67
Eclipse	0.52	LDA	$C=0.01$	0.50	0.5	0.2
	0.31	SLDA	$K=2$	0.30	0.23	0.2
	0.53	SLDAX	$K=2$	0.50	0.50	0.80
Mozilla	0.53	LDA	$C=0.01$	0.50	0.50	0.82
	0.51	SLDA	$K=3$	0.48	0.49	0.87
	0.52	SLDAX	$K=3$	0.50	0.50	0.95

from 0.50 to 0.80 for LDA, from 0.48 to 0.82 for SLDA and, finally, from 0.36 to 0.50 for SLDAX. In general, the best accuracy value is obtained by LDA but, since there is a great variability of values, this model could not bee considered as affordable concerning the accuracy. However, it is important to note that accuracy is a misleading measure for imbalanced class distributions. In the case of our experimentation, the two classes are not equally distributed. Furthermore, it is evident that the minority class (SLOW) has more importance in the context of software maintenance, because of its larger impact in terms of cost/effectiveness. Consequently, if it is assumed that a higher recall (proportion of true positives of all SLOW bugs) is a more sensible target, the SLDAX model has the best performance, even better than those obtained by SLDA [3]. Overall, these results show that the use of a supervised topic model with covariates lightly improves the recall of bug-fix time prediction.

5   Threats

This section discusses the main threats to the validity of our study.

- Dataset. The number of software systems considered and the generalization of the results obtained are certainly an issue. The set considered is composed of five systems, and, therefore, it is smaller than the population of all software systems. Therefore, we cannot speak of the generalization of systems in this sense. To mitigate, but only in part, this threat, we have chosen for our study all systems that are constantly evolving, with a very long history, and characterized by different dimensions, domains, sizes, time intervals, and the number of bugs. Furthermore, the amount of data considered is really enormous, because for each system we have collected the entire bug life history.
- Non-open-source projects. There is no guarantee that the proposed model is effective for non-open-source projects. Typically, in fact, in proprietary projects a specific group is responsible for fixing given bugs based on corresponding features.
- Outliers and noises. Dataset could contain bug reports whose fixing time is not fit with other bug reports because, for example, it is extremely long. These bug reports, called outliers, should be removed to both improve the quality of the data and, maybe, generate a positive impact on the accuracy of the predictions. Moreover, a possible noise in the dataset could be represented by a bug CLOSED more than one time. BTS, in fact, permits that a CLOSED bug could be reopened at any time. When this happens the calculation of the time resolution is not more coherent with the time necessary to fix a bug. Another threat in our experiment concerns the so-called problem of "proportion of inconsistent samples". Two bug reports are inconsistent if they have the same characteristics but, one is marked as positive class and the other is marked as negative class. A possible way to tackle this problem is reported in [12], where the authors aim to reduce, by incorporating the activity information and time information of bug activity transfer, the proportion of inconsistent samples. This method of bug feature extraction and model construction is based on a LSTM-based deep learning model which can not only achieve sequence prediction, but also learn sequences interaction through the attention mechanism to

improve prediction accuracy. The results are promising even if they are obtained on only one open data set Firefox.

- Bug-fixing time. A strong assumption about bug-fixing time was made. The actual amount of time spent by developers and the distribution in terms of hours per day to fix a bug are not publicly declared on Bugzilla. It is assumed, therefore, a uniform distribution of developers' work and calculated effort spent in calendar days. These assumptions hide and ignore the real efforts made by the developers to complete the fixing work.
- Number of developers involved. The number of developers involved in fixing a bug is not publicly known. It represents another limitation in calculating the bug-fixing time. For example, if different bugs have the same calendar days value, it does not imply that the time spent to fix them is the same.

6   Conclusion

A significant amount of time is spent by software developers investigating bug reports. To this aim, predicting when a new bug report will be closed, could help software teams to better allocate resources for their work. Several studies have been conducted to address this problem in the past decade. However, these approaches do not classify an individual bug report within the collection in terms of how "relevant" it is to each of the discovered topics. A topic is considered to be a set of individual words and phrases that, taken together, suggest if the bug-fixing time is SLOW or FAST. This paper proposes an automatic binary bug-fixing time prediction model based on three different generative topic models, that are LDA (unsupervised latent Dirichlet allocation), SLDA (supervised latent Dirichlet allocation) and SLDAX (supervised latent Dirichlet allocation with covariates). The last model, SLDAX, provides the best results for recall that can be considered a good result. Accuracy, instead, is lower and, considering all the models used, not so good. SLDAX jointly incorporates a latent variable measurement model of text and a structural regression model to allow the latent topics and other manifest variables to serve as predictors of an outcome. These results are aligned with the need to maximize recall to detect SLOW classes as much as possible and the acceptance that the negative class (FAST) plays a secondary role.

In the future, we will work on a more fine-grained prediction for bug fixing time, such as the exact time spent resolving the bugs. We also will increase in the SDLAX model the number of variables included in the manifest to explore more estimates of the bug-fixing time.

References

1. Alenezi, M., Banitaan, S., Zarour, M.: Using categorical features in mining bug tracking systems to assign bug reports. arXiv preprint arxiv:1804.07803 (2018)
2. Anvik, J., Hiew, L., Murphy, G.C.: Who should fix this bug? In: Osterweil, L.J., Rombach, H.D., Soffa, M.L. (eds.) 28th International Conference on Software Engineering (ICSE 2006), Shanghai, China, 20–28 May 2006, pp. 361–370. ACM (2006). https://doi.org/10.1145/1134285.1134336

3. Ardimento., P., Boffoli., N.: A supervised generative topic model to predict bug-fixing time on open source software projects. In: Proceedings of the 17th International Conference on Evaluation of Novel Approaches to Software Engineering - ENASE, pp. 233–240. INSTICC, SciTePress (2022). https://doi.org/10.5220/0011113100003176

4. Ardimento, P., Dinapoli, A.: Knowledge extraction from on-line open source bug tracking systems to predict bug-fixing time. In: Proceedings of the 7th International Conference on Web Intelligence, Mining and Semantics (WIMS 2017). Association for Computing Machinery, New York (2017). https://doi.org/10.1145/3102254.3102275

5. Ardimento, P., Mele, C.: Using BERT to predict bug-fixing time. In: 2020 IEEE Conference on Evolving and Adaptive Intelligent Systems, EAIS 2020, Bari, Italy, 27–29 May 2020, pp. 1–7. IEEE (2020). https://doi.org/10.1109/EAIS48028.2020.9122781

6. Blei, D.M.: Probabilistic topic models. Commun. ACM **55**(4), 77–84 (2012). https://doi.org/10.1145/2133806.2133826

7. Blei, D.M., Kucukelbir, A., McAuliffe, J.D.: Variational inference: A review for statisticians. arXiv preprint arxiv:1601.00670 (2016)

8. Blei, D.M., McAuliffe, J.D.: Supervised topic models. In: Platt, J.C., Koller, D., Singer, Y., Roweis, S.T. (eds.) Advances in Neural Information Processing Systems 20, Proceedings of the Twenty-First Annual Conference on Neural Information Processing Systems, Vancouver, British Columbia, Canada, 3–6 December 2007, pp. 121–128. Curran Associates, Inc. (2007). https://proceedings.neurips.cc//paper/2007/hash/d56b9fc4b0f1be8871f5e1c40c0067e7-Abstract.html

9. Blei, D.M., McAuliffe, J.D.: Supervised Topic Models (2010)

10. Blei, D.M., Ng, A.Y., Jordan, M.I.: Latent dirichlet allocation. J. Mach. Learn. Res. **3**, 993–1022 (2003). https://jmlr.org/papers/v3/blei03a.html

11. Du, J., Ren, X., Li, H., Jiang, F., Yu, X.: Prediction of bug-fixing time based on distinguishable sequences fusion in open source software. J. Softw.: Evol. Process (2022). https://doi.org/10.1002/smr.2443

12. Du, J., Ren, X., Li, H., Jiang, F., Yu, X.: Prediction of bug-fixing time based on distinguishable sequences fusion in open source software. J. Softw.: Evol. Process e2443 (2022). https://doi.org/10.1002/smr.2443

13. Eclipse: Bugzilla installation for eclipse project (2022). https://bugs.eclipse.org/bugs/. Accessed 7 Sept 2022

14. Giger, E., Pinzger, M., Gall, H.C.: Predicting the fix time of bugs. In: Holmes, R., Robillard, M.P., Walker, R.J., Zimmermann, T. (eds.) Proceedings of the 2nd International Workshop on Recommendation Systems for Software Engineering, RSSE 2010, Cape Town, South Africa, 4 May 2010, pp. 52–56. ACM (2010). https://doi.org/10.1145/1808920.1808933

15. Hamdy, A., El-Laithy, A.R.: Semantic categorization of software bug repositories for severity assignment automation. In: Jarzabek, S., Poniszewska-Marańda, A., Madeyski, L. (eds.) Integrating Research and Practice in Software Engineering. SCI, vol. 851, pp. 15–30. Springer, Cham (2020). https://doi.org/10.1007/978-3-030-26574-8_2

16. Kim, S., Whitehead, E.J.: How long did it take to fix bugs? In: Proceedings of the 2006 International Workshop on Mining Software Repositories (MSR 2006), pp. 173–174. Association for Computing Machinery, New York (2006). https://doi.org/10.1145/1137983.1138027

17. LibreOffice. Bugzilla installation for livecode project (2022). https://quality.livecode.com/. Accessed 7 Sept. 2022

18. Marks, L., Zou, Y., Hassan, A.E.: Studying the fix-time for bugs in large open source projects. In: Proceedings of the 7th International Conference on Predictive Models in Software Engineering, pp. 1–8 (2011)

19. Meng, D., et al.: Bran: Reduce vulnerability search space in large open source repositories by learning bug symptoms. In: Cao, J., Au, M.H., Lin, Z., Yung, M. (eds.) ASIA CCS '21: ACM Asia Conference on Computer and Communications Security, Virtual Event, Hong Kong, 7–11 June 2021. pp. 731–743. ACM (2021). https://doi.org/10.1145/3433210.3453115

20. Mogotsi, I.C.: Christopher D. Manning, Prabhakar Raghavan, and Hinrich Schütze: Introduction to information retrieval, vol. 482, pp. 192–195. Cambridge University Press, Cambridge (2008). ISBN: 978-0-521-86571-5. Inf. Retr. **13**(2) (2010). https://doi.org/10.1007/s10791-009-9115-y

21. Mohsin, H., Shi, C.: SPBC: A self-paced learning model for bug classification from historical repositories of open-source software. Expert Syst. Appl. **167**, 113808 (2021). https://doi.org/10.1016/j.eswa.2020.113808

22. Mozilla: Bugzilla installation for mozilla project (2022). https://bugzilla.mozilla.org/home. Accessed 7 Sept. 2022

23. NetBeans: Bugzilla installation for netbeans project (2022). https://bz.apache.org/netbeans/. Accessed 7 Sept. 2022

24. Novell: Bugzilla installation for novell project (2022). https://bugzilla.novell.com/index.cgi. Accessed 7 Sept. 2022

25. Panjer, L.D.: Predicting eclipse bug lifetimes. In: Proceedings of the Fourth International Workshop on Mining Software Repositories (MSR 2007), p. 29. IEEE Computer Society, USA (2007). https://doi.org/10.1109/MSR.2007.25

26. RProject: The r project for statistical computing (2022). https://www.r-project.org/. Accessed 7 Sept. 2022

27. Silva, C.C., Galster, M., Gilson, F.: Topic modeling in software engineering research. Empir. Softw. Eng. **26**(6), 1–62 (2021)

28. Sontag, D.A., Roy, D.M.: Complexity of inference in latent dirichlet allocation. In: Shawe-Taylor, J., Zemel, R.S., Bartlett, P.L., Pereira, F.C.N., Weinberger, K.Q. (eds.) Advances in Neural Information Processing Systems 24: 25th Annual Conference on Neural Information Processing Systems 2011. Proceedings of a meeting held 12–14 December 2011, Granada, Spain. pp. 1008–1016 (2011). https://proceedings.neurips.cc/paper/2011/hash/3871bd64012152bfb53fdf04b401193f-Abstract.html

29. Sun, X., Zhou, T., Li, G., Hu, J., Yang, H., Li, B.: An empirical study on real bugs for machine learning programs. In: Lv, J., Zhang, H.J., Hinchey, M., Liu, X. (eds.) 24th Asia-Pacific Software Engineering Conference, APSEC 2017, Nanjing, China, 4–8 December 2017, pp. 348–357. IEEE Computer Society (2017). https://doi.org/10.1109/APSEC.2017.41

30. Wallach, H.M., Murray, I., Salakhutdinov, R., Mimno, D.M.: Evaluation methods for topic models. In: Danyluk, A.P., Bottou, L., Littman, M.L. (eds.) Proceedings of the 26th Annual International Conference on Machine Learning, ICML 2009, Montreal, Quebec, Canada, 14–18 June, 2009. ACM International Conference Proceeding Series, vol. 382, pp. 1105–1112. ACM (2009). https://doi.org/10.1145/1553374.1553515

31. Wilcox, K.: psychtm: Text mining methods for psychological research (2022). https://cran.r-project.org/web/packages/psychtm/. Accessed 7 Sept. 2022

32. Wilcox, K., Jacobucci, R., Zhang, Z., Ammerman, B.: Supervised latent Dirichlet allocation with covariates: A Bayesian structural and measurement model of text and covariates. PsyArXiv (2021). https://doi.org/10.31234/osf.io/62tc3

33. Zhang, H., Gong, L., Versteeg, S.: Predicting bug-fixing time: an empirical study of commercial software projects. In: Notkin, D., Cheng, B.H.C., Pohl, K. (eds.) 35th International Conference on Software Engineering, ICSE '13, San Francisco, 18–26 May 2013. pp. 1042–1051. IEEE Computer Society (2013). https://doi.org/10.1109/ICSE.2013.6606654

Challenges and Novel Approaches
to Systems and Software Engineering
(SSE)

Pull Requests Integration Process Optimization: An Empirical Study

Agustín Olmedo[1]([✉])[ID], Gabriela Arévalo[2], Ignacio Cassol[1][ID], Quentin Perez[3][ID], Christelle Urtado[3][ID], and Sylvain Vauttier[3][ID]

[1] LIDTUA (CIC), Facultad de Ingeniería, Universidad Austral, Buenos Aires, Argentina
`aolmedo@austral.edu.ar`
[2] DCyT (UNQ), CAETI (UAI), CONICET, Buenos Aires, Argentina
[3] EuroMov Digital Health in Motion, Univ. Montpellier and IMT Mines Ales, Ales, France

Abstract. Pull-based Development (PbD) is widely used in collaborative development to integrate changes into a project codebase. In this model, contributions are notified through Pull Request (PR) submissions. Project administrators are responsible for reviewing and integrating PRs. In the integration process, conflicts occur when PRs are concurrently opened on a given target branch and propose different modifications for a same code part. In a previous work, we proposed an approach, called *IP Optimizer*, to improve the Integration Process Efficiency (IPE) by prioritizing PRs. In this work, we conduct an empirical study on 260 open-source projects hosted by GitHub that use PRs intensively in order to quantify the frequency of conflicts in software projects and analyze how much the integration process can be improved. Our results indicate that regarding the frequency of conflicts in software projects, half of the projects have a moderate and high number of pairwise conflicts and half have a low number of pairwise conflicts or none. Futhermore, on average 18.82% of the time windows have conflicts. On the other hand, regarding how much the integration process can be improved, *IP Optimizer* improves the IPE in 94.16% of the time windows and the average improvement percentage is 146.15%. In addition, it improves the number of conflict resolutions in 67.16% of the time windows and the average improvement percentage is 134.28%.

Keywords: Collaborative software development · Distributed version control system · Pull-based development · Pull request · Integration process efficiency · Software merging · Merge conflicts

1 Introduction

Distributed Version Control Systems (DVCSs) have transformed collaborative software development [26]. Each developer has a personal local copy of the entire project history. Changes are first applied by developers to their local copy and then integrated into a new shared version. If they exists, conflicts between concurrent changes must be solved during this integration process [23].

The Pull-based Development (PbD) model is widely used in collaborative software development [15, 17]. In this model, developments are performed on new branches, forked from the latest version currently available on the main development branch [7].

H. Kaindl et al. (Eds.): ENASE 2022, CCIS 1829, pp. 155–178, 2023.
https://doi.org/10.1007/978-3-031-36597-3_8

Contributors work separately using individual copies of project files. When the development is finished, they submit a *Pull Request* (PR) so that the core team members (aka project administrators) integrate it into the main development branch.

Project administrators must review and integrate opened PRs in the project. While trying to integrate different PRs, project administrators might have to deal with conflicting changes between them. Conflicting changes are changes that modify the same part of the code (*i.e.,* same lines of the same file) in the versions to be integrated. When two PRs are concurrently opened on a given target branch, proposing different modifications for identical code parts, a *pairwise conflict* exists. In such case, only one PR can be integrated automatically, while the other requires conflict resolution (CR).

The integration process is defined as the PR integration sequence according to the chronological order. In a previous work, we proposed an approach to improve the Integration Process Efficiency (IPE) by automatically prioritizing Pull Request integration [24], considering integration process efficiency as the fact that for a given integration cost (*i.e.,* number of pairwise conflicts to be solved) the highest possible gain is reached (*i.e.,* the largest number of PRs are integrated) and taking as an hypothesis that all pairwise conflict resolutions have the same mean cost. In this paper, we refer to this work as Integration Process Optimizer (*IP Optimizer*).

In this paper, we present an empirical study conducted on 260 open-source projects hosted by GitHub[1] that use PRs intensively with the aim of quantifying the frequency of conflicts in software projects and analyzing how much the integration process can be improved in software projects. We perform this analysis with a sliding time window approach. For each time window, we extract the historical integration sequence corresponding to the integrated PRs in the window ordered chronologically by integration date and apply *IP Optimizer* to that set of PRs.

Our results indicate that, regarding the frequency of conflicts in software projects, half of the projects have a moderate to high number of pairwise conflicts and the other half have a low number of pairwise conflicts or none. Futhermore, on average 18.82% of the time windows have conflicts. On the other hand, regarding how much the integration process can be improved, *IP Optimizer* improves the integration process compared to the historical one by 94.16% of the time windows and the average improvement percentage is 146.15%. In addition, it improves the number of conflict resolutions in 67.16% of the time windows and the average improvement percentage is 134.28%.

We also perform the analysis for time windows of different sizes and confirm our intuition that the larger the size of the window, the greater the percentage of time windows with conflicts but also found that the larger the size of the time window the better *IP Optimizer* improves the integration process as compared to the historical one. This verifies what the practice of continuous integration indicates [6]: integrating the PRs quickly is the best way to avoid conflicts and this make the integration process more efficient.

The remainder of this article is structured as follows. Section 2 includes background knowledge and definitions. Section 3 introduces the research questions. Section 4 explains the design of the empirical study. Section 5 reports the results. Section 6 discusses the results and answers the research questions. Section 7 contains the threats to

---

[1] https://github.com/.

validity. Related works are included in Sect. 8 before providing our conclusions and perspectives for this work.

2 Background

In collaborative software development, contributors choose or are provided a *ticket* to deal with. Tickets are stored in an issue tracking system (IST) such as Jira[2] and define a task to correct, maintain or improve the software. To take the ticket into account, a contributor creates a dedicated development branch in his/her local repository from the latest software version (fetched from the main development branch in the shared project repository), check-out this version to get a working copy and make the needed changes. These changes can then be committed on the dedicated development branch in the local repository to enact them. When the development is finished, the versions locally commited on the dedicated development branch are checked-in (pushed) to the remote shared repository. A last step is to submit a PR to ask the project administrators to merge the changes into the project's main development branch.

A PR is a request to the project administrators to pull versions from a branch to another one. Therefore, a PR contains a source branch from which versions are pulled from and a target branch to which versions are pushed. Project administrators must review the opened PRs. As a result of the review process, PRs can be closed as accepted or rejected.

The accepted PRs are integrated, that is, the changes commited on the source branch since it was forked from the target branch, *i.e.,* the changes in the last version on the source branch, are merged into the target branch. If versions have been commited on the target branch since the source branch of the PR was forked, there may be merge conflicts since the head version of the source branch do not derive anymore from the head version of the target branch. We consider changes to be text file modifications like Git does [8]. So, merge conflicts between changes are due to the fact that the same line(s) of the same file are modified in both branches.

When there are merge conflicts between the changes of the source branch and the changes of the target branch of a PR, the PR is considered as a conflicting PR. Conflicting PRs require a conflict resolution to integrate their changes into the target branch whereas for unconflicting PRs, the changes are automatically integrated. In the PbD model, a pairwise conflict exists between two PRs when the integration of a PR would entail a future conflict when integrating the other one to their shared target branch (and reciprocally). Figure 1 shows a simple pairwise conflict scenario where two PRs conflict with each other.

3 Research Questions

The goal of this work is to quantify the frequency of conflicts in software developments based on DVCSs and to analyze to what extent the integration process can be optimized in these projects. To achieve this goal, we aim to answer the following research questions.

---

[2] https://www.atlassian.com/en/software/jira.

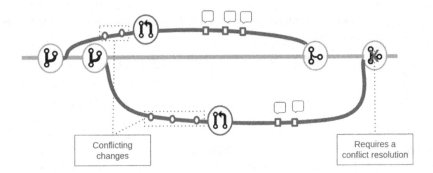

Fig. 1. Pairwsie conflict scenario where two PRs conflict with each other.

Research Question 1 (RQ1): To what extent do conflicts occur in software projects managed with DVCS?

In order to answer this question, we obtain the pairwise conflicts from the history of projects that use PRs intensively and analyze how many pairwise conflicts there are in the history of each project and how they are distributed over time considering integration time windows of different sizes.

Research Question 2 (RQ2): How much can the integration process of software projects be optimized?

To answer this question, we perform a sliding window analysis. Specifically, we obtain the number of time windows in which *IP Optimizer* improves the IPE and the number of conflict resolutions compared to the historical integration sequence and in what proportion this improvement occurs. For this, we obtain for each time window the historical integration sequence and the PR group integration sequence obtained by *IP Optimizer* for the set of PRs in the time window. Afterwards, we calculate the IPE and the number of conflict resolutions corresponding to the historical integration sequence and the PR group integration sequence obtained by *IP Optimizer*. Based on this information, we obtain the number of time windows in which *IP Optimizer* improves the IPE and the number of conflict resolutions with respect to the history of each project. We also calculate the IPE improvement percentage and the improvement percentage of the number of conflict resolutions that *IP Optimizer* achieves with respect to the historical one.

4   Empirical Study Setup

We set up an empirical study on projects hosted in GitHub that use PRs intensively. We extracted the information on projects and their PRs from the GHTorrent[3] dataset [14]. All the scripts and data used in this study are available in our online appendix [1].

Figure 2 illustrates the study design consisting of three stages. The first stage filters and extracts the project data from the GHTorrent dataset according to four selection criteria. The second stage obtains all the pairwise conflicts of each of the projects. The

---

[3] https://ghtorrent.org/.

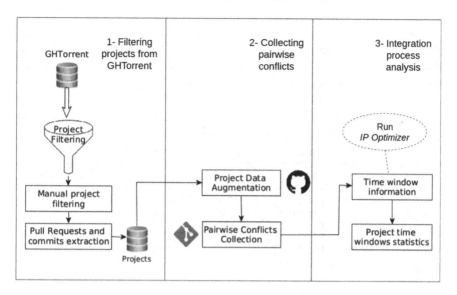

Fig. 2. Study design.

third stage performs an integration process analysis that consists of extracting N-days time windows and comparing the related historical integration sequence data with the PR group integration sequence data for the time window obtained using *IP Optimizer*. Then, from the time windows data, we calculate statistical data for each project.

We conduct the reproducibility assessment for our empirical study according to the methodological framework of González-Barahona and Robles [13]. For reasons of space we include it in the online appendix [1].

4.1 Stage 1: Project Filtering and Project Data Extraction

Project Selection Criteria. We defined four selection criteria that are described below. Figure 3 shows the filter funnel applied to the GHTorrent dataset.

Official Projects. Consider only the official / original projects, that is, not the forked projects. The reason of this filter is that forked projects are not project by themselves; they are usually only used to contribute to the official projects.

Active Projects. Consider only active projects. Many inactive projects are temporary or discontinued projects. Moreover, most of these are deleted after a period of time and deleted projects are not accessible. Thus, we filter deleted projects or projects that have not had a commit in the last year[4].

Software Projects. Consider only software projects. Software projects involve a software development process and thus are of interest to evaluate the integration process. So, we filter projects by their main programming language. We select the projects that

---

[4] Since the GHTorrent dataset has data up to 2019-06-01, last year corresponds to 2018-06-01 and after.

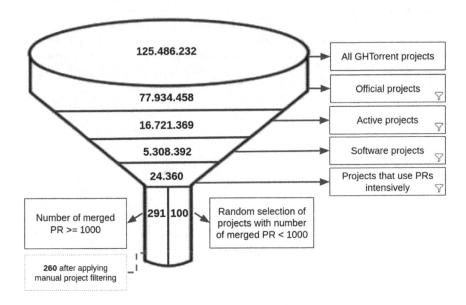

Fig. 3. GHTorrent filter funnel and filtering criteria.

are implemented in the 25 most popular programming languages according to the PYPL ranking [2]: Python, Java, JavaScript, C#, C/C++, PHP, R, TypeScript, Objective-C, Swift, Matlab, Kotlin, Go, Rust, Ruby, VBA, Ada, Scala, Visual Basic, Dart, Abap, Lua, Groovy, Perl, Julia.

Projects that Use PRs Intensively. Consider only the projects that use PRs intensively, that is, projects that have at least 100 PRs. Therefore, we filter projects that have less than 100 PRs.

We are interested in projects that use PRs. On GHTorrent there are 704711 projects that have at least one PR, of which there are 208949 projects (29.65%) that have only one PR. In addition, most of the projects (96.54%) have less than 100 PRs. The projects that have few PRs do not provide much relevant information for our analysis since, in many cases, they do not have pairwise conflicts or they have very few. That is why we decided to take projects that have at least 100 PRs to avoid data disturbances.

Since getting pairwise conflicts for a project requires a lot of resources and time, we consider to study projects that have more than or equal 1000 merged PRs because that is a large enough number of PRs that will allow us to find all kinds of scenarios and the number of projects is significant for evaluating the integration process. In addition, these merged PRs correspond to PRs where the source branch and the target branch are in the same repository because it is not possible to obtain the historical pairwise conflicts of merged PRs from the project repository where the source branch is in a different repository.

To avoid any kind of bias by only analyzing in detail the projects that have more than 1000 merged PRs, we made a random selection of 100 projects that have less than 1000 merged PRs. In this way we verify that the results remain the same even if we take a larger set of projects.

Manual Project Filtering. After applying the filters described above automatically, we obtain 291 projects with at least 1000 PRs. Some of these projects do not meet the proposed criteria because the GHTorrent dataset has outdated data or because the main programming language defined on GitHub is not correct. Specifically, we find that there are projects that have defined one of the programming languages that interest us as the main programming language, but the project is not a software project. On the other hand, there are projects that are no longer on GitHub and the project history cannot be accessed. This is why we had to manually apply the *software projects* and *active projects* filters on the 291 projects obtained with the automatic filtering. As a result of the manual filtering, there are 260 projects that meet the defined criteria.

Pull Requests and Commit Extraction. We extract the PRs and commits of the selected projects from the GHTorrent database to be able to obtain the pairwise conflicts in stage 2.

4.2   Stage 2: Collecting Pairwise Conflicts

Project Data Augmentation. GHTorrent is missing information needed to obtain pairwise conflicts. In particular, we need the *default branch* of the project and the *target branch* of the PRs. So we use the GitHub API to do so.

Pairwise Conflicts Collection. We obtain the pairwise conflicts for merged PRs of each project. The conditions for the existence of a pairwise conflict are:

1. The target branch of the involved PRs must be the same.
2. PRs must be open simultaneously for a period of time.
3. The changes applied in the versions of the source branches of the involved PRs must conflict.

Therefore, to obtain the pairwise conflicts of a given PR, we search for PRs that have the same target branch defined (first condition) and that have been opened or closed while the PR is open (second condition). Figure 4 shows the PRs that are candidates to have a pairwise conflict with a given PR according to the second condition. Then, we check if there are conflicts between the given PR and each candidate PRs (third condition) by performing an in-memory merge[5] of the head version[6] of the source branch of each PR.

4.3   Stage 3: Integration Process Analysis

Based on project data extracted from GHTorrent and the pairwise conflicts, we conduct a similar analysis to the one we performed on the Antlr4 project in our previous work [24]. We extract historical integration sequences from N-days time windows. An

---

[5] https://git-scm.com/docs/git-merge.
[6] Version in which the PR was created.

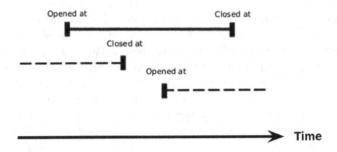

Fig. 4. Candidate PRs (dashed lines) to have a pairwise conflict with a given PR (solid line) according to the second condition.

historical integration sequence corresponds to the merged PRs in a given time window sorted by the chronological order in which the PRs were merged. We also calculate the PR group integration sequence related to the time window using *IP Optimizer*. *IP Optimizer* receives as input a set of PRs and returns a sequence of groups of PRs where the PRs of each group do not conflict with each other and the number of groups is minimal.

Given an integration sequence, we obtain the cumulative gain G_k and the cumulative cost C_k for each integration step k as shown in (1) where g_i is the number of PRs integrated in the integration step i and c_i is the number of pairwise conflicts solved in the integration step i.

$$G_k = \sum_{i=1}^{k} g_i \qquad k = 1, ..., \#PRs$$

$$C_k = \sum_{i=1}^{k} c_i \qquad k = 1, ..., \#PRs \tag{1}$$

Next, we map the integration steps onto a cumulative gain / cumulative cost plot. Each coordinate (x,y) is an integration step and the line between points corresponds to the cost of the integration step. The trajectory obtained models the integration sequence. The area under the trajectory represents the IPE because a larger area means that a higher gain is achieved at a lower cost. Figure 5 shows an example of an integration trajectory.

As the popularity of PRs grew over time [15,39], projects incorporated their use at a certain point in their lives. That is why we start calculating the time windows of a project from the merge date of the first PR and we calculate them until the date we have data. Figure 6 shows how we extract the historical integration sequences of a given project.

Time Window Information. For each project, we extract 7-days, 14-days, 28-days, 60-days and 90-days time windows. From each time window we calculate the following information.

Number of PRs (#PRs). It is the number of PRs merged between the start and end dates of the time window.

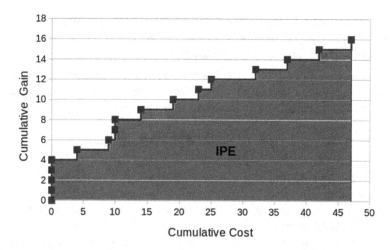

Fig. 5. Example of an integration sequence mapped onto a cost/gain trajectory. The area under the trajectory represents the IPE.

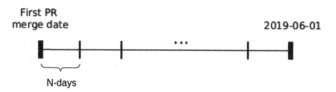

Fig. 6. Historical integration sequences extraction.

Number of Pairwise Conflicts (#PC). It is the number of pairwise conflicts that involve PRs merged in the time window. In (2) it is shown how the number of pairwise conflicts is calculated, where n is the number of merged PRs in the time window.

$$\#PC = \sum_{j=i+1}^{n} Exists\_PC(PR_i, PR_j) \quad i = 1, ..., n-1$$

$$Exists\_PC(P, Q) = \begin{cases} 1 & \text{if exists pairwise conflict between PR P and PR Q} \\ 0 & otherwise \end{cases} \tag{2}$$

Number of Historical CRs (Historical_CR). It is the number of conflict resolutions that actually occurred in the history of the project for the time window. In (3) it is shown how we calculate the number of conflict resolutions where n is the number of integration steps and c_k is the cost for the integration step k.

$$CR = \sum_{k=1}^{n} f(c_k)$$

$$f(c) = \begin{cases} 1 & c > 0 \\ 0 & otherwise \end{cases} \tag{3}$$

Number of Optimized CRs (Optimized_CR). It is the resulting number of conflict resolutions in the PR group integration sequence, obtained by *IP Optimizer*, for the time window. Formula (3) is also used to calculate this value.

CRs Improvement Percentage (CR_IP). It is the percentage of improvement in the number of conflict resolutions between the PR group integration sequence obtained by *IP Optimizer* and the historical one. It is calculated using formula (4).

$$CR\_IP = \left(\frac{Historical\_CR}{Optimized\_CR} - 1 \right) * 100 \tag{4}$$

Historical IPE. It is the Integration Process Efficiency of the historical integration sequence for the time window. In (5) it is shown how we calculate the IPE, where n is the number of integration steps, G_k is the cumulative gain for the integration step k and C_k is the cumulative cost for the integration step k. Note that this formula calculate the area under the cost/gain trajectory by adding the area of the rectangles where the base is the integration step cost and the height is the cumulative gain of the step.

$$IPE = \sum_{i=0}^{n-1} G_i * (C_{i+1} - C_i) \tag{5}$$

Optimized IPE. It is the Integration Process Efficiency of the PR group integration sequence, obtained by *IP Optimizer*, for the time window. This value is also calculated using formula (5).

IPE Improvement Percentage (IPE_IP). It is the improvement percentage of the IPE between the PR group integration sequence obtained by *IP Optimizer* and the historical one for the time window. It is calculated using formula (6).

$$IPE\_IP = \left(\frac{Optimized\_IPE}{Historical\_IPE} - 1 \right) * 100 \tag{6}$$

Project Time Windows Statistics. Once the information of the time windows of the projects has been calculated, we calculate the following statistical information of each project by time window size (7-days, 14-days, 28-days, 60-days and 90-days).

Number of Time Windows. It is the number of time windows between the merge date of the first merged PR to the date we have data.

Number and Percentage of Time Windows Without Conflicts. Corresponds to the number and the percentage of time windows in which there is no pairwise conflict.

Number and Percentage of Time Windows With Conflicts. Corresponds to the number and the percentage of time windows in which there is at least one pairwise conflict.

The following statistical information is calculated considering only the time windows that have pairwise conflicts.

Mean Number of Pairwise Conflicts. It is the mean number of pairwise conflict for a time window.

Number and Percentage of Time Windows that Improve the Historical Number of CRs.
It is the number and percentage of time windows in which the number of conflict resolutions obtained by *IP Optimizer* is better than the historical one.

Number and Percentage of Time Windows that Maintain the Historical Number of CRs.
It is the number and the percentage of time windows in which the number of conflict
resolutions obtained by *IP Optimizer* is equal to the historical one.

It should be noted that since *IP Optimizer* obtains groups of PRs that do not conflict
with each other, there will only be conflict resolutions for each group that is integrated
except the first one that is integrated without conflicts. Since the number of groups
calculated by *IP Optimizer* is minimal, then the number of conflict resolutions of the
integration process obtained by *IP Optimizer* is minimal. This is why we do not calculate a measure where *IP Optimizer* worsens the number of conflict resolutions compared
to the historical integration process.

Number and Percentage of Time Windows that Improve the Historical IPE. It is the
number and percentage of time windows in which the IPE obtained by *IP Optimizer* is
better than the historical IPE.

Number and Percentage of Time Windows that Worsen the Historical IPE. It is the
number and the percentage of time windows in which the IPE obtained by *IP Optimizer*
is worse than the historical IPE.

Number and Percentage of Time Windows that Maintain the Historical IPE. It is the
number and the percentage of time windows in which the IPE obtained by *IP Optimizer*
is equal to the historical IPE.

Mean Percentage of Improvement in the Number of CRs. It is the mean percentage of
improvement in the number of conflict resolutions between the integration sequence
obtained by *IP Optimizer* and the historical one.

Mean Percentage of IPE Improvement. It is the mean percentage of IPE improvement
between the integration sequence obtained by *IP Optimizer* and the historical one.

5   Results

In this section, we report the main results achieved in our work. We first analyze the
distribution of pairwise conflicts in the projects and the proportion of time windows with
and without pairwise conflicts for each project. Next, we make a comparative analysis
of the historical integration process and the one obtained by *IP Optimizer* on the time
windows with pairwise conflicts. The results are shown in detail for time windows of
14 d because it is both the usual sprint length in agile methodologies such as Scrum [9]
and the size of the merge window used in the Linux kernel project [11]. In addition, in
Sect. 5.3 we make a comparative analysis of the results obtained using time windows of
different sizes.

Table 1. Percentage and number of projects by pairwise conflict quantity.

Category	Projects (%)	# Projects
no conflict	20.00%	52
low amount of conflicts	30.00%	78
moderate amount of conflicts	28.85%	75
high amount of conflicts	21.15%	55

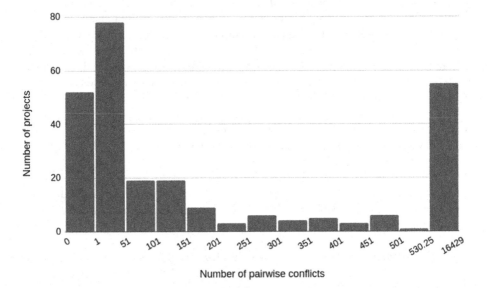

Fig. 7. Pairwise conflicts histogram.

5.1 Projects Time Windows: Pairwise Conflicts

Figure 7 shows a histogram of pairwise conflicts. We can see 52 projects without pairwise conflicts (20%), 78 projects (30%) with less than 50 pairwise conflicts in their entire history, 75 projects (28.85%) with a moderate number of conflicts (between 51 and 530 pairwise conflicts) and finally 55 projects (21.15%) with a large number of pairwise conflicts. Therefore, we classify projects as **no conflict, low amount of conflicts, moderate amount of conflicts** and **high amount of conflicts**. Table 1 shows the percentage and number of projects for each category.

For the rest of the analysis we do not take into account the projects that do not have any pairwise conflicts since they do not provide relevant information for the analysis. Considering the remaining projects, on average 18.82% of the time windows have pairwise conflicts while the remaining 81.18% are time windows without conflicts.

Figure 8 shows the percentage of time windows with and without pairwise conflicts per project ordered by the highest percentage of time windows with pairwise conflicts. So on the right we have the projects (3.85%) that have no time window with pairwise conflicts. Then, on the left, we can see the projects that have the highest proportion

Table 2. Percentage and number of projects by amount of conflicting time windows category.

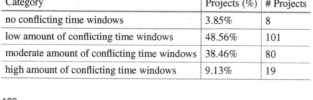

Category	Projects (%)	# Projects
no conflicting time windows	3.85%	8
low amount of conflicting time windows	48.56%	101
moderate amount of conflicting time windows	38.46%	80
high amount of conflicting time windows	9.13%	19

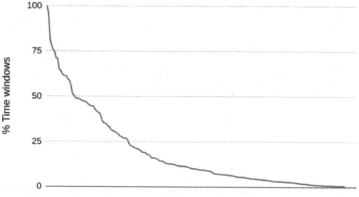

Fig. 8. Percentage of time windows with and without pairwise conflicts by project.

of time windows with pairwise conflicts: 9.13% of the projects have more than 50% of the time windows with conflicts; 17.31% have between 25% and 50% of time windows with conflict. It is followed by 21.15% of projects that have between 10% and 25% conflicting time windows. And finally, 48.56% of projects that have less than 10% of time windows with conflicts. Therefore, we classify projects as **no conflicting time windows, low amount of conflicting time windows, moderate amount of conflicting time windows** and **high amount of conflicting time windows**. Table 2 shows the percentage and number of projects for each category.

5.2   Time Windows with Pairwise Conflicts

In this section, we analyze in detail the time windows with pairwise conflicts since for the time windows without pairwise conflicts the historical integration sequence and the PR group integration sequence obtained by *IP Optimizer* both give the same IPE and the same number of CRs and do not provide any relevant information.

IPE.   Considering the time windows of all the remaining projects, *IP Optimizer* improves the historical IPE for 94.16% of the time windows; for the 3.83% of the time windows *IP Optimizer* achieves the same IPE compared to the historical one and only for 2.01% *IP Optimizer* worsens the historical IPE.

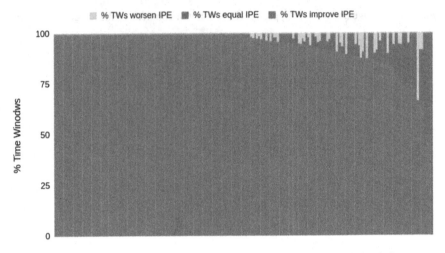

Fig. 9. Percentage of time windows that improves, maintains and worse the historical IPE by project.

Table 3. Percentage and number of projects by percentage range of time windows in which the IPE is improved.

Percentage range of time windows in which the IPE is improved	Percentage of projects	Number of projects
= 100%	52.00%	104
>= 90%, <100%	25.00%	50
>= 75%, <90%	18.00%	36
>= 50%, <75%	4.50%	9
= 0%	0.50%	1

Figure 9 shows the percentage of time windows where *IP Optimizer* improves, worsens or mantains the same IPE compared to the historical one per project ordered by the percentage of time windows that improve the historical IPE. Table 3 shows the percentage and number of projects in which the IPE is improved. We can see that *IP Optimizer* improves all the time windows for 52% of the projects. 25% of the projects improves more than 90% of the time windows and 18% improves between 75% and 90% of the time windows. 4.50% improves between 50% and 75% of the time windows. Only one project (0.50%) mantains the same IPE for all the time windows, but this project only has one time window with pairwise conflicts.

Regarding the magnitude of the improvement of the historical IPE achieved by *IP Optimizer*, the average of the mean improvement of the historical IPE of all the projects is 146.15%. That is, on average, the IPE obtained by *IP Optimizer* is 146.15% higher than the historical IPE.

Figure 10 shows the mean IPE improvement achieved by *IP Optimizer* compared to the historical one per project ordered by the highest mean number of pairwise conflicts.

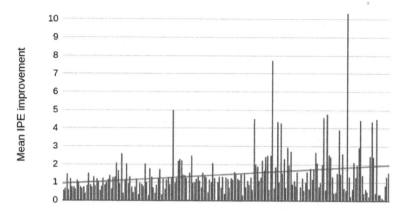

Fig. 10. Mean IPE improvement by project.

Table 4. Percentage and number of projects by range of mean improvement of the IPE.

Mean IPE improvement range	Projects (%)	# Projects
< 1	37.50%	75
>= 1, <2	42.00%	84
>= 2, <3	14.00%	28
>3	6.50%	13

Table 4 shows the percentage and number of projects by range of mean improvement of the IPE. For 37.50% of the projects, the mean IPE improvement is less than 1. This means that the mean improvement percentage is between 0% and 100%. In 42% of the projects, *IP Optimizer* improves on average the historical IPE between 1 and 2 times, that is, the mean IPE improvement percentage is between 100% and 200%. Then 14% of the projects have a mean IPE improvement between 2 and 3 times and 6.50% of the projects have a mean IPE improvement higher than 3 times. There is a project where *IP Optimizer* improves on average the historical IPE more than 7 times and another project that *IP Optimizer* improves on average the historical IPE more than 10 times.

It should be noted that when the number of pairwise conflicts is larger, the IPE tends to improve less than when the number of pairwise conflicts is smaller. The green line shows this trend.

Number of CRs. Considering the time windows of all the projects, *IP Optimizer* improves the historical number of CRs for 67.16% of the time windows and achieved the same number of CR for 32.84% of the time windows.

Figure 11 shows the percentage of time windows where *IP Optimizer* improves or mantains the number of CRs with respect to the historical one per project, ordered by the percentage of time windows that improves the CRs number. Table 5 shows the per-

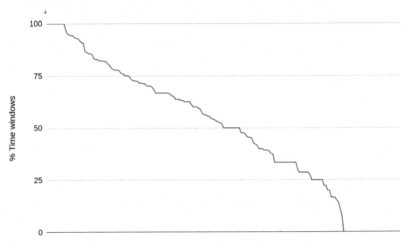

Fig. 11. Percentage of time windows that improves and maintains the number of CRs by project.

Table 5. Percentage and number of projects by percentage range of time windows in which the number of CRs is improved.

Percentage range of time windows in which the number of CRs is improved	Percentage of projects	Number of projects
= 100%	5.50%	11
>= 75%, <100%	18.50%	37
>= 50%, <75%	31.00%	62
> 0 %, <50%	29.00%	58
= 0%	16.00%	32

centage and number of projects in which the number of CRs is improved. The projects in which *IP Optimizer* improves the number of CRs for all time windows (5.50%) and those in which the same number of CRs is maintained compared to the historical one for all time windows (16%) have few time windows with pairwise conflicts. There is 18.50% of projects in which the number of CRs is improved for more than 75% of the time windows and 31% that improve between 50% and 75% of the time windows. Finally, for 29% of the projects, the number of CRs is improved in less than 50% of the time windows.

Regarding the magnitude of the improvement of the historical number of CRs achieved by *IP Optimizer*, the average of the mean improvement of the historical number of CRs of all the projects is 134.28%. That is, on average, the number of CRs obtained by *IP Optimizer* is 134.28% lower than the historical one.

Figure 12 shows the mean number of CRs improvement achieved by *IP Optimizer* compared to the historical one per project ordered by the highest mean number of pairwise conflicts. Table 6 shows the percentage and number of projects by range of mean improvement of the number of CRs. For 48.50% of the projects, the mean number of CRs improvement is less than 1. This means that the mean improvement percent-

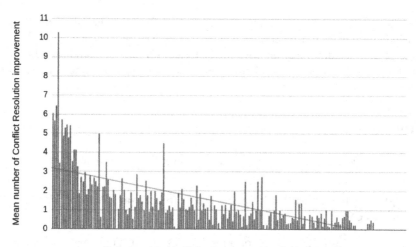

Fig. 12. Mean number of CR improvement by project.

Table 6. Percentage and number of projects by range of mean improvement of the number of CRs.

Mean number of CR improvement range	Projects (%)	# Projects
< 1	48.50%	97
>= 1, <2	29.50%	59
>= 2, <3	12.50%	25
>3	9.50%	19

age is between 0% and 100%. In 29.50% of the projects, *IP Optimizer* improves on average the historical number of CRs between 1 and 2 times, that is, the mean number of CRs improvement percentage is between 100% and 200%. Then, 12.50% of the projects have a mean number of CRs improvement between 2 and 3 times and 9.50% of the projects have a mean number of CR improvement higher than 3 times. There is a project where *IP Optimizer* improves on average the historical number of CRs more than 10 times.

It should be noted that when the number of pairwise conflicts is larger, the number of CRs tends to improve more than when the number of pairwise conflicts is smaller. The green line shows this trend.

5.3 Comparison of Time Windows of Different Sizes

In this section, we make a comparison of the main results obtained using different time window sizes. Table 7 shows the results for 7-days, 14-days, 28-days, 60-days and 90-days time windows. These results correspond to the average of all the projects that have at least one time window with conflicts.

We can see that, not surprisingly, as the window size is greater, the percentage of time windows with pairwise conflicts is also greater. The same happens with the percentage of time windows that improve the historical IPE and the number of historical CRs. Moreover, the magnitude of that improvement is also greater when the time window size is greater.

6 Discussion

In this section, we disccuss the results and we answer the research questions.

6.1 RQ1. to What Extent Do Conflicts Occur in Software Projects Managed with DVCS?

To answer this question, we focus on Figs. 7 and 8. From Fig. 7, we can extract the number of pairwise conflicts that the projects have throughout their history and in Fig. 8 we can see how they are distributed over time by analyzing how many integration time windows are affected by conflicts.

We see that half of the projects have a moderate and high number of pairwise conflicts and the other half have a low number of pairwise conflicts or no conflict. We also see that, on average, 18.82% of project time windows have conflicts of which 47.59% of projects have a moderate to high number of conflicting integration time windows and the rest of the projects (52.41%) have a low number of integration time windows with pairwise conflicts or no conflict.

Therefore, in 50% of the projects, conflicts are very frequent while in the other half they occur infrequently. This can depend on many factors such as the way the projects are managed, the size of the projects or the number of contributors that deserve a study exclusively dedicated to this topic.

On the other hand, Table 7 shows how the percentage of time windows with pairwise conflicts increases when the size of the window is larger. This means that if the integration process is prolonged, that is, if it takes a long time to integrate the PRs, there is possibly more conflicts. This information verifies what continuous integration

Table 7. Comparison of the main results obtained for different time window sizes.

Time window size	7-days	14-days	28-days	60-days	90-days
# Time windows (avg)	226.61	113.88	57.22	27.06	18.04
% Time windows with conflicts	12.57%	18.82%	26.79%	35.35%	41.63%
% Time windows without conflicts	87.43%	81.18%	73.21%	64.65%	58.37%
% Time windows that improve historical IPE	89.83%	94.16%	96.88%	98.28%	98.58%
% Time windows that do not change historical IPE	7.39%	3.83%	2.12%	0.95%	0.90%
% Time windows that worsen historical IPE	2.78%	2.01 %	1.00%	0.77%	0.52%
% Time windows that improve historical number of CR	59.55%	67.16%	72.76%	76.65%	77.30%
% Time windows that do not change historical number of CR	40.45%	32.84%	27.24%	23.35%	22.70%
Mean IPE improvement percentage	128.69%	146.15%	178.25%	186.40%	211.69%
Mean number of CR improvement percentage	95.21%	134.28%	198.10%	306.84%	385.08%

practice proposes, which suggests integrating changes as soon as possible, even several times a day. In this way, it is avoided that the code where the programmer is working is very outdated and therefore conflicts are avoided.

6.2   RQ2. How Much Can the Integration Process of Software Projects Be Optimized?

We answer this question by considering two factors of the integration process: the efficiency and the number of CRs. So we compare the integration process efficiency and the number of CRs obtained by *IP Optimizer* with the historical ones.

In previous section, we mentioned that *IP Optimizer* improves the integration process efficiency (IPE) by an average of 146.15% and reduces the number of CRs by an average of 134.28%.

In addition, *IP Optimizer* improves the efficiency of the historical integration process for most (94.16%) of the time windows. This indicates the level of usefulness of the proposal since it not only improves efficiency but also achieves it most of the time. Something similar, but to a lesser extent, occurs with the number of CRs. For 67.16% of the time windows, *IP Optimizer* reduces the number of CRs while it remains the same for the remaining time windows.

For 64.50% of the projects, *IP Optimizer* improves the integration process efficiency by more than double, and for 51.50% of the projects, it reduces the number of CRs by half or more.

Something interesting to note about Fig. 10 and Fig. 12 is that, while the IPE improvement is greater when there are fewer pairwise conflicts, the reduction in the number of CRs is greater when there are more pairwsie conflicts. The IPE trend according to the number of pairwise conflicts has little slope, that is to say that the difference between there being many pairwise conflicts or few does not modify the IPE improvement to a great extent. On the other hand, in the case of the number of CRs, the trend is very steep, so there is a great difference in the reduction of the number of CRs according to the number of pairwise conflicts.

Table 7 shows how *IP Optimizer* further improves the historical IPE and the number of historical CRs when the size of the windows increases. This makes a lot of sense since there are more conflicts and the project administrator does not have the information on the existence of conflicts between the PRs to be integrated, so the decisions made about the integration order of the PRs do not take into account the efficiency of the integration process.

7   Threats to Validity

We carefully analyzed the threats to validity based on the work of Feldt and Magazinius [10] and did our best to mitigate them.

7.1   Threats to Construct Validity

To obtain the pairwise conflicts from the project history, we use the version from which the branch to be integrated was forked and the version in which the PR was created. In many cases, it happened that when looking for one of these versions they were not in the repository. This may be because the versions to be integrated have been squashed when integrating[7]. In these cases, if there was a conflict, we could not find it. This issue was mitigated by the number of projects we used to validate the proposal since the number of conflicts we found is large enough to have relevant data.

7.2   Threats to Internal Validity

It would be argued that the analysis was not performed on all software projects that have more than 100 PRs. We prioritize projects with the most number of merged PRs (those with more than 1000) because they include all relevant cases. To mitigate this risk, we performed the analysis on 100 randomly selected projects that have less than 1000 merged PRs and verified that the results do not provide relevant information.

7.3   Threats to Conclusion Validity

We are validating *IP Optimizer* in static scenarios. We take the merged PRs in a time window of the project's history and apply *IP Optimizer* on that set of PRs, comparing the efficiency of the historical integration sequences and that obtained by *IP Optimizer*. However, further studies are needed in a dynamic environment. That is, to implement a tool integrated with the code repositories and evaluate it in real time considering all the open PRs and offering the information to the project administrator so that she/he can carry out the integration process efficiently.

7.4   Threats to External Validity

Due to the fact of having to take the merged PRs where the source branch and the target branch are in the same repository, we were not able to evaluate projects that use the Forking workflow[8], which are very popular in open source software development. Likewise, we consider that we were able to evaluate the proposal in a sufficiently large number of projects which allows us to generalize the results to apply them to projects that use this workflow as well.

8   Related Work

In a previous work [24], we proposed an approach to optimize the efficiency of the integration process through the prioritization of PRs and we validated it by analyzing 7 representative historical integration sequences of the Antlr4 project[9]. In the present work, we conduct an empirical study that seeks to understand how frequent conflicts are in software projects managed with DVCS and analyze how much the integration process carried out in the history of software projects can be improved establishing as baseline the results obtained by *IP Optimizer*.

---

[7] https://git-scm.com/docs/git-merge#Documentation/git-merge.txt---squash.

[8] https://www.atlassian.com/git/tutorials/comparing-workflows/forking-workflow.

[9] https://www.antlr.org/.

In recent years, several empirical studies have been conducted to understand how contributors and project administrators work with the PbD model from a general perspective, or from the perspective of contributors, project aministrators or contributions [15–17,29,30]. The results obtained in our work have a direct implication for project administrators, although they also provide information about the development process in general and thus increase the body of knowledge on software engineering practices.

Some works study latency factors [15,20,33,35,38] proposing different quantitative / qualitative analyzes to identify latency factors in the PR review process. In our work, we find that the latency in the integration of the PRs can cause more conflicts. There are works that seek to reduce latency by recommending the most suitable project administrator for reviewing a given PR [18,19,28,32,34]. Other works seek to lower the latency of the most important PRs, prioritizing them by response and acceptance likelihood [4,5,31]. Zhao *et al.* [40] also propose a learning-to-rank approach to prioritize PRs that can be quickly reviewed by project administrators in order to review more PRs in a period of time or be able to review any PR when they have a few minutes. Recently, Saini and Britto [27] use a Bayesian Network to prioritize PRs based on acceptance probability, change type (*i.e.,* bug fixing, new feature, refactoring) and presence or absence of merge conflicts. Their main goal is to decrease the overall lead time of code review process along with helping to reduce the workload of project administrators.

Other works study the PR acceptance factors [17,21,25,29,36] identifying and analyzing the social and technical factors behind PR acceptance or rejection. Gousios *et al.* [15] indicate that 27% of rejected PRs are conflicting PRs. Our work indicates that there are integration processes that reduce the number of conflict resolutions, so the acceptance rate can also be improved according the integration process.

Finally, there are works that study conflicts in software projects. Some works [22,37] analyze the frequency and the difficulty of resolution. Accioly *et al.* [3] conduct an empirical study that analyze the effectiveness of two types of code changes as conflict predictors in open-source Java projects. Ghiotto *et al.* [12] study the merge conflicts found in the histories of 2731 open-source Java projects. They characterize merge conflicts in terms of number of chunks, size, and programming language constructs involved, classify the manual resolution strategies that developers use to address these merge conflicts, and analyze the relationships between various characteristics of merge conflicts and chosen resolution strategies. Our work also performs an analysis of merge conflicts but between PRs. Furthermore, our analysis is independent of the code structures, so we are not limited to evaluating a single programming language.

9   Conclusions

In this paper, we conduct an empirical study on 260 open-source projects hosted in GitHub that use PRs intensively to understand how frequent pairwise conflicts are in the Pull-based Development model and evaluate our integration process optimization proposal.

We find that half of the projects have a moderate and high number of pairwise conflicts and the other half have a low or none number of pairwise conflicts. Futhermore, on average, there is a 18.82% of the time windows that have conflicts.

Regarding how much the integration process can be improved, *IP Optimizer* improves the historical integration process for 94.16% of the time windows and does so on average by 146.15%. In addition, it reduces the number of CRs for 67.16% of the time windows and does so on average by 134.28%. Therefore, we can conclude that the integration process can be greatly improved.

It should be noted that the analysis performed is in a static environment and the real environment is dynamic. In addition, the application of the proposal in a real environment could have side effects on work habits of the involved people in the project. Therefore, we plan to develop a tool integrated into platforms that support PbD (*e.g.,* GitHub, Bitbucket), in order to evaluate *IP Optimizer* in a real environment and study the side effects on work habits when using our approach.

We also plan to further study the occurrence of conflicts in projects that use PbD, in order to discover the factors for some projects to be more conflictive than others. Finally, it is also a perspective for our work to study accurate models for the evaluation of the cost and gain of PR merges.

References

1. Online Appendix. https://anonymous.4open.science/r/pull-request-conflicts-7884/docs/index.md
2. PYPL Popularity of Programming Language. https://pypl.github.io/PYPL.html
3. Accioly, P., Borba, P., Silva, L., Cavalcanti, G.: Analyzing conflict predictors in open-source java projects. In: Proceedings of the 15th International Conference on Mining Software Repositories, pp. 576–586 (2018)
4. Azeem, M.I., Panichella, S., Di Sorbo, A., Serebrenik, A., Wang, Q.: Action-based recommendation in pull-request development. In: Proceedings of the International Conference on Software and System Processes, pp. 115–124 (2020)
5. Azeem, M.I., Peng, Q., Wang, Q.: Pull request prioritization algorithm based on acceptance and response probability. In: 2020 IEEE 20th International Conference on Software Quality, Reliability and Security (QRS), pp. 231–242. IEEE (2020)
6. Beck, K.: Extreme Programming Explained: Embrace Change. Addison-Wesley (2000)
7. Bird, C., Zimmermann, T.: Assessing the value of branches with what-if analysis. In: Proceedings of the ACM SIGSOFT 20th International Symposium on the Foundations of Software Engineering, pp. 1–11 (2012)
8. Chacon, S., Straub, B.: Pro git. Springer Nature (2014)
9. Diebold, P., Ostberg, J.-P., Wagner, S., Zendler, U.: What do practitioners vary in using scrum? In: Lassenius, C., Dingsøyr, T., Paasivaara, M. (eds.) XP 2015. LNBIP, vol. 212, pp. 40–51. Springer, Cham (2015). https://doi.org/10.1007/978-3-319-18612-2_4
10. Feldt, R., Magazinius, A.: Validity threats in empirical software engineering research-an initial survey. In: SEKE, pp. 374–379 (2010)
11. German, D.M., Adams, B., Hassan, A.E.: Continuously mining distributed version control systems: An empirical study of how linux uses git. Empiric. Softw. Eng. **21**(1), 260–299 (2016)
12. Ghiotto, G., Murta, L., Barros, M., Van Der Hoek, A.: On the nature of merge conflicts: A study of 2,731 open source java projects hosted by github. IEEE Trans. Softw. Eng. **46**(8), 892–915 (2018)
13. González-Barahona, J.M., Robles, G.: On the reproducibility of empirical software engineering studies based on data retrieved from development repositories. Empir. Softw. Eng. **17**(1–2), 75–89 (2012)

14. Gousios, G.: The ghtorrent dataset and tool suite. In: Proceedings of the 10th Working Conference on Mining Software Repositories (MSR 2013), pp. 233–236. IEEE Press, Piscataway (2013). https://dl.acm.org/citation.cfm?id=2487085.2487132

15. Gousios, G., Pinzger, M., Deursen, A.v.: An exploratory study of the pull-based software development model. In: Proceedings of the 36th International Conference on Software Engineering, pp. 345–355 (2014)

16. Gousios, G., Storey, M.A., Bacchelli, A.: Work practices and challenges in pull-based development: The contributor's perspective. In: 2016 IEEE/ACM 38th International Conference on Software Engineering (ICSE), pp. 285–296. IEEE (2016)

17. Gousios, G., Zaidman, A., Storey, M.A., Van Deursen, A.: Work practices and challenges in pull-based development: The integrator's perspective. In: 2015 IEEE/ACM 37th IEEE International Conference on Software Engineering, vol. 1, pp. 358–368. IEEE (2015)

18. Jiang, J., Lo, D., Zheng, J., Xia, X., Yang, Y., Zhang, L.: Who should make decision on this pull request? analyzing time-decaying relationships and file similarities for integrator prediction. J. Syst. Softw. **154**, 196–210 (2019)

19. Jiang, J., Yang, Y., He, J., Blanc, X., Zhang, L.: Who should comment on this pull request? Analyzing attributes for more accurate commenter recommendation in pull-based development. Inf. Softw. Technol. **84**, 48–62 (2017)

20. Kononenko, O., Rose, T., Baysal, O., Godfrey, M., Theisen, D., De Water, B.: Studying pull request merges: A case study of shopify's active merchant. In: Proceedings of the 40th International Conference on Software Engineering: Software Engineering in Practice, pp. 124–133 (2018)

21. Legay, D., Decan, A., Mens, T.: On the impact of pull request decisions on future contributions. arXiv preprint arXiv:1812.06269 (2018)

22. Ma, P., Xu, D., Zhang, X., Xuan, J.: Changes are similar: Measuring similarity of pull requests that change the same code in GitHub. In: Li, Z., Jiang, H., Li, G., Zhou, M., Li, M. (eds.) NASAC 2017-2018. CCIS, vol. 861, pp. 115–128. Springer, Singapore (2019). https://doi.org/10.1007/978-981-15-0310-8_8

23. Mens, T.: A state-of-the-art survey on software merging. IEEE Trans. Softw. Eng. **28**(5), 449–462 (2002)

24. Olmedo, A., Arévalo, G., Cassol, I., Urtado, C., Vauttier, S.: Improving integration process efficiency through pull request prioritization. In: ENASE 2022–17th International Conference on Evaluation of Novel Approaches to Software Engineering, pp. 62–72. SCITEPRESS-Science and Technology Publications (2022)

25. Rahman, M.M., Roy, C.K.: An insight into the pull requests of github. In: Proceedings of the 11th Working Conference on Mining Software Repositories, pp. 364–367 (2014)

26. Rodríguez-Bustos, C., Aponte, J.: How distributed version control systems impact open source software projects. In: 2012 9th IEEE Working Conference on Mining Software Repositories (MSR), pp. 36–39. IEEE (2012)

27. Saini, N., Britto, R.: Using machine intelligence to prioritise code review requests. In: 2021 IEEE/ACM 43rd International Conference on Software Engineering: Software Engineering in Practice (ICSE-SEIP), pp. 11–20. IEEE (2021)

28. Thongtanunam, P., Kula, R.G., Cruz, A.E.C., Yoshida, N., Iida, H.: Improving code review effectiveness through reviewer recommendations. In: Proceedings of the 7th International Workshop on Cooperative and Human Aspects of Software Engineering, pp. 119–122 (2014)

29. Tsay, J., Dabbish, L., Herbsleb, J.: Influence of social and technical factors for evaluating contribution in github. In: Proceedings of the 36th International Conference on Software Engineering, pp. 356–366 (2014)

30. Tsay, J., Dabbish, L., Herbsleb, J.: Let's talk about it: Evaluating contributions through discussion in github. In: Proceedings of the 22nd ACM SIGSOFT International Symposium on Foundations of Software Engineering, pp. 144–154 (2014)

31. Van Der Veen, E., Gousios, G., Zaidman, A.: Automatically prioritizing pull requests. In: 2015 IEEE/ACM 12th Working Conference on Mining Software Repositories, pp. 357–361. IEEE (2015)
32. Ying, H., Chen, L., Liang, T., Wu, J.: Earec: Leveraging expertise and authority for pull-request reviewer recommendation in github. In: 2016 IEEE/ACM 3rd International Workshop on Crowd Sourcing in Software Engineering (CSI-SE), pp. 29–35. IEEE (2016)
33. Yu, Y., Wang, H., Filkov, V., Devanbu, P., Vasilescu, B.: Wait for it: Determinants of pull request evaluation latency on github. In: 2015 IEEE/ACM 12th Working Conference on Mining Software Repositories, pp. 367–371. IEEE (2015)
34. Yu, Y., Wang, H., Yin, G., Wang, T.: Reviewer recommendation for pull-requests in github: What can we learn from code review and bug assignment? Inf. Softw. Technol. **74**, 204–218 (2016)
35. Yu, Y., Yin, G., Wang, T., Yang, C., Wang, H.: Determinants of pull-based development in the context of continuous integration. Sci. China Inf. Sci. **59**(8), 1–14 (2016)
36. Zampetti, F., Bavota, G., Canfora, G., Di Penta, M.: A study on the interplay between pull request review and continuous integration builds. In: 2019 IEEE 26th International Conference on Software Analysis, Evolution and Reengineering (SANER), pp. 38–48. IEEE (2019)
37. Zhang, X., et al.: How do multiple pull requests change the same code: A study of competing pull requests in github. In: 2018 IEEE International Conference on Software Maintenance and Evolution (ICSME), pp. 228–239. IEEE (2018)
38. Zhang, Y., Yin, G., Yu, Y., Wang, H.: A exploratory study of @-mention in github's pull-requests. In: 2014 21st Asia-Pacific Software Engineering Conference, vol. 1, pp. 343–350. IEEE (2014)
39. Zhang, Y., Yin, G., Yu, Y., Wang, H.: Investigating social media in github's pull-requests: A case study on ruby on rails. In: Proceedings of the 1st International Workshop on Crowd-based Software Development Methods and Technologies, pp. 37–41 (2014)
40. Zhao, G., da Costa, D.A., Zou, Y.: Improving the pull requests review process using learning-to-rank algorithms. Empir. Softw. Eng. **24**(4), 2140–2170 (2019)

Identify Javascript Trends in Crowdsourcing Small Tasks

Ioannis Zozas$^{(\boxtimes)}$ ⓘ, Iason Anagnostou, and Stamatia Bibi ⓘ

Department of Electrical and Computer Engineering, University of Western Macedonia, Kozani, Greece
{izozas,sbibi}@uowm.gr

Abstract. A popular alternative non-conventional model for software development is crowdsourcing, which aims at decomposing software project into tasks that assigns them to individual stakeholders, through an open call for participation. A major challenge is to ensure community participation in developing high-quality solutions by each individual stakeholder. It is of high importance to be aware of the skills that can be acquired by the crowd, especially in cases of constantly evolving development environments, such as the JavaScript programming language and its applications. In the current paper, we aim at exploring trends in crowdsourcing JavaScript small tasks as an attempt to unveil a) popularity as the core technological skills and the functionalities that are more frequently crowdsourced, b) success as the relationship between the technological skills and the functionalities crowdsourced, and d) the monetary reward differences between these technological skills and the functionalities relationships. We have analyzed contest data collected from the Bountify crowdsourcing platform, resulting that while JavaScript small task development focuses on multiple technologies, frameworks, and libraries, that frequently overlap or complement each other, popularity, success, and monetary reward of the latter, in most cases are not associated.

Keywords: JavaScript · Crowdsourcing · Small tasks · Bountify

1 Introduction

Crowdsourcing is a non-conventional software development method to outsource development tasks to individual stakeholders (crowd) with a specific skill or domain knowledge [26]. This development model aims at decomposing a project into tasks and recruiting stakeholders for each one, in order to lower the overall cost, reduce defect rates, minimize time-to-market, and alleviate existing knowledge gaps in a form of collective intelligence [3, 14]. This enables extreme scalability for completing self-contained small tasks (or microtasks) of a larger project. These tasks are considered to be more reliable and efficient than a large task development scheme [15]. A common industrial practice today is to handle them via crowdsourcing, as to acquire missing knowledge and expertise instead of outsourcing the whole development as one big task, which may risk the success of the project [29].

Crowdsourcing today is an emerging market, in which the industry relies on for a variety of operations. Today, many platforms related to crowdsourcing have been operational, with some of them operating for more than 10 years. Most notable crowdsourcing platforms include Amazon Mechanical Turk, StackOverflow, uTest, TopCoder, and Bountify. Out of these, TopCoder has hosted more than 400 million competitions. uTest incorporated more than 100 thousand testers. StackOverflow includes answers for more than 16 million programming-related tasks.

On the other hand, JavaScript (JS) is currently among the most popular programming languages for all-purpose development today [5]. JavaScript today presents a constantly expanding development eco-system, which includes a variety of applications, including front-end, client-side, server-side, and Internet-of-things. It is a high-level dynamic language, that supports object-based and multi-paradigm development, and is characterized as interpreted and weakly type language. A most important feature which supports the language's popularity is the leverage of a variety of technologies, frameworks,and libraries. This high interoperability has led to the development of an expanding and evolving ecosystem. Today large number of small tasks in development are based on JavaScript due to the fragmentation of related technologies and required skills. A most common way to handle these tasks, which is a difficult process to handle, is distributing them to an arbitrarily larger crowd via crowdsourcing [9].

On this basis, the current study aims at exploring JavaScript small task development, taking into consideration that each task represents a unique form of crowdsourcing activity, which does not belong to a network of micro-tasks on a crowdsourced project. Thus, by analyzing crowdsourced task data, the goal of this study is to:

- Explore the trends related to both the *technology* (i.e., frameworks) and the associated *programming languages* that these tasks use, as well as the *functionality* that the tasks implement and the *platforms* (i.e., applications, operating systems) on which these tasks are deployed.
- Associate *JavaScript technologies to domain functionality, in an attempt to optimize small task completion efficiency.* As the JavaScript eco-system is considered to be volatile, these trends can provide further information on the language current and future domain utilization [17] as well as reveal industrial requirement skills for developers to master [15].
- Investigate monetary trends in crowdsourcing JavaScript small tasks, aiming at providing an overview of the industrial workforce skills demands [17].

For the purpose of our research, we decided to focus on the Bountify crowdsourcing platform. This platform specialized solely on providing small tasks to participant works, while covering a variety of required programming languages, including JavaScript. Bountify is currently a popular question-and-answer platform with a decade lifespan. It has been successfully employed in order to improve crowdsourced small coding tasks. On the contrary to other crowdsourcing platforms, participant seek to only provide source code solutions and crowd-base support. Moreover, the platform implements and optional requirement of a payment or charity donation as a form or reward, apart from regular monetary reward. Furthermore, it is open source, supports free access to all users or visitors, and utilizes a tag-based filter to store data. But most importantly, the platform focuses on hosting small crowdsourced tasks, that lack the cognitive requirement to belong to a large project [15]. For these reasons, Bountify was chosen for our research.

The current research effort is an extension to our previous work [30] based on the same platform but to an extended dataset. To further extend our initial work, this study aims at:

- *Extending* our research including monetary reward
- Indicating maximized reward crowdsourcing job opportunity trends for employees/developers
- Exploring minimized cost crowdsourcing opportunity trends for employers/crowdsourcers
- Associating crowdsourcing success, job skill and monetary rewards

The rest of the paper is structured as follows. In Sect. 2 reviews of the current related work regarding investigating trends in JavaScript small tasks are presented and in Sect. 3 the case study design we utilized to locate and analyze trends is described. The results of the statistical analysis process are presented in Sect. 4. Furthermore, in Sect. 5 we discuss the results, implications to researchers and practitioners, and present threats to validity of our research. The conclusion of the paper is presented in Sect. 6.

2 Related Work

Crowdsourcing software development has been a hot research topic in the last decade, concentrating the interest of the community. One of the first research efforts was conducted by Yuen et al. [28]. They performed a survey on crowdsourcing development models, resulting in the categorization of crowdsourcing types into four groups: application, algorithm, performance and dataset. On this basis, Hetmak [10] examined the nature of crowdsourcing systems as well as the typical design aspects, by conducting a systematic literature review. To a further extend, Alt et al. [1] after examining the concept of crowdsourcing, they designed and implemented a prototype crowdsourcing platform which incorporated the parameter of worker location in order to distribute tasks among the digital workers. To face task decomposition, in the prototype platform, small tasks of a project are being broadcasted to the crowd by placing open calls for solutions, concluding that as a concept, crowdsourcing can be feasible. Tong et al. [25] also focused on the crowdsourcing task decomposition problem. To achieve the minimal cost at a desired reliability level, they proposed a series of efficient approximation algorithms. The latter utilized a greedy strategy over an optimal priority queue data structure as to discover a near-optimal solution based on cost and time rather than skills.

Apart from prototype platforms or concepts, many research efforts focus on real time productive crowdsourcing platforms, with most notably the Amazon's Mechanical Turk micro-task market. Most notably, Kittur et al. [12] examined this platform as a potential paradigm for a) engaging many users, b) minimizing monetary costs and c) shortening time-to market. The results showed that there is a need for further research in order to determine effective techniques for both promoting useful user participation and ensuring overall effectiveness. On the same track, Weidema et al. [27] concluded that even though each small task in the crowdsourcing platforms can be considered of limited scope, several participant workers rate them as difficult to handle.

Apart from the task decomposition problem, another major issue that crowdsourcing faces is task allocation to the crowd. Many research efforts focus on the latter. In order to address the challenge of crowdsourcing to determine the most efficient allocation of small tasks to crowd workers, Boutsis et al. [4] proposed a prototype crowdsourcing system. To achieve the most efficient allocation, variables like worker skills and characteristics were taken into consideration. On the same track, Bibi et al [3] analyzed a plethora of worker characteristics including individual profiles, performance and competencies, with respect to the application domain of the crowdsourced task. Furthermore, Machado et al. [16] conducted an empirical study aiming at identifying the difficulty in tally stakeholder programming skills on specific domain tasks. However, Kittur et al. [13] indicated that there is a potential danger in cases of replacing some forms of skilled with unskilled labor in the task decomposition and allocation process. They concluded that, task assignment, in relation to each stakeholder's ability, is considered to be an important success factor for crowdsourcing labor economics, with an imminent effect on quality, efficiency, job satisfaction and overall cost [24].

Combining crowdsourcing and JavaScript is a research trend in the latest years, due to the fact that, JavaScript is one of the most popular programming languages today. Most notably, Gude et al [8] was one of the first to perform an empirical study on JavaScript feature utilization. Their work suggested possible future directions in the field. Moreover, Delcev et al. [6] performed a survey on frameworks, while recording trends in the emerging JavaScript web technologies. Furthermore, both Sun et al. [24] and Rauschmayer [20] explored both JavaScript development and researched current trends. In the same direction, Zozas et al. [30] explored trends in crowdsourcing small tasks developed in Javascript, aiming to associate domain functionality and JavaScript related technology and frameworks, in a large-scale study. The results showed that in general, JavaScript crowdsourced tasks are successful, and the expanded language ecosystem is not focused on a single technology but rather on a series of technologies, frameworks, and libraries that in most cases either overlap or complement each other. In the current study, we aim at extending our latter research effort to include, apart from success on trends, the monetary reward evaluation as to indicate trends in managing cost for both crowdsourcing employees and employers.

3 Case Study Design

In order to investigate empirically and detect possible trends in crowdsourcing JavaScript small tasks, we have performed a case study on 771 JavaScript coding tasks posted on Bountify platform between 2014–2021. The case study is performed according to the guidelines of Runeson et al [21].

3.1 Research Questions

Under the Runeson et al [21]. Guidelines, for the purpose of our research, we have formulated the following four research questions:

- **RQ1:** Which are the *JavaScript frameworks and technologies* mostly used by the crowdsourced tasks?

The purpose of this RQ is threefold: a) to identify trends regarding the development *frameworks* and the *technologies* (i.e., *programming languages)* when crowdsourcing JavaScript tasks, b) to research whether the *success* of JavaScript crowdsourced tasks presents significant differences with respect to the technologies and programming languages used, and finally c) to explore whether the *monetary reward* of the JavaScript crowdsourced tasks presents significant differences with respect to technologies and programming languages used.

- **RQ2:** Which *types of functionalities* do the crowdsourced tasks mostly implement?

The purpose of this RQ is also threefold, in the same principles as the previous: a) to identify trends related to the *functionalities* that are mostly implemented by the crowdsourced tasks and the *platforms* on which the tasks will operate (i.e., *operating systems, container applications-facebook, wordpress,* etc.) b) to research whether the *success* of JavaScript crowdsourced tasks presents significant differences with respect to the functionalities required and the platform with which they are related to, and finally c) to explore whether the *monetary reward* of the JavaScript crowdsourced tasks present significant differences with respect to the functionalities required and the platform with which they are related to.

- **RQ3:** Is there a correlation between the *JavaScript frameworks and technologies* used by the crowdsourced tasks and the *functionalities* implemented?

The goal of the third research question is to investigate the existence of significant correlations between *frameworks and technologies*, as well as *functionalities and platforms*. Furthermore, to identify trends on the combination of technologies with functionalities in successful crowdsourcing.

- **RQ4:** Is there a trend in the monetary reward between the correlated JavaScript *frameworks and technologies* and *functionalities* implemented?

In the fourth research question, we investigate whether there is a significant trend in the monetary reward of each microtask, between the correlated *frameworks and technologies*, as well as *functionalities and platforms*. Our goal is to identify monetary trends towards the correlation as investigated in the previous research question.

3.2 Data Collections and Units of Analysis

We have collected data from tasks posted for crowdsourcing in the Bountify platform during. For the purpose of our research, we have collected all tasks for the lifetime of the platform, covering the period from 2014 to January 2022. The collection process was performed with the use of a custom data crawler software developed by the second author, and is available online[1].

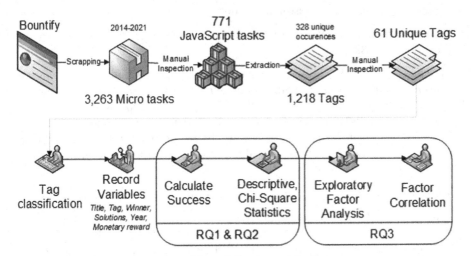

Fig. 1. Overview of Data Collection and Analysis process.

During the data collection process, we have collected a total of 3,263 tasks from the Bountify platform. A number of variables were recorded for each individual task, which were the following:

- *Title*
- *Tag*
- *Winner*
- *Number of solutions*
- *Year of announcement*
- *Monetary reward*

In the next step, we examined the tags and the titles of the tasks, and kept the tasks that included related keywords (i.e., js, javascript), in order to isolated tasks related to JavaScript technology. In order to ensure the accuracy of the results, this process was performed by two individual researchers of our team, resulting in a total sum of 771 tasks. In order to perform the statistical analysis, we applied a Boolean representation on each tasks targeting the appearance or absence of each tag to the task. Thus, a representation of 0 for absence and 1 for appearance. By this representation, a mathematical categorization of tags contained in tasks was possible. During this process, a total number of 328 individual tasks were identified among all 771 tasks. The users of the Bountify platform declare freely tags in every task they add, and as such, a large number of similar tags were traced concerning the same item (e.g., "node" and "nodejs", "angular" and "angularjs", etc.) or concerning different versions of an item (e.g., "boostrap" and "bootstrap-3"). Therefore, the methodology we performed to group these items is to manually inspect

---

[1] https://github.com/zozas/Bountify.

every record and summarize them. This process produced 61 individual tags. The latter occurred a total of 1,218 times in all tasks, as accordingly presented in the expanded Table 2. and Table 3. [30] to include monetary rewards.

Apart from the recorder variables, the additional variable *task success* was calculated, in order to indicate whether at least one winning contribution exists or not, for each task under study. Thus, this variable was calculated as Boolean. Under this scope, a posted task can be considered a successfully fulfilled task in each case it includes at least one winning contributor to it. As such, for each unique tag we have calculated the **success** percentage that is described in Eq. (1). According to the latter, N_{solved} is the total occurrences of the particular tag in the tasks that acquire at least one acceptable solution, and N_{total} is the total tag occurrences of the particular tag in all contests analyzed.

$$Success_\% = N_{solved}/N_{total} \tag{1}$$

The last step of the data collection process is tag classification. Four groups were formed in order to classify each tag: *frameworks* (JavaScript frameworks), *technologies (programming languages), functionalities* (i.e., visualization, data handling, security), and *platforms* (operating systems, container applications). An overview of the Data Collection and Analysis process, as presented, is presented in Fig. 1.

3.3 Data Analysis Methods

The applied methodology utilizes common statistical methods used by literature. In order to answer the first and second RQ, we have calculated standard descriptive statistics, *observations,* and *frequencies,* and performed a *chi-square* test [22]. Thus, we were able to determine whether each tag is associated with the *success* variable described by Eq. (1). Furthermore, we calculated the minimum, maximum and average monetary reward for each tag.

In order to answer the third RQ, Exploratory Factor Analysis (EFA) [22] was performed as to determine the underlying dimensionality of tags based on the correlation among each. EFA is a popular statistical approach used to examine the internal reliability of a measure and investigate the theoretical constructs, or factors, that might be represented by a set of items – in our case tags. For this purpose, we performed Principal Component Analysis (PCA) to decide the total number of factors. This methodology aims at discovering the factor structure of a measure, in order to examine the measure internal reliability, usually when no hypotheses exist about the nature of the underlying factor structure [22]. We followed the steps described in [22] as to perform EFA and subsequently determine the components of the related tags (in the context of the JavaScript crowdsourced development). The PCA factoring extraction was performed with the adaption of the Varimax rotation of the data. To determine the total number of factors, we only selected factors corresponding to an eigenvalue higher than 1. A cutoff value of 0.5 was applied to examine the commonality of each tag. As a result, concerning the cases where the cut-off value was lower than 0.5, the model was refitted. Apart from the above, to answer the third RQ, to explore potential correlations between the derived *frameworks and technologies* factors, and the *functionality and platform* factors, we have performed Spearman correlation.

Last but not least, to answer the last RQ, based on the previous results, we have calculated the average monetary reward for each component extracted during the PCA extraction process.

4 Results

4.1 Research Question 1

In this RQ we will identify which JavaScript frameworks and technologies (i.e., programming languages related to JavaScript) are mostly used in crowdsourced small tasks. Furthermore, we will research the success of these tasks. Last but not least, we will explore significant differences on the monetary reward of each task with respect to technologies and programming languages used. For this purpose, we analyzed the tags that are used by the contest providers to describe each crowdsourced task and define the skills required to address it. The expanded Table 1. [30] presents the frequency, the percentage frequency, and the success percentage for each tag identified along with the results of the chi-squared test performed for each tag and the *success* variable, including the minimum, maximum and average monetary reward based on the percentage frequency of each tag.

Concerning **frameworks and technologies**, a large diversity can be identified by the results for both client and server-side technologies. The most dominant development frameworks are *"jQuery"*, *"bootstrap"* and *"nodejs"*. We should mention that the *"jslibrary"* tag do not represent a single framework, rather than a merged group of frameworks. This merge occurred naturally during the tag frequency analysis process, in which we observed a large number of frameworks with low frequency (commonly single or twice appearance in the data set). This group include popular frameworks like Parsley.js, Popper.js, Chart.js, etc. Although the combined frequency of all these frameworks is high, each single frequency is too low compared to other tags. This is an indication of the wide diversity in framework usage in JavaScript development. This can be considered as a limitation to our research, and a possible future further analysis on larger datasets should indicate whether these libraries should be merged or not. Furthermore, an emphasis should be placed upon *"nodejs"* due to the fact that it supports server-side scripting in contrast to the majority of other frameworks.

Regarding **programming languages,** the most common languages featured in JavaScript development are *"css"*, *"html"* and *"php"* scripting languages, followed by *"json"*, *"ajax"* and *"xml"*. This list is a typical full-stack development toolset and under this scope, the findings are reasonable, due to the fact that many tasks are not implemented in any particular framework. The majority of the available JavaScript frameworks are oriented to directly manipulate the overall application output. The absence of framework usage in development requires relevant output formatting languages (as CSS, HTML) to be incorporated. Furthermore, the JavaScript interoperability with other full-stack development programming languages, *"php"* is the most prominent, followed by "ruby", *"python"* and *"java"*. Furthermore, an interesting outcome is that concerning data manipulation, *"json"* and *"xml"* are the most common technologies used for data retrieval.

Table 1. JavaScript Frameworks & Technologies tags.

Framework	N	%	Success	χ^2	p_{05}	Monetary Reward		
						Min	Max	Avg
jquery	182	23.61	96.70	1.93	0.16	1	100	25.08
bootstrap	79	10.25	94.94	0.01	0.91	1	100	**36.58**
jslibrary	61	7.91	93.44	0.20	0.65	1	100	22.57
nodejs	42	5.45	83.33	11.36	**0.01**	1	100	21.19
angular	20	2.59	85.00	3.82	0.05	1	100	**29.10**
react	18	2.33	83.33	4.71	**0.03**	1	50	23.44
meteor	12	1.56	91.67	0.22	0.63	1	100	19.25
typescript	9	1.17	77.77	5.16	**0.02**	1	50	22.33
vue	7	0.91	100	0.39	0.52	1	100	**45.85**
Languages	N	%	Success	χ^2	p_{05}	Monetary Reward		
						Min	Max	Avg
css	123	15.95	93.50	0.40	0.52	1	100	26.13
html	108	14.01	94.44	0.01	0.90	1	100	23.87
php	37	4.80	86.49	5.18	**0.02**	1	100	30.89
json	27	3.50	92.59	0.24	0.62	1	100	20.81
ajax	14	1.82	92.86	0.09	0.75	1	100	**36.50**
xml	9	1.17	100	0.51	0.47	**5**	100	19.44
ruby	8	1.04	77.78	6.22	**0.01**	1	100	20.50
python	7	0.91	100	0.39	0.52	1	100	23.00
java	5	0.65	60.00	12.02	**0.01**	1	100	**40.40**
perl	3	0.39	100	0.16	0.68	**10**	100	**45.00**
c	2	0.26	100	0.11	0.73	1	1	1.00

On the success rate, tasks related to the tag *"typescript"*, *"jquery"* and *"bootstrap"* present a higher percentage of success. Tasks implemented in *"nodejs"*, *"react"* and *"angular.js"* present also high success rate. It is clear that the least successful tasks are concerning programming languages, related to *"ruby"* and *"python"*, and for frameworks *"vue.js"*. To further examine whether the tasks implemented in the various frameworks and technologies present a significant difference with respect to *success*, a chi-square test was conducted between each individual related tag and the success variable. We calculated a χ^2 value with an asymptotic 2-sided significance p-value over 0.05 for most tasks. However few frameworks present a significant difference with respect to *success*. These include concerning **frameworks and technologies** *"nodejs"*, *"react"* and *"typescript"*, while concerning **programming languages** *"php"*, *"ruby"* and *"java"*.

We conclude that there are no significant differences in success percentages of the tasks regardless of the frameworks and programming languages.

Regarding the monetary reward, all tags have a minimum reward of 1 while "*xml*" is 5. However, the size of tasks for "*xml*" is too low compared to the dataset to support a differentiation. As for the maximum reward, all tasks present 100 while "*react*" and "*typescript*" present 50. In the case of "*typescript*" the data size is too low. However, concerning "*react*" is considerable. On the average reward, concerning **frameworks and technologies,** we cannot conclude that "*vue*" has the maximum average since the population of task is too small. On the other hand, "*bootstrap*" and "*angular*" are the highest rewarded tasks, while "*meteor*" and "*nodejs*" are the least. Concerning **programming languages**, all tags have a minimum reward of 1 and a maximum of 100, with the exception of "*xml*", "*perl*" and "*c*". In the case of the latter two, as previously mentioned, the dataset is too small to support evidence for a trend. On the average reward, the same thing applied for "*java*" and "*perl*". Thus "*ajax*" and "*php*" are among the top rewarded tags, while "*xml*", "*json*" and "*ruby*" the least.

In summary, Fig. 2 presents the 10 most frequently appearing framework and technology tags for the time period 2012 to 2020. On the popularity, a large shift in framework utilization is presented where *jQuery* which was a dominant framework until 2010 decreases, while *React* is increasing. The overall task posting on the platform peaked in 2013, and since then, follows a decreasing trend.

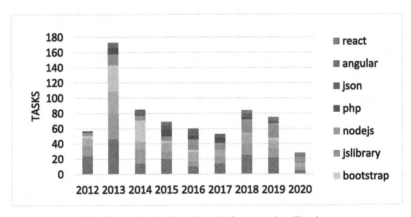

Fig. 2. Analysis of small tasks framework utilization.

In Fig. 3 we observe the average reward of each tag compared to the total mean of the group. The majority of the tags tend to be lower than the average 47.46.

4.2 Research Question 2

In the same direction as the previous RQ, we will first identify which applications and the functionalities are mostly used in crowdsourced small tasks. The next step is to explore whether the task success, as described previously, presents significant differences within each type of functionality, application, and platform. The tag descriptive statistics results

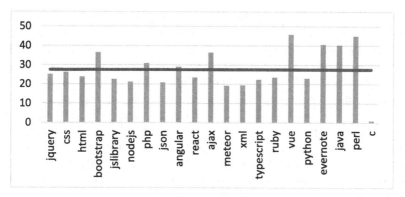

Fig. 3. Frameworks and Languages tag monetary reward and mean.

as well as the results of the chi-square tests are presented in the expanded Table 2. [30]. Furthermore, in Fig. 4 we present the 10 most frequent platform and functionality tags from 2012 to 2020.

Regarding **platforms and applications**, *"wordpress"* is the dominant content management platform, as expected, as today holds the largest market share against other content management systems (*"cms"*) observed. In the case of service providers, *"google"* is the dominant platform. On the contrary, there is a limited demand for tasks related to operating systems, which include the related tags *"windows"*, *"linux"*, *"android"* and *"ios"*, a case that might explain the latest shift towards the cloud computing paradigm, where Software-as-a-Service operational models override the client operating system [22]. As for the case of **core functionality**, the dominant functionality is visual representation by grouping the related tags *"layout"*, *"canvas"*, *"image"*, *"design"*, and *"table"*. Even though JavaScript frameworks are included in the dataset, like "wordpress", a large number of contests do not include any framework for the task. For this reason, visual representation tags as *"layout"*, *"canvas"*, *"image"*, *"design"*, and *"table"*, score high frequencies, and tags like *"graphics"* present low number of tags. We can observe another significant tag group related to logic supporting web development, including tags *"algorithms"* and *"regex"* (regular expressions) with a noticeable frequency. Furthermore, another group with high frequency is e-commerce related, including tags like *"epayments"*, *"sales"* and *"form"*. This group indicates that on the one hand, JavaScript client-side technologies are applied in order to minimize data transitions from clients to servers, ensuring both safety and data privacy, as well as an intense interest in e-commerce applications and digital money.

Last but not least, Fig. 4 presents the demand for specific functionalities and applications over years. This demand does not remain stable, showing that the most popular tags, present a declining trend as new tags appear over the years and concentrate higher popularity (i.e., the *"responsive"* which refers to web representation on mobile devices).

Regarding the monetary reward, the data show a shift compared to the results of the previous RQ. While the majority hold a minimum reward of 1 and a maximum of 100, there are significant differences. In the case of **platforms and applications**, "evernote", "excel" tend to have higher minimum rewards, by taking notice and the higher frequency of these tags, while *"android"*, *"youtube"*, *"web"* and *"videogame"* have the lowest maximum. As for **core functionality**, the minimum reward presents a uniformity while the top 6 most popular tags have the same maximum reward. In the case of the least popular, the maximum reward varies and tends to be lower. As an example, *"analytics"*, *"geolocation"*, *"api"* and *"audio"* have maximum reward as low as 25.

Concerning the average monetary reward, in the case of **platforms and applications**, "evernote", "mobile" and "google" are the most rewarding tasks. The tag *"twitter"* presents a high reward but we cannot take it into notice since there is only one appearance in the data list. On the contrary, *"android"*, *"facebook"* and *"web"* present a low reward. In the case of *"android"*, the maximum reward is quite low compared to other tags (10,00) while the average reward is even lower (6.14). Comparing to *"ios"* there is a huge difference, by taking into considerations that both tags present a similar frequency in the dataset. Either there is low demand for android developers or employee offering is large enough to lower the total reward. As for **core functionality**, tags related to e-commerce (including *"epayments"*, *"form"*, *"regex"*, *"sales"*) tend to have the highest rewards compared to visual representation (including *"design"*, *"responsive"*, *"layout"*, *"canvas"*) which has the lowest. Tags *"graphics"* and *"audio"* present the lowest average reward, depicting a low demand for artistic skills.

Table 2. Tags analysis.

Monetary Reward								
Platform & Application	N	%	Success	χ^2	P .05	Min	Max	Avg
wordpress	24	3.11	91.7	0.44	0.50	1	100	28.91
google	23	2.98	91.3	0.53	0.46	1	100	**33.26**
browser	14	1.82	92.9	0.09	0.75	1	100	30.50
cms	11	1.43	81.8	3.66	0.05	1	100	25.63
mobile	10	1.30	90.0	0.44	0.50	1	100	**35.00**
android	7	0.91	85.7	1.12	0.28	1	**10**	6.14
evernote	7	0.91	100	0.39	0.52	**5**	100	**40.71**
facebook	6	0.78	100	0.34	0.56	**5**	100	23.33
ios	6	0.78	83.3	1.54	0.21	1	100	28.66
excel	6	0.78	100	0.34	0.56	**5**	100	29.16
youtube	5	0.65	100	0.28	0.59	1	**50**	33.00
linux	5	0.65	80.0	2.15	0.14	**10**	100	31.00
web	5	0.65	80.0	2.15	0.14	**5**	**50**	20.00

(continued)

Table 2. (*continued*)

Monetary Reward

Platform & Application	N	%	Success	χ^2	p .05	Min	Max	Avg
videogame	4	0.52	100	0.22	0.63	1	**50**	26.50
pdf	3	0.39	100	0.16	0.68	10	100	40.00
windows	3	0.39	66.6	4.69	**0.03**	10	**25**	15.00
twitter	1	0.13	100	0.05	0.81	100	100	100.00

Monetary Reward

Core functionality	N	%	Success	χ^2	p .05	Min	Max	Avg
layout	34	4.41	100	1.99	0.15	1	100	24.20
canvas	26	3.37	96.2	0.11	0.73	1	100	22.00
database	24	3.11	83.3	6.33	**0.01**	1	100	32.16
image	21	2.72	90.5	0.75	0.38	1	100	30.38
epayments	19	2.46	94.7	0.00	0.99	1	100	**36.89**
form	16	2.08	93.8	0.02	0.86	1	100	**36.31**
design	15	1.95	93.3	0.05	0.81	1	**50**	16.86
table	14	1.82	100	0.80	0.37	1	100	30.50
algorithm	18	2.33	83.3	4.71	**0.03**	1	100	30.88
regex	21	2.72	100	1.21	0.27	1	100	**36.71**
video	12	1.56	100	0.68	0.08	1	100	14.83
security	10	1.30	90.0	0.44	0.50	1	**50**	18.20
analytics	9	1.17	100	0.51	0.47	1	**25**	13.55
geolocation	8	1.04	75.00	6.22	**0.01**	1	**25**	12.00
responsive	8	1.04	100	0.45	0.50	1	**50**	11.00
sales	8	1.04	87.5	0.82	0.36	1	100	**45.75**
api	7	0.91	100	0.39	0.52	**5**	**25**	14.28
audio	7	0.91	100	0.39	0.52	1	**25**	6.28
messaging	7	0.91	71.4	7.58	**0.00**	**5**	100	**52.14**
datatransfer	6	0.78	100	0.34	0.56	1	**50**	27.66
graphics	6	0.78	100	0.34	0.56	1	**25**	8.50
performance	5	0.65	100	0.28	0.59	**5**	100	33.00
mail	4	0.52	100	0.22	0.63	**10**	100	36.25

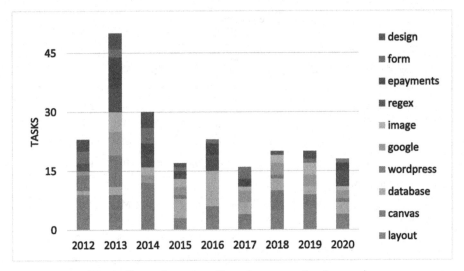

Fig. 4. Comparison of top 10 tag frequency of each category.

Furthermore, in Fig. 5 we observe the average reward of each tag compared to the total mean of the group. As in the previous research question, the average mean monetary reward is 28.14, and the majority of the tags tend to be lower than the average.

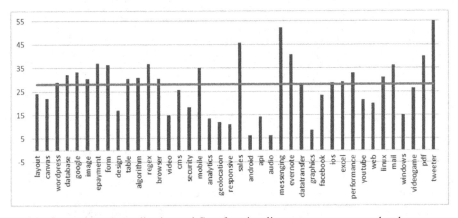

Fig. 5. Platform & Application and Core functionality tag monetary reward and mean.

4.3 Research Question 3

To identify trends on the combination of technologies with functionalities in successful crowdsourcing, we focus on forming components of related tags based on one hand on different platforms, frameworks and technologies, and on the other, on different

Table 3. Frameworks and Technologies factor analysis.

Component	Initial Eigenvalues			Success %	Monetary Reward	Tags
	Total	% Variance	Cumulative %			
1	1.76	8.39	8.39	100	23.00	python, perl, c
2	1.60	7.62	16.01	94.3	20.13	xml, json
3	1.48	7.06	23.08	93.3	30.14	html, css, java
4	1.42	6.77	29.86	85.4	20.22	nodejs, meteor
5	1.29	6.14	36.00	87.0	22.89	react, typescript
6	1.19	5.69	41.70	89.4	28.35	perl, c, php, ajax
7	1.18	5.65	47.35	95.6	32.79	bootstrap, jquery, angular, java
8	1.06	5.08	52.44	87.8	22.53	c,ajax, ruby, angular
9	1.02	4.89	57.33	91.5	36.28	jslibrary, java, vue

applications and functionalities implemented. The last step of this process is to examine if the formed components are correlated.

The expanded Table 3. [30] presents the components formed based on the *JavaScript frameworks and technologies* group including the related *success* percentage for each. As each component includes several tags, the calculation of the success percentage is based on the mean of cumulative success rates of each task containing at least the corresponding tag. The tag inclusion in each task is based on the process described in Sect. 3.2, while the success percentage is calculated according to Eq. (1). In the case of multiple tags for a task, for each tag, success is calculated based on the success task in which it is included. Furthermore, the expanded Table 3. includes the mean monetary reward for the group of tags on each component.

The components presented in Table 3. [30] are in descending order of importance. The latter is based on the percentage of the explained variance. A total variance of 57.3% is identified among the total 9 components, with each eigenvalue consisting of one to four tags. The Kaiser-Meyer-Olkin (KMO) measure of sampling adequacy scored 0.521, while all sampling adequacies were above the commonly recommended value of 0.5. The Bartlett's test of sphericity was statistically significant scoring $x^2(210) = 1,046.96$ for $p < 0.001$. All eigenvalues score high on success with a rate over 87%. The extracted factors revealed highly related as well as distinguishable frameworks and technologies tags, found in tasks.

On the monetary reward, components 3 (*"html"*, *"css"*, *"java"*), 7 (*"bootstrap"*, *"jquery"*, *"angular"*, *"java"*) and 9 (*"jslibrary"*, *"java"*, *"vue"*) present high average reward over 30, mostly as *"java"* and *"perl"* tags, as presented also in Table 1. [30]. The components with the lowest average reward are 2 (*"xml"*, *"json"*) and 4 (*"nodejs"*, *"meteor"*), including mostly framework-related or core data manipulation operations.

Table 4. Functionalities factor analysis.

Component	Initial Eigenvalues			Success %	Monetary Reward	Tags
	Total	% Variance	Cumulative %			
1	2.44	6.11	6.11	93.3	30.50	table, browser
2	1.88	4.70	10.81	94.1	20.20	windows, linux, android, ios
3	1.62	4.05	14.86	93.8	13.93	design, responsive
4	1.47	3.68	18.54	91.3	25.49	android, datatransfer mobile, ios
5	1.41	3.52	22.07	98.0	29.90	layout, excel, form
6	1.37	3.44	25.52	89.5	32.04	sales, database, security
7	1.32	3.31	28.83	92.6	23.77	google, api
8	1.30	3.25	32.09	87.5	22.22	analytics, algorithm
9	1.23	3.09	35.18	100	18.60	api, performance, graphics
10	1.21	3.03	38.22	100	29.79	facebook, mail
11	1.20	3.01	41.23	94.7	68.45	tweeter, epayments
12	1.15	2.88	44.12	100	17.50	videogame, graphics
13	1.14	2.85	46.97	96.1	18.45	layout, image, youtube, canvas
14	1.12	2.82	49.79	90.3	30.65	mobile, ios, security, evernote
15	1.08	2.70	52.50	82.4	38.89	messaging, cms

(*continued*)

Table 4. (*continued*)

Component	Initial Eigenvalues			Success %	Monetary Reward	Tags
	Total	% Variance	Cumulative %			
16	1.05	2.64	55.14	85.7	16.00	web, geolocation
17	1.02	2.56	57.70	95.6	32.82	wordpress, regex
18	1.01	2.52	60.23	100	14.83	video
19	1.00	2.51	62.74	100	21.50	regex, audio
20	1.00	2.50	65.25	100	40.00	pdf

The results of the performed PCA analysis in order to identify factors based on the types of functionalities and applications implemented, are presented in the expanded Table 4. [30], including the mean monetary reward for the group of tags on each component. A total variance of 65.26% is identified among the total 20 components, with each eigenvalue consisting of one to four tags. On these results, the KMO measure of sampling adequacy on the *Functionalities* is 0.527. All sampling adequacies present values above the recommended which is 0.5. The Bartlett's test of sphericity is statistically significant $x^2(780) = 3,499.98$ for $p < 0.001$. Moreover, all eigenvalues score high on success over 82%.

On the monetary reward, component 11 related to e-commerce (*"tweeter"*, *"epayments"*) appear to have by far the highest average reward, followed by 15 (*"messaging"*, *"cms"*). Component 20 should not be taking into consideration, as component 18, since they are composed out of one tag, and the freqauency into the database is low. On the other hand, component 3 (*"design"*, *"responsive"*) hase the lowest average reward.

In order to identify significant correlations between the above derived components on *framework/technology*, and *functionality/application*, we performed a correlation analysis between the latter. The results of this analysis are presented in Table 5. [30]. The Spearman's rho coefficient for $p < 0.001$ indicates statistical significance, and the results are presented in Table 5. [30]. A total of twenty statistically significant correlations are revealed. By examining the statistically significant correlated from the previous table, the most interesting findings are the following:

- C1.1 component (*"python"*, *"perl"*, *"c"*)

  - Out of the framework and technology dataset, it is the most correlated component, currently presenting association with 6 functionality and application components. These three programming languages appear to be used as a supplementary option to JavaScript, in order to perform a variety of functionalities related to operating systems components. These include components C2.1 (*"table"*, *"browser"*), C2.2 (*"windows"*, *"linux"*, *"android"*, *"ios"*), regular expressions component C2.17

Table 5. Tag component correlation analysis.

JavaScript Frameworks and Technologies		Functionalities		rho	Success %
C1	Tags	C2	Tags		
9	jslibrary, java, vue	13	layout, image, youtube, canvas	.287	95.0
6	perl, c, php, ajax	6	sales, database, security	.241	90.4
4	nodejs, meteor	6	sales, database, security	.214	86.6
5	react, typescript	8	analytics, algorithm	.214	86.0
4	nodejs, meteor	2	windows, linux, android, ios	.187	87.9
5	react, typescript	1	table, browser	.187	91.1
1	python, perl, c	20	pdf	.186	100
2	xml, json, evernote	14	mobile, ios, security, evernote	.179	91.5
1	python, perl, c	19	regex, audio	.173	100
1	python, perl, c	2	windows, linux, android, ios	.152	95.6
4	nodejs, meteor	14	mobile, ios, security, evernote	.138	87.5
5	react, typescript	13	layout, image, youtube, canvas	.138	94.3
1	python, perl, c	17	wordpress, regex	.128	96.0
1	python, perl, c	4	android, mobile, datatransfer, ios	.124	93.3
7	bootstrap, java, jquery, angular	19	regex, audio	-.113	95.9
4	nodejs, meteor	4	android, mobile, datatransfer, ios	.112	87.8
5	react, typescript	4	android, mobile, datatransfer, ios	.112	88.1
4	nodejs, meteor	15	messaging, cms	.107	86.8
5	react, typescript	14	mobile, ios, security, evernote	.107	87.7
3	html, css, java	19	regex, audio	-.106	94.1

(continued)

Table 5. (*continued*)

JavaScript Frameworks and Technologies		Functionalities		rho	Success %
C1	Tags	C2	Tags		
8	c, ajax, ruby, angular	6	sales, database, security	.105	89.0
1	python, perl, c	14	mobile, ios, security, evernote	.100	92.1
6	perl, c, php, ajax	7	google, api	.099	89.8
7	bootstrap, java, jquery, angular	14	mobile, ios, security, evernote	-.096	94.9

$P < 0.001$, C for Component

> ("*wordpress*", "*regex*") and mobile data transferring and security handling components C2.4 ("*android*", "*mobile*", "*datatransfer*", "*ios*") and C2.14 ("*mobile*", "*ios*", "*security*", "*evernote*")

- C1.4 ("*nodejs*", "*meteor*") and C1.5 ("*react, "typescript*") components

  - Both components are correlated to the mobile data transfer functionalities component C2.4 ("*android*", "*mobile*", "*datatransfer*", "*ios*"). Furthermore, C1.4 ("*nodejs*", "*meteor*") is correlated to back-office operations component C2.6 ("*sales*", "*database*", "*security*") and content management component C2.15("*messaging*", "*cms*").

- C1.5 component ("*react*", "*typescript*")

  - The component is also apart from the prementioned, related to both user interface functionalities components C2.1 ("*table*", "*browser*") and C2.13 ("*layout*", "*image*", "*youtube*", "*canvas*"), as well as to more demanding tasks related to analytics and algorithms component C2.8 ("*analytics*", "*algorithm*").

- C1.6 component ("*perl*", "*c*", "*php*", "*ajax*")

  - The component correlates to back-office functionalities component C2.6 ("*sales*", "*database*", "*security*") and functionalities related to the interaction with external sources component C2.7 ("*google*", "*api*").

- C1.7 component ("*bootstrap*", "*java*", "*jquery*", "*angular*")

  - The current component correlates to functionalities components related to regular expressions (including the tag "*regex*").

- All correlations are over 84% *successful*. This indicated that the majority of the contests in the dataset, which are related to the technologies and functionalities and include these components, have managed to acquire at least one winning solution. More specifically, in the case of the combination of components C1.1 (*"perl"*, *"python"*, *"c"*) with C2.17 (*"regex"*, *"audio"*) or C2.20 (*"pdf"*), a 100% *success* rate is indicated.

4.4 Research Question 4

In this last RQ, we will investigate whether there is a significant trend in the monetary reward of each microtask, between the correlated *frameworks and technologies*, as well as *functionalities and platforms*. For this reason, for each correlated component formed in the previous RQ, we calculated the average monetary reward in order to compare between. The expanded Table 6. [30] presents the results of the monetary reward of each component, from highest to lowest.

By examining the results from the previous table, the most interesting findings are the following:

- C2.2 component (*"windows"*, *"linux"*)

  - More rewarding functionalities component is C1.4 (*"nodejs"*, *"meteor"*) rather than C1.1 (*"python"*, *"perl"*, *"c"*).

- C2.4 component (*"android"*, *"mobile"*, *"datatransfer"*, *"ios"*)

  - Both C1.1 (*"python"*, *"perl"*, *"c"*) and C.1.5 (*"react"*, *"typescript"*) prove to be equal rewarding.

- C2.6 component (*"sales"*, *"database"*, *"security"*)

  - Component C1.8 (*"c"*, *"ajax"*, *"ruby"*, *"angular"*) is the most rewarding component.

- C2.13 component (*"layout"*, *"image"*, *"youtube"*, *"canvas"*)

  - Component C1.5 (*"react"*, *"typescript"*) tend to be more rewarding towards C1.9 (*"jslibrary"*, *"java"*, *"vue"*). We should mention that in the case of C1.9, it includes the grouped tag *"jslibrary"*. A possible split to further frameworks with lower frequencies in the dataset will increase dramatically this difference.

- C2.14 component (*"mobile"*, *"ios"*, *"security"*, *"evernote"*)

  o Both C1.1 (*"python"*, *"perl"*, *"c"*) and C.1.5 (*"react"*, *"typescript"*) prove to be equal rewarding.

- C2.19 component (*"regex"*, *"audio"*)

  - C1.1 (*"python"*, *"perl"*, *"c"*) tends to be more rewarding than C.1.7 (*"bootstrap"*, *"java"*, *"jquery"*, *"angular"*).

Table 6. Tag component correlation cost.

JavaScript Frameworks and Technologies		Functionalities		Average Monetary Reward
C1	Tags	C2	Tags	
1	python, perl, c	20	pdf	43.18
1	python, perl, c	14	mobile, ios, security, evernote	40.89
5	react, typescript	14	mobile, ios, security, evernote	40.84
1	python, perl, c	2	windows, linux, android, ios	39.45
2	xml, json, evernote	14	mobile, ios, security, evernote	36.83
5	react, typescript	1	table, browser	36.55
5	react, typescript	4	android, mobile, datatransfer, ios	35.78
1	python, perl, c	4	android, mobile, datatransfer, ios	35.32
5	react, typescript	8	analytics, algorithm	34.24
8	c, ajax, ruby, angular	6	sales, database, security	33.94
4	nodejs, meteor	14	mobile, ios, security, evernote	33.21
4	nodejs, meteor	2	windows, linux, android, ios	30.84
4	nodejs, meteor	4	android, mobile, datatransfer, ios	29.48
1	python, perl, c	19	regex, audio	28.88
4	nodejs, meteor	6	sales, database, security	27.42
4	nodejs, meteor	15	messaging, cms	27.30
7	bootstrap, java, jquery, angular	14	mobile, ios, security, evernote	26.49
5	react, typescript	13	layout, image, youtube, canvas	25.19
7	bootstrap, java, jquery, angular	19	regex, audio	24.47

(continued)

Table 6. (*continued*)

JavaScript Frameworks and Technologies		Functionalities		Average Monetary Reward
C1	Tags	C2	Tags	
6	perl, c, php, ajax	7	google, api	22.65
6	perl, c, php, ajax	6	sales, database, security	22.20
1	python, perl, c	17	wordpress, regex	21.69
9	jslibrary, java, vue	13	layout, image, youtube, canvas	21.24
3	html, css, java	19	regex, audio	18.96

5 Discussion

5.1 Interpretations of Results

Based on the above results, we are able to identify several trends concerning crowd-sourcing JavaScript micro-tasks. In Sect. 4.1 (*frameworks and* technologies), *Node.JS* and *Meteor* technologies are widely used for crowdsourcing a variety of tasks, with most notably *business* and *data-oriented* tasks on several platforms, as well as *mobile deployment* and *security-related* tasks. *React* and *TypeScript* technologies are also used in *multiple platform development*, but emphasize more in *layout and user interface* micro-tasks. *Python, Perl* and *C* languages are often utilized supplementary with JavaScript for development, in order to handle tasks related to *operating systems* and for *regular expression manipulation*.

In Sect. 4.2 (*functionalities and applications*), tasks related to *mobile applications* and *security* are more frequent and are being implemented by applying a disperse variety of technologies. These may include other programming languages (e.g., *Python*), frameworks (e.g., *React, Bootstrap*) and data distribution technologies (e.g., *XML, JSON*). *Sales transactions, database manipulation* and *security tasks* rely on server-side technologies (e.g., *Node.JS, Meteor*), and other programming languages in conjunction with JavaScript (e.g., *C, PHP*). In the latter case, we should mention that these technologies also pose a trend in mobile data operations as well as mobile platforms, with most notably *Android*. Furthermore, concerning mobile platform development, in the case of *Android*, most preferred JavaScript technologies are *Node.JS, Meteor, React,* and *TypeScript*, while for *iOS*, are *Bootstrap, jQuery,* and *Angular*.

In Sect. 4.3 we conclude that the expanded eco-system of JavaScript crowdsourced micro-tasks is not focused on a single technology but rather on a series of technologies, frameworks, and libraries. These, in most cases, either overlap or complement each other. Moreover, JavaScript micro-tasks are related to the implementation of a variety of functionalities. Most successful of the latter are *user-interface handling, layout tasks,* and *regular expression manipulation*. These tasks can be considered small and light-weight. Concerning tasks that are more demanding in the sense that they require more specialized skills (e.g., *operating systems, business logic,* and *algorithms*), these tend to present lower success percentages than light-weight, but still above 80% in most of the cases.

In Sect. 4.4 we examine all tasks in relation to the monetary reward. Interesting indications can be extracted in the case of combining the above prementioned task success with the reward perspective. *Python, Perl* and *C,* tend to be the most rewarding technologies that accompany JavaScript development, either for desktop or *mobile* environments. However, in the case of desktop development, *NodeJS* and *Meteor* tend to be more successful. Furthermore, a variety of JavaScript libraries and frameworks are applied in low frequencies each, but high when grouping into a single tag, indicating the high dispersion in the JavaScript framework eco-system. In the case of *user-interface handling* tasks, *React* and *TypeScript* are the most rewarding. In combination to the previous research question, these technologies are also among the most successful. Specifically for mobile development, the prementioned technologies tend to be equal popular and rewarding. Last but not least, concerning *business logic* and *sales* related tags, which presented a lower success rate, most rewarding technologies tend to be *Angular.* The latter in most cases is included in the highest rewarding tasks with the most success. On the opposite of the above, *Java* is included mostly in successful tags with low rewards.

5.2 Implications to Researchers and Practitioners

Both researchers and practitioners can benefit from the results of the current study. The findings of our study indicate that crowdsourcing JavaScript small tasks, can be successful at high rate, since out of all the contests examined, the majority of them acquire at least one winning solution. This is an indication that *researchers* can work on models concerning the decomposition of large JavaScript applications, into a series of small tasks, in order to be easily crowdsourced, with high rate of success at a minimal cost. An indication for the need of new frameworks or libraries, is presented in Table 5. [30], where JavaScript functionalities like audio and video handling, or regular expression manipulation, are crowdsourced in combination to a variety of both frameworks as well as programming languages.

Crowdsourcing has been a popular research topic in the last decade. However, most research efforts focus on the Amazon Mechanical Turk crowdsourcing platform [12]. A future replication of our study, including alternative or different crowdsourcing platforms, contributors, tasks and employers could further reveal trends in JavaScript frameworks, technologies and functionalities. Regarding *Practitioners*, the current findings indirectly indicate industrial demands on skills. Professionals may benefit from the job market demands by acquiring corresponding skills that correspond to present and future industry demands.

5.3 Threats to Validity

To this point, we will discuss the threats to validity identified in this study, based on the categorization of Runeson et al. [21].

Regarding Construct Validity, we need to mention that the outcome of the overall findings may be affected by the described metrics we apply in this study, as well as the tags of each small task we collected. Moreover, the evaluation of alternative metrics to the ones presented in the current research should be included in the future. Candidate metrics to be included may be workforce characteristics, experience, skills, past behavior or participation, as well as trends in JavaScript development technologies [18].

Regarding Internal Validity, the purpose of our research is to detect trends. Our study attempts to solely detect trends. For this reason, we cannot claim that the current findings present any form of causality.

Regarding Reliability, in Sect. 3 we have presented a detailed process which we followed in order for anyone to easily reproduce our research. The presented Case Study Design is fully documented and we believe that a future replication of the study is safe, and the reliability is ensured.

Regarding External Validity, there may occur changes or alternations in future findings, in cases of alternative data sets or alternative platforms. A future replication of the current study would be valuable in order to be able to verify the findings of our research, as well as to support the generalizability supposition.

6 Conclusions

In the current study, we explored trends in crowdsourcing JavaScript small tasks. We aim to associate domain functionality with JavaScript related technologies and frameworks, under the scope of both task completion success and monetary reward. We have analyzed 771 small tasks crowdsourced and hosted in the Bountify platform. The results show that the majority of the tasks are successful but the monetary reward differs based on domain functionality and technologies incorporated. A series of frameworks (*jQuery, Bootstrap, Node.JS*) and languages (*HTML, CSS, XML*) are employed for implementing tasks related to visualization (*user interfaces, layout*), data manipulation (*security, databases, algorithms*) and platform deployment (*iOS, Windows, Android*). Frameworks and languages result in high monetary reward and success, but frameworks tend to be more popular. Both visualization and data manipulation result in high popularity and success but lower monetary reward, while platform deployment results in higher rewards but low popularity and success. The expanded ecosystem of JS crowdsourced microtasks is focused on a series of technologies, frameworks, and libraries that in most cases either overlap or complement each other. However, the popularity and success of the associate domain functionality or technologies in many cases, do not share the same monetary reward, and are not associated.

References

1. Alt, F., Shirazi, A., Schmidt, A., Kramer, U., Nawaz, Z.: Location-based crowdsourcing: extending crowdsourcing to the real world. In: 6th Nordic Conf. on Human-Computer Interaction, Association for Computing Machinery, NY, USA, pp. 13–22 (2010)
2. Archak, N.: Money, glory and cheap talk: Analyzing strategic behavior of contestants in simultaneous crowdsourcing contests on TopCoder.com. In: 19th International Conference on WWW, NY, USA, pp. 21–30 (2010)
3. Bibi, S., Zozas, I., Ampatzoglou, A., Sarigiannidis, P.G., Kalampokis, G., Stamelos, I.: Crowdsourcing in software development. IEEE Access **8**, 58094–58117 (2020)

4. Boutsis, I., Kalogeraki, V.: On task assignment for real-time reliable crowdsourcing. In: IEEE 34th International Conference on Distributed Computing Systems, Spain, pp. 1–10 (2014)
5. Chatzimparmpas, A., Bibi, S., Zozas, I., Kerren, A.: Analyzing the evolution of javascript applications. In: 14th International Conference on Evaluation of Novel Approaches to Software Engineering, vol. 1, pp. 359–366 (2019)
6. Delcev, S., Draskovic, D.: Modern javascript frameworks: a survey study. In: Zooming Innovation in Consumer Technologies Conference, Serbia, pp. 106–109 (2018)
7. Difallah, D., Catasta, M., Demartini, G., Ipeirotis, P., Cudré-Mauroux, P.: The dynamics of micro-task crowdsourcing: the case of Amazon MTurk. In: 24th International Conference on WWW, Switzerland, pp. 238–247 (2015)
8. Gude, S., Hafiz, M., Wirfs-Brock, A.: JavaScript: the used parts. In: IEEE 38th Annual Computer Software and Applications Conference, Sweden, pp. 466–475, (2014)
9. Guittard, C., Schenk, E., Burger-, T.: Crowdsourcing and the evolution of a business ecosystem. In: Garrigos, F.J., Gil-, I., Estelles, S. (eds.) Advances in Crowdsourcing, pp. 49–62. Springer, Cham (2015). https://doi.org/10.1007/978-3-319-18341-1_4
10. Hetmank, L.: Components and functions of crowdsourcing systems – a systematic literature review. In: Wirtschaftsinformatik Proceedings, vol. 4 (2013)
11. 1061–1998: IEEE Standard for a Software Quality Metrics Methodology, IEEE Standards, IEEE Computer Society, 31 December 1998 (reaf. 9 December 2009), (Accessed 21 July 2022)
12. Kittur, A., Chi, E., Suh, B.: Crowdsourcing user studies with Mechanical Turk. In: Conference on Human Factors in Computing Systems, NY, USA, pp. 453–456 (2008)
13. Kittur, A., et al.: The future of crowd work. Conference on Computer supported cooperative work, pp. 1301–1318. Association for Computing Machinery, NY, USA (2013)
14. Lakhani, K., Garvin, D., Lonstein, E.: TopCoder(A): Developing software through crowdsourcing. Harvard Business School Case (2010)
15. LaToza, T., Van der Hoek, A.: Crowdsourcing in software engineering: models, motivations, and challenges, IEEE Softw. 33(1), 74–80 (2016)
16. Machado, M., Zanatta, A., Marczack, S., Prikladnicki, R.: The good, the bad and the ugly: an onboard journey in software crowdsourcing competitive model. In: 4th International Workshop on Crowd Sourcing in Software Engineering, Buenos Aires, Argentina, pp. 2–8 (2017)
17. Mao, K., Capra, L., Harman, M., Jia, Y.: A survey of the use of crowdsourcing in software engineering. J. Syst. Softw. 126, 57–84 (2017)
18. Meldrum, S., Licorish, S., Savarimuthu, B. Crowdsourced knowledge on stack overflow. In: 21st International Conference on Evaluation and Assessment in Software Engineering. Association for Computing Machinery, NY, USA, pp. 180–185 (2017)
19. Papoutsoglou, M., Mittas, N., Angelis, L.: Mining people analytics from stackoverflow job advertisements. In: 43rd Euromicro Conference on Software Engineering and Advanced Applications, Austria, pp. 108–115 (2017)
20. Rauschmayer, A.: The Past, Present, and Future of JavaScript. O'Reilly Media, Inc. (2012)
21. Runeson, P., Höst, M.: Guidelines for conducting and reporting case study research in software engineering. Empir. Softw. Eng. 14, 131 (2009)
22. Sharma R., Sood M. Cloud SaaS: Models and Transformation. Advances in Digital Image Processing and Information Technology. CCIS, vol 205. Springer (2011). https://doi.org/10.1007/978-3-642-24055-3
23. Snook, S., Gorsuch, R.: Principal component analysis versus common factor analysis: A Monte Carlo study. Psychol. Bull. 106, 148–154 (1989)
24. Sun, K., Ryu, S.: Analysis of javaScript programs: challenges and research trends. ACM Comput. Surv. 50(4), Article 59, 34 (2017)

25. Tong, Y., Chen, L., Zhou, Z., Jagadish, H.V., Shou, L., Lv, W.: SLADE: A smart large-scale task decomposer in crowdsourcing. In: 35th IEEE International Conference on Data Engineering, ICDE Macau, China, pp. 2133–2134 (2019)

26. Wang, H., Wang, Y., Wang, J.: A participant recruitment framework for crowdsourcing-based software requirement acquisition. In: 9th IEEE International Conference on Global Software Engineering, pp. 65–73 (2014)

27. Weidema, E., López, C., Nayebaziz, S., Spanghero, G., Van der Hoek, A.: Toward microtask crowdsourcing software design work. In: 3rd International Workshop on Crowd Sourcing in Software Engineering, NY, USA, vol. 2016, pp. 41–44 (2016)

28. Yuen, M., King, I., Leung, K.: A survey of crowdsourcing systems. In: 3rd International Conference on Privacy, Security, Risk & Trust, MA, USA, pp. 766–773 (2011)

29. Zanatta, A., Machado, L., Steinmacher, I.: Competence, collaboration, and time management: barriers and recommendations for crowdworkers. In: 5th International Workshop on Crowd Sourcing in Software Engineering (CSI-SE), Gothenburg, Sweden, 9–16, (2018)

30. Zozas, I., Anagnostou, I., Bibi, S.: Trends on crowdsourcing javascript small tasks. ENASE **2022**, 85–94 (2022)

Assessing Sustainability Impacts of Systems: SuSAF and the SDGs

Ian Brooks[1] , Norbert Seyff[2(✉)] , Stefanie Betz[3,4] , Dominic Lammert[3],
Jari Porras[4] , Leticia Duboc[5] , Ruzanna Chitchyan[6] , Colin C. Venters[7] ,
and Birgit Penzenstadler[4,8]

[1] University of the West of England, Bristol, UK
ian.brooks@uwe.ac.uk
[2] FHNW and University of Zurich, Windisch, Switzerland
norbert.seyff@fhnw.ch
[3] Furtwangen University, Furtwangen , Germany
{besi,lado}@hs-furtwangen.de
[4] LUT University, Lappeenranta, Finland
jari.porras@lut.fi
[5] La Salle - University Ramon Llull, Barcelona, Spain
l.duboc@salle.url.edu
[6] University of Bristol, Bristol, UK
r.chitchyan@bristol.ac.uk
[7] University of Huddersfield, Huddersfield, UK
c.venters@hud.ac.uk
[8] Chalmers, Gothenburg, Sweden
birgitp@chalmers.se

Abstract. The United Nations Sustainable Development Goals (SDGs) identify key topics where action is required to transform our world towards sustainability. We call for the extensive integration of the SDGs into Software Engineering to support this transformation. This will require the creation of methods and tools for the analysis of software system impacts on the SDGs. To show how this integration might be achieved, we report on a mapping to the SDGs from an existing software sustainability assessment tool, the Sustainability Assessment Framework (SusAF). We find that there is a good mapping between SusAF and the SDGs but that mapping to some specific SDG targets may be dependant on the expertise of the analysts. Mapping of case study systems will be needed for empirical validation.

Keywords: Sustainability · Sustainable Development Goals · Requirements Engineering Software Engineering · SusAF

1 Introduction: SDGs and Software

"The Sustainable Development Goals are the blueprint for achieving a better and more sustainable future for all. They address the global challenges we face, including those related to poverty, inequality, climate change, environmental degradation, peace and

H. Kaindl et al. (Eds.): ENASE 2022, CCIS 1829, pp. 205–219, 2023.
https://doi.org/10.1007/978-3-031-36597-3_10

justice. The 17 Goals are all interconnected, and in order to leave no one behind, it is important that we achieve them all by 2030." [28]

The Sustainable Development Goals (SDGs) (see Fig. 1) inspire change and were made more actionable with the help of specific targets to achieve a more sustainable future. The SDGs are not geared towards software systems and software development. However, software is an integral part of modern societies and the anticipated transformation of our world also needs to be driven by it. This means that software systems can be developed to specifically support one or more SDGs. We are already seeing more and more software systems to do so. For example, the app "Too Good to Go" directly supports food waste prevention (SDG12)[1].

Developing such systems is challenging, and software engineers ideally would have support in understanding whether and to what extent a software system supports or undermines the Sustainable Development Goals and Targets. Unfortunately, we are not aware of widely used systematic methods and tools (see Sect. 2) that support software engineers in carrying out such an analysis.

We see the development of software systems that incorporate the considered design of their impacts on the SDGs as key to changing our world. However, most of the software systems developed are created without SDGs or sustainability in mind [6]. Nevertheless, these "ordinary" software systems will have an impact (positive or negative) on the world and the SDGs.

Motivated by this reasoning, the main question for our ongoing work is: How can software engineers understand the impact of software systems on the SDGs?

A novel solution which supports software engineers in understating the impact of software systems on sustainability in general is the Sustainability Awareness Framework (SusAF) [7,8]. This framework has been developed and validated by the authors of the present chapter and is used for supporting software developers and system stakeholders in raising their awareness of the potential effects of software systems on the social, economic, environmental, technical and individual aspects of sustainability.

We consider SusAF to be a starting point for answering our main research question. Therefore, in our current research, we explore whether and to what extent SusAF helps in identifying the impacts of software systems on the SDGs.

We expect that, in the longer term, the outcome of investigating and answering this question will be a novel framework supporting software engineers to understand and analyse the relation of a software system to the SDGs. Meanwhile, this chapter takes the first step towards such an understanding.

This paper is organized as follows: Sect. 2 discusses the use of SDGs. In Sect. 3 we present our overall vision on how to make consideration of sustainability a key aspect for all software systems. Section 4 provides an introduction to the Sustainability Awareness Framework (SusAF). In Sect. 5, we present the results of mapping SusAF to the SDGs. Section 6 discusses lessons learned and Sect. 7 concludes the chapter and discusses next steps.

This chapter builds on our previous paper [24] and extends it with a more detailed report on the mapping of SusAF to SDGs at target level reported in the extended version of Step 2 in Sect. 5, represented in Fig. 3. We also add an additional step of exploring

---

[1] https://2030.builders/articles/doing-business-with-an-impact-too-good-to-go/.

Fig. 1. The 17 SDGs of the UN.

the direct mapping of SusAF to three selected SDG targets where no mapping had been identified in the previously published work and discuss the implication of these new findings. This new material is reported in the new Step 3 of Sect. 5 and on the fourth finding of Sect. 6.

2   Related Work

The 17 SDGs, which are broken down into 169 targets, represent "the world we want" by 2030 [28]. Together, they have the potential to change the nature of human development by making environmental and social sustainability a defining feature of economic activity [27].

The United Nations SDGs have been analysed from different angles and integrated into different analytical frameworks. Filho et al., for example, explored the usage of the SDGs to better understand sustainability challenges in the context of policy making [9].

Morton et al. [17] argue that using and prioritising the SDGs requires the application of systems thinking. They note that the SDGs can be divided into five areas of importance (people, planet, prosperity, peace and partnership). However, researchers also note that the SDGs must be analysed within the context of each system: for instance, the way that different countries deal with the SDGs varies depending on how their impact is locally assessed on other goals [10]. This means that the analysis of SDGs requires an understanding of each individual goal and the interaction between goals. Researchers from different fields have started working on the analysis of these possible interactions between goals regarding both positive and negative effects. It is commonly assumed that the SDGs and targets are mutually supportive, i.e. progress in one area requires progress in other areas [20].

Researchers and policy makers have already pointed out that there can be both conflict and support between the SDGs. For example, in the work of Nilsson et al. [19] seven different types of interactions between the SDGs are discussed - from inseparable to cancellation. Nilsson et al. also show the impact of their framework in different contexts (governance, geographical and temporal) in different application areas (health, energy and oceans) [18]. Furthermore, they propose a web-based knowledge platform considering their research and policy-making.

Singh et al. [25] conduct research on SDG14 (Life below water) which depicts the full complexity of cross-SDG impacts. They are able to identify 267 relationships (both positive and negative, as well as presupposed and optional) between SDG14 targets and other SDGs.

Similar types of interactions can also be observed in other areas such as health [16]. Furthermore, there exists an SDG integration framework for the corporate value chain – although this approach does not emphasise accountability as done by Morton et al. [17]. Finally, Stafford-Smith et al. [26] discuss SDG interactions across different domains, societal actors, and countries.

It is important to question how claims of SDG impact can be validated. Is it sufficient to assert that a business or a system has a positive impact at the goal level or should impact only be recognised at the level of specific targets or indicators? Claims at the level of the 17 goals are at high risk of greenwashing or "SDG-washing" because the goal titles are very general in nature [12,21]. The more widely-adopted approach is to seek to identify impact at the level of the 169 targets, since the targets were an explicit part of the UN General Assembly motion which adopted the SDGs in 2015 [28]. Many sustainability reporting organisations recommend working at target level [11]. There is an argument to be made for seeking impact at the level of the 231 unique indicators which were adopted by the United Nations in 2017 for national statistical reporting on progress towards the SDGs, but these are less appropriate for a business context [29]. Some researchers have sought to identify a subset of targets and indicators which are more relevant to business [5]. In this work we have focused on the target level, all 169, and not attempted to identify impact at the indicator level.

In summary, the SDGs and their interaction have been analysed by different researchers from different fields. To provide a more detailed overview, we have started a literature review of work on the SDGs and software and requirements engineering. Our initial analysis results suggest that there are only a few studies or models that link the SDGs to software systems development or the impact of software systems on the SDGs such as [4]. Although these results are initial, they have strongly motivated us to conduct the research described in this chapter.

3   Vision: Sustainability for All Software Systems

Software systems play an essential role in today's society. Many of these systems also have the power to strengthen the Sustainable Development Goals, even though they are not explicitly built having the support of an SDG in mind. However, this connection is often not recognised by software engineers. They fail to realise that the systems they build also have an effect on sustainability. Even when software engineers build a software system to support one or more SDGs and to consider sustainability aspects, it is challenging to fully understand how the system will affect different SDGs and which software development process can be used to best do so.

The software system's main purpose (implemented as its key features) is the obvious place to look at when starting a discussion about the impact of the system on the SDGs it is intended to support. This approach allows for a deep understanding of how the system supports or does not support the intended SDGs, and to change and adjust the purpose of the system to better align it to these SDGs. In particular, this approach also allows identifying contributions of software systems to the SDGs that the system was not initially intended to support.

Take, for example, a software system to aid teaching at a university. This system has a clear link to SDG4 (Quality Education). There is a scenario in which this system is developed from scratch, taking SDG4 into account. In this scenario, the purpose of the system could then be analysed and discussed, ensuring that the system is well aligned with this particular SDG4. However, if the system already existed, a comparison of its key features with SDG4 and other SDGs could be used to understand how the system contributes to sustainable development. These comparisons can inspire the evolution of the system and help to better align the system features with the SDGs.

We observe that the support for/impact on one or more SDGs is often closely linked to the overall purpose of a software system. The SDGs can help developers to conceptualise and build software systems that are geared toward sustainability. We also note that this level of consideration is not sufficient and that there is a need for methods and tools enabling software engineers to investigate and understand the potential sustainability effects of systems that have not been built with sustainability in mind. This also allows relating these systems to the SDGs. Analyzing features and requirements for these features allows software engineers to better understand their potential effects on sustainability [2] and to make any software system more sustainable.

4   SusAF–The Sustainability Awareness Framework

There are methods and tools that allow the discussion of sustainability effects of common software systems (e.g. [1,13,23]). The basis for our research is the Sustainability Awareness Framework (SusAF) [8]. It is well documented and its relevant artifacts are publicly available with Creative Commons license [22].

SusAF [8] supports software engineers in raising awareness of the link between software systems and sustainability. In particular, it supports the identification and discussion of the potential effects of software systems on five sustainability dimensions: economic, environmental, social, individual, and technical (discussed in Table 1).

Key artifacts of SusAF include a set of questions, a visualisation tool, guidelines and examples. Together, they serve to support the identification and discussion of potential effects of a software system on sustainability.

The set of questions is assigned to the five sustainability dimensions and the topics depicted in Table 1. Key results of the application of SusAF can be visualised in the so-called Sustainability Awareness Diagram (SusAD). It is an adapted radar chart showing five areas representing the five sustainability dimensions. In addition, SusAD includes the visualisation of three concentric areas to show different orders of effects:

Table 1. Coverage and Questions of the Five Sustainability Dimensions in the SusAF based on [8].

Dimensions: Topics	Coverage and Questions
Economic: value, CRM, supply chain, governance, innovation	The financial aspects and business value. The questions are about how the system creates or destroys value, how it affects the relationship between businesses and customers, whether it alters a business supply chain, governance, processes, or R&D
Environmental: material & resources, waste & pollution, biodiversity, energy and logistics	The use and stewardship of natural resources. The questions are about how the system may affect the consumption of resources, the production of waste, pollution and emissions and biodiversity
Social: community, trust, inclusiveness, equity and participation	The relationships between individuals and groups. The questions are about how the system may affect people's sense of belonging, their trust in its surroundings, their perception of others, how they participate in social groups, or whether they are receiving the same treatment as others
Individual: Health, lifelong learning, privacy, safety & agency	The individual's ability to thrive, exercise their rights, and develop freely. The questions are about how the usage of the system may affect the individual themselves, that is, a person's physical and mental health, on their level of knowledge, on their privacy, safety and ability to act on their surroundings
Technical: maintainability, usability, adaptability, security & scalability	The technical system's ability to accommodate changes. The questions aim to identify how the system is maintained and used over time, and to illustrate the system's ability of change and adaptability of the functionalities into the change environment, and whether the security of the system and privacy of its users are considered

immediate, enabling and systemic (see Table 2). In this way, software engineers can discuss potential chains of effects that describe how effects can lead to other effects over time. The guidelines and examples provided by SusAF help software engineers to better understand how to use SusAF.

5   Mapping SusAF and the SDGs

Based on our ongoing research, we have made a pilot mapping between the SDGs and SusAF. This mapping is based on a thematic analysis of the topics and questions covered by the SusAF framework (as shown in Table 1) and the SDGs. This mapping was carried out by one of the authors of this chapters in the form of a deductive qualitative content analysis based on [15]. The coding guides or category system was based on the

Table 2. Definition of the order of effects [3].

Order of effects	Definition
Immediate (or 'first order') effects	"Are concerned with the immediate impacts resulting from the production, use and disposal of software systems, such as energy use. This can be measured using metrics based on performance requirements or network bandwidth, for example"
Enabling (or'second order') effects	"Are concerned with the benefits and impacts of ongoing use of the software system. E.g. This might be, for example, how a web search engine reduces the cost of access to information"
Structural (or'third order') effects	"Are concerned with changes resulting from the use of software systems by a very large number of people over medium to long term, leading to substantial changes in societal structures such as new laws, politics, or social norms, or economic structures such as the networked economy"

SusAF topics and the targets for all SDGs. In terms of process, the analysis was carried out in three steps. In a first step, the general feasibility of the mapping was investigated. In a second step, a detailed pilot mapping was carried out. A third step involved a direct mapping of three selected SDG targets to all of the SusAF questions.

Step 1: The general feasibility of the mapping.

In Step 1, one of the authors of this chapter analysed the 25 SusAF topics[2] and the SusAF questions for each topic to determine their relationship to the 169 targets of the 17 SDGs. If at least one of the SusAF topic questions were considered related to an SDG target, the topic was linked to the SDG. For example, for the social dimension of SusAF and the topic of equity, the question "Can the system make people be treated differently from each other?" was mapped to SDG target 5.1 "End all forms of discrimination against all women and girls everywhere." This target is part of SDG5 (Gender Equality). The author performing the mapping concluded that discrimination against women and girls is an example of how 'people can be treated differently'. As a result, the SusAF theme "Equity" was linked to SDG5 (Gender Equality). Using this approach, all SusAF topics were linked to one or more SDGs.

Step 2: The detailed mapping.

After the general relatedness of the concepts (i.e. SusAF and the SDGs) had been established, a more detailed pilot mapping by the same author was carried out in a second step. The main aim of conducting this second step was to analyse whether SusAF covers all points of the SDGs at the target level in detail.

---

[2] These are listed under Dimensions:Topics heading of Table 1.

Therefore, this author used the maxqda tool[3] to conduct a systematic and transparent deductive qualitative content analysis. This involved independently coding the 95 SusAF questions and the 169 SDG targets into semantic categories, which were then compared. The topic belonging to that question and the SDG belonging to that target were mapped if the same code occurred in both the code set of the SusAF question and the SDG target.

For example, the code "Nature: plants and animals" is found in both the SusAF question "Can the system impact the plants or animals around it?" (topic biodiversity of the environmental domain) and in SDG Target 15.4 "By 2030, ensure the conservation of mountain ecosystems, including their biodiversity, in order to enhance their capacity to provide benefits that are essential for sustainable development" of SDG15 (Life on Land). This detailed mapping confirmed that SusAF is largely in line with the SDG targets. [14] provides further details regarding the mapping.

This detailed pilot mapping found no direct link between five SusAF topics and SDG targets. These topics are Maintainability, Adaptability, Security and Scalability (Technical Dimension) and Trust (Social Dimension). We suspect that the topics from the Technical dimension of SusAF relate to the specific technical solutions through which many of the SDGs may be achieved. However, as technical solutions are not discussed at the level of abstraction of the SDGs, the direct links were not immediately apparent. Furthermore, Trust, although essential for social sustainability and functioning of society, is largely implicit in the SDG targets.

Furthermore, the author conducting the mapping could not find a direct link between 37 SDG targets (i.e. 22% of the overall targets) to SusAF questions. We suspect that one possible reason is that many of these targets are partly focused on developing countries and specific industry sectors. An example for this are the targets "10.a ...special and differential treatment for developing countries..." and "3.a ...Tobacco control in all countries...". Another potential reason is that SusAF is intentionally not meant to be comprehensive; it is meant to provide an initial exploration of the potential effects of technology products and services on sustainability; the exploration of the more detailed aspects of each system would follow this initial exploration [7].

The diagrams in Fig. 2 and 3 show the mapping results. Two tables of targets and questions that could not be mapped are included in [14]. The diagram in Fig. 2 can be read from the inside out as follows:

– The inner circle depicts the five interrelated dimensions that SusAF targets: Individual, Social, Economic, Technical, and Environmental.
– The second circle depicts the topics that determine the questions for each of the five dimensions. For example, the individual dimension is about privacy, agency, safety, lifelong learning, and health.
– The third (outer) circle lists the SDGs for which we found a mapping between the SusAF topic and the SDG target level. More details on the mapping results can be found in the data folder for this chapter [14]. For example, health in the individual dimension can be linked to six SDGs: SDG1 (No Poverty), SDG3 (Good Health and Well-Being), SDG5 (Gender Equality), SDG6 (Clean Water and Sanitation), SDG9 (Industry, Innovation and Infrastructure) and SDG12 (Responsible Consumption and Production).

---

[3] https://www.maxqda.com/.

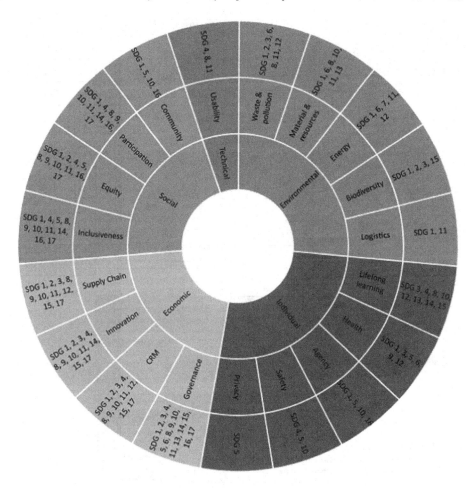

Fig. 2. Mapping between SusAF and the SDGs [24].

The diagram in Fig. 3 shows the intensity of the mapping from SusAF questions to the SDG targets. The cells below each SDG represent that SDG's targets in order. The number within the cell shows the frequency of the mapping between that target and code list where there is also a SusAF mapping. The cells in deeper green show more intensity of mapping. The cells in red are those where no mapping was identified between SusAF questions and that SDG target.

Step 3: Sample target mapping. Given that there were 37 SDG targets in Step 2 where we did not find a mapping, we undertook a third step of exploration. For this, we mapped a sample of these targets directly to the SusAF questions using four potential outcomes that assessed the potential relation between them. The selected targets included a range of environmental, social, and economic sustainability issues:

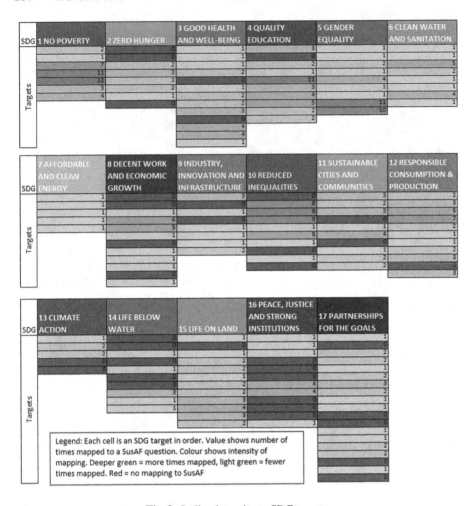

Fig. 3. Coding intensity to SDG targets.

- 2.c "Adopt measures to ensure the proper functioning of food commodity markets and their derivatives and facilitate timely access to market information, including on food reserves, in order to help limit extreme food price volatility"
- 14.1 "By 2025, prevent and significantly reduce marine pollution of all kinds, in particular from land-based activities, including marine debris and nutrient pollution"
- 16.4 "By 2030, significantly reduce illicit financial and arms flows, strengthen the recovery and return of stolen assets and combat all forms of organized crime"

Each target was assigned to a separate pair of experienced sustainable technology researchers. For each SusAF question, the individuals considered the mapping between the SusAF question to their SDG target with four potential outcomes:

- (A) Always: every system assessed must have a direct impact on the SDG target (regardless of whether positive or negative).

- (M) May: a system may conceivably have a direct impact but is dependant on details of the system or implementation context
- (N) Never: no system would conceivably have a direct impact on the target
- (C) Cannot Assess: the researcher does not have the experience to evaluate the direct impact.

Following independent individual evaluation, the pair discussed their answers to arrive at an agreed outcome, with an additional option of (X) if agreement could not be reached. The outcome of Step 3 is shown in Table 3. This showed that even for SDG targets where no mapping was shown in Step 2, experienced researchers could identify a very high likelihood of a direct mapping although this was completely dependent on the application domain.

It is worth noting that the SDG target 14.1 had been selected because of the low coding intensity in Step 2 to the targets in SDG 14 Life Below Water. In Step 3, we found that although the SusAF questions cover biodiversity in general and soil impacts specifically, there is no explicit mention of the marine environment. Yet, we observe that SusAF can indeed map to the SDG 14 targets depending on the application domain. Yet we suggest to include explicit mention of marine environment in the SusAF questions in future versions of this framework.

Table 3. Step 3 SusAF to SDG target mapping.

SDG target	(A) Always	(M) May	(N) Never	(C) Cannot assess	(X) No agreement
2.c	0	81	0	15	0
14.1	0	96	0	0	0
16.4	0	92	3	1	0

6   Findings

We have gained several insights from conducting this pilot mapping:

1. **Common Concerns That Promote Transparency and Accountability.** The vast majority of issues considered in both frameworks are the same, although SusAF focuses on the analysis of technical products and services and the SDGs address country or planetary level issues. Therefore, there is a clear commonality between these frameworks, for which the mapping presented in Fig. 2 may help to identify how a software system may affect particular SDGs. This leads to transparency and accountability for software and requirements engineers and allows them to under-stand which SDGs they impact through their software development activities.
2. **SusAF Is at a Different Level of Abstraction than the SDGs.** The SDGs set out the overarching goals and targets that countries must work towards, they do not address comprehensively the specific technical or other solutions that would be used

to achieve the goals set. This is evidenced by the fact that the Step 2 of our exploration did not find a direct map between the SDGs and most of the topics in the technical dimension: Maintainability, Adaptability, Security and Scalability. However, the impact of the technical solutions themselves on all the SDGs must be considered.

3. **The Connection between Technical Systems and the SDGs May Not Be Obvious at First Glance.** Based on the mapping, we suggest that technical systems, independent of their main purpose, have positive and/or negative effects on the SDGs. For example, it has been reported that, Airbnb, a peer-to-peer short-term rental platform, may have led to racialised gentrification in New York. This negatively impacts SDG 10 (Reduce inequalities) and in particular target 10.2 ("promote the social, economic and political inclusion of all, irrespective of age, sex, disability, race, ethnicity, origin, religion or economic or other status") [30]. SusAF may help to identify potential hidden impacts of technical systems on the SDGs.

4. **Domain Dependency and the Need for Empirical Validation.** The Steps 1 and 2 of the mapping between SusAF and SDGs have been carried out without case study-based validation. As we have observed in Step 3, experienced researchers were able to find potential mapping between previously unrelated SusAF topics and SDG targets, when considering the domain of a software system. Consider, for example the target 2.c ("Adopt measures to ensure the proper functioning of food commodity markets [...] and facilitate timely access to market information, [...]). At first sight, there is no clear relationship between this target and the topic of "trustin the social dimension of SusAF. However, if we are talking about a software for helping to stabilise and regulate food commodity markets and this relies on the self-reporting of food production and prices, then trust is key to information access and price volatility. Therefore some SusAF - SDG mappings are highly dependent on the domain of the software application. For the more generic mapping, shown in Fig. 2, empirical evidence with real case studies are needed to validate the conceptual relationship between SusAF topics and SDG targets.

5. **Threats to Validity.**
The work presented in this chapter promotes a better understanding of how the choice of software solutions (as exemplified by SusAF) can contribute to or detract from the SDGs. While presenting these preliminary findings, we note that there are several threats to validity that must be taken into account.

   – As mentioned earlier, the mapping was conducted without case studies for validation. It is possible that we have overlooked and/or misrepresented areas where SusAF questions can support the identification of software systems' impacts on the SDGs. Therefore, the mapping needs to be validated using case studies.

   – As discussed in the Related Work section of this chapter, researchers have described interactions (positive and negative) between the SDGs. However, interactions have not yet been included in our mapping process, which will likely result in future updates of the presented mapping.

   – No SDG experts were involved in Steps 1 and 2 of the mapping process. As that mapping was done from the perspective of a single person, this may have led to a biased representation of the impact and interpretation of the mapping.

Two other authors of the chapter did review and iterate upon the initial mapping. Nevertheless, a more thorough validation of the results, e.g. by experts in specific SDGs, needs to be undertaken. Step 3 showed us that this may require a significant time commitment.

Despite the possible bias of researchers and validators, this chapter shows that it is broadly possible to see substantial commonality between SusAF and the SDGs. The initial mapping described in this chapter can help software and requirements engineers to connect impacts and contributions of their software systems to the SDGs and sustainability.

7   Conclusion

In this chapter, we present a pilot mapping study across SusAF questions and SDG targets. This mapping shows a strong link between SusAF and the SDGs and can support the identification of a software system's impact on specific SDGs.

Our work aims at helping software engineers to understand how their work and the functions and qualities they want to include in a software system support or undermine specific SDGs. We intend to further validate the initial findings presented and refine them within a case study (together with an industry partner). This application will help to validate our mapping in the context of a specific system and domain.

Furthermore, we intend to extend Step 3 of the mapping, discussed above, to evaluate the SDG targets which are not yet mapped in Step 2, involving multiple authors and SDG experts. An area identified for improvement from the Step 3 work is the explicit inclusion of marine environment impacts in a future update to the SusAF questions or facilitator guidance, even though it is implicitly included in the current biodiversity question. However, we are aware that any mapping may have a subjective character influenced by the opinions and knowledge of the people involved.

We foresee, that with the help of the mapping and the results provided by our research (i.e. SusAF) software engineers will be better equipped to consider how their systems contribute to the SDGs and take more responsibility for the systems they develop or use.

It is important to stress that with this work we do not claim that software systems are the only means to achieve the SDGs. However, they are one of the tools in the toolbox at hand, supporting the transition to sustainability. We hope this work will stimulate a deeper discussion on how to operationalise the SDGs. Furthermore, we would like to encourage the software engineering community to develop new methods and tools to contribute to the SDGs through software.

Acknowledgements. This research is partially funded by the UK EPSRC Refactoring Energy Systems Project (EP/R007373/1) and the Digitaldialog 21 Project.

References

1. Alharthi, A., Spichkova, M., Hamilton, M.: Susoftpro: Sustainability profiling for software (08 2018). https://doi.org/10.1109/RE.2018.00072

2. Becker, C., et al.: Requirements: The key to sustainability. IEEE Softw. **33**(1), 56–65 (2016). https://doi.org/10.1109/MS.2015.158

3. Betz, S., et al.: Sustainability debt: A metaphor to support sustainability design decisions. In: CEUR Workshop Proceedings, vol. 1416, pp. 55–63 (2015)

4. Brooks, I.: The united nations sustainable development goals in systems engineering: Eliciting sustainability requirements. In: 7th International Conference on ICT for Sustainability (ICT4S2020), pp. 196–199. Association for Computing Machinery (ACM) (06 2020)

5. Calabrese, A., Costa, R., Gastaldi, M., Levialdi Ghiron, N., Villazon Montalvan, R.A.: Implications for sustainable development Goals: A framework to assess company disclosure in sustainability reporting. J. Cleaner Product. **319**, 128624 (2021). https://doi.org/10.1016/j.jclepro.2021.128624, https://go.exlibris.link/zC0tF6t0

6. Chitchyan, R., et al.: Sustainability design in requirements engineering: State of practice. In: 2016 IEEE/ACM 38th International Conference on Software Engineering Companion (ICSE-C), pp. 533–542 (2016)

7. Duboc, L., et al.: Do we really know what we are building? raising awareness of potential sustainability effects of software systems in requirements engineering. In: 2019 IEEE 27th International Requirements Engineering Conference (RE), pp. 6–16 (Sep 2019). https://doi.org/10.1109/RE.2019.00013

8. Duboc, L., et al.: Requirements engineering for sustainability: an awareness framework for designing software systems for a better tomorrow. Requirements Eng. **25**(4), 469–492 (2020). https://doi.org/10.1007/s00766-020-00336-y

9. Filho, W., Tripathi, S.K., Andrade Guerra, J.B., Gine, R., Orlovic Lovren, V., Willats, J.: Using the sustainable development goals towards a better understanding of sustainability challenges. Int. J. Sustainable Developm. World Ecol. **26**(2), 179–190 (2019). https://doi.org/10.1080/13504509.2018.1505674

10. Fleming, A., Wise, R., Hansen, H., Sams, L.: The sustainable development goals: A case study. Mar. Policy **86**, 94–103 (2017). https://doi.org/10.1016/j.marpol.2017.09.019

11. GRI, Un Global Compact, PwC: Business Reporting on the SDGs. An analysis of the goals and targets. Tech. rep., GRI and UN Global Compact, New York (2018). https://www.pwc.com/gx/en/sustainability/publications/assets/sdgs-business-reporting-analysis.pdf

12. Heras-Saizarbitoria, I., Urbieta, L., Boiral, O.: Organizations' engagement with sustainable development goals: From cherry-picking to SDG-washing?. Corporate Soc.-Responsib. Environm. Manag. **29**(2), 316–328 (2022). https://doi.org/10.1002/csr.2202, https://go.exlibris.link/61XNyfVw

13. Hilty, L., Aebischer, B.: ICT for Sustainability: An Emerging Research Field, vol. 310, pp. 3–36 (2015). https://doi.org/10.1007/978-3-319-09228-7_1

14. Lammert, D., Betz, S.: ENASE Data Folder. https://figshare.com/s/ce84deccfd049670d0b6 (2021)

15. Mayring, P.: Qualitative content analysis. Forum Qualitative Sozialforschung / Forum: Qualitative Social Research, vol. 1(2) (Jun 2000). https://doi.org/10.17169/fqs-1.2.1089, https://www.qualitative-research.net/index.php/fqs/article/view/1089

16. Morton, S., Pencheon, D., Bickler, G.: The sustainable development goals provide an important framework for addressing dangerous climate change and achieving wider public health benefits. Public Health **174**, 65–68 (2019). https://doi.org/10.1016/j.puhe.2019.05.018

17. Morton, S., Pencheon, D., Squires, N.: Sustainable development goals (sdgs), and their implementation: A national global framework for health, development and equity needs a systems approach at every level. British Med. Bull. **124**, 1–10 (2017). https://doi.org/10.1093/bmb/ldx031

18. Nilsson, M., et al.: Mapping interactions between the sustainable development goals: lessons learned and ways forward. Sustain. Sci. **13**(6), 1489–1503 (2018). https://doi.org/10.1007/s11625-018-0604-z

19. Nilsson, M., Griggs, D., Visbeck, M.: Policy: Map the interactions between sustainable development goals. Nature **534**, 320–322 (2016). https://doi.org/10.1038/534320a

20. Nilsson, M., Griggs, D., Visbeck, M., Ringler, C., McCollum, D.: A framework for understanding sustainable development goal interactions. a guide to sdg interactions: From science to implementation. International Council for Science (2017)

21. Nishitani, K., Nguyen, T.B.H., Trinh, T.Q., Wu, Q., Kokubu, K.: Are corporate environmental activities to meet sustainable development goals (SDGs) simply greenwashing? An empirical study of environmental management control systems in Vietnamese companies from the stakeholder management perspective. J. Environ. Manage. **296**, 113364 (2021). https://doi.org/10.1016/j.jenvman.2021.113364

22. Penzenstadler, B., et al.: The SusA Workshop - improving sustainability awareness to inform future business process and systems design (Jan 2020). https://doi.org/10.5281/zenodo.3632486

23. Seyff, N., et al.: Tailoring requirements negotiation to sustainability, pp. 304–314 (Aug 2018). https://doi.org/10.1109/RE.2018.00038

24. Seyff, N., et al.: Transforming our world through software: mapping the sustainability awareness framework to the un sustainable development goals. In: Proceedings of the 17th International Conference on Evaluation of Novel Approaches to Software Engineering - ENASE, pp. 417–425. Scitepress (apr 2022). https://doi.org/10.5220/0011063200003176, https://www.scitepress.org/PublicationsDetail.aspx?ID=cKzXxvbUC1w=&t=1

25. Singh, G., et al.: A rapid assessment of co-benefits and trade-offs among sustainable development goals. Marine Policy **93** (2017). https://doi.org/10.1016/j.marpol.2017.05.030

26. Stafford-Smith, M., et al.: Integration: the key to implementing the Sustainable Development Goals. Sustain. Sci. **12**(6), 911–919 (2016). https://doi.org/10.1007/s11625-016-0383-3

27. Stevens, C., Kanie, N.: The transformative potential of the sustainable development goals (SDGs). Int. Environm. Agreem. Politics, Law Econom. **16**(3), 393–396 (2016). https://doi.org/10.1007/s10784-016-9324-y

28. United Nations General Assembly: Transforming our world: the 2030 Agenda for Sustainable Development (2015). http://www.un.org/ga/search/view_doc.asp?symbol=A/RES/70/1&Lang=E

29. United Nations General Assembly: Work of the Statistical Commission pertaining to the 2030 Agenda for Sustainable Development (2017). https://upload.wikimedia.org/wikipedia/commons/9/9d/A_RES_71_313_E.pdf

30. Wachsmuth, D., Weisler, A.: Airbnb and the rent gap: Gentrification through the sharing economy. Environm. Planning Econ. Space **50**(6), 1147–1170 (2018). https://doi.org/10.1177/0308518X18778038

Exploiting Metadata Semantics in Data Lakes Using Blueprints

Michalis Pingos$^{(\boxtimes)}$ ⓘ and Andreas S. Andreou ⓘ

Department of Computer Engineering and Informatics, Cyprus University of Technology, Limassol, Cyprus

{michalis.pingos,andreas.andreou}@cut.ac.cy

Abstract. Smart processing of Big Data has been recently emerged as a field that provides quite a few challenges related to how multiple heterogeneous data sources that produce massive amounts of structured, semi-structured and unstructured data may be handled. One solution to this problem is manage this fusion of disparate data sources through Data Lakes. The latter, though, suffers from the lack of a disciplined approach to collect, store and retrieve data to support predictive and prescriptive analytics. This chapter tackles this challenge by introducing a novel standardization framework for managing data in Data Lakes that combines mainly the 5Vs Big Data characteristics and blueprint ontologies. It organizes a Data Lake using a ponds architecture and describes a metadata semantic enrichment mechanism that enables fast storing to and efficient retrieval. The mechanism supports Visual Querying and offers increased security via Blockchain and Non-Fungible Tokens. The proposed approach is compared against other known metadata systems utilizing a set of functional properties with very encouraging results.

Keywords: Data lakes · Smart data processing · Heterogeneous data sources · Data lakes · Semantic metadata · Data blueprints · Visual query · Blockchain · NFTs

1 Introduction

Big Data is a term referring to the large amounts of digital data constantly generated by tools and machines, as well as by the global population and is nowadays called the "new gold" [1]. Big Data analysis is at the center of modern science and business [2]. According to Oracle [3], the concept of big data itself is relatively new, but large data sets can be traced back to the 1960s and 1970s when the world of data was just getting started with the first data centers and relational databases. The amount of data users generate through Facebook, YouTube and other online services started to become apparent around 2005. During the same year, Hadoop, an open-source framework designed to store and analyze large data sets, was developed. During the same period, NoSQL started gaining popularity. It is projected that the speed and frequency by which digital data is produced and collected will increase exponentially. According to [4], in 2020,

H. Kaindl et al. (Eds.): ENASE 2022, CCIS 1829, pp. 220–242, 2023.
https://doi.org/10.1007/978-3-031-36597-3_11

each person generated 1.7 megabytes in just a second, while an estimated 2.5 quintillion bytes of data were generated every day by Internet users. It is clear that the growing volume of data, coupled with its tremendous social and economic value, is driving a global data revolution [5, 6]. Big Data has been called also "the new oil" since, when properly gathered and analyzed, can provide valuable insights into many aspects of our everyday lives and, moreover, can allow us to predict what will happen in the future [7].

The majority of Big Data comes from heterogeneous sources with irregular structures [8]. The process of transforming Big Data into Smart Data in the sense making them valuable and transforming them into meaningful information, is called Smart Data Processing (SDP) and includes a series of actions and techniques. The latter support the processing and integration of data into a unified view from disparate Big Data sources. More specifically, this field includes adaptive frameworks and tool-suites in support of smart data processing by allowing the best use of streaming or static data, and may rely on advanced techniques for efficient resource management. The analytic solutions, which rely on the smart data processing and integration techniques, are called Systems of Deep Insight (SDI). These solutions enable optimization of asset performance in SDI and are geared towards systems of insight. In addition, they sift through the data to discover new relationships and patterns by analyzing historical data, assessing the current situation, applying business rules, predicting outcomes, and proposing the next best action. It remains a challenging and unsolved problem to treat Big Data produced by multiple heterogeneous data sources despite the many drastic solutions proposed in recent years.

This chapter extends and enhances previous work on the topic [7, 31] which adopts the basic principles of manufacturing blueprints [31] and modifies their purpose and meaning to reflect the description and characterization of sources and the data they produce via the utilization of the 5V 5Vs Big Data characteristics. These characteristics describe data sources by means of specific types of blueprints through an ontology-based description representation. Big Data sources will thus be accompanied by a blueprint metadata description before they become part of a Data Lake (DL). The DL follows a pond architecture, while the data source selection process and retrieval are performed via a dedicated Visual Querying environment. Additional security characteristics are induced in this scheme by utilizing Blockchain. Specifically, for each selected source, a mint function is called through a smart contract which is responsible for creating Non-Fungible Tokens (NFTs) for that source and storing them in the Blockchain.

The rest of the chapter is organized as follows: Sect. 2 discusses related work and the areas of SDP, DLs, Semantic Enrichment and Blockchain. Section 3 presents the proposed semantically enriched mechanism, starting with a short overview of the technical background and moving to describing the approach and architecture of the mechanism, discussing its main components. Section 4 provides the details of the anticipated attributes of a DL's metadata system and compares them with a number of already published works. The chapter is wrapped up in Sect. 5, which provides the conclusions and discusses possible future work possibilities.

2 Related Work

Common fields of SDP are semantic models, structured data configurations, DLs, Data Warehouses, Machine Learning (ML) and ontologies. One of the most significant findings in these studies is the importance of using DLs architecture to store large amounts of relational and non-relational data, sometimes combining them with traditional data warehouses. Another notable finding is the exploitation of ontology frameworks to manage heterogenous data sources that produce large amounts of data and make them part of DLs, while privacy and security is yet another challenge in DLs architecture.

As stated in [21], a DL holds a vast amount of raw data in its native format while fast data is defined as a time-sensitive structured and unstructured "in-flight" data that should be gathered and acted upon right away. The authors conclude that not all Big Data is fast, as well as not all fast data is big.

DL architecture is one of the arguable concepts appeared in the era of Big Data as presented in [19]. The idea of a DL was originated from the business field instead of the academic. As DL is a newly conceived idea with revolutionized concepts, it brings many challenges for its adoption. However, the potential to change the data landscape makes the research on DLs worthwhile.

Fang discusses the concept of DLs and shares his thoughts and practices on the subject [30]. The main goal of that paper was to examine and provide answers to a series of questions, such as what a DL is, or how does it help with the challenges posed by Big Data. The author concludes that the data warehouse is a wise choice for a company dealing with Big Data challenge and outlines the best practices of DL implementations.

The authors in [22] provide a comprehensive state of the art of the different approaches to DL design. They particularly focus on DL architectures and metadata management, which are key issues for their successful implementation. The authors also discuss the pros and cons of DLs and their design alternatives. Finally, they classify metadata and introduce the features that are necessary to achieve a full metadata system and report the major and challenging issues facing DL, two of which are particularly useful and are outlined in this paper:

- The lack of descriptive metadata and of mechanisms for maintaining metadata leads to a swamp of data;
- Due to the nature of the DL, data in it can be replaced without the need for oversight of its contents, both in terms of security (privacy) and access control.

The work in [33] mentions that the digitization of the industry requires information models that describe assets of companies to enable the semantic integration and interoperable exchange of data. The proposed model is centered around machine data and describes all relevant assets, key terms and relations in a structured way. The paper evaluates the proposed approach with stakeholders on two case studies. While the stakeholders find the advantages of semantic technologies appealing, the lack of ready-to-use business solutions, industrial ontologies and available IT personnel is halting efforts to move forward.

Mehdi et al. [34] report that industrial rule-based diagnostic systems are often data-dependant in the sense that they rely on specific characteristics of individual pieces of equipment. This dependence poses significant challenges in rule authoring, reuse, and maintenance by engineers. That work addressed the aforementioned problems by proposing a semantic rule language, sigRL, where sensor signals are considered first class citizens. Their evaluation shows that up to 66% of the time is saved when employing ontologies and that execution of semantic rules is efficient and scales well to real-world complex diagnostic tasks.

A new and alternative paradigm called manufacturing blueprints is presented in [29] based on ontologies and semantics, which allows manufacturers to move from a traditional product-centric business model to a fully digital, knowledge-based and service-centric one. Using this paradigm, manufacturers are able to combine manufacturing and equipment data and knowledge, production systems and processes to form a smart manufacturing network to diversify products and build new markets.

To address the highly complex problem of dealing with heterogeneous data sources, the authors in [7] propose a novel standardization framework combining mainly the 5Vs Big Data characteristics, blueprint ontologies, and DL architecture, offering a metadata semantic enrichment mechanism that enables fast storage to and efficient retrieval from a DL. A set of functional characteristics or properties are used to compare the proposed mechanism with existing metadata systems, and the results indicate that it is indeed a promising approach.

In [31], the authors present DLMetaChain, an extended DL metadata mechanism that integrates heterogeneous data sources with IoT data. Recently, the Blockchain technology has been introduced as a promising solution for building trust between entities, where trust has been either undeveloped or non-existent, and for addressing security and privacy concerns. The extended mechanism emphasizes on developing an architecture that ensures that the data in the DL will not be modified or altered.

Digital twin technology should be adopted by the manufacturing industry in order to modernize their operations, outputs, and services, according to [32]. A number of advanced technologies have been seamlessly synchronized with the digital twin paradigm since then, including the Internet of Things, artificial intelligence, big and streaming data analytics, deep learning, software-defined cloud environments, and Blockchain, among others.

3   A Semantic Enrichment Metadata Mechanism via Blueprints

This section describes the proposed semantic enrichment mechanism. It starts by providing a brief overview of the necessary technical notions this chapter builds upon, outlining the different forms of data available today and discussing how to distinguish and handle them, introducing also the notion of blueprints as a way for semantically describing data sources. It then focuses on describing the semantic mechanism, providing details on its architecture and how it is used for managing storing and retrieval of heterogeneous data in a DL.

3.1   Technical Background

SDP and SDI are frequently integrated with human beings, other smart systems, networks of big data, and the environment (natural, artificial, and social). The ability of a system to provide (and employ) cognitive support to (and from) its environment is a necessary (or extrinsic) condition for its intelligence. The development of "smartness" is based on system functionality. The associated functions that may induce intelligence in systems usually perform sensing, smart data processing, knowledge-based data communication, aggregation, and interoperability, as well as decision making and human-like perception and behavior.

The term Smart Data is used to emphasize the latent value inherent in widely dispersed and unconnected data sources. The aim here is to extract meaning from data, consider multiple scenarios and provide decision-makers with high value information and services that help them make the best possible decisions and solve complex problems. Smart data exhibits the following properties:

- Normalized Data – conflict-free, homogenized data retrieved from multiple related data sources and diverse representations that can be interpreted in a specific context.
- Contextualized Data – normalized data providing meaning and contextual awareness to enable orchestration and improved decision-making.
- Orchestrated Data – cross-correlated secure contextualized data across a specific domain (e.g., healthcare, manufacturing, smart cities, etc.) that can be turned with AI support to actionable tasks at the speed of business.

Predictability and prescriptiveness are the two main characteristics that SDI aspire to achieve. The key idea behind predictability is that learning can be thought of as inferring plausible models to explain observed data. Probability theory provides a solid framework where a decision may depend on the amount of uncertainty. The dominant paradigm for representing such probabilistic models with variants is examined in [9]. Traditionally, the problem of integration over the various plausible outcomes has been considered a source of high computational burden. However, recent advances in the field, including black-box variational approximations [10] and stochastic gradient Markov chain Monte-Carlo (SG-MCMC) [11] have completely ameliorated these issues, by rendering Bayesian probabilistic models amenable to large-scale data analytics applications. In addition, probabilistic programming constitutes a recent culmination on the aforementioned research efforts, allowing the use of computer programs to represent Bayesian probabilistic models. There is a growing number of probabilistic programming languages currently under active development, with the work reported in [12] and [13] being a few such examples.

Prescriptiveness refers to the ability to prescribe an action so that the decision-maker can take insight information and act. Prescriptive analytics require a predictive model able to predict the possible consequences based on different choices of actions. In the context of systems of deep insight, the work in [14] considers the problem of planning an action that maximizes the potential of short-term gain based on historical data, while gathering new information for improving goodness between actions and long-term effects. This dilemma is typically formulated as a contextual multi-armed bandit problem.

where each arm corresponds to one possible course of action. The optimal strategy is to use the arm with the maximum expected reward as regards contextual information on each trial, and then to maximize the total accumulated reward for the whole series of trials.

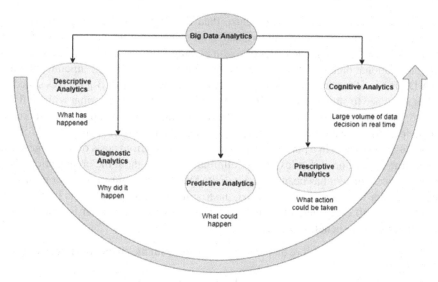

Fig. 1. The evolution of Big Data Analytics.

Predictability and prescriptiveness are led by Machine Learning (ML), with the application of existing and new algorithms. Recently, a series of algorithms for contextual multi-armed bandit problems have been reported with promising performance under different settings, including unguided exploration, for example, ε-greedy [15] and epoch-greedy [16], and guided exploration, such as Thompson Sampling [17]. These existing algorithms take the contextual information as input and predict the expected reward for each arm, assuming the reward is invariant under the same context. Finally, other methods that capture the time varying behaviors of the reward in contextual multi-armed bandit problems have also been proposed in [18].

It is important to mention that predictiveness and prescriptiveness are the evolution of descriptiveness and diagnosis. Utilizing big data and big data analytics, and smart data processing techniques is not enough to report what has happened or what was the cause, but it is possible to predict what would happen under what actions and, therefore, be able to make decisions in real time with large volumes of data (see Fig. 1).

A significant contribution of this study is the use of DLs to support the desired level of Big Data processing and ultimately develop SDP. Therefore, we propose a standardization framework for storing data (and data sources) in a DL, as well as a meta-data enrichment mechanism able to handle Big Data from disparate and heterogeneous sources effectively and efficiently. Data is generated from these sources at various frequencies and the proposed mechanism is applied to both the ingestion of the data into a DL and the extraction of knowledge and information from it.

The term "Big Data processing" refers to the preparation of data that is heterogeneous in type and may include structured, semi-structured, as well as unstructured data. There are many different types of raw data that can be stored in a DL, including many different types of raw data in their native format. DLs are also centralized repositories where structured, semi-structured, and unstructured data can be stored, selected and organized at any scale. There is no need to organize data before performing different types of analytics, including dashboards and visualizations and real-time analytics, as well as machine learning to help guide better decision making. DLs can also combine relational and non-relational data with traditional data warehouses to store large amounts of data.

A DL is one of the arguable concepts that appeared in the era of Big Data as stated in [19]. It is a place to store practically every type of data in its native format with no fixed limits on account size or file, offering at the same time high data quantity to increase analytic performance and native integration. In a DL, data is moved in its original format instead of being placed in a purpose-built data store. The upfront costs of data ingestion, such as transformation and indexing, are eliminated. Throughout the organization, data can be analyzed once it has been placed into the DL [20]. In contrast to a hierarchically organized Data Warehouse, a DL is a flat, unstructured database. Metadata information is associated with every data element in a DL and a unique identifier is assigned for each. The following benefits can be derived from DLs:

- It has become easier to store disparate information with the advent of storage engines like Hadoop;
- DLs do not require enterprise-wide schemas to model data;
- Analyses become more accurate as data volume, quality, and metadata increase;
- Business agility is offered by DLs;
- Predictions can be made with the help of machine learning and artificial intelligence;
- A DL offers a competitive advantage to the organization implementing it.

The idea of a DL is originated from the business field instead of the academic and constitutes a quite new data storage architecture linked with Big Data processing with unsolved challenging problems [19] such as:

- Lack the ability to determine data quality or the lineage of findings;
- They accept any data without oversight and governance;
- There is no descriptive metadata or a mechanism to maintain metadata leading to data swamp [21];
- Data need to be analyzed from scratch every time;
- Performance cannot be guaranteed;
- Security (privacy and regulatory requirements) and access control (weakness of metadata management) suffer as data can be replaced without oversight of the contents.

In a DL, a data pond is a subdivision that deals with specific types of data [22]. In essence, a data pond is a data mart built using Big Data technology for a single purpose or project. Typically, it is the first step in adopting Big Data technology.

There are five main and innate characteristics of Big Data that can be referred to as the 5Vs (see Fig. 2). A change in one dimension may result in a change in another dimension. By understanding the 5Vs, data scientists can get more value from their data, while becoming more customer-centric [24]. A widely-accepted definition of Big Data was articulated in 2001 by Doug Laney as 3Vs of Big Data [25]:

- Volume - the amount of data produced by data sources;
- Velocity - the fast rate which data produced;

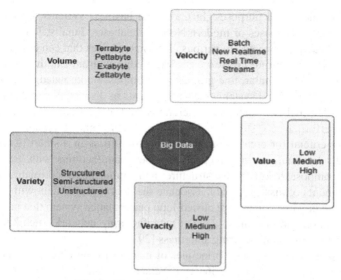

Fig. 2. The 5Vs big data characteristics.

- Variety – the different type of data produced;

Other dimensions of Big Data are reported in addition to the 3Vs. Among them are [26]:

- Veracity: Based on IBM's definition, it represents the unreliability inherent in some sources of data [27];
- Value: Was introduced by Oracle as a defining attribute of Big Data [28].

The main sources of Big Data are social media, cloud computing, the web, traditional business management systems (e.g., ERPs), and the internet of things (IoT). Data from these primary sources includes structured, unstructured, and semi-structured information (see Fig. 3) as presented in [7]. Structured data may be stored in a fixed field within a file or record, while nowadays structured data resides in a relational database management system (RDBMS). Data models define what types of data are present and how they should be used. The term unstructured refers to any data that is not structured, that is, there is no predefined structure, though it may have a native, internal structure; there is no data model, the data is stored in its native format. Typical examples of unstructured data include rich media, text, social media activity, surveillance imagery, etc. Data that does not fit into a relational database's formal structure is called structured data. While it does not match the description of structured data entirely, tags are still used to separate elements and enable searching. A self-describing structure can also describe this type of data.

Media includes social networks and interactive platforms such as Google, WhatsApp, Facebook, Tik Tok, Twitter, YouTube, and Instagram, as well as generic media such as videos, audios, and images that provide qualitative and quantitative information about user interaction. Whether private or public, cloud storage can store real-time or on-demand business data. Any data available on the Internet or the Web can be used for commercial or individual purposes. In traditional business systems, business data is stored in relational databases or modern NoSQL databases. Finally, IoT includes data from sensors that are connected to various electronic devices that can emit data.

Manufacturing blueprints create a basic knowledge environment that provides manufacturers with more granular, fine-grained and composable knowledge structures and approaches to correlate and systematize vast amounts of dispersed manufacturing data, associate the "normalized" data with operations, and orchestrate processes in a more closed-loop performance system that delivers continuous innovation and insight. Such knowledge is crucial for creating manufacturing smartness in a smart manufacturing network [29]. A manufacturing blueprint provides manufacturers with granular, fine-grained and composable knowledge structures and approaches to correlate and systematize vast amounts of dispersed data, associate the "normalized" data with operations, and orchestrate processes in a more closed-loop performance system that provides continuous innovation and insight. In a smart manufacturing network, such knowledge is essential for creating manufacturing smartness [29].

This chapter adopts the basic principles of manufacturing blueprints and modifies their purpose and meaning to describe and characterize data sources and the data they generate. To describe Big Data sources, a framework based on the five aforementioned characteristics (5Vs) is proposed. Through an ontology-based description, these characteristics will guide the characterization of data sources. The blueprint description will accompany Big Data sources before they become part of a DL.

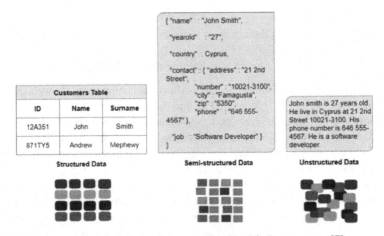

Fig. 3. Different types of data produced by Big Data sources [7].

3.2 Approach and Architecture

As mentioned in the previous section, data processing (storing and retrieval) in DLs organized with pond architecture will be facilitated by integrating the 5Vs Big Data characteristics and blueprint ontologies. Storing and retrieval of data sources will be supported by visual querying providing Digital Twin characteristics. The ownership of the selected data sources will be recorded during DL storing in the Blockchain as a NFT.

Using the pond architecture, a DL consists of a set of data ponds each hosting/referring to a particular type of data. Based on the data type, each pond contains a specialized storage system and data processing. As presented on Fig. 4, a DL with pond architecture uses dedicated ponds to store structured, unstructured, and semi-structured data from each source. As will be demonstrated later, the innate pond architecture is particularly useful for extracting information from the DL via Visual Query.

First, Big Data sources are filtered and selected by the DL owner using a Visual Query environment before they become part of the DL as shown in Fig. 4. Since data sources that are candidates for inclusion in the DL are characterized according to the blueprint attributes shown in Fig. 5, their selection is performed by defining specific values for these attributes.

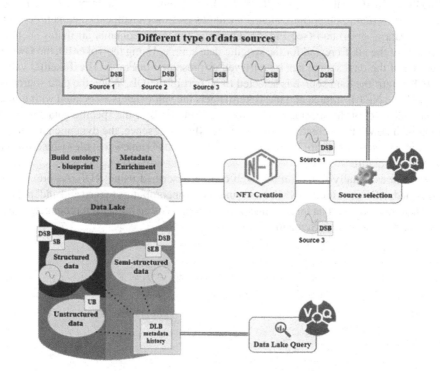

Fig. 4. Visual Querying data sources selection metadata enrichment mechanism using 5Vs.

Data Source Blueprint (DSB) is a metadata enrichment mechanism [7] that identifies and characterizes a candidate source before it becomes member of a DL as shown in Fig. 4. Volume, Variety, Veracity, Value, and Velocity are the five basic characteristics of Big Data we use that contribute to this characterization. Basically, there are two parts in the blueprint mechanism: the stable blueprint and the dynamic blueprint. The stable blueprint records the Source Name, the Variety type and Type of data, Value of the data, Velocity, and Veracity. As presented in Fig. 5, these attributes can be assigned using

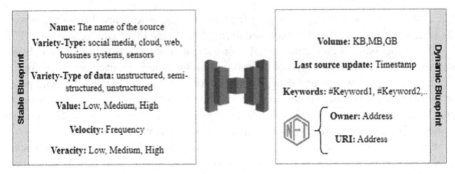

Fig. 5. Data source blueprints description.

standard linguistic values, such as Low, Medium, High, or a custom property, such as frequency. Dynamic blueprint contains attributes that may change as data is processed or new data is generated (see Fig. 5). Dynamic blueprint contains attributes such as TokenID of the NFT created for the specific data source. Using the TokenID, the Owner and URI of the data source can be retrieved as presented in Fig. 5. The TokenID value is NULL until the data source is selected to be part of the DL. When the data source is selected, the NFT is minted and the TokenID gets the value that is associated with of the Owner and URI of the specific NFT. Every time the DSB of the specific data source is modified a new URI is created pointing to the NFT. In essence, the dynamic and stable blueprints form the DSB are RDF (Resource Description Framework) files which follow the XML structure.

Resources usually found on the Web can be described using RDF. As previously mentioned, RDF is written in XML and is intended for computers to read and understand. RDF is a standard for data interchange used for representing highly interconnected data that is part of the W3C's Semantic Web Activity.

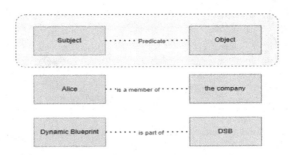

Fig. 6. The basic semantic RDF triple model with examples.

Typically, RDF statements consist of three parts, with each part identified by a URI. RDF allows Artificial Intelligence (AI) systems to identify, disambiguate, and connect information easily. Based on the theory of triples (subject, predicate, object), the authors in [7] describe the blueprint of a source as an instance of this model, with a stable and dynamic scheme (see Fig. 6).

Let us assume that we have for example three data sources which produce energy data and are candidate to be part of a DL, which bear the characteristics listed in Tables 1, 2 and 3. SPARQL (Protocol and Query Language), as well as Visual Query that builds SPARQL via a visual interface, enables us to query all RDF resources prior to or after their ingestion into the DL. SPARQL queries can be run without technical knowledge in a Visual Query environment. In order to query these sources from the visual environment, each data source's description must be in RDF form as mentioned previously, which can be obtained by a public API (RDF API). Using the blueprint ontology description, Fig. 7 illustrates the RDF files written in XML for Source 1. Based on the characteristics of each source, the XML follows the same structure. As presented in Fig. 7 and Tables 1, 2 and 3, attributes Owner and URI are NULL, due to the fact that the specific data source has not been selected yet to be a member of the DL. Once this selection is made, it will lead to creating an NFT for that particular source.

For each selected source, a mint function is called through a smart contract which is responsible for creating NFTs for that source and storing it in the Blockchain. The function receives as parameters a Blockchain address representing the source, which is used for verifying the ownership of the source, and a URI that is automatically created from the system and used for storing the metadata of the source to IPFS (Inter Planetary File System). IPFS is a peer-to-peer distributed file system [39] for storing and accessing files, and it is widely used for NFTs due to its high robustness, availability, and immutability. In order to verify the ownership of a specific data source, the NFTs of the data sources can be retrieved through the smart contract. The smart contract is developed in Solidity [38], which is a high-level object-oriented programming language for implementing mainly Ethereum Virtual Machine (EVM)-compatible smart contracts. It is published in the Rinkeby Test Network, which is an EVM-compatible testing Blockchain network.

```
Source 1 Stable Blueprint
<?xml version="1.0"?>

<rdf:RDF
xmlns:rdf="http://www.w3.org/1999/02/22-rdf-syntax-ns#"
xmlns:si="https://www.blueprints.com/source1">

<rdf:Description
rdf:about="https://www.blueprints.com/stable">
  <cd:name>SourceE1</cd:name>
  <cd:varietytype>Business Systems</cd:varietytype>
  <cd:varietypeof>Structured</cd:varietypeof>
  <cd:value>High</cd:value>
  <cd:velocity>3600s</cd:velocity>         Source 1 Dynamic Blueprint
  <cd:veracity>High</cd:veracity>          <?xml version="1.0"?>
</rdf:Description>
                                           <rdf:RDF
</rdf:RDF>                                  xmlns:rdf="http://www.w3.org/1999/02/22-rdf-syntax-ns#"
                                           xmlns:si="https://www.blueprints.com/source1">

                                           <rdf:Description
                                           rdf:about="https://www.blueprints.com/dynamic">
                                             <cd:volume>GB</cd:volume>
                                             <cd:lastupdate>11/08/2022 07:50</cd:lastupdate>
                                             <cd:keywords>
                                               <li>#Energy Prices</li>
                                               <li>#Energy Autonomy</li>
                                             </cd:keywords>
                                             <cd:owner>NULL</cd:owner>
                                             <cd:uri>NULL</cd:uri>
                                           </rdf:Description>

                                           </rdf:RDF>
```

Fig. 7. DSB for Source 1 written in XML.

Let us now assume that the three sources described in Tables 1, 2 and 3 are candidate to become members of the DL. Therefore, the DL owner needs first to build a specific SPARQL, through the Visual Query environment, according to his/her preferences for the data sources characteristics. For example, if the DL owner wants to insert into the DL data sources with *Variety* type of data Structured OR Unstructured, *Value* High, *Veracity* Medium OR High, and with *keywords* #Energy Autonomy, a source selection middleware is fed with these preferred conditions and executes the query after the following SPARQL query is built by the Visual Querying environment presented in Fig. 8:

SELECT ?sources
    WHERE{? Source
        $<$ has varietytypeof $>$ (Structured $||$ Semi $-$ structured) &&
        $<$ has value $>$ (High) &&
        $<$ has veracity $>$ (Medium $||$ High) &&
        $<$ has keyword $>$ #Energy Autonomy}

Table 1. Source 1 DSB attributes.

Stable Blueprint	Value	Dynamic Blueprint	Value
Name	Source-E1	Volume	GB
Variety-Type	Bus. Systems	Last Update	11/08/2022 07:50
Variety-Type of data	Structured	Keywords	# Energy Prices # Energy Autonomy
Value	High	TokenID	Null
Velocity	3600 s		
Veracity	High		

Table 2. Source 2 DSB attributes.

Stable Blueprint	Value	Dynamic Blueprint	Value
Name	Source-E2	Volume	MB
Variety-Type	Web	Last Update	11/08/2022 07:40
Variety-Type of data	Semi-Structured	Keywords	#Weather Conditions
Value	High	TokenID	Null
Velocity	1800 s		
Veracity	Medium		

Table 3. Source 3 DSB attributes.

Stable Blueprint	Value	Dynamic Blueprint	Value
Name	SourceE3	Volume	GB
Variety-Type	Sensors	Last Update	11/08/2022 07:30
Variety-Type of data	Semi-structured	Keywords	# Energy Production # Energy Autonomy
Value	High	TokenID	Null
Velocity	10 s		
Veracity	Medium		

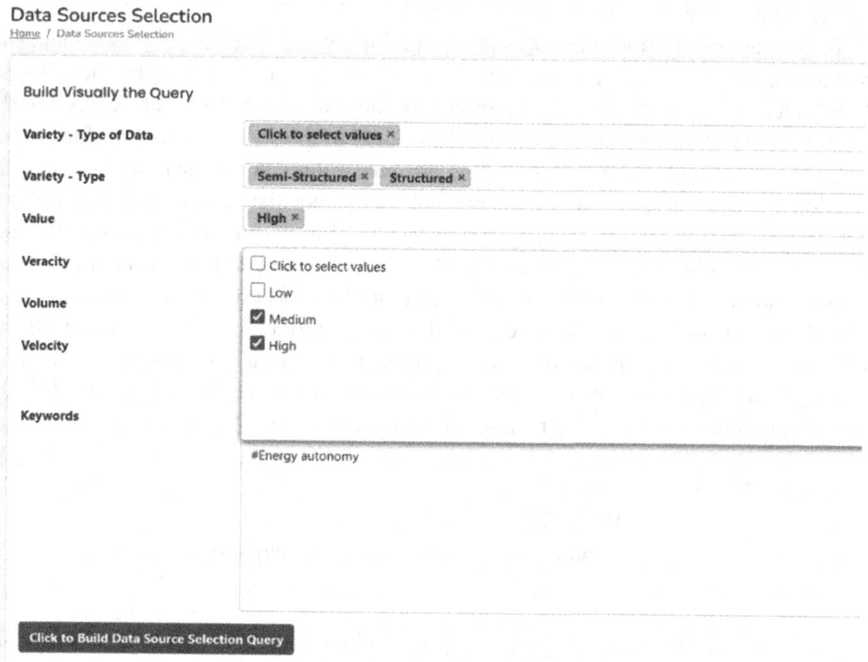

Data Sources Selection
Home / Data Sources Selection

Build Visually the Query

Variety - Type of Data	Click to select values ×
Variety - Type	Semi-Structured × Structured ×
Value	High ×
Veracity	☐ Click to select values
Volume	☐ Low
	☑ Medium
Velocity	☑ High
Keywords	
	#Energy autonomy

Click to Build Data Source Selection Query

Fig. 8. Visual Querying environment source selection.

The execution of the query will result in the creation of the NFTs for Sources 1 and 3, the stable and dynamic blueprints of which will be added to the DL's RDF schema. Therefore, the DSBs of the selected sources become part of the DL and contribute to the DL's metadata semantic enrichment, something which is necessary for their efficient retrieval from the DL. The selected data sources are then distributed to the specific DL Pond according to the variety type attribute of the DSB. Their DSB is added to

Structured Blueprint (SB), Semi-structured Blueprint (SEB) and Unstructured Blueprint (UB) according to the DL Pond to which it is distributed. Essentially, SB, SEB and UB constitute the DLB metadata history as presented in Fig. 4. In essence, this process and its associated characterization helps to manage and enrich the metadata of multiple and diverse sources before and after they become members of the DL. The DL uses the DLB metadata history for filtering and retrieving data based on blueprints and their metadata as soon as a data source is added. This involves characteristics like the type of data produced, the size, the speed, the accuracy, the significance of the data produced by the sources, etc. DSB, as well as the DLB metadata history, provide effective guidance for retrieving, via Visual Querying environment, data from the DL. As presented in the example that follows, the Visual Querying environment is fed with DLB metadata history; as a result, the DL owner is able to query the DL according to the attribute(s) included to the DLB metadata history. It is important to note that in the case of the dynamic blueprint, this part of the metadata will be dynamically updated in the DLB metadata history whenever new data is produced by the sources, or as deemed necessary (e.g., if the location of an associated pond is changed).

To further demonstrate the applicability and the value that the proposed metadata mechanism brings to supporting the data actions in a DL, and in particular the retrieval of data, let us use once again use the example of the sources given earlier. As previously mentioned, the selected data sources are distributed to the specific DL pond for further processing according to the corresponding attribute values. After the completion of the selection process, the retrieval process is based on the metadata DLB metadata history – RDF schema of the DL encoded in the blueprints. Let us now assume that after the selection process Source 1 is a member of the pond with structured data and that Source 3 is also a member of the pond with semi-structured data as presented in Fig. 4.

If the DL owner wishes to retrieve all the energy production data from our DL by the Visual Querying environment in the application layer of a system that uses the DL, then in the simplest case all that needs to be done is to create the following SPARQL query through the Visual Querying environment (see Fig. 9):

> **SELECT**? Dlsources
> **WHERE**{
> ? source < has keyword > #Energy production
> }

As shown in Fig. 9, the Visual Querying environment is fed with DLB metadata history, so DL owners can query DLs using only the attributes in the metadata history.

In essence, Visual Querying essentially retrieves data from the DL and pushes all data sources with the Product Delivery keyword to the application layer. This results in a large volume of data and a greater complexity of filtering after retrieval. Using the metadata provided by the semantic enrichment mechanism, we can refine the type of information sought in the DL and get the results we need through the Visual Querying environment. Of course, more guided queries can be built using such DLB metadata history existing attributes. These guided queries from the Visual Querying environment can range from simple to more sophisticated by utilizing partly or fully the spectrum of the 5Vs data characteristics mentioned in Fig. 2. Thus, they allow not only data scientists

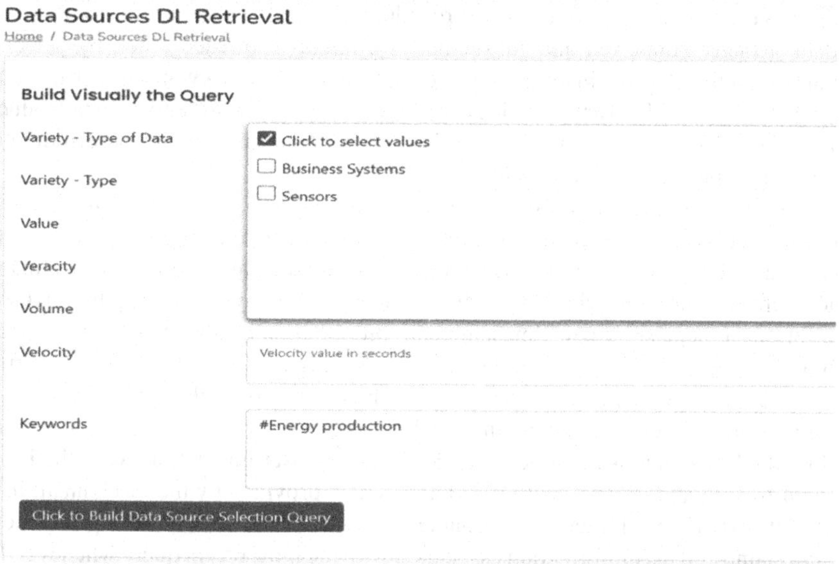

Data Sources DL Retrieval

Home / Data Sources DL Retrieval

Build Visually the Query

Variety - Type of Data	☑ Click to select values
Variety - Type	☐ Business Systems
	☐ Sensors
Value	
Veracity	
Volume	
Velocity	Velocity value in seconds
Keywords	#Energy production

Click to Build Data Source Selection Query

Fig. 9. Visual Querying environment source selection.

but also DL owner without IT knowledge to derive more value from their data and to define custom levels of granularity and refined information in the data sought as required. Essentially, this SPARQL query process and the associated characterization support the handling and management of multiple and diverse types of data sources residing in a DL in a simple yet efficient way. Finally, this latter ensures and vests in the owner ownership of the source by creating NFT data sources after selected to be part of the DL.

4   Preliminary Validation

Based on the analysis presented in [35], DL metadata systems should provide the following characteristics as a minimum: Semantic Enrichment (SE), Data Indexing (DI), Link generation and conservation (LG), Data Polymorphism (DP), Data Versioning (DV) and Usage Tracking (UT). Below we provide a short description for each characteristic:

A SE process uses knowledge bases, such as ontologies, to describe the context of data (e.g., tags). Using semantic enrichment, data from the DL is summarized and linked so that it can be understood and identified. Linking data can be done, for instance, when the tags are the same. This characteristic is met by our mechanism similarly as presented in [7, 31] using both the dynamic and stable blueprints provided in Figs. 5, 6 and 7.

As described in [35], the second major functionality is DI, which involves setting up a data structure based on keywords or patterns for retrieving datasets. DL querying is optimized through keyword filtering using this feature. As illustrated in Figs. 4, 5 and 9, our metadata semantic enrichment mechanism offers this characteristic via the attribute *Variety* - type of data, which is used to distribute data sources and data ponds based on their structure and the keyword attribute within the stable blueprint.

The LG characteristic defined as the procedure to identify data clusters, that is, groups of data strongly connected and substantially different from each other, by detecting similarity relationships or integrating pre-existing links. The keyword properties in the dynamic blueprint, which are modified each time a new data source or new data produced by a registered source are posted to the DL, are the main instruments describing how our system implements this capability.

DV refers to the capability of the metadata system to handle data changes during processing in the DL, while DP refers to the storage of various representations of the same data. When sources in the DL alter or produce new data, our metadata semantic enrichment technique provides these functional qualities by preserving the metadata description - blueprint. A new timestamped representation of the newly pushed data is built and stored in the DL, alongside with pre-existing representations and blueprints. The suggested approach changes the dynamic blueprint, particularly the keywords, as needed, during the data processing in the DL.

Finally, UT, which is the process of documenting user interactions with the DL, is the final functionality mentioned in [35] and is also provided by the mechanism in [7, 31] and its extension reported in this chapter. In essence, the dynamic blueprint records the timestamp and user information associated with the most recent query whenever data is accessed, and this information is also added in the DLB metadata history.

In addition, [35] compares 15 metadata systems in a synthetic way. Using the set of functional characteristics introduced in [7] and some new extra characteristics that were added in this chapter also reported in [37], we compare CoreKG [36] and MEDAL [35], the two most fully developed systems examined in [35] and DLMetachain [37], with our extended metadata data mechanism. DL metadata quality and efficiency can be assessed synthetically based on these extra characteristics, which are:

- Granularity (GR) [7]
- Ease of storing/retrieval (ESR) [7]
- Size and type of metadata (STM) [7]
- Expandability (EX) [7]
- Security and Ownership (SO)
- Process Mining readiness (PR) [37]

Granularity is defined in [7] as the ability to refine what type of information is necessary to retrieve, for example, using keywords. Information sought can be defined at a variety of fine-grained levels using the metadata mechanism.

Ease of storing/retrieval describes the ease of storing or retrieving data in the DL using the metadata mechanism. Retrieval action is assumed to be efficient enough to return the desired parts of the information. For the process of storing and retrieving data items, this characteristic is reflected in the number of steps required.

The *Size and type of metadata* [7] are defined as the volume and type of metadata that the mechanism produces, needed for efficient and accurate retrieval. In general, the greater the size and/or the complexity of the type of data required, the less efficient and suitable the metadata mechanism is.

Expandability [7] refers to the ability to add additional functional features and other approaches to the metadata mechanism. As expected, the better the expanding mechanism, the more open it must be.

Security and Ownership refers to the ability of the DL mechanism to ensure that the data in the DL has not been modified and to enable the sharing of data contained in DLs with verified owners.

Finally, *Process Mining Readiness* as presented in [37] is measured by the number of steps that are needed after the query is executed to provide data suitable for process mining. Using a Likert linguistic scale with the values Low, Medium, and High, these characteristics are assessed in this chapter as defined in Table 4.

As previously mentioned, we use the suggested characteristics to provide a short comparison between our extended metadata enrichment mechanism proposed in this chapter with the two top existing metadata mechanisms suggested by [35], that is, MEDAL and CoreKG, as well as DLMetachain presented in [31].

Table 4. Definition of Low, Medium, High of each characteristic.

Characteristic	Low	Medium	High
Granularity	1 Level	2 Levels	3 or more Levels
Ease of storing and retrieval	5 or more Actions	3–4 Actions	2 Actions max
Size of metadata	KB	MB	GB
Expandability	No	Normal	Limited
Security & Ownership	None	One of them	Both
Process Mining Readiness	5–4 Actions	3–2 Actions	1 Action max

MEDAL follows a graph-based organization based on the idea of an object and a typology of metadata falling in three categories: intra-object, inter-object, and global metadata. It corresponds to a representation and version of an object contained within the hypernode. The nodes in MEDAL are further connected by oriented edges that perform transformations and updates. Several ways can be used to link hypernodes of the mechanism, such as edges for modeling similarity relationships and hyperarcs for translating parenthood relationships. In addition, global resources are present in the form of knowledge bases, indexes, or event logs. SE, DI, LG, DP, DV, and UT are provided by this concept and operation of the framework. MEDAL can be described as having High GR, Medium ESR using Indexes and Event Logs, Medium STM, and an Undefined EX, SO and PR since no reference was made related to these characteristics.

A complete Data and Knowledge Lake Service is offered by CoreKG, which provides researchers and developers with a single REST API for organizing, curating, indexing and querying data and metadata. Using CoreKG's DL service, Web developers can produce data-driven applications using relational and NoSQL databases. Within the DL, these datasets can be created, read, updated, and deleted, and federated search can be applied on top of various islands of data. As well as providing built-in capabilities for authenticating, controlling, and encrypting data, it enhances traceability and provenance. DL's raw data is curated and prepared for analysis by CoreKG on top of the DL layer. Extractions, summaries, enrichments, linking, and classifications are included in this layer. The concept of Knowledge Lake is another component of this mechanism. It is a centralized repository of virtually inexhaustible amounts of raw data, as well as contextualized data. As a result, it provides the foundation for Big Data analytics by automatically curating raw data into data islands, which can provide insights from vast amounts of local, external, and open data that are constantly growing. This service is open-source and offers SE, DI, LG, DP, and UT. According to the suggested property scheme, CoreKG can be assessed as having High GR, Medium ESR utilizing the single API, with Medium STM, and High EXP because it utilizes the Hadoop ecosystem, Medium SO provided by the aforementioned built-in capabilities, and Undefined PR.

The metadata enrichment mechanism of DLMetachain provides DI, LG, DP, DV and UT [31], which is an extension of the mechanism presented in [7]. Both the proposed mechanism of this chapter and DLMetachain offer High GR and High ESR, both using the Stable and Dynamic DSB, with Medium STM, and High EXP. These values are attributed as follows: The use of keywords that specify the sources and the values of the blueprints provide High GR. This gives the user the ability to define specific levels of the properties these keywords offer and the type of blueprint characteristics for which values are preserved. The features set provided by both mechanisms may be regarded as being extremely comprehensive for enabling data retrieval based on precise query-like information. The blueprint description of the DL achieves the High ESR because each time data sources are pushed to the DL, a variety of types of data attributes are produced, aiding the mechanisms' placement of the sources to a particular pond based on the structure of the data involved (structured, semi-structured and unstructured). The DL's source distribution by both mechanisms makes it straightforward and convenient to store and retrieve information. Both systems are distinguished by the Low number of actions to select and query data sources in accordance with Stable and Dynamic blueprint and push data into particular DL Ponds. Due to the creation of the metadata description of the DL each time new sources or data are pushed to the DL, as well as the DV characteristic that the blueprint provides in both mechanisms, the STM produced by the mechanisms has the maximum value. Additionally, because both of DL implementation approaches are built on the Hadoop ecosystem, they offer High EXP. It should be noted here that EXP of the mechanism proposed in this chapter can be traced in the application of visual querying using the simple semantic enrichment and blueprint ontologies during the source selection or data retrieval.

Both mechanisms aim to enhance the privacy, security, and data governance of DLs and, as a result, deal with some of the major challenges encountered in DLs. By storing the descriptive metadata information on the Blockchain, DLMetachain satisfies the SO requirement. This allows for the storage of encrypted metadata information and ensures the immutability of the metadata. This functionality provided by this mechanism offers Medium SO as Ownership is not guaranteed in contrast to the mechanism of this chapter that provides also this characteristic offering High SO. Finally, none of the mechanisms refers to the ability to prepare the data for process mining, but this can be provided by extending the data blueprints.

The information from the brief qualitative comparison between the four mechanisms made in this section is summarized in Table 5. It is evident that the proposed mechanism appears to function better that MEDAL and CoreKG in various characteristics, and that

Table 5. Evaluation and comparison of the mechanisms.

Mechanism/Characteristic	GR	ESR	STM	EXP	SO	PR
Medal	High	Medium	Medium	Medium	Undefined	Undefined
CoreKG	High	Medium	Medium	High	Medium	Undefined
DLMetachain	High	High	Medium	High	Medium	Undefined
Proposed Mechanism	High	High	Medium	High	High	Undefined

is equal in performance with DLMetachain, while outperforming the latter in terms of the SO feature.

5   Conclusions and Future Work

This chapter was involved with a major challenge in DLs, namely the standardization of the processes for storing/retrieving data generated by heterogeneous sources. In this context, it proposed a novel framework for managing data inputted to or outputted from a DL organized with ponds architecture. The proposed framework relies on a semantic enrichment mechanism that utilizes blueprints comprising a set of properties in the form of metadata. This mechanism essentially produces and organizes meta-information describing a data source that will be included in a DL. The meta-information is divided into two categories, each being realized by a dedicated blueprint, which are structured around the 5Vs Big Data characteristics Volume, Velocity, Variety, Veracity and Value: The first blueprint includes static information, that is, information that does not change over time, such as, the name of the source and its velocity of data production. The second encloses descriptors that vary with time as data is produced by the source, such as the volume and date/time of production.

Each time a new data source or a new piece of data are pushed in or out of a DL, the properties in the abovementioned stable and dynamic blueprints are updated and transactions are recorded for historical purposes. The description of the sources offered by the blueprints essentially supports the management of many, multiple, and different types of data sources by contributing to enriching a DLs' metadata information before and after these sources become members. In case a new data source becomes part of the DL, the metadata schema is used to update the description of the whole DL ontology. Therefore, filtering and retrieving data relies solely on this metadata mechanism, mainly utilizing properties and descriptors based on the 5Vs, such as last source updates and keywords.

Two new significant features have been added in the proposed mechanism compared to previous work on the topic. The first revolves around making the approach more usable and easier to learn by using Visual Querying when selecting and retrieve data sources. The second deals with security and integrates the mechanism with NFTs and Blockchain to claim and record ownership of the data sources.

A short evaluation cycle was performed by comparing qualitatively this approach to other existing metadata systems. The results indicated that there is high potential of our approach as it provides a complete and thorough way to characterize the data sources including a set of key properties usually met in literature which is further expanded in this chapter. Finally, the evaluation proved that the proposed approach offers the required tools for efficient and fast retrieval of the information sought.

Future research will concentrate on extending the implementation of the proposed mechanism to a fully-fledged tool to handle the metadata information and the associated blueprints to describe sources with structured, semi-structured and unstructured data. This, in turn, will offer the ability for a more comprehensive evaluation of the proposed framework, as well as its assessment against other existing systems with the use of dedicated performance metrics. Finally, we plan to emphasize more on improving privacy, security, and data governance in DLs by extending the use of Blockchain and smart contracts to cover issues such as ownership transfer.

Acknowledgement. This chapter is part of the outcomes of the CSA Twinning project DESTINI. This project has received funding from the European Union's Horizon 2020 research and innovation program under grant agreement No. 945357. Special thanks are due to Stelios Mappouras for his valuable suggestions on the Blockchain application development.

References

1. Chen, M., Mao, S., Liu, Y.: Big data: a survey. Mob. Netw. Appl. **19**(2), 171–209 (2014)
2. Singh, D.S., Singh, G.: Big data-a review. Int. Res. J. Eng. Technol. **4**(04), 2395-0056 (2017)
3. What is Big Data? Oracle. https://www.oracle.com/big-data/what-is-big-data/. Accessed 01 Aug 2022
4. 25+ impressive Big Data Statistics for 2022. https://techjury.net/blog/big-data-statistics. Accessed 01 Aug 2022
5. Bertino, E.: Big data - opportunities and challenges: panel position paper. In: IEEE 37th Annual Computer Software and Applications Conference 2013, pp. 479–80. IEEE Computer Society (2013)
6. Günther, W.A., Mehrizi, M.H.R., Huysman, M., Feldberg, F.: Debating big data: a literature review on realizing value from big data. J. Strateg. Inf. Syst. **26**(3), 191–209 (2017)
7. Pingos, M., Andreou, A.: A data lake metadata enrichment mechanism via semantic blueprints. In: Proceedings of the 17th International Conference on Evaluation of Novel Approaches to Software Engineering, pp. 186–196 (2022). ISBN 978-989-758-568-5, ISSN 2184-4895
8. Blazquez, D., Domenech, J.: Big data sources and methods for social and economic analyses. Technol. Forecast. Soc. Chang. **130**, 99–113 (2018)
9. Koller, D., Friedman, N.: Probabilistic Graphical Models: Principles and Techniques. MIT press, Cambridge (2009)
10. Ranganath, R., Gerrish, S., Blei, D.: Black box variational inference. In: Artificial intelligence and statistics 2014, pp. 814–822. PMLR (2014)
11. Chen, C., Carlson, D., Gan, Z., Li, C., Carin, L.: Bridging the gap between stochastic gradient MCMC and stochastic optimization. In: Artificial Intelligence and Statistics 2016, pp. 1051–1060. PMLR (2016)
12. Tran, D., Hoffman, M.D., Saurous, R.A., Brevdo, E., Murphy, K., Blei, D.M.: Deep probabilistic programming. arXiv preprint arXiv:1701.03757 (2017)
13. Salvatier, J., Wiecki, T.V., Fonnesbeck, C.: Probabilistic programming in Python using PyMC3. PeerJ Comput. Sci. **2**, e55 (2106)

14. Li, Q., Han, Z., Wu, X.M.: Deeper insights into graph convolutional networks for semi-supervised learning. In: Thirty-Second AAAI Conference on Artificial Intelligence (2018)
15. Tokic, M.: Adaptive ε-greedy exploration in reinforcement learning based on value differences. In: Dillmann, R., Beyerer, J., Hanebeck, U.D., Schultz, T. (eds.) KI 2010. LNCS (LNAI), vol. 6359, pp. 203–210. Springer, Heidelberg (2010). https://doi.org/10.1007/978-3-642-16111-7_23
16. Langford, J., Zhang, T.: The epoch-greedy algorithm for contextual multi-armed bandits. Adv. Neural Inf. Process. Syst. **20**(1), 96–1 (2007)
17. Chapelle, O., Li, L.: An empirical evaluation of thompson sampling. Adv. Neural Inf. Process. Syst. **24** (2011)
18. Krishnamurthy, A., Langford, J., Slivkins, A., Zhang, C.: Contextual bandits with continuous actions: Smoothing, zooming, and adapting. J. Mach. Learn. Res. **21**(1), 5402–5446 (2020)
19. Khine, P.P, Wang, Z.S.: Data lake: a new ideology in big data era. In: ITM Web of Conference 2018, vol. 17, p. 03025. EDP Sciences (2018)
20. Farid, M., Roatiş, A., Ilyas, I F., Hoffmann, H.F., Chu, X.: CLAMS: bringing quality to data lakes. In: Proceedings of the ACM SIGMOD International Conference on Management of Data 2016, pp. 2089–2092. ACM (2016)
21. Miloslavskaya, N., Tolstoy, A.: Big data, fast data and data lake concepts. Procedia Comput. Sci. **88**, 300–305 (2016)
22. Sawadogo, P., Darmont, J.: On data lake architectures and metadata management. J. Intell. Inf. Syst. **56**(1), 97–120 (2020). https://doi.org/10.1007/s10844-020-00608-7
23. The Enterprise Big Data Lake (O'Reilly Online Learning). https://www.oreilly.com/library. Accessed 04 Aug 2022
24. Bell, D., Lycett, M., Marshan, A., Monaghan, A.: Exploring future challenges for big data in the humanitarian domain. J. Bus. Res. **131**, 453–468 (2021)
25. Kościelniak, H., Puto, A.: BIG DATA in decision making processes of enterprises. Procedia Comput. Sci. **65**, 1052–1058 (2015)
26. Gandomi, A., Haider, M.: Beyond the hype: Big data concepts, methods, and analytics. Int. J. Inf. Manag. **35**(2), 137–144 (2015)
27. Luckow, A., Kennedy, K., Manhardt, F., Djerekarov, E., Vorster, B., Apon, A.: Automotive big data: applications, workloads and infrastructures. In: IEEE International Conference on Big Data 2015, pp. 1201–1210. IEEE (2015)
28. Kim, Y., You, E., Kang, M., Choi, J.: Does big data matter to value creation? based on oracle solution case. J. Inf. Technol. Serv. **11**(3), 39–48 (2012)
29. Papazoglou, M.P., Elgammal, A.: The manufacturing blueprint environment: Bringing intelligence into manufacturing. In: International Conference on Engineering, Technology and Innovation (ICE/ITMC) 2017, pp. 750–759. IEEE (2017)
30. Fang, H.: Managing data lakes in big data era: what's a data lake and why has it became popular in data management ecosystem. In: IEEE International Conference on Cyber Technology in Automation, Control and Intelligent Systems (IEEE-CYBER) 2015, pp. 820–824 (2015). IEEE (2015)
31. Pingos, M., Christodoulou, P., Andreou, A. S.: DLMetaChain: an IoT data lake architecture based on the blockchain. In: Information, Intelligence, Systems and Applications Conference (IISA) 2022
32. Raj, P.: Empowering digital twins with Blockchain. Adv. Comput. **121**, 267–283 (2021)
33. Petersen, N., Halilaj, L., Grangel-González, I., Lohmann, S., Lange, C., Auer, S.: Realizing an RDF-based information model for a manufacturing company – a case study. In: d'Amato, C., et al. (eds.) ISWC 2017. LNCS, vol. 10588, pp. 350–366. Springer, Cham (2017). https://doi.org/10.1007/978-3-319-68204-4_31

34. Mehdi, G., et al.: Semantic rule-based equipment diagnostics. In: d'Amato, C., et al. (eds.) ISWC 2017. LNCS, vol. 10588, pp. 314–333. Springer, Cham (2017). https://doi.org/10.1007/978-3-319-68204-4_29

35. Sawadogo, P.N., Scholly, É., Favre, C., Ferey, É., Loudcher, S., Darmont, J.: Metadata systems for data lakes: models and features. In: Welzer, T., et al. (eds.) ADBIS 2019. CCIS, vol. 1064, pp. 440–451. Springer, Cham (2019). https://doi.org/10.1007/978-3-030-30278-8_43

36. Beheshti, A., Benatallah, B., Nouri, R., Tabebordbar, A.: CoreKG: a knowledge lake service. In: Proceedings of the VLDB Endowment 2018, pp. 1942–1945. ACM (2018)

37. Pingos, M., Andreou, A.S.: A smart manufacturing data lake metadata framework for process mining. In: International Conference on Software Engineering Advances (ICSEA) (2022)

38. Solidity Programming Language. https://soliditylang.org/. Accessed 05 Aug 2022

39. IPFS Powers the Distributed Web. https://ipfs.tech/. Accessed 08 Aug 2022

The Ugly Side of Stack Overflow: An In-depth Exploration of the Social Dynamics of New Users' Engagement and Community Perception of Them

Abdullah Al Jobair[1]([⊠])[iD], Suzad Mohammad[2,3][iD], Zahin Raidah Maisha[2,3],
Md. Jubair Ibna Mostafa[2,3], and Md. Nazmul Haque[2,3]

[1] Department of Computer Science and Engineering, United International University, United City, Madani Avenue, Badda, Dhaka, Bangladesh
aljobair@iut-dhaka.edu
[2] Software Engineering Lab (SELab), Islamic University of Technology (IUT), OIC, Gazipur, Dhaka, Bangladesh
{suzadmohammad,zahinraidah,jubair,nazmul.haque}@iut-dhaka.edu
[3] Department of Computer Science and Engineering, Islamic University of Technology (IUT), OIC, Gazipur, Dhaka, Bangladesh

Abstract. Stack Overflow (SO) is the most popular knowledge-sharing platform for novice to experienced programmers. It is growing gradually with its rapidly expanding community of new users. However, the hostile environment towards new users has been a burning issue for several years, which hinders the enhancement of a skillful community. In this research, we study a subset of users registered in the last 45 days or have a reputation of less than or equal to 50 and term them "neophytes." We study if neophytes experience an unwelcoming environment when cooperating on Stack Overflow; if so, we determine the potential reasons behind this problem and determine how much adverse situation affects neophytes' activity. According to our findings, neophytes face difficulty while cooperating on the platform and 9 potential reasons (such as deletion or closing of posts, no answer to the post, rude comments, misconception of SO rules and culture, and steep learning curve) are responsible behind this difficulty. Moreover, the activeness of regular users is 6.71 times more than the neophytes who face adverse situations. It depicts that facing adverse situations reduces the activeness of neophytes. The study aims to address the problems and pathways to maintain a friendly environment for all. The findings of our research study can be used to develop guidance in making the SO community more user-friendly and aid researchers in future studies to improve the Stack Overflow environment.

Keywords: New user · Unwelcoming environment · Hostility · Stack Overflow(SO) · Stack overflow data mining · SE platform · Crowdsourced knowledge sharing · User profiles

1 Introduction

Stack Overflow is the most renowned Q&A platform designed for developers to assist one another and exchange their programming knowledge. The platform has a massive

H. Kaindl et al. (Eds.): ENASE 2022, CCIS 1829, pp. 243–265, 2023.
https://doi.org/10.1007/978-3-031-36597-3_12

user base of 18.4 million users, registering an average of 3370 users and posting around 11,203 posts every day[1] (based on a query run in August 2022). The community's continuous development since 2008 has resulted in today's vast collection of 21 million questions and 31 million answers on Stack Overflow [14]. SO significantly influences its users' willingness to actively contribute and develop the community as a whole.

Maintaining the culture of such an enormous platform is very crucial because it significantly influences its users to actively contribute and develop the community as a whole. However, there have been accusations regarding community health from the very beginning. Although the problem persists on a continual basis, a few lights are shed on the topic with appropriate research and study.

The work of Toth *et al.* [19] is amongs the few studies. According to the study, ambiguity in closing posts create frustrations, especially in less experienced users, and ultimately makes the environment unsupportive to them. Another study [1] by Abbas identified unanswered questions, negative feedback, and deleted questions as the cause of a significant demotivating influence on users. Moreover, new users' posts are getting removed and receiving no response at a higher rate compared with regular users [18].

In addition to researchers, the SO community also expresses concern regarding this pressing matter. As indicated by the annual site satisfaction survey[2] conducted within the community, the unwelcoming environment represents the most frustrating and unappealing element for users of the SO platform. The result of the surveys claims as following -

"The toxic nature of the community .... Scares people from even signing up let alone asking questions"

We address the problem in our study. The study comprises two parts where part one is the hurdle analysis of new users, and part two is the activity or longevity analysis of new users. In the first part of the study [4], we define a specific group of new users called *"neophytes"*. With the help of neophytes data, we validate the authenticity of the problem, i.e., the unwelcoming nature of the SO community, and identify the potential reasons behind this problem. The second part of the study focuses on analysing the activity of both the neophytes and regular users and making a further clustering of neophytes to inspect their reaction to adverse situations.

We organized our study into three research questions -

1. **RQ-1: Do Neophytes Face Hurdles While Collaborating in Stack Overflow?**
   - The question answers the validity of the problem both qualitatively and quantitatively. The investigations provided an affirmative response to the question.

2. **RQ-2: What Are the Potential Reasons for Neophytes Facing Hurdles While Collaborating in Stack Overflow?**
   - Our study identify 9 potential reasons i.e. posts being deleted, rude comments, closed etc. that are accountable for neophytes facing hurdles while collaborating in SO community.

---

[1] https://data.stackexchange.com/stackoverflow/query/1541382.

[2] https://stackoverflow.blog/2020/01/22/the-loop-2-understanding-site-satisfaction-summer-2019/.

3. **RQ-3: How Much Adverse Situation Impacts on the Activeness of Neophytes?**
- An analysis to see the gradual activity of neophytes after facing hurdle. Moreover, a comparison is made to understand the activity among neophytes and regular users.

The remaining sections of the paper are discussed in a manner that Sect. 2 discusses some motivation behind working with this problem. Then we defined the specific group of new users, neophytes. Section 4 discusses some related work on SO. Section 5 is the deliberative discussion on the process we followed to perform the study. The outcome of the process is mentioned in Sect. 6. Section 7 informs about the validity of the study, and lastly, Sect. 8 concludes the study by mentioning some future directions for further investigations.

2 Motivation

Stack Overflow, the largest platform for software developers, has been criticized for its hostile community environment since the beginning. The accusation is proclaimed with numerous pieces of evidence on various blog sites. Even the SO officials and community people are vocal against the issue through meta-discussions, official blogs, and surveys. The continual nature of the problem till today lightens the need to analyze the topic.

Meta Stack Exchange is a Q&A website that discusses the policy related to Stack Exchange websites. A question asked in Meta Stack Exchange in 2008 is now the most upvoted post[3] on the "new user" tag, which asks for the community to be nicer to new users, depicted in Fig. 1. The *"Exception Catcher"*, a renowned blog, states that SO is a difficult community to participate[4].

Fig. 1. Most Upvoted post on Meta Stack Exchange.

Fig. 2. Blog of Jay Hanlon

In addition to that, Slegers' qualitative analysis yields a conclusion on the hostility of Stack Overflow, with the vital claim being that *"Stack Overflow hates new users"*[5].

---

[3] https://meta.stackexchange.com/questions/9953/could-we-please-be-a-bit-nicer-to-new-users.

[4] https://theexceptioncatcher.com/blog/2012/09/stackoverflow-is-a-difficult-community-to-participate-in/.

[5] https://hackernoon.com/the-decline-of-stack-overflow-7cb69faa575d.

As shown in Fig. 2, Jay Hanlon, former Executive Vice President of Culture and Experience of SO also stressed the unwelcoming environment Stack Overflow has and how urgently it needs to change[6].

The hostile environment on Stack Overflow has been there for a long time and shows no signs of change. The Stack Overflow community conducts a site satisfaction survey to learn more about the site users' pain points[7]. In this survey, users were asked this question:

"What do you find most frustrating or unappealing about using Stack Overflow?"

Among 2,942 responses, an unwelcoming community was the top concern. As shown in Fig. 3, according to the data, around 10.6% of the respondents identified the **unwelcoming community** as the most significant factor that makes the SO platform unappealing. The situation remains the same in 2020[8].

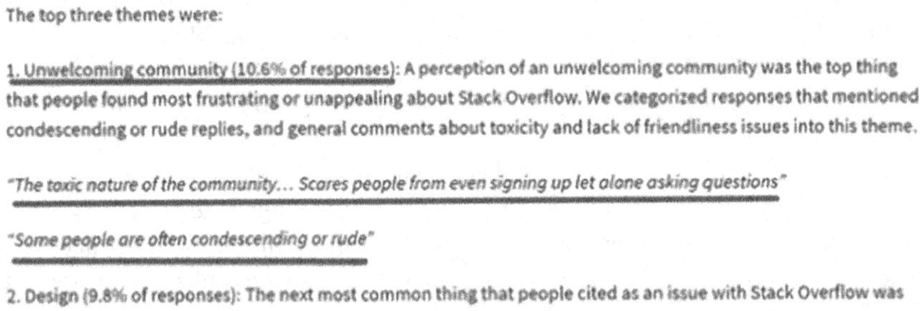

The top three themes were:

1. Unwelcoming community (10.6% of responses): A perception of an unwelcoming community was the top thing that people found most frustrating or unappealing about Stack Overflow. We categorized responses that mentioned condescending or rude replies, and general comments about toxicity and lack of friendliness issues into this theme.

"The toxic nature of the community... Scares people from even signing up let alone asking questions"

"Some people are often condescending or rude"

2. Design (9.8% of responses): The next most common thing that people cited as an issue with Stack Overflow was

Fig. 3. Site Satisfaction Survey 2019.

According to developer survey of 2019[9] and 2020[10] we can clearly see that scenario remain same as previous year. The survey of 2019 presents that 73% users say the situation remains the same as previous year. Whereas, the survey of 2020 (Fig. 4) shows 70.6% vote.

All these resources depict an evident concern among related stakeholders of SO that the community environment is negatively impacting many users.

3   Defining Neophyte

Stack Overflow is the most reliable online platform because of the contributions of people at all skill levels, from beginners to experts [13]. Our research focuses on a fixed set of users labeled as "Neophytes" who have registered in SO in the last 45 days or have

---

[6] https://stackoverflow.blog/2018/04/26/stack-overflow-isnt-very-welcoming-its-time-for-that-to-change/.

[7] https://stackoverflow.blog/2020/01/22/the-loop-2-understanding-site-satisfaction-summer-2019/.

[8] https://insights.stackoverflow.com/survey/2020.

[9] https://insights.stackoverflow.com/survey/2019.

[10] https://meta.stackexchange.com/questions/310881/.

Compared to Last Year, How Welcome Do You Feel on Stack Overflow?

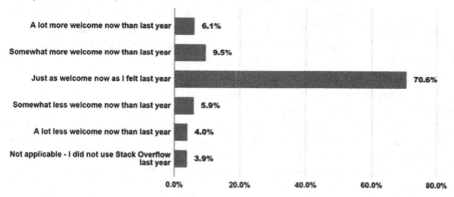

Fig. 4. Developer Survey 2020 [4].

a reputation of less than or equal to 50. We evaluate people who have signed up for SO during the previous 45 days since Stack Overflow considers them *"New users"*(See footnote 10). Although it is a valid sign that new users have joined the platform, it says nothing about their contributions to the site. A condition on reputation is added to check neophytes' contributions to the site.

After a thorough investigation, we arrive at two reputation thresholds of 38 and 50. A study by slag et al. [18] used 38 reputation because they believed it to be the typical reputation of medium-active users. However, a person with a 38 reputation cannot comment, which is an essential feature[11]. On the other hand, if a user reaches 50 reputation, Stack Overflow permits practically all fundamental actions including asking, replying, commenting, and upvoting (except from downvoting, reserved for the reputed users). Thus, 50 reputation is chosen over 38 in order to ensure that users have a significant presence in SO.

Therefore, a user will be considered a neophyte for any one of the aforementioned condition being fulfilled. Other than neophytes, all other users in SO are termed "regular users" throughout the paper.

Algorithm 1. Algorithm to find neophytes from registered user pool [4].

```
1: procedure FINDINGNEOPHYTES(reg_users)
2:     neophytes = []
3:     for each user in reg_users do
4:         if (user.reputation ≤ 50) or (user.registration_day ≤ 45) then
5:             neophytes.add(user)
6:         end if
7:     end for
8:     return neophytes
9: end procedure
```

---

[11] https://stackoverflow.com/help/privileges.

Algorithm 1 is designed to separate neophytes from the pool of registered users [4]. The algorithm is constructed to accept *"reg_users"* as a parameter, which encompasses all registered users' characteristics on the platform. The resulting output is a distinct list of *"neophytes"* separated from the registered user pool. The algorithm begins by initializing an empty list of neophytes in line-2. Next, each registered user is evaluated based on two constraints stipulated in line-4: their reputation score must be below or equal to 50 or their registration date should be within the last 45 days. Users who fulfill either of these conditions are added to the neophytes list. This algorithmic process can be used to analyze the behavior of new users and aid in developing targeted interventions to improve their experience and engagement within the Stack Overflow community. Based on our definition of neophytes, a staggering 89.9%[12] of total users in the Stack Overflow 2020 data dump - equivalent to 14,897,718 individuals - qualify as neophytes.

4   Related Work

After the SO dataset was made available for study, several studies were done. Regularly, several studies were conducted on different disciplines of Stack Overflow.

4.1   The Overall Stack Overflow Environment

The overall Stack Overflow consists of users interacting with each other through questions, answers, comments, and voting. Posts Analysis is one of the research domains related to Stack Overflow with the highest density of research. Among the factors Haifa Alharthi *et al.* discussed in their study to estimate question scores, duplicate question is a significant factor [5]. Users with less expertise are more likely to post duplicate queries, yet duplicate responses to those questions usually contain helpful information for the askers [2].

In a study, Sarah Nadi *et al.* developed four methods for locating crucial sentences in Stack Overflow responses [16]. They demonstrated that no strategy is always effective by contrasting the various approaches even though the theory was proven wrong later on [10].

Studies that categorize comments show how the remarks support learning and skill development [17]. One recent study on SO looked at the platform's comment management and found that 97.3% of the replies are in the hidden comments portion [21]. These comments may be examined to learn more about gender hospitality in Stack Overflow [7].

4.2   New Users and the Atmosphere They Face

Since the creation of SO, several study on "user badge", "reputation", and "engagement on SO" has enhanced the Stack Overflow *User* domain. In a research study on "user badge", Stav Yanovsky *et al.* [20] examined the relationship between user activity and

---

[12] https://data.stackexchange.com/stackoverflow/query/1384160/.

badge accomplishment. Additionally, the writers fabricated the idea that earning badges would boost user engagement. The research of Amiangshu Bosu *et al.* [6], which offered advice to new users on quickly boosting their reputation, is a much-needed contribution for the new users. The relationship between a user's reputation and the diversity of tags associated with their contribution was examined by Laura MacLeod *et al.* [12].

The engagement patterns of people with high and low reputations are strongly correlated. It is known that people with a very high reputation are the primary source of responses, especially good responses [15]. Complete profiles are associated with users that submit more high-quality material and have a more favorable reputation [3].

Numerous studies express worry about the Stack Overflow ecosystem. According to a study on identifying and categorizing offensive words, SO makes itself unwelcoming by employing such language [9]. In a previous study, the authors looked at a subset of users known as "one-day flies" or individuals who left after only making one post [18]. They found that new users commonly submit duplicate queries, frequently post on obscure topics, and receive fewer views. An analysis of the news and debate website "Slashdot" reveals that it has implemented a distributed moderation mechanism to provide feedback on the quality of its contributions [11]. The study discusses three hypotheses regarding users joining a new online community: learning transfer from prior experiences, member observation, and member feedback. Another study of four significant comment-based news sites shows that negative feedback leads to significant behavioral changes that are bad for the community [8].

4.3 Adaptation of Users Based on Environment

Tóth *et al.* [19] discussed the site's professionalism issues and investigated the conflict between emphasizing quantity and quality of questions. Moutidis *et al.* analyze the shifts in prominence of diverse programming languages and frameworks on Stack Overflow over time. According to the study of user data, users frequently stick to one community or receive no score at all [14].

5 Methodology

A brief overview of our research methodology is presented in Fig. 5. The figure consists of 2 separate parts, where the top part represents the *"Hurdles analysis"* of neophytes [4], and the bottom part represents the *"Adaptation/Longevity analysis"* of neophytes. The top part is a synopsis of our previous work [4], and the bottom is our extended work.

For the *"Hurdles analysis"* of neophytes, the neophytes' and regular users' data is extracted from the official SO data dump of 2020. Then, qualitative and quantitative analyses are carried out to answer RQ-1 and RQ-2. Along with the manual analysis, the qualitative analysis involves considering posts, blogs, and surveys. The quantitative analysis comes after the qualitative analysis. A query-based statistical analysis is performed for quantitative analysis.

After the *"Hurdles analysis"* of neophytes, we perform the *"Adaptation/ Longevity analysis"* of neophytes. At first, we extracted 300 regular users' data, 300 neophytes' data who did not face adverse situations, and 300 neophytes' data who faced adverse situations from the SO data dump of 2015. The collected data covers the range from January 2015 to December 2021. Following that, a query-based comparative analysis is conducted on the users' activity to answer RQ-3. The following subsections describe our method with further details.

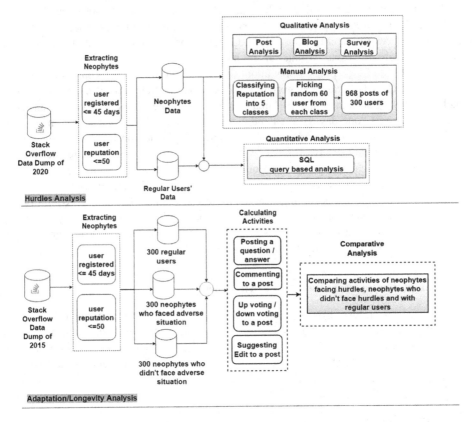

Fig. 5. An Overview of Methodology.

5.1   Data Extraction

The June 2020 database of Stack Overflow was initially used for the analysis. Stack Exchange Archive[13] provides the database. However, we had to select another data source because some tables important to our study were missing from the data dump (e.g., CloseAsOffTopicReasonTypes, CloseReasonTypes, FlagTypes, PendingFlags, SuggestedEdit, PostFeedback, etc.). These tables indicate neophytes facing difficulty in the community; without them, the study loses a substantial amount of weight.

Hence, the "*Stack Exchange Data Explorer*" has been utilized. The Stack Exchange Data Explorer is an online platform intended to facilitate the execution of SQL queries

---

[13] https://archive.org/download/stackexchange.

by utilizing publicly available data linked to the Stack Exchange Network. The data were acquired during the month of August 2021, when we conducted our analysis. Table 1 provides a succinct overview of the dataset [4].

Table 1. An overview of dataset for hurdle analysis [4].

	Dataset
Total Posts	4,456,062
Neophytes' Posts	1,161,701
Data Duration	1st January - 31st December, 2020

A timeframe of 1st January 2020 to 31st December 2020 is selected for the queries to comprehend the current situation. The 2021 dump was omitted to avoid anomalies as it was not completely published then. The one-year timeframe consists of a total of 4,456,062 posts. Among these posts, 1,161,701 posts are posted by 619,171 neophytes. This represents a neophyte posting an average of 1.88 posts. On the contrary, on average, 3,294,361 posts are posted by 458,745 regular users, meaning each regular user posts 7.18 posts. Since most of the study used data ranging from 6 months to 1 year, the data used in this study is sufficient. We use Python for our statistical analysis. Our analysis is conducted entirely through the SQL Server database because Stack Overflow stores its data dumps in SQL Server databases.

The following sections discuss the analysis and methodologies used to answer the research questions in detail.

5.2   RQ-1: Do Neophytes Face Hurdles While Collaborating in Stack Overflow?

Both qualitative and quantitative analyses have been conducted to investigate whether the hurdles encountered by neophytes are a myth or an empirical reality. According to our definition (in Sect. 3), a large portion of 89% of users of SO are neophytes. So, the outcomes of this question will be highly significant.

Qualitative Analysis. The whole process of qualitative analysis is divided into two types of inspections. One is the analysis of Posts, blogs, and surveys. Another is the manual analysis.

Starting from the Meta Stack Exchange posts to the official blogs and surveys[14], [15], the unwelcoming environment of SO is evident. From this evidence, we get some influencing factors to make the environment of SO hostile.

The second part is the manual analysis conducted on 300 randomly selected neophytes. While selecting the neophytes, we have clustered the reputation boundary into 5 classes (0–10, 11–20, 21–30, 31–40, and 41–50 reputations). Now, from each of the reputation classes, 60 random neophytes are selected. In this way, we accumulate a total

---

[14] https://tinyurl.com/424h7w4j.

[15] https://theexceptioncatcher.com/blog/2012/09/stackoverflow-is-a-difficult-community-to-participate-in/.

of 300 neophytes. The reputation boundary-wise selection process avoids biases. These 300 neophytes posted a total of 968 posts. The manual analysis consists of this dataset, and a prospective list of reasons is accumulated by manually investigating the posts.

Quantitative Analysis. The quantitative analysis consists of a query-based investigation on "Stack Exchange Data Explorer". It contains a statistical analysis comparing total neophytes and total users, posts of neophytes with posts of all users. Furthermore, the number of downvoted posts and if the first post is negatively scored is also inspected.

5.3 RQ-2: What Are the Potential Reasons for Neophytes Facing Hurdles While Collaborating in Stack Overflow?

Finding potential reasons not only requires identifying the reasons but also validating them. This necessitates both qualitative and quantitative analysis. The qualitative analysis is for finding prospective reasons, and the quantitative analysis is for statistically confirming the reasons. Thus, the quantitative analysis is performed only after conducting the qualitative analysis.

The steps performed to answer RQ-2 are listed below -

1. Qualitative analysis to identify prospective reasons for neophytes facing hurdles in Stack Overflow.
2. Quantitative analysis to statistically authenticate the prospective reasons.

Qualitative Analysis. The qualitative analysis is performed to fetch out a list of prospective reasons. To do so, we used the same dataset of 968 posts of randomly chosen 300 neophytes which have been used to answer RQ-1. A rigorous analysis is done not only over the 968 posts but also on the 300 neophytes' profiles. Profile analysis is necessary to acknowledge the hurdles they are facing.

The profile analysis includes the following inspections -

- Gradual activity of user.
- Number of badges of user.
- Analysis of acquired badges.
- Total posts.
- Date different between first and last post.
- Date difference between highest negative scored post and immediate next post.

After observing the aforementioned scopes, we put an observation comment against a user. The observation comment tells about whether the user is facing hurdles and the probable reasons for such hurdles.

Quantitative Analysis. The quantitative analysis is organized fully with numerous query-based statistical analyses. Several queries are formulated to understand and authenticate the prospective reasons obtained from "*Qualitative Analysis*". The queries try to understand the user's situation against each reason. The Stack Overflow data dump of 2020 (as described in Sect. 5.1) has been used to investigate the process.

5.4   RQ-3: How Much Adverse Situation Impacts on the Activeness of Neophytes?

To assess the activeness of neophytes after being faced with an adverse situation, we analyzed their gradual activity on SO and how much they contribute under unpleasant scenarios. We try to figure out a comparative analysis among three distinct groups of users' activity in this platform, i.e., continuous activity of regular users, continuous activity of neophytes who did not face any adverse situation, and continuous activity of neophytes who faced adverse situations.

Defining "Activity".   In order to perform the comparative analysis, first, the term *"activity"* needs to be defined. A considerably more wide-ranging dataset must be extracted to examine the progressive change in activity. Under activity, we have considered the following criteria of a user:

- Posting a question / answer
- Commenting to a post
- Up voting / down voting to a post
- Suggesting Edit to a post

Dataset Collection.   Initially, we worked with the 2020 Stack Overflow Data Dump, which was also used for RQ-1 and RQ-2. However, for RQ-3, the dataset proved to be too small. A much more diverse dataset is needed to evaluate the gradual change in activity. So, the data dump from January 2015 to December 2021 was selected for analysis. From the data dump, 300 regular users were randomly selected, along with 300 neophytes who faced an adverse situation and 300 neophytes who did not face an adverse situation. The data have been picked randomly to eliminate any biases in obtaining a collection of 900 users.

The 50 points of the neophytes' reputation border, which serves as the selection criteria, are segregated into 50 classes, each symbolizing a single reputation. From each reputation, 6 randomly selected users are chosen. This is done until reputation 50 to accumulate 300 random neophytes. On the contrary, for the accumulation of 300 random regular users' sets, we randomly selected users with reputations above 50. This ensures that users from all reputation ranges get included in the dataset.

Comparative Analysis.   A query-based comparative analysis is performed to observe each accumulated user's gradual activity. For each user, we checked if the user performed any activity on the activity list mentioned in *"Defining Activity"*. Their number of activity, activity type, and year of activity is tracked. This process is performed over 900 users divided into 3 sets. Each set contains 300 users (one set for 300 neophytes facing adverse situations, another for 300 neophytes without any adverse situation, and the last for 300 regular users). The quantitative analysis result provides crucial statistics on the effects of adverse situations on neophyte activity, which are displayed in the RQ-3 result section.

6   Result Analysis

6.1   Result of RQ-1

Out of the 968 posts, 62 posts are closed, and 47 are marked to be duplicated. 110 posts received no response, even though the posts' score is 0. A total of 123 posts are negatively scored without mentioning any reason. A massive amount of 254 posts are negatively scored. The results of the quantitative analysis are depicted in Figure The results of the quantitative analysis is depicted in Fig. 6. According to the analysis, a total of 49% of posts are evident of facing hurdles. While calculating the total number of posts facing hurdles, we avoid 123 posts that negatively scored without reasoning posts because those are already included in the 254 negatively scored posts.

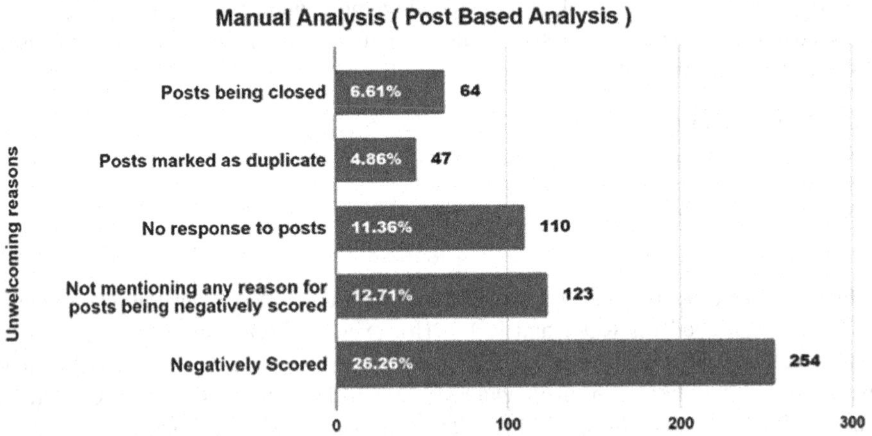

Manual Analysis (Post Based Analysis)

Fig. 6. Post based Manual analysis [4].

A total of 1,161,701 posts are posted by neophytes in 2020, which is 26.07% of the total posts in 2020. Among these 26.07% posts, 9.35% (108,568) posts are negatively scored. Although the ratio seems normal, however, it declines to only 3% when it comes to the case of regular users.

All the findings are depicted in Fig. 6. It leads us to conclude that neophytes face hurdles in Stack Overflow while participating.

Key Findings of RQ-1.

Based on the results of the qualitative analysis, nearly half (49%) of the total 968 posts of neophytes are identified to be afflicted by various issues (such as duplication, closure, and negative scoring). The findings of the quantitative analysis indicate that neophytes' total 9.35% of posts received a negative score, whereas regular users' only 3% of posts received a negative score. The analysis clearly illustrates that neophytes encounter hurdles when collaborating on Stack Overflow.

6.2   Result of RQ-2

The analysis starts with the qualitative analysis and then the quantitative analysis. The qualitative analysis provides a list of 9 potential reasons. Later on, quantitative analysis validates the reasons. However, some reasons do not have proper data to authenticate them. The privacy policy of Stack Overflow keeps those data private, and this caused us to rely only on qualitative analysis for those reasons. A statistical evidence of unwelcoming reasons is depicted in Fig. 8.

Qualitative Analysis. From the profile analysis of 300 neophytes, 77 were found to get the "*Informed*" badge. Stack Overflow provides the badge to those who have gone through the entire tour page. It indicates that the user is informed about SO rules. Only 25.67% of neophytes are acquainted with SO rules. 13.67% of neophytes halted posting after their posts got negative scores. The numerical value of this group is 41 among the 300 neophytes. The vital criterion to realize the participation of neophytes in SO is to inspect whether a neophyte is a one-day fly or not [18]. 62 neophytes are found to be one day fly which is 20.67%. Further analysis of these 62 one-day flies shows that 44 of them got zero or negatively scored in their first post. An overview of profile-based analysis is depicted in Fig. 7

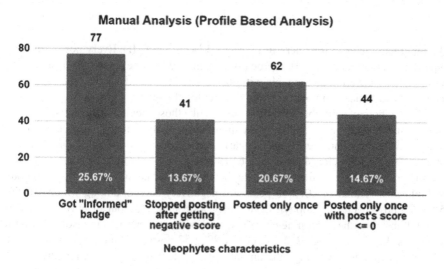

Fig. 7. Profile based manual analysis [4].

The qualitative analysis also provides us with 9 prospective reasons for neophytes' facing hurdles. The prospective reasons are listed below -

– Post being closed.
– Posts marked as duplicate.
– Not mentioning any reason for posts being negatively scored.
– No response to posts.
– Unaware of Stack Overflow rules and culture
– Deletion of Posts
– Moderation without proper reasoning
– Rude comments
– Steep learning curve

The last four points (Deletion of Posts, Moderation without proper reasoning, Rude comments, and Steep learning curve) remained unsubstantiated because of keeping the data private by SO.

Quantitative Analysis. A number of queries are executed to validate the reasons identified in the qualitative analysis of RQ-2. One such query is given below -

```
1  select count (p.Id)
2  from Posts p
3  inner join Users u
4  on p.OwnerUserId=u.Id
5  inner join PostLinks pl
6  on pl.PostId=p.Id
7  where (u.Reputation<=50 or u.CreationDate>=getdate()-45)
8  and (p.CreationDate between datefromparts(2020,01,01) and
       datefromparts(2020,12,31))
9  and (pl.LinkTypeId=3)
```

Listing 1.1. Query to find posts marked as duplicate [4]

The input parameter of the query in Listing 1.1 [4] is a post ID. Every post with Link-TypeId 3 is a duplicate post. The same point is checked in line 9. To take posts of only neophytes, we have joined the table with the "Users" table and checked the reputation, account creation date, and post creation date within the query.

With the help of a number of similar queries like those mentioned above, the statistical quantitative analysis is executed. The quantitative analysis helps build a comparison between neophytes and the overall scenario of SO, depicted in Table 2 [4]. Out of a total of 104,461 total closed posts, 52,761 (50.5%) posts belong to neophytes. 48.96% (38,508 posts out of a total of 78,652 duplicate posts) of neophytes' posts are marked as duplicates. A total of 207,508 posts got negatively scored, among which 108,568 (52.32%) posts were of neophytes. Similarly, 44.8% (25,421 out of 56,717 posts) of the total posts that have been negatively scored without mentioning reasons belong to neophytes. Lastly, 18.29% (212,457 out of 892,557 posts) of total responseless posts belong to neophytes. Although the amount seems quite fine, actually, neophyte posts much less in comparison to regular users. So, the ratio of neophytes' posts facing hurdles in comparison to regular users is many folds.

Posts Being Closed. The quantitative analysis shows that about 50.5% of closed posts are of neophytes, which looks normal. However, the alarming fact is 4.54% of the total posts of neophytes are getting closed, whereas the ratio is only 1.57% for regular users. The clear distinction between the ratio of neophytes' posts getting closed and that of regular users shows the impact of this reason. The frequent closure of posts is one reason that frustrates the users and hurls them away from the community.

Posts Marked as Duplicate. Although compared to total posts, 48.96% of duplicate posts are from neophytes, the ratio of making a duplicate post is 3 folds compared to regular users. 3.31% of posts of neophytes are marked duplicates. The ratio declines to 1.3% for regular users.

Table 2. Comparison of total posts and neophytes posts [4].

Unwelcoming Reasons	Total Posts	Neophytes Posts
Posts being closed	104,461	52,761 (50.5%)
Posts marked as duplicate	78,652	38,508 (48.96%)
Negative scored posts	207,508	108,568 (52.32%)
Not mentioning any reason for posts being negatively scored	56,717	25,421 (44.8%)
Posts getting no response at all	892,557	212,457 (18.29%)

The community often reacts negatively to duplicate posts. However, Abric et al. [2] show that repeated inquiries and replies often contain helpful information for the asker in their research. The goal of the original inquiry, even if it is flagged as a duplicate question, is not served. The neophytes are frustrated by this because they did not receive assistance and, on top of that, had to deal with strict moderation.

Not Mentioning Any Reason for Posts Being Negatively Scored. One strategy that helps maintain the platform's quality is downvoting posts. However, the goal is not achieved if it is done without a justification for what went wrong with the post.

A total of 25,412 posts of neophytes in 2020 were found negatively scored without mentioning any reason. About 2.19% of posts of neophytes have received this fate. Even though it may appear insignificant, such conduct severely discourages neophytes from continuing to make contributions to the site.

Posts Got No Response at All. A total of 212,457 posts of neophytes in 2020 remained completely responseless. That is, those posts are not closed or answered and contain no comments, flags, or edit suggestions.

The alarming fact is that 112,486 neophytes halted posting further after their posts got no response. It is 53.81% of total neophytes whose posts got no response.

Unaware of Stack Overflow Rules and Culture. 2,174,619 neophytes (15.15%) did not go through the tour page of SO. The number is a huge amount, and the tour page is the first step that introduces SO to a newly registered user.

Neophytes frequently provide irrelevant solutions, security-vulnerable responses, opinion-based inquiries, request debugging and break Stack Overflow rules. All of these result from being uninformed about SO culture and rules. Neophytes are frequently unaware of Stack Overflow conventions, which causes misunderstandings between neophytes and regular users. Regular users see this undermining SO's integrity because the site becomes flooded with repetitive and pointless posts. However, the outcome of this dynamic frequently dissuades neophytes from participating further in this platform.

Deletion of Posts. It is tough to perform any quantitative research on deleted posts because Stack Overflow keeps all information pertaining to post-deletion confidential[16]. However, counting the number of neophytes earning the "Peer Pressure" badge can provide insight into the deletion of posts. Users can get the "Peer Pressure" badge by deleting their own posts with a score of −3 or below. According to the quantitative analysis, there were 153,515 neophytes with the "Peer Pressure" badge in 2020.

Deleted posts are one of the significant factors hindering users from participating in Stack Overflow [1]. Posts by One Day Fly make up 15.4% of all posts that have been deleted [18].

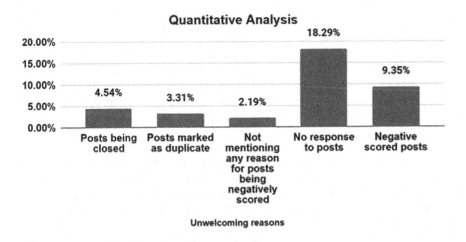

Fig. 8. Quantitative analysis [4].

Moderation Without Proper Reasoning. Users in SO receive responses relatively quickly, usually within 21 min[17]. Because of Stack Overflow's lightning-fast moderation, queries are often closed, deleted, or given negative feedback in less than 10 min(See footnote 17). Users may become frustrated as a result of this easily. As a result, it is one of the key elements that hinders communication between experienced users and neophytes.

Rude Comments. Rude Comments are promptly flagged and removed. However, users still read insulting remarks about them even in that case. This phenomenon serves as a source of frustration and alienation for individuals new to the Stack Overflow community and unfamiliar with its cultural norms. We discovered multiple instances throughout our analysis of the profiles of neophytes that suggest a neophyte ceased contributing after receiving unfavorable feedback on their contributions. Rude remarks made to neophytes make them unhappy and cause them to quit the community.

---

[16] https://stackoverflow.com/questions/56770820/.
[17] https://meta.stackexchange.com/questions/61301/.

Steep Learning Curve. In contrast to the majority of question-and-answer websites, Stack Overflow aims to establish a useful developer knowledge base. The learning curve for participation in SO is steep to retain such efficacy. This brings up the idea that it takes time to comprehend SO's goals or interact with the community appropriately. By then, neophytes are inundated with downvotes, closure deletions, and other lousy feedback.

Key Findings of RQ-2.
The factors that contribute to the hurdles faced by neophytes in Stack Overflow are - posts being closed, posts marked as duplicate, not mentioning any reason for posts being negatively scored, no response to posts, the misconception of Stack Overflow rules and culture, deletion of posts, moderation without proper reasoning, rude comments, steep learning curve.

6.3 Result of RQ-3

The accumulated results of RQ-3 are portrayed in 3 different tables. Each table represents each group of users' activity. Table 3 represents the year-wise activity of regular users. Table 4 represents the year-wise activity of neophytes who did not face adverse situations, whereas Table 5 represents the year-wise activity of neophytes who faced adverse situations. Each table consists of 6 columns, i.e., "*year*" represents activity year, "*total participation*" represents the total number of unique users showed their activity within that corresponding year, "*total activity count*" represents the total number of activity within that year by participated users, "*maximum count*" represents the maximum number of activity by a user on that year, "*minimum count*" represents the minimum number of activity by a user on that year and "*standard deviation*" represents the deflection of activity count within that year.

According to the quantitative analysis, the activity count of 300 regular users is 8786 from January 2015 to December 2021, depicted in Table 3. We can observe from Table 4 that the count decreases to 2351 for neophytes without facing any adverse situation. In contrast, the activity number declines to only 1306 (in Table 5) for neophytes facing adverse situations.

Table 3. Year wise activity of Regular User.

Year	Regular User				
	total participation	total activity count	maximum count	minimum count	standard deviation
2015	236	3190	174	0	20.78879938
2016	160	1641	126	1	14.50232984
2017	156	1298	73	1	10.1992961
2018	119	937	81	1	11.35300649
2019	102	669	106	1	12.5757692
2020	87	688	54	1	11.12783247
2021	70	363	41	1	6.930907164
		Total = 8786			

Table 4. Year wise activity of neophytes not in adverse situation.

Year	Neophytes Not in Adverse Situation				
	total participation	total activity count	maximum count	minimum count	standard deviation
2015	226	1350	92	1	8.88590412
2016	67	280	18	1	4.277939794
2017	66	283	16	1	3.011593759
2018	49	173	11	1	2.836532807
2019	28	78	11	1	2.266619981
2020	36	139	44	1	7.464785052
2021	20	48	6	1	1.353358396
		Total = 2351			

Table 5. Year wise activity of neophytes facing adverse situation.

Year	Neophytes Facing Adverse Situation				
	total participation	total activity count	maximum count	minimum count	standard deviation
2015	191	527	51	1	4.345362089
2016	67	261	55	1	7.383713298
2017	45	127	12	1	2.470635628
2018	36	160	36	1	7.361849319
2019	39	94	10	1	2.325125336
2020	25	87	31	1	6.318755152
2021	18	50	8	1	2.101975417
		Total = 1306			

The comparative analysis outcome is precisely depicted in Fig. 9, where each activity curve line represents each set of users separately. Although the activity curve of 300 regular users shows a slight declining nature, it is much more consistent compared with the other two groups. The amount of activity is much higher in every year. We can observe from Fig. 9 that the activity curve of 300 neophytes who did not face any difficulties shows a stable nature. However, the activity count is significantly less than regular users. Finally, the quantitative analysis of 300 neophytes facing adverse situations leads us to a slanting curve line of their gradual activity. The pattern shows a high range of activity at the beginning and a gradual decrease with time progress.

A total of 3190 activities were noted in 2015 by 300 regular users, depicted in Table 3. The standard deviation of activity count is 20.79 in that same year. The standard deviation of activity count becomes 14.50 with 1641 activities in the next year, 2016. In 2017, the standard deviation of activity count turned to 10.19, with a total count of 1298 activities. The following year accounts for a total activity of 937 posts where the standard deviation of count increases to 11.35. In 2019, the standard deviation of

Regular User Activity VS Neophytes (not in adverse situation) Activity VS Neophytes (facing adverse situation) Activity

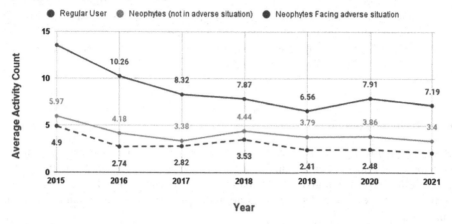

Fig. 9. Gradual activity curve of regular users, neophytes not in adverse situation and neophytes facing adverse situation.

activity count ended up at 12.57, with a total count of 669 posts. The standard deviation of activity count is 11.12 and 6.93 for the following 2020 and 2021, respectively. The total activity in 2020 and 2021 is 688 and 363, respectively.

The standard deviation of activity count for neophytes not facing adverse situations was 8.88 in 2015, presented in Table 4. A total of 1350 activities are observed in that year. The count exceedingly decreases in the following two years, i.e., 2016 and 2017. The standard deviation of activity count is 4.27 and 3.01, with a total activity of 280 and 283, respectively. The standard deviation of activity count roams around 2.83 and 2.26 for the following years, with a total activity count of 173 and 78, respectively. The standard deviation of activity count following 2020 and 2021 accounted for 7.46 and 1.35, respectively. During the tenure, the total activity is numbered 139 and 48 in the following years.

Table 5 presents that the standard deviation of activity count started at 4.34 in 2015. The count was unstable in the following years. In 2016 the value increased to 7.38. A little spike was noticed in 2017 and 2018, with a standard deviation of activity count of 2.47 and 7.36, respectively. However, the declining slope continues in the following year. The standard deviation of activity counts for 2019, 2020, and 2021 are 2.32, 6.31, and 2.10, respectively. The year-wise total activity count is 527, 261, 127, 160, 94, 87, and 50 in the year 2015, 2016, 2017, 2018, 2019, 2020, and 2021 respectively. The amount of activity depicts the significantly declining nature with the progress of time. Even the activities are much less compared to the regular users' activity.

The results indicate that for the neophytes who face adverse situations, the activity is almost as half as that of those who do not face adverse situations or difficulties. In comparison, regular users' activity is 6.71 times more than neophytes facing adverse situations. This shows how significant the effect of an unwelcoming situation is on the activity of neophytes and how it discourages them from participating.

> **Key Findings of RQ-3.**
> The information shows that regular users' activity count is 6.71 times compared to neophytes facing hurdles. Furthermore, neophytes not facing adverse situations have twice the activity count compared to neophytes facing adverse situations. So, it is evident that with facing a hurdle, the activity ratio declines, and facing a hurdle is a factor that reduces the activeness of neophytes.

6.4   Recommendation

Based on the findings of the research questions presented above, it is evident that the creation of an improved environment within Stack Overflow requires the implementation of effective collaborative efforts and initiatives from both neophytes and the platform itself. We recommend some necessary initiatives for the SO community based on our findings.

- Stack Overflow is recommended to utilize a pre-post automated prediction tool for closed posts, which can effectively anticipate the likelihood of a post being closed before its publication. This tool will be able to anticipate the reasons for the closure of posts and provide corresponding recommendations for their closure. As a result, the number of closed posts within the SO community is expected to diminish.
- In order to foster transparency and accountability, it is recommended that the SO requests moderators and privileged users to provide a suitable explanation for downvoting posts when no cause has been explicitly stated. This could facilitate users in recognizing and addressing their flaws.
- Rude comments must be identified through SO moderation before they are made public. This can be performed by an automated tool. This will suppress offensive words from users' views and, in turn, lessen the aggression.
- It is recommended that, in instances where posts lack any form of response, Stack Overflow should prompt its privileged users to review them. Moreover, necessary measures are to be implemented to detect post-quality. An automated tool can also facilitate routing the responseless posts to the most appropriate recipients.
- Neophytes should take greater care when posting. They must adhere to SO's policies and guidelines. The new users' familiarity with the rules and regulations should be checked through an inspection.

7   Threats to Validity

Internal Validity

- Stack Overflow withholds any information pertaining to the removed posts. The only way to obtain this information is by importing older data and comparing it to the current data, which is not a feasible and tangible task. As a result, our research lacked quantitative analysis on deleted posts due to the unavailability of this data.

– Significant data like closed posts, flags, and proposed revisions to posts in the Stack Exchange Archive are not accessible by Stack Overflow (offline database). As a result, we were motivated to utilize the online version of the SO data dump, specifically the Stack Exchange Data Explorer. However, we faced the constraint of working within a specific time frame due to the frequent updates of online data dumps. This was necessary to avoid potential abnormalities in our data.

External Validity

– We restricted our research to Stack Overflow solely in order to preserve consistency. Therefore, the research's findings could not accurately represent the state of other contemporary Q&A websites (such as Reddit and Quora). To comprehend the general state of new users and their environment, an investigation of these sites is also necessary.
– We examined only the 2020 Stack Overflow database for new users. Databases from covid pre-pandemic and post-pandemic periods could be compared. It may reveal the impact of covid on SO atmosphere and neophyte characteristics.

8   Future Work and Conclusion

Despite years of discussion and minimal action, unwelcoming behavior toward neophytes still exists. Our study addresses this issue with definitive data and statistics by confirming its authenticity, determining potential reasons behind this problem, and finding out the effect of facing adverse situations on neophytes' activeness. The findings will contribute to creating a welcoming environment by bringing together all user groups. It will motivate new users to engage proactively in this popular platform.

Effective research would include analyzing the sentiment of neophytes and determining how rude comments affect their collaboration to SO. The comprehensive investigations will yield optimal recommendations for Stack Overflow to address the issue, thus creating a healthy, welcoming platform for users.

References

1. Abbas, A.E.: Investigating 'one-day flies' users in the stackoverflow: why do and don't people participate? In: 2019 International Conference on ICT for Smart Society (ICISS), vol. 7, pp. 1–5 (2019). https://doi.org/10.1109/ICISS48059.2019.8969815
2. Abric, D., Clark, O.E., Caminiti, M., Gallaba, K., McIntosh, S.: Can duplicate questions on stack overflow benefit the software development community? In: 2019 IEEE/ACM 16th International Conference on Mining Software Repositories (MSR), pp. 230–234 (2019). https://doi.org/10.1109/MSR.2019.00046
3. Adaji, I., Vassileva, J.: Towards understanding user participation in stack overflow using profile data. In: Spiro, E., Ahn, Y.-Y. (eds.) SocInfo 2016. LNCS, vol. 10047, pp. 3–13. Springer, Cham (2016). https://doi.org/10.1007/978-3-319-47874-6_1

4. Al Jobair, A., Mohammad, S., Maisha, Z.R., Mostafa, Md.N., Haque, Md.J.I.: An empirical study on neophytes of stack overflow: how welcoming the community is towards them. In: Proceedings of the 17th International Conference on Evaluation of Novel Approaches to Software Engineering - ENASE, pp. 197–208. INSTICC, SciTePress (2022). https://doi.org/10.5220/0011081100003176. ISBN 978-989-758-568-5. ISSN 2184-4895

5. Alharthi, H., Outioua, D., Baysal, O.: Predicting questions' scores on stack overflow. In: Proceedings of the 3rd International Workshop on CrowdSourcing in Software Engineering. p. 1–7. CSI-SE 2016. Association for Computing Machinery, New York, NY, USA (2016). https://doi.org/10.1145/2897659.2897661

6. Bosu, A., Corley, C.S., Heaton, D., Chatterji, D., Carver, J.C., Kraft, N.A.: Building reputation in stackoverflow: an empirical investigation. In: 2013 10th Working Conference on Mining Software Repositories (MSR), pp. 89–92 (2013). https://doi.org/10.1109/MSR.2013.6624013

7. Brooke, S.: condescending, rude, assholes: framing gender and hostility on stack overflow. In: Proceedings of the Third Workshop on Abusive Language Online, pp. 172–180 (2019)

8. Cheng, J., Danescu-Niculescu-Mizil, C., Leskovec, J.: How community feedback shapes user behavior. In: Eighth International AAAI Conference on Weblogs and Social Media (2014). https://doi.org/10.1007/978-3-030-72376-7_2

9. Cheriyan, J., Savarimuthu, B.T.R., Cranefield, S.: Towards offensive language detection and reduction in four software engineering communities. In: Evaluation and Assessment in Software Engineering, pp. 254–259 (2021). https://doi.org/10.1145/3463274.3463805

10. Hart, K., Sarma, A.: Perceptions of answer quality in an online technical question and answer forum. In: Proceedings of the 7th International Workshop on Cooperative and Human Aspects of Software Engineering, pp. 103–106. CHASE 2014. Association for Computing Machinery, New York, NY, USA (2014). https://doi.org/10.1145/2593702.2593703

11. Lampe, C., Johnston, E.: Follow the (slash) dot: effects of feedback on new members in an online community. In: Proceedings of the 2005 International ACM SIGGROUP Conference on Supporting Group Work, pp. 11–20. GROUP 2005. Association for Computing Machinery, New York, NY, USA (2005). https://doi.org/10.1145/1099203.1099206

12. MacLeod, L.: Reputation on stack exchange: tag, you're it! In: 2014 28th International Conference on Advanced Information Networking and Applications Workshops, pp. 670–674 (2014). https://doi.org/10.1109/WAINA.2014.108

13. May, A., Wachs, J., Hannák, A.: Gender differences in participation and reward on stack overflow. Empirical Softw. Eng. 24(4), 1997–2019 (2019)

14. Moutidis, I., Williams, H.T.: Community evolution on stack overflow. Plos one 16(6), e0253010 (2021). https://doi.org/10.1371/journal.pone.0253010

15. Movshovitz-Attias, D., Movshovitz-Attias, Y., Steenkiste, P., Faloutsos, C.: Analysis of the reputation system and user contributions on a question answering website: stackoverflow. In: 2013 IEEE/ACM International Conference on Advances in Social Networks Analysis and Mining (ASONAM 2013), pp. 886–893 (2013). https://doi.org/10.1145/2492517.2500242

16. Nadi, S., Treude, C.: Essential sentences for navigating stack overflow answers. In: 2020 IEEE 27th International Conference on Software Analysis, Evolution and Reengineering (SANER), pp. 229–239 (2020). https://doi.org/10.1109/SANER48275.2020.9054828

17. Sengupta, S., Haythornthwaite, C.: Learning with comments: an analysis of comments and community on stack overflow. In: Proceedings of the 53rd Hawaii International Conference on System Sciences (2020)

18. Slag, R., de Waard, M., Bacchelli, A.: One-day flies on stackoverflow - why the vast majority of stackoverflow users only posts once. In: 2015 IEEE/ACM 12th Working Conference on Mining Software Repositories, pp. 458–461 (2015). https://doi.org/10.1109/MSR.2015.63

19. Tóth, L., Nagy, B., Gyimóthy, T., Vidács, L.: Why will my question be closed? nlp-based pre-submission predictions of question closing reasons on stack overflow. In: 2020 IEEE/ACM 42nd International Conference on Software Engineering: New Ideas and Emerging Results (ICSE-NIER), pp. 45–48 (2020)
20. Yanovsky, S., Hoernle, N., Lev, O., Gal, K.: One size does not fit all: a study of badge behavior in stack overflow. J. Assoc. Inf. Sci. Technol. **72**(3), 331–345 (2021). https://doi.org/10.1002/asi.24409
21. Zhang, H., Wang, S., Chen, T.H.P., Hassan, A.E.: Are comments on stack overflow well organized for easy retrieval by developers? ACM Trans. Softw. Eng. Methodol. **30**(2) (2021). https://doi.org/10.1145/3434279

Systems and Software Quality

Better Understanding Diverse End User Website Usage Challenges with Browser-Based Augmented Reality Approaches

Minh Hieu Vu, Joshua (Shuki) Wyman, John Grundy(✉) ⓘ, and Anuradha Madugalla

Department of Software Systems and Cybersecurity, Faculty of IT, Monash University, Clayton, Australia
{john.grundy, anu.madugalla}@monash.edu
https://www.monash.edu/it/humanise-lab

Abstract. Software engineers are usually quite different from their end users, especially those with a variety of accessibility related usage challenges. These include, but are not limited to, sight, hearing, cognitive, mobility, hand control, age, language and many others. A popular approach to assist developers in understanding and designing for these diverse end user accessibility challenges are 'Augmented Reality' (AR) browser-based plug-ins. These attempt to mimic how a user with a particular challenge or set of challenges will perceive viewing and interacting with a target web site. We review work on developing such plug-ins, summarise some of the popular AR brower-based plug-ins designed to support accessibility design and evaluation, and report results of a developer survey we conducted on their requirements and usage of such tools. We then report a detailed heuristic evaluation of a popular example, Funkify, and discuss the performance of several of its simulators on commonly used web site exemplars. Finally we identify and report a range of future research needs in this area.

Keywords: Human computer interaction · Accessibility · Human aspects · Disability simulation · Software engineering

1 Introduction

Many end users of web sites have accessibility-related challenges. An estimated 1 in 6 Australians lives with some form of disability [14]. Increasingly, modern life requires greater online access to education, work, leisure and government services – much more since the COVID-19 pandemic. Therefore it is imperative for websites to accommodate these diverse end users accessibility challenges. Unfortunately, there are still many issues in this front. Almost all of the top 1,000 free Android apps have shown to have severe accessibility issues for many of their target end users [4]. The top 100 banking websites in the US have approximately 6 accessibility violations each on average [35]. Analysis of a large number of app user reviews have shown many accessibility and other human aspects are not catered for [11]. The US saw 3,500 website accessibility lawsuits filed in 2020, and the rate has risen 64% in the first half of 2021 [3,22].

Accessibility research has a high focus on development of design guidelines and tools to aid accessibility. These tools focus on automating issue identification and verifying compliance with accessibility guidelines (eg: Web Content Accessibility Guidelines (WCAG)) [2]. Despite these works, the lack of support on web sites for accessibility related challenges of diverse end users continues to exist as a critical problem [2]. One likely cause for this is the lack of understanding amongst developers about the issues faced by people who are different to them [15,34]. Developers may lack the experience, training and insight to fully grasp how different types of end users interact with web sites, which makes it difficult to design and build suitably accessible websites [6,34].

Several researchers have developed Augmented Reality (AR) browser-based plug-ins which mimic accessibility-related challenges faced by diverse end users when using web sites. In this paper, we survey few of these approaches. These are a commonly used to provide developers with an understanding of how diverse end users interact with their web-based systems. We view key related work in this area, summarise some popular AR browser-based plug-ins designed to support accessibility design and evaluation, and evaluate the performance of a particular example – the Funkify simulator. In contrast to other researches, which focus on design guidelines and suggesting changes or accessibility improvements to these tools by working with real end users, our aim is to understand (i) how such tools may elicit a lasting empathetic response from the developer to their diverse end users' accessibility-related needs, and (ii) if they provide a deeper understanding of their users' needs. We also wanted to compare the Funkify simulator's behaviour to prior studies with real end users and published studies on how users with the simulated challenges actually perceive technology.

In this research, we evaluated Funkify Premium as the free version of Funkify limits simulators features e.g. the colour-blindness simulator to a single type of colour blindness. Funkify Premium is available on a subscription basis and provides access to 4 additional simulators - or 'personas', the ability to manually adjust the sensitivity of each of the personas, and the ability to define new personas using a combination of any of the simulators. For example, Funkify Premium allows the user to select between 7 different types of colour blindness to filter the screen for.

The rest of this paper is organised as follows. Section 2 discusses related work on supporting accessibility for diverse end user challenges. Section 3 summarise the key research questions we wanted to answer, Sects. 4, 5 and 6 present our practitioner survey, Funkify evaluation design and Funkify evaluation results respectively. We then discuss key findings and future work directions in Sect. 7 discusses key findings and recommendations from the work and Sect. 8 key limitations and needed future research recommendations. Section 9 surveys some key related work and finally Sect. 10 summarises the paper.

2   Background

2.1   Human Aspects

Humans are different and many have diverse challenges when making use of software solutions [15]. Some of these are related to physical and mental challenges of the users and software not designed taking these into account will suffer accessibility problems [16,29]. Currently software engineers lack tools and techniques for adequately modelling end users with diverse challenges that impact accessibility [15]. A few examples include:

Blurred Vision. Blurred vision can have a negative effect on a persons' entire line of sight or partially affect one's vision. It includes peripheral vision issues, and it is also possible to experience blurred vision in one eye only. It is often caused by refractive errors (nearsightedness, farsightedness), abrasions to the cornea, age-related macular degeneration, migraine, trauma or injuries to the eye, infectious retinitis [38]. A person with blurred vision can have their functional status and overall well-being severely impacted [23].

Dyslexia. Dyslexia is considered as a language-based learning difference that affects the organization in the brain which controls the ability to process the way language is heard, read, spelled, or spoken. Dyslexia can also have negative effects on a person's working memory, attention, and organization. Davis's research reported 37 common traits of a dyslexic that spans across vision, speech, hearing, writing, motor, math and time management, cognition, behaviour, and personality. Davis stated that people with dyslexia exhibit several common traits and behaviours and these characteristics vary inconsistently [9]. They include reading or writing repetition, transpositions, omissions, reversals or substitutions of letters, numbers and/or words, distraction, movement of letters/words and various others. Mistakes and symptoms increase dramatically with confusion, time pressure, emotional stress, or poor health.

Tremor. Tremor is characterised by shaking movements in a part of the body caused by involuntary muscle contractions. One of the most common neurological diseases, tremor can occur on its own or in conjunction with another neurological disease such as Parkinson's, MS, or stroke. For Parkinson's alone, 1 in every 100 Australians over the age of 60 lives with the disease [10]. Tremors are classified as either rest or action, with action further subdivided to give 7 types of tremors, each with their own typical frequency and amplitude [32]. Designing apps to support people with tremor has been shown to be challenging [37].

Tunnel Vision. Tunnel vision is a colloquial name for peripheral vision loss, a narrowing of the field of view to the extent that the individual can only see directly ahead [1] It is most commonly seen in patients with retinitis pigmentosa or glaucoma, with glaucoma alone affecting over 300,000 Australians. Limited work to date has been done on design guidelines and support for users suffering from tunnel vision [21].

Cognition. Some users have ADHD, autism, cognitive decline and other neurological challenges. Most software developers are unfamiliar with the challenges these can bring, and like Dyslexia, these manifest in different ways for different people [12].

Age. Differently aged users may have very different experiences and expectations of their software [20,25]. Most software engineers are male, relatively young and relatively affluent. When designing for children, elderly or those from different education, cultural, language and other backgrounds to themselves they may struggle to understand needed software differences [20].

2.2   Browser Plug-ins for Accessibility Analysis

A great many browser plugins exist providing web and app accessibility support[1] Only a few seem to use augmented reality-like simulation of end user challenges. Some provide a range of accessibility issue analysis and/or simulation support, whereas others focus on a small range of end user challenges. Table 1 summaries a few examples.

Table 1. Examples of browser plug-ins to assist with web accessibility.

Tool	Description
WAVE	WAVE is a popular Chrome plug-in that highlights potential accessibility issues in a web page
IBM Equal Access Accessibility Checker	Uses IBM's accessibility rule engine to check web site issues and highlight issues
ChromeLens	Provides a range of tools for visual accessibility issue detection
Tenon	Accessibility-as-a-service that scans web site to highlight issues
Chromatic Vision Simulator	Simulator showing impact of various forms of colour blindness
Toptal Colour Blind Web Page Filter	Shows a web page after filtering illustrating different colour blindness impacts
Silktide	Web site accessibility simulator including simulated screenreader
Web Disability Simulator	Plug-in simulating the impact on web site usage of colour blindness, low vision, dyslexia

2.3   Funkify

Funkify is a publicly available extension for Google Chrome that offers a range of simulators for vision, motor, and cognition impairment as well as dyslexia [13]. The extension breaks users down into personas, with each representing a class of challenged end users. Some available personas are shown in Fig. 1. These include vision personas, cognition personas, dyslexia and motor personas. The premium version has some support for combining multiple persona challenges in a simulation. The tool does not support adding new simulators, additional persona information e.g. user stories, demographics etc., or multiple developers sharing persona configurations if working on the same project. To use Funkify, a Chrome browser is installed. The developer then enables a simulator - tagged as a 'persona' - and makes use of their software. The browser plug-in intercepts keyboard input and browser display to mimic how a user with the selected simulator and its configuration settings might experience using the web site.

3   Research Questions

The research was divided into answering four major Research Questions:
RQ1: What Do Developers Think about the Use of Augmented Reality Browser-based Plug-ins for Supporting Design Of Web Sites for Their Accessibility Challenged End Users? To answer this we conducted a survey of developer current usage and opinion on augmented reality browser-based plug-in approaches to help them support diverse user accessibility challenges.

---

[1] A large list is provided by W3.org – https://www.w3.org/WAI/ER/tools/.

Fig. 1. Examples of Funkify Personas (from [34]).

RQ2: Can a Browser-based Augmented Reality Simulation Tool Such as Funkify Personas Give Software Engineers a Useful Experience Of Diverse end User Web Accessibility Challenges? We identified a range of exemplar websites requiring diverse end user accessibility. We identified a range of Funkify personas representing diverse end users with quite different accessibility challenges.

RQ3: How Comparable Are Funkify's Simulations to Documented Experiences of Web Accessibility Challenges? We then designed and carried out an evaluation of Funkify Premium personas on these representative websites and tasks. We looked to see how the simulator's mimiced challenged end user experience compared to those documented by earlier studies with real challenged end users and documented medical literature relating to the simulated challenge.

RQ4: What Extensions to Tools Such as Funkify Would Enhance Their Usability for More Human-centric Software Engineering? We identified a range of needed improvements to the current state of Funkify and related augmented reality browser-based plug-ins.

4 Developer Survey

4.1 Purpose

We conducted this survey to answer the first research question. We achieve this by trying to understand (i) Developers current usage of augmented reality browser-based plug-ins in websites to support accessibility; and (ii) Developers opinions about using such plugins to support accessibility.

4.2 Procedure

The survey consisted of two main sections: demographics and open ended questions. Demographic questions focused on user characteristics, qualifications, job role, domain, expertise and experience in software development. The open ended questions focused on developer's current practices to support accessibility, their understanding and usage of augmented reality browser-based plug-ins to support accessibility and general feedback on software accessibility.

We created the survey in Qualtrics platform and launched it via social media and Prolific platforms. We obtained 30+ responses in a duration of 2 months.

4.3   Results

Participants. We had 30 usable responses whose results we report here, 24 male and 6 female. Ages ranged from 20–29 (16), 30–39 (9), 40–49 (1), 50–59 (2) and 2 not specified. Locations were Europe (19), Africa (9), North America (4), Oceania (4) and South America (3). Most (25) has a Bachelors degree, and most areas were Computer Science (12) or Information Technology (12). Years of experience were 0–3 (20), 4–6 (4), 7–9 (4) and 10+ (2). We asked about job roles (past and present) and domains of work. These are summarised in Table 2. Figure 2 shows a summary of the key survey findings.

Table 2. Survey Participant Role and Domains.

Role and Domain (past and present)	Number of Participants
Project Manager	9
Requirements Engineer	7
Software Architect	4
User Interface Designer	12
Programmer	40
Tester	15
Operations	6
Other	3
Finance	12
Social Media	5
Transport & Logistics	5
Education	4
Insurance	2
Other	7

Fig. 2. Summary of survey findings.

Processes and Tools Used. We asked what development processes participants used to help address diverse end user challenges, and any tools they use to aid them. 11 focused on accessibility in the design stage with 5 adopting User-Focused Design and 6 designing based on Guidelines. 7 considered accessibility after development with 5 focusing on gaining user feedback and 2 using different testing methods such as user acceptance testing. 6 claimed did not use any specific approaches to address diverse end user challenges while 7 explained general software development approaches such as MVC patterns which showed lack of awareness on accessibility.

"We do research and monitor accessibility by building products that can adapt and change when we have feedback from our users" [P23]

"Follow accessibility guidelines by the Web Content Accessibility Guidelines (WCAG)" [P16] and *"Reading WCAG guidelines to understand accessibility needs"* [P25]

"for every stage ... I make sure that I test with the user, ... enable[s] me to know exactly what the user expects" [P6]

"Using screen readers during QA process" [P25] and *"Screen reader functionality"* [P4]

In terms of tools, very few participants used augmented-reality based browser plug-ins to aid them in these tasks, with only 5 naming specific support tools. These included AR tools such as PlugXR, ARKit, WebXR and other browser based plugins such as Cisco Web Assist,Web Developer, Google translate, Hiver, Session Manager, IE Tab and CSSViewer.

Focused End-user Challenges. Only a small number of diverse end user challenges were named by our participants who had used AR-based web browser plug-ins.

"Free tester tools for screen readers are key for us" [P25]

"better UI designs for the visually impaired, the option for audio-description for those who may have trouble reading, and various language translation to limit language barrier" [P27]

"Enlarged texts and textures mostly, maybe we should give better try by image contrast [P23]

Most named sight challenges as those addressed e.g. *"especially people that have accessibility issues, such as sight problems"* [P10], *"varying font sizes options to help sight-challenged users"* [P12], *"Maybe the bigger fonts could help users who couldn't see very well"* [P21] and *"Sight impairments"* [P28]. A few named other challenges e.g. *"The aurally impaired"* [P4], age based issues *"content for users of all ages"* [P24].

Some noted they followed design practices without needing to use AR-based tools to help them e.g. *"We didn't use any plugin to address color blindness, we simply follow guidelines and do user experience tests to validate the correctness of the implementation"* [P19] and *"Our aim was always to make the UI as intuitive and easy-to-read as possible (bigger fonts, colors, etc.), we didn't consider that maybe some of our users could be sight-challenged"* [P21]

Participants felt some issues are not commonly addressed and those are, physical impairments and technical skills *"non-technology inclined individuals"* [P27]. It was noted that navigation was also a challenge for many users. *"Interaction navigating and finding People navigate and find content using different strategies and approaches depending on their preferences, skills, and abilities."* [P16], and that tools could help most/all users have an improved interaction experience, *"I believe it is beneficial to all"* [P10].

Support for some issues was claimed not to be helped by current AR-based plug-ins, *"It does not support anything outside of hearing, speech and vision"* [P20]

Suggested Improvements. The improvements can be categorised to two: *tool feature improvements* and *general improvements* to help developers better support diverse end user needs.

Several suggested improvements to AR-based browser plug-in tool features. These included *"I think there could be some sort of bot which guide us through website"* [P11], better support in installation and support for graphic accessibility. One participant gave many interesting suggestions for improved web site design/AR-plugin support: *"[supporting] customized fonts and colours:changing the font types, sizes, colors, and spacing to make text easier to read"*, *"Document outline:representation of the content that only shows the headings and relevant structures"*, *"simplified summaries for passages of text ... Progressive disclosure:design technique that involves showing only the least amount of information or functions necessary for a given task or purpose"*, *"Reduced interface: representation of the content that only shows most relevant information or more frequently used functions"* [P16]. They also suggested supporting use of symbols instead of text in some situations, and use of sign language to indicate both content and emotions/intensity. Other improvements suggested included *"Live transcriptions for deaf people or clear speech relays"* [P23], and *"Understanding graphs for sight challenge users"* [P3].

The general suggestions to help developers better address accessibility challenged end user issues can be categorised in to three, Awareness, Involvement and Support. Under *Awareness*, more knowledge and training with such tools was suggested, e.g. *"more advertising to make developers aware of the presence of such tools"* and *"Make it easier to access them and have them taught in varsity"* [P17]. It was noted there are sometimes clashes between accessibility needs and e.g. security e.g. *"As a bank we thought of using voice prompts but it's not practical as some sensitive data can be intercepted"* [P9].

Under *Involvement*, the need to engage with diverse end users throughout the design process was emphasised by a four respondents, whatever development support tools are used e.g. *"Constant engagement with individuals with the accessibility challenged end user"* [P2], *"...conduct a study about end users with accessibility issues. Short-sighted people, hearing impaired, etc."* [P21], and getting feedback from diverse end users.

For *Support*, participants believed that developers need to be better supported to adapt these plugins. They suggested providing open source code of the plugins to allow developers to make changes as needed [P6] and providing public APIs for accessibility services [P20].

5   Funkify Evaluation Study Design

We carried out an evaluation of the Funkify augmented reality browser-based plug in to see how well it supports developers understanding end user web based interface usage challenges. The range and number of personas and websites that we evaluated were chosen with regards to a diverse, representative set of digital services needed by many in the community and relatively common end user accessibility challenges.

5.1 Funkify Persona Selection

Personas are fictional profiles of characters, created to represent different types of users with the aim to provide a perspective, or observations about different challenges or experiences diverse users face, ultimately building empathy from developers and designers towards their end users [27]. In our research, these personas represent users with a disability or multiple disabilities that affects the users' experience while interacting with software, whether they be visual, motor and/or cognitive impairments. Our set of target personas were selected on the basis of (i) covering a wide range of user's challenges, and (ii) relatively common disabilities that would have the most effect on users' experience and would be difficult to simulate effectively and thoroughly with an augmented reality tool such as Funkify. From the 10 personas Funkify provides, 4 personas were selected for our evaluation – tremor, tunnel vision, blurred vision and dyslexia.

5.2 Target Websites

To perform the evaluation on the selected personas, a set of target websites were chosen. Our approach to choosing these websites were to cover a wide range of topics, layouts, content of the sites (content-heavy news sites, websites with a lot of interactions, pictures...) The websites were chosen to also differ in user needs when using them, spanning from recreational purposes to daily fundamental needs. In the end, a set of 3 such target websites were selected:

Commonwealth NetBank. Commonwealth Bank of Australia (CBA) is one of the most popular banks in the country and has an online system to support all the fundamental banking tasks like checking your balance, making a transaction, finding an ATM or branch, and so on. These are tasks that most people do almost every day, and can have direct detrimental effects on a person who is unable to do them effectively and accurately.

Reddit. Reddit is a social news platform with a large user community, covering a wide range of topics and subjects. Its website is very content-heavy consisting of mainly text and pictures with a lot of interactions between interactions. Reddit was selected to assess the experiences of diverse end users on a content-heavy site where most of the interactions and content are casual using a lot of colloquial language.

Amazon. Amazon is the world's largest e-commerce website with more than 1.5 million transactions every day. Amazon was selected to evaluate how one of the largest and most visited websites in the world design their platform in regard to accessibility for diverse end users.

5.3   Evaluation Method

We conducted a heuristics evaluation of our selected personas using Funkify Premium applying a set of evaluation criteria, including:

– What range of diverse end user challenges does Funkify support? How do such challenges manifest in the browser?
– How well does the tool work with our selected websites when performing tasks?
– How is the AR environment produced by the tool for developers comparable to the documented experiences of end users with these challenges?
– Does the modification of website interaction appear to be based on actual evidence or literature?
– Do Funkify personas provide a software developer a good idea of how someone using the website with this challenge would find the experience? Can the software developer "empathise" with this target end user's accessibility-related challenges?
– Can users with multiple accessibility-related challenges be addressed, and how feasible and efficient does the tool address users with such multiple challenges?
– What new challenges (combination of challenges) are we able to add to the tool? What challenges are not possible to add?

To support the evaluation of this set of criteria, we conducted cognitive walk-throughs with each persona on all the target websites. From the results of the cognitive walk-throughs, we assessed how effective the persona's challenges manifest in the browser with Funkify, what the notable limitations of the tool for a persona/target website are, and how the personas challenges relate to real users' experience based on existing accessibility studies and literature on the disabilities. From these we identified opportunities for improvement in Funkify's augmented reality approach for better supporting software engineers in designing and building interfaces for diverse end users.

5.4   Cognitive Walk-through

Cognitive walk-through is a method primarily used in usability evaluation to look for usability issues in interactive systems, with a focus on task completion for novice users [8]. Its emphasis is on studying how easy it is for new or infrequent users to learn a system. It was first used as a tool to evaluate systems such as ATMs or interactive exhibits in museums where users will generally have little to no prior experience or training. Due to its ease of use and feasibility, the method's usage has been extended to complex software systems including CAD and software development tools [28].

Cognitive walk-throughs were conducted, one for each selected persona and website combination. We chose a set of tasks for each website and conducted the walk-throughs. Our approach to selecting these tasks for each target website was to select those that were the most basic and relevant for all the websites (e.g., logging on, registering) and the most major tasks for each site (e.g., make a transaction). A series of 4–6 major tasks were chosen for each of the target websites. The next step was to define a goal or success criteria for each of the tasks to determine how effective can the task be done in the augmented environment created using Funkify for each of the personas. After finalising the tasks and their respective definition of success, we would then conduct the walk-throughs for each of the personas on all the target websites and tasks.

Each persona was be assessed as to how it affects the tasks' feasibility, whether the task could still be done with the Funkify filter active at different intensity settings or if it proved to be impossible to complete the task when Funkify is active, based on the defined success criteria. The results of each task and target website from the walk-throughs could then be generalised into the feasibility and effectiveness of the Funkify persona in terms of how well it achieves the simulation of the persona's challenges and what the major limitations of the tool are or in general the limitations of augmented reality tools in simulating diverse end users' experience.

The evaluators of the websites and Funkify personas were software engineering students with real-world software practitioner experience. Each has expertise in software engineering processes and tools, UX/UI design, web and app development, but no particular training in designing for accessibility.

5.5 Website Tasks

All of the target websites have similar tasks for logging on and registering a new user where the definition of success is straightforward and consistent among all websites. Key tasks which differ across the websites are as follows:

Commonwealth NetBank Tasks

Make a transaction: this is the most common and fundamental task to be completed on a banking website. The definition of success was to be able make a transaction for the correct amount of money from a specific account to the correct recipient. The user needs to navigate to the transaction page, choose the correct 'To' and 'From' accounts and input the correct amount to complete the task.

Find a branch or ATM: Commonwealth NetBank provides a feature to show a map of ATM or branches nearby or to selected set of filter options. How this task is considered as done can vary between use cases, so we chose to define success for this task to be able to navigate around the map effectively and be able to find a specific CBA branch on the map.

Reddit Tasks

Join and navigate subreddits: Reddit is a social news platform where each subreddit represents a community that focuses on a specific category or topic. It was difficult to define a tangible success criterion for navigating through the subreddits, so we focused on joining a subreddit while assessing how the Funkify filters affect the experience of navigating through subreddits.

Read Comments on Posts: comments are a large proportion of all content and interactions on Reddit posts. Users need to successfully read comments, navigate through all comments and replies, and be able to follow and understand comment threads.

Post on Subreddit: A Reddit post can be simple as a sentence or it can consist of pictures, links, various font options... We decided to assess the task's completion on the user's accessibility and effectiveness in using these additional options when posting.

Post Comments: this task involves composing a comment relating to a post and is relatively simple, so a definition of success is not required.

Amazon Tasks.

Find a Product (example - an HDMI Cable): Being an e-commerce site, Amazon's most fundamental task would be to find a product. The definition of success was to be able to search for a product (an HDMI cable was selected for this task) and effectively compare all the search results (in terms of descriptions, prices, quantities...).

Buy a Product: conventionally buying a product on Amazon involves selecting the product, comparing and choosing the products' options if any, adding it to the user's cart, and checking out with the required user billing details. For this research, we define this task as completed when user has selected the right product, read its descriptions effectively, compared between product's options, and add it to their cart.

6   Funkify Evaluation Results

For each persona we describe how Funkify attempts to simulate the underlying accessibility issue, report key findings from the cognitive walk-throughs [RQ1], and discuss the extent to which the experience provided by Funkify mirrors the documented experiences of diverse end users with these challenges [RQ2]. Notably, Funkify only augments the browser window underneath the title bar, so any changes to the url or open tabs are not concealed. A limitation of the tool is that it only applies to the view within the page so all the other components in the browser UI are not affected such as tabs' names, browser menu, settings. This is of course not consistent with the real-world experience of a person with blurred vision.

6.1   Blurred Vision Augmentation

Blurred vision is the most common sight challenge, but varies in level. Funkify applies a blur filter to the entire window, with intensity being able to be varyied on a 0–10 scale. Figure 3a shows the persona and Fig. 3b how this manifests for the CommBank website ATM locator page.

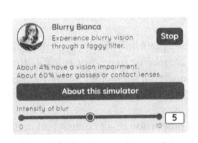

(a) Blurry Bianca Persona   (b) NetBank ATM search dropdown

Fig. 3. (a) Blurry Bianca simulator and (b) example of applying to NetBank web site (from [34]).

While there were isolated instances like Fig. 3b of components such as drop-down selections appearing as normal on top of the filter, overall the simulator performed

(a) Reddit with Blurry Bianca filter, 2.5 intensity

(b) NetBank login colour highlights the most important interactions

Fig. 4. Examples of Blurry Bianca simulations (from [34]).

consistently well. It immersed the user in the persona and allowed them to identify areas where the site design led to user frustration.

For content-heavy websites like Amazon and Reddit (Fig. 4a), the visual strain made browsing particularly difficult and tiring. However, fatigue was also experienced when navigating NetBank, with lower information density. Amazon, with many busy pages, description blocks and copious amounts of small, clickable, text was very taxing to navigate. Product titles and costs, as the top elements of Amazon's typographic hierarchy, are the only readable parts of the page at 1.5 intensity. Even Amazon's captcha posed a difficulty. Although the registration process allows the user to select an audio challenge, the explanation of what is required is shown in unreadably small font.

As navigation was tiring, accessible and bold design choices stood out for their ease of use. The use of contrasting and vibrant colours drew the user's focus more easily, and was used to good effect by NetBank's yellow log in button as shown in Fig. 4b. It also highlighted the benefit of iconography and logos as opposed to reliance on text. Reddit's login modal has the Google and Apple logos alongside their login options. The text became unreadable at 1.8 intensity, whereas the logos remained recognisable until 3.0, reducing the cognitive strain.

The experience produced by the tool was very comparable to that of a short-sighted person when not using prescription glasses. A noticeable takeaway is that for most of the evaluated websites and tasks, it is almost impossible to read any content or text on the screen when the intensity reaches 3.0, so a large portion of the intensity spectrum will yield the same results when using this augmentation. And the characteristic of the blur filter is the same for all the websites and all the intensity levels (a blur effect to the entire screen) which might not be the experience for all users with blurred vision (partial blurred vision, left or right blurred vision, short-sightedness compared to age-related causes...).

6.2   Tunnel Vision Augmentation

The Tunnel Toby Funkify persona, shown in Fig. 5a, shrinks the visible area in the browser window to either a circle or rectangle centered at the current position of the user's mouse. The remainder of the window is covered by an opaque black filter. A sensitivity slider from 0–10 is provided to change the amount of vision loss desired. We evaluated the circular option intended to simulate peripheral vision loss.

(a) Tunnel Toby Persona   (b) NetBank login button placement

Fig. 5. (a) Tunnel Toby simulator and (b) example of its impact (from [34]).

Evaluating this simulator was found to be a very confronting and intensely uncomfortable experience. Although solely isolated to the browser window, and with the user able to stop at any time, prolonged exposure to this persona repeatedly led the evaluators to spikes of anxiety and claustrophobia. On unfamiliar sites navigation times were dramatically slowed due to the need to systematically scan each page, building a mental picture of the structure and ensuring key details were not overlooked.

To compensate, there was a noted reliance on established UI norms. For example, assuming a button to login would be in the top right corner of the window (shown in Fig. 5b). Similarly, visual identifiers of page structure helped with maintaining an understanding of position. As shown in Fig. 6a, Reddit displays its nested comment hierarchy with parallel vertical lines signifying the level of indentation, where clicking on a line navigates the user to the parent comment of that level. Without such a visual aid it would be extremely difficult to follow conversations.

This confusion manifested when evaluating Amazon's product search. Products were arranged inconsistently, alternating between a single product per row and three separate products side-by-side. Advertisements and sponsored products were interlaced at unpredictable intervals. Product images were larger than the visible circle, and product names were long and technical in nature. All of these factors combined to make comparisons between products difficult.

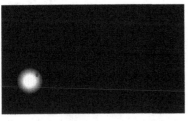

(a) Reddit hierarchy lines   (b) Tunnel Toby sensitivity 10

Fig. 6. Examples of Tunnel Toby simulations (from [34]).

A number of bugs were identified with Funkify's tunnel vision augmentation. When using the persona, the mouse could not enter the Reddit login modal and lagged significantly when Reddit posts were opened. Scrolling on a page moved the visible area in tandem, as opposed to it sticking to the mouse position. This resulted in most scrolling occurring with an entirely black screen, only refreshing on mouse move.

Funkify provides a 0–10 slider for amount of vision loss, however this scale is quite a narrow range. 0 is no vision loss at all, but 0.1 is already significant impairment. 10, demonstrated in Fig. 6b is almost complete vision loss. To better reflect reality this range should be much wider, with lower numbers just showing some darkening around the edges of the screen and gradually decreasing the vision.

6.3 Dyslexia Augmentation

Funkify attempts a simulation of dyslexia by scrambling text on the web page. Scrambling is localised to a word with the exact characters swapping at random. Figure 7a illustrates this persona.

(a) Dyslexia Dani Persona

(b) Browsing Reddit with Dyslexia Dani

Fig. 7. (a) Dyslexia Dani and (b) an example of its impact (from [34]).

It was found that content-heavy sites such as Amazon are difficult to read, and small site elements escalate the challenge. It became difficult to ascertain and remember product names when trying to find a product that had been seen previously. Evaluating Reddit (Fig. 7b) exposed a set of challenges around comprehending slang and internet colloquialisms, which proved to be barriers to entering the conversation.

The simulator only changes page text, and therefore it does not scramble any text in images, branding, tooltips, and certain buttons. It fails to work on Reddit's login modal and seems to not scramble two-digit numbers, even when they appear as text. Additionally text typed into websites remains unaltered. Figure 9 shows the ATM search stage of a NetBank evaluation, where neither the input text or dropdown list are scrambled. These limitations cumulatively limit the immersive experience of the simulator, as in Fig. 8 where the focal point of the screen is text embedded in an image.

With each letter generally not moving far relative to their correct position; words with 2 or less characters stay the same during the simulation. The tool's capability is only limited to the visual aspects of dyslexia, so it is not comprehensible enough to generalize the whole set of challenges a dyslexic person experiences. The tool is not able to cover other aspects related to the persona including hearing, writing, motor, especially behavioral traits. It is not clear that all people with dyslexia experience reading in this manner, and some have simulated dyslexia by removing lines from normal lettering [5].

Fig. 8. Amazon home page - banner unaffected by dyslexia filter (from [34]).

Fig. 9. Dropdown item and form inputs do not scramble (from [34]).

6.4   Tremor Augmentation

The Trembling Trevor Funkify persona simulates tremor by moving the mouse involuntarily and unpredictably in all directions. As the mouse continues to move without user input it would be classified as a resting tremor, as is commonly seen in Parkinson's disease. The amount of tremor is adjustable on a 0–10 scale. Figure 10a shows the persona from Funkify.

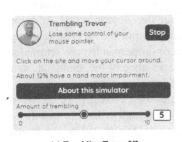

(a) Trembling Trevor UI   (b) Amazon sign out button

Fig. 10. (a) Trembling Trevor simulator and (b) challenges when activated (from [34]).

While using the persona, accurately selecting small targets posed a significant challenge. This was most prevalent in the Amazon walk-through, due to the abundance of clickable text. When searching for products the filter options are inaccessibly small, as is the breadcrumb navigation in the user profile section.

Critically, signing out of an account necessitates clicking on a small piece of text at the bottom of a dropdown menu, as shown in Fig. 10b. It requires fine motor control to accurately click the correct button, with the additional frustration that unintended movements that cause the cursor to move outside of the box results in the dropdown menu collapsing.

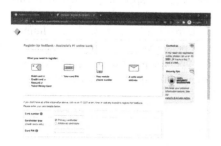

(a) NetBank registration form radio buttons

(b) Amazon profile page

Fig. 11. Examples of impact of Trembling Trevor simulator (from [34]).

Similarly, when applying to register for NetBank (Fig. 11a), the user is prompted to select between radio button options, which were basically unclickable with this Funkify persona enabled. The most accessible pages had large, separated buttons, like on Amazon's user profile page shown in Fig. 11b.

The sensitivity adjustment is a 10-point sliding scale of an ill-defined "amount of trembling". Although probably sufficient to emulate the experience of navigating with a tremor, this could be broken down into frequency and amplitude to better align with the medical literature. An advanced feature set could also break it down by tremor type.

7 Discussion

Cognitive walk-throughs with Funkify provided both valuable insights into accessibility issues on the evaluated sites and also a lasting impression on the evaluators of the constraints experienced by end-users who live with the examined disabilities. The lessons learned were applicable beyond the local scope of one website, and the tool elicited the desired empathetic response above and beyond accessibility issue identification. We recommend its use in further research that can explore this relationship further and to identify whether it can lead to improved long-term improved accessibility outcomes.

Funkify as it currently exists is a straightforward and easy to use extension that offers flexibility and customisation across a wide range of disabilities. Personas are toggled with a single button click and any combination of existing simulators can be combined into a new persona. Having all of the functionality neatly packaged in a single plugin allows Funkify to add value if included in future projects that use personas to model diverse end users. However, a number of potential limitations were found, and a number of extensions to Funkify identified that would enhance its suitability as a basis for future research [RQ3].

7.1 Expanded Personas

Prior research on the use of personas to understand end users includes more biographical and emotional context than Funkify currently allows. Other work has proposed personas that are tailored to the needs of the development team and express the background, goals, and frustrations of the modelled end user to specific problem domains [24]. We propose that another button be created underneath"About this simulator" for each Funkify persona, where the user will be able to read and edit more of the human aspects of the persona. This ability to enrich Funkify personas by defining more contextual data would improve the quality and utility of the personas for testing purposes, and simultaneously provide a mechanism by which to instantly simulate the perspective of the previously text-based persona.

7.2 Sharing Capability

As a Chrome extension, any custom personas or changes to sensitivity settings are localised to a single account. To facilitate repeatable testing and consistency amongst team members, support is needed for sharing personas with other Funkify users. This could be combined with extending persona human aspects to provide richer, more contextual personas.

7.3 Predefined Intensities

At present, Funkify Premium always allows the user to adjust the simulator intensity. However as we move to richer personas we may, for consistency, want to specify the exact desired values and disable the ability of users to deviate from it. Therefore we suggest that the screen to make or edit a new persona should contain a field for whether the intensity values are locked. It will always be possible to return to the edit screen to unlock them, but this feature would prevent accidental miscalibration. If this is not possible, we would suggest a button in the persona window that would return all values to a preset default.

7.4 Broader Range of Intensities

A finding of our cognitive walk-throughs was that the range of intensity options provided for each persona was too narrow, often resulting in the user solely utilising the lower end of the spectrum. For example the minimum amount of vision loss (0.1) for the Tunnel Toby persona shown in Fig. 6b is already quite advanced peripheral vision loss whereas the circle size in upper half of the range (>5) is too small to be useful. The sensitivity range should be re-calibrated to allow the minimums to represent a far more gentle form of the disability.

7.5 Combining Personas

Funkify provides a limited ability to define new personas and some target end users have multiple challenges that would be good to be able simulate concurrently. As Funkify uses different approaches to its augmented reality-based simulations, this may be difficult if not impossible for some multiple challenge personas. This may require a more sophisticated augmented reality-based approach.

7.6 New Simulators

Finally, we would add new simulators to Funkify targeting aspects of dyscalculia, hearing impairment, and developmental disabilities including autism. While these conditions may not be able to be replicated precisely, we would implement targeted parts of their documented end user experience from other studies and medical literature. As above, we would aim to leverage Funkify's ability to combine simulators in order to scaffold a more holistic persona from constituent symptom personas.

8 Limitations and Future Work

One major limitation in this research was limiting our evaluation to Funkify. This opens further potential research paths and questions as to whether all of the personas provided by Funkify yield the same evaluation results as other comparable tools, or if there are better performing tools compared to Funkify to simulate diverse end users' experience for some challenges. Although our selection approach was to cover the widest range of personas and websites possible, there are of course many other widely used websites and tasks that could be evaluated with Funkify's augmentation approaches. The small number of people doing the cognitive walk-through-based evaluations is also a limitation. This can result in the lack of integrity between each cognitive walk-throughs as members would have had some prior experience with the target websites and tasks. With the evaluation only done internally by research team members with experience in software engineering, UI/UX and web development, this may not reflect actual experience of target end users. However a major aim of our work was to see how software engineers perceived the augmented browser-based interfaces, and whether they could help identify key usability challenges for such target end users. We also wanted to see if software engineers could gain a more empathetic understanding of these target end users by using Funkify's persona and augmented browser-based interface approach.

Another limitation in our study was the lack of real end user involvement. This can be overcome in the future by conducting user studies with actual visual-impaired users. It would also help to overcome the limitation of possible bias in current participants since they were from a software engineering background. A comparison of task completion between real versus simulated user groups may reveal further interesting insights. However, we did compare Funkify's augmented interfaces to the impacts of different user challenges reported in prior studies and medical literature. Further studies into evaluating a wide range of users at different levels/manifestations of the disabilities are also necessary to assess the impact on their web usage and study different UI solutions required to cater to different range of users with the same disabilities (e.g., different levels of tunnel vision, different manifestations of dyslexia).

The effect on software developers and designers after using tools such as Funkify on their design process is an important area to study. Some studies have shown having able-bodied people experience disability simulators can reinforce negative stereotypes and attitudes to these challenged people.[26]. It would be interesting to see how developers assess their existing UI designs using the Funkify personas, and how this might influence their designs to better accommodate more diverse challenged end users and empathise better with them after experience with these tools. A notable perspective raised by Huynh et al. was the use of personas of developers with their own challenges [17], and how they would diagnose and fix UI problems differently to other developers. Future research could use such different software engineer personas to evaluate Funkify.

9   Related Work

Alshayban et al. [4] developed an automated accessibility evaluation tool that they used to evaluate 1135 free Android applications and conducted a follow-up survey of Android developers. They found that accessibility issues are prevalent and pervasive throughout all categories of apps, and that these issues are not limited to affecting a single type of user disability. Although they surveyed a relatively small sample of 66 developers, it was found that the respondents lacked awareness of accessibility issues or training to address them. It's noteworthy that the minimum amount of development experience among respondents was 0.25 years, a very short amount of time that may raise questions about the ability to generalise this result. An interesting observation was that no existing accessibility analysis tools are prioritising issues by severity or importance, leading developers to either overlook critical flaws or be overwhelmed with the quantity and variety. They identified accessibility issues within half of the templates provided directly by Android Studio. Developers view these templates as a trustworthy foundation and build their apps around them, thereby propagating the issues. This raises the question of whether a similar phenomenon may be occurring in the website space, for example with front-end component libraries or popular website templates. However, they only evaluated free Android apps, and it would be interesting to investigate whether the same reliance on templates is present in popular paid apps that presumably have higher development budgets.

Bai et al. [5] investigated and compared six accessibility testing methods for software development teams. They evaluated these methods in terms of their usefulness, satisfaction, ease of use and ease of learning to determine the methods that would yield the best engagement for the participants, investigated how different software roles and development phases would affect the choice of appropriate testing methods. The sample size of participants was relatively small (53 participants) with 74% were male, and it would be interesting to see how this fact relates to the empathy of developers towards end-users. A notable observation was that there are no set rules to determine the types of issues a testing method best identifies, which made it difficult to choose a method and resulted in developers neglecting testing entirely. The de facto method for the participants was WCAG walk-through. However, the assessment of this method yielded the lowest result in terms of satisfaction and ease of use with a hostile attitude in many responses. This poses a question of whether enforcing use of a specific testing method is appropriate to engage the developers. Their work highlights how different software roles prefer different methods. They identfied that the methods assessed were valuable and easy to use, except for the WCAG walk-through.

Schulz and Fuglerud [30] introduced methods to create personas more comprehensively. They presented the potential barriers, proposed multiple techniques, and discussed the application in their studies. A notable observation made was that if personas are simply recycled or imitated, then the empathy and engagement from developers is lost. Also, personas are not complete replacements of true end users, and misconceptions are possible when personas are developed without prior real interactions. Schulz and Fuglerud provided in-depth details to some commonly known methods and conducted research on real-world use cases. They made suggestions for persona creators to be mindful when using different Assistive Technology versions, and aim at creating personas with the same learning attitudes as focus groups.

Several design approaches have been developed specifically for visually impaired and blind users, encompassing a range of sight related accessibility challenges [18,31]. Dyslexia is another accessibility challenge faced by a range of users but with limited research on solutions to date [36]. A number of recent works have looked to to help software engineers take better account of diverse end users during development. This includes use of enhanced personas capturing user differences that allow software engineers to more easily examine accessibility considerations at all stages of development without requiring the overhead of finding many varied live users [24]. It also includes work extending modelling languages documenting different end user accessibility-related and other human-centric related challenges [20]. Recent work has investigated how to support users with mild cognitive impairments [19].

Some work has investigated use of augmented reality-based interfaces to aid improved accessibility in software development. Biswas et al. [7] discussed different user modelling approaches in regard to designing inclusive interfaces for elderly and disabled people. They proposed a simulator to address the limitations of existing modelling techniques in predicting likely interaction patterns and estimating the time needed to complete an action for users with disabilities. Stearns at al. [33] design and evaluate an AR-based magnification aid for sight challenged end users to improve accessibility. Such approaches aim to fill the gaps in limited existing user modelling techniques by breaking interactions up into smaller components and combining different approaches in each component, while considering the needs of challenged people with visual or mobility impairments. In Biswas et al., roughly 30% of situations had more than 50% relative error. This raises the question of whether these case studies are sufficient to determine the validity of such simulators. Their research showed that developing models for simulators of people with disabilities is valuable. However, it needs further research and development to be sufficient on its own and replace other qualitative techniques for assessing diverse target end user experience.

10 Summary

Augmented reality browser-based plug-ins have the potential to assist software engineers in identifying accessibility challenges in web-based applications for their diverse end users. We identified a number of challenges that developers have in addressing these issues from a practitioner survey. We then evaluated a representative tool, Funkify, to see how well several of its simulators work when using banking, e-commerce and social media web applications. We identified a number of promising further research and development enhancements that may better assist software engineers in understanding and empathising with their diverse end user accessibility challenges.

Acknowledgements. Grundy and Madugalla are supported by ARC Laureate Fellowship FL190100035.

References

1. Tunnel vision: What peripheral vision loss feels like - https://www.webmd.com/eye-health/common-causes-peripheral-vision-loss (2019)
2. Abascal, J., Arrue, M., Valencia, X.: Tools for web accessibility evaluation. In: Yesilada, Y., Harper, S. (eds.) Web Accessibility. HIS, pp. 479–503. Springer, London (2019). https://doi.org/10.1007/978-1-4471-7440-0_26
3. Alcántara, A.M.: Lawsuits over digital accessibility for people with disabilities are rising (2021). https://www.wsj.com/articles/lawsuits-over-digital-accessibility-for-people-with-disabilities-are-rising-11626369056
4. Alshayban, A., Ahmed, I., Malek, S.: Accessibility issues in android apps: state of affairs, sentiments, and ways forward. In: ICSE, pp. 1323–1334. IEEE (2020)
5. Bai, A., Stray, V., Mork, H.: What methods software teams prefer when testing web accessibility. Adv. Hum.-Comput. Interact. 1–14 (2019)
6. Bi, T., Xia, X., Lo, D., Grundy, J.C., Zimmermann, T., Ford, D.: Accessibility in software practice: a practitioner's perspective. ACM Trans. Softw. Eng. Methodol. **31**(4), 1–26 (2022)
7. Biswas, P., Robinson, P., Langdon, P.: Designing inclusive interfaces through user modeling and simulation. Int. J. Hum. Comput. Interact. **28**(1), 1–33 (2012)
8. Blackmon, M.H., Polson, P.G., Kitajima, M., Lewis, C.: Cognitive walkthrough for the web. In: CHI, pp. 463–470 (2002)
9. Davis, R.: The gift of dyslexia. Educ. Horizons **8**(3), 12–13 (2004)
10. Dorsey, E.A., et al.: Projected number of people with parkinson disease in the most populous nations, 2005 through 2030. Neurology **68**(5), 384–386 (2007)
11. Fazzini, M., et al.: Characterizing human aspects in reviews of covid-19 apps. In: Proceedings of the 9th IEEE/ACM International Conference on Mobile Software Engineering and Systems, pp. 38–49 (2022)
12. Fletcher-Watson, S., Pain, H., Hammond, S., Humphry, A., McConachie, H.: Designing for young children with autism spectrum disorder: a case study of an IPAD app. Int. J. Child-Comput. Interact. **7**, 1–14 (2016)
13. Funkify: Funkify - a disability simulator for the web - https://www.funkify.org/ (2021)
14. Green, C., Dickinson, H., Carey, G., Joyce, A.: Barriers to policy action on social determinants of health for people with disability in Australia. Disabil. Soc. 1–25 (2021)
15. Grundy, J.C.: Impact of end user human aspects on software engineering. In: ENASE, pp. 9–20 (2021)

16. Harper, S., Chen, A.Q.: Web accessibility guidelines. World Wide Web **15**(1), 61–88 (2012)
17. Huynh, K., Benarivo, J., Da Xuan, C., Sharma, G.G., Kang, J., Madugalla, A., Grundy, J.: Improving human-centric software defect evaluation, reporting, and fixing. In: COMPSAC, pp. 408–417. IEEE (2021)
18. Jacko, J.A., Sears, A.: Designing interfaces for an overlooked user group: considering the visual profiles of partially sighted users. In: ACM Conference on Assistive Technologies, pp. 75–77 (1998)
19. Jamieson, M., Cullen, B., Lennon, M., Brewster, S., Evans, J.: Designing appltree: usable scheduling software for people with cognitive impairments. Disabil. Rehabil. Assist. Technol. **17**(3), 338–348(2020)
20. Jim, A.Y., et al.: Improving the modelling of human-centric aspects of software systems: a case study of modelling end user age in wireframe designs. In: ENASE, pp. 68–79 (2021)
21. Kamikubo, R., Higuchi, K., Yonetani, R., Koike, H., Sato, Y.: Exploring the role of tunnel vision simulation in the design cycle of accessible interfaces. In: 15th International Web for all Conference, pp. 1–10 (2018)
22. Lazar, J.: The potential role of us consumer protection laws in improving digital accessibility for people with disabilities. U. Pa. JL Soc. Change **22**, 185 (2019)
23. Lee, P.P., Spritzer, K., Hays, R.D.: The impact of blurred vision on functioning and well-being. Ophthalmology **104**(3), 390–396 (1997)
24. Li, C., et al.: A human-centric approach to building a smarter and better parking application. In: COMPSAC, pp. 514–519. IEEE (2021)
25. McIntosh, J., et al.: Evaluating age bias in e-commerce. In: 2021 International Conference on Cooperative and Human Aspects of Software Engineering (CHASE), pp. 31–40. IEEE (2021)
26. Nario-Redmond, M.R., Gospodinov, D., Cobb, A.: Crip for a day: the unintended negative consequences of disability simulations. Rehabil. Psychol. **62**(3), 324 (2017)
27. Pruitt, J., Grudin, J.: Personas: practice and theory. In: Designing for User Experiences, pp. 1–15 (2003)
28. Rieman, J., Franzke, M., Redmiles, D.: Usability evaluation with the cognitive walkthrough. In: Human Factors in Computing Systems, pp. 387–388 (1995)
29. Rutter, R., et al.: Web Accessibility: Web Standards and Regulatory Compliance. Apress (2007)
30. Schulz, T., Skeide Fuglerud, K.: Creating personas with disabilities. In: Miesenberger, K., Karshmer, A., Penaz, P., Zagler, W. (eds.) ICCHP 2012. LNCS, vol. 7383, pp. 145–152. Springer, Heidelberg (2012). https://doi.org/10.1007/978-3-642-31534-3_22
31. Sierra, J.S., Togores, J.: Designing mobile apps for visually impaired and blind users. In: 5th International Conference on Advances in Computer-human Interactions (2012)
32. Sirisena, D., Williams, D.R.: My hands shake: Classification and treatment of tremor. Aust. Family Phys. **38**(9), 678–683 (2009)
33. Stearns, L., Findlater, L., Froehlich, J.E.: Design of an augmented reality magnification aid for low vision users. In: SIGACCESS, pp. 28–39 (2018)
34. Vu, M.H., Wyman, J.S., Grundy, J.: Evaluation of an augmented reality approach to better understanding diverse end user website usage challenges. In: ENASE, pp. 50–61 (2022)
35. Wentz, B., Pham, D., Feaser, E., Smith, D., Smith, J., Wilson, A.: Documenting the accessibility of 100 us bank and finance websites. Univ. Access Inf. Soc. **18**(4), 871–880 (2019)
36. Wery, J.J., Diliberto, J.A.: The effect of a specialized dyslexia font, opendyslexic, on reading rate and accuracy. Ann. Dyslexia **67**(2), 114–127 (2017)
37. Zhong, Y., Weber, A., Burkhardt, C., Weaver, P., Bigham, J.P.: Enhancing android accessibility for users with hand tremor by reducing fine pointing and steady tapping. In: Proceedings of the 12th International Web for All Conference, pp. 1–10 (2015)
38. Zhou, S., Carroll, E., Nicholson, S., Vize, C.J.: Blurred vision. BMJ **368** (2020)

An Exploration of Technical Debt over the Lifetime of Open-Source Software

Arthur-Jozsef Molnar(✉) and Simona Motogna

Faculty of Mathematics and Computer Science, Babeş-Bolyai University,
Cluj-Napoca, Romania
{arthur.molnar,simona.motogna}@ubbcluj.ro
http://www.cs.ubbcluj.ro/

Abstract. Technical debt represents unwanted issues that result from decisions made to speed up the design or implementation of software at the expense of resolving existing issues. Like financial debt, it consists of the principal and an interest. Debt is usually paid back through code rewrites, refactoring, or the introduction of test code. When unchecked, interest can accumulate over time and lead to development crises where focus and resources must be shifted to resolve existing debt before the development process can be resumed. Existing software tooling allows practitioners to quantify the level of debt and identify its sources, allowing decision makers to measure and control it. We propose a detailed exploration of the characteristics of source code technical debt over the lifetime of several popular open-source applications. We employed a SonarQube instance configured for longitudinal analysis to study all publicly released versions of the target applications, amounting to over 15 years' worth of releases for each. We found that a small number of issue types were responsible for most of the debt and observed that refactoring reduced debt levels across most application packages. We observed increased variance in technical debt distribution and composition in early application versions, which lessened once applications matured. We addressed concerns regarding the accuracy of SonarQube estimations and illustrated some of its limitations. We aim to continue our research by including additional tools to characterize debt, leverage existing open data sets and extend our exploration to include additional applications and types of software.

Keywords: Technical debt · Software evolution · Longitudinal case study · Open-source software · Refactoring · Software maintenance

1 Introduction

Introduced by Cunningham in 1992 [50], technical debt (TD) is an indicator of all hidden quality issues overlooked during development at the expense of adding new functionalities to the system. Neglecting accumulated technical debt may have serious consequences on the overall system, with modification and further development requiring more resources.

Size and time can add extra complexity to TD handling: big applications developed by large teams over significant periods of time can have an important impact over TD

© The Author(s), under exclusive license to Springer Nature Switzerland AG 2023
H. Kaindl et al. (Eds.): ENASE 2022, CCIS 1829, pp. 292–314, 2023.
https://doi.org/10.1007/978-3-031-36597-3_14

issues. Hence, strategic management of debt is needed. It should take into consideration the diffusion of debt [5] across applications and packages, its prevalence, composition and distribution [27,36], as well as how these change over time [33].

Important results have been obtained in the last 10 years are were reflected in TD estimation models such as SQALE [28], CAST [10], SIG [38], and also implemented in different tools such as SonarQube, NDepend or Kiuwan, which provide useful TD estimates for practitioners. Even so, TD management and prioritization remain open problems [8,30], as several studies reported the prevalence of ad-hoc and non-formal management decisions [25].

Providing accountable case study results related to long-term TD characterization can improve decision making in technical debt management and increase trust in existing estimation and monitoring tools. As a consequence, the current study adds to the body of existing knowledge related to TD, especially due to the longitudinal perspective that covers the entire lifespan of the studied applications.

Addressing open source software systems is key to such investigations as access to target application source code enables manual examination of detected trends or patterns, while the transparency of the development history in terms of commits and releases allows researchers to examine how source code-level artifacts translate to a working program.

The main goal of this study was to analyze the prevalence, characteristics, and evolution of TD through the entire lifetime of the target applications. The main contributions were to (i) provide a characterization of source code technical debt in complex open-source software; (ii) compare the results obtained when employing a manually curated, extended ruleset over using the default tool configuration; (iii) investigate debt prevalence, composition and evolution over the entire lifetime of the target applications and (iv) investigate the effects of refactoring on debt prevalence, distribution and composition.

2 Preliminaries

2.1 Computational Models for Technical Debt

This section synthesizes the most prevalent estimation models for TD based on existing literature surveys [3,16,22,25], together with a selection of software tools implementing each model.

The **SQALE** [28] method was introduced in 2010 and is currently the most widely used [4] method for estimating TD. Given its prevalence, as well as our use of the method within the present research we reserved the following section for a more detailed presentation.

The **Checking Quality Model (CQM)** [21] was developed by Kiuwan and focuses on the idea of extracting source code analytics that correspond to quality factors that are associated with the ISO 25010 software quality model. These analytics are based on computing metrics, checking rules based on metrics, and in the end assessing indicators to provide a TD estimation. The CQM evaluates indicators for security, reliability, efficiency, maintainability and portability.

The most well-known tool to implement the CQM is *Kiuwan*[1]. Its reputation was built on its security analysis as a tool from OWASP's[2] recommended list. It computes TD as an *"effort to target"*, namely to achieve the desired values for quality indicators without advocating for a complete elimination of existing debt. While its most powerful features are security-related, Kiuwan also proposes some strong points in TD estimation, such as risk analysis and the ability to construct a remediation action plan for the effort required to reach the desired quality target for each characteristic.

CAST [10] proposes a model for estimating both the TD principal and interest. The model was applied for scientific analysis of an extensive database of enterprise applications selected from companies worldwide for over five years. The insight obtained from analyzing the data was used to formulate TD as an expression depending on severity, number of occurrences, time and cost needed to fix each violation. The considered quality factors are performance, robustness, security, transferability (equivalent to reusability) and changeability.

The model was implemented in the *CAST - AIP*[3] software tool, which is available for over 60 languages and which a recent survey found to be particularly popular within the scientific literature [4]. One of its strengths is the *"Appmarq"*, a large repository of analyzed applications that enables offering benchmark services supporting organizational decisions-making on software product quality. TD is estimated using a formula that is relative to a threshold computed based on 50% high severity, 25% medium severity, respectively 10% low severity violations.

The keypoint of the method proposed by Marinescu [29] is the hypothesis that **design flaws** are responsible for introducing TD. The model assumes four steps: select relevant design flaws, associate rules for detecting them, evaluate the influence of each flaw occurrence, and determine an overall score. The so called design disharmonies are evaluated and then the overall debt symptoms index is computed. The initial paper describing the model was referring to the *inFusion* tool that appears to no longer be available. However, the model offers a unique perspective, which is to consider design flaws as the root of TD. Some authors refer to this as *"architectural technical debt"* [48].

Defined as an empirical model for TD principal and interest, the **SIG** model [38] was proposed in 2011 by the Software Improvement Group as an alternative to the deprecated Maintainability Index [47]. Its evaluation starts from source code level metrics such as lines of code, cyclomatic complexity, code duplication, unit size and unit testing. It addresses ISO 25010 defined sub-characteristics of maintainability such as analyzability, changeability, stability and testability in order to quantify TD through two metrics: estimation of the repair effort and of the maintenance effort. While the model includes an evaluation of the return on investment for the remediation effort, it still suffers from neglecting some important software characteristics such as reliability, security or performance.

---

[1] Kiuwan - https://www.kiuwan.com/.

[2] Open Web Application Security Project - https://owasp.org/.

[3] CAST Application Intelligence Platform - https://www.cast-software.com/products/application-intelligence-platform.

Most of the tools implementing these models use static code analysis to detect issues based on some rules associated with quality attributes. There exist significant differences between computation methods, associated rules and quality attributes between all proposed models. As such, the domain poses important research questions that remain open. Several recent studies [23, 27, 36] also reported that estimation may sometime lack accuracy and that detected issues do not always correspond to actual software faults.

2.2   The SQALE Method

As stated in its proposal [28], the SQALE method proposes to define, estimate, analyse and prioritize technical debt. The computation is based on rules corresponding to nine quality factors and sub-factors: testability, reliability, changeability, efficiency, usability, security, maintainability, portability and reusability. The final value is weighted by severity. SQALE provides a configurable rating scale of at least five values, such as from A to E, with the application ranked according to the remediation cost calculated in relation to its development cost [28]. As such, a rating of A might correspond to less than 1% of the development time required to address TD issues. These are the most popular software tools that implement the SQALE method [4]:

- *SonarQube*[4] is the most popular tool to monitor software quality and security. According to [4], its strong points reside in the large number of supported languages as well as its availability as a stand-alone application, cloud-based solution or linter. On the downside, the set of rules associated with its key features differs significantly between analyzed languages; for instance, version 9.5 includes 613 Java rules, 392 C# rules and 196 rules for Python.
- *Squore*[5] was developed for project monitoring analytics. Its main advantages relate to result visualization and the inclusion of rules for compliance against standards such as MISRA or HIS metrics that might be useful for embedded projects.
- *NDepend*[6] is a static analysis tool dedicated to the .NET platform and includes TD estimation. It appears to be the most popular such tool for .NET practitioners [4], it includes a significant set of useful references and is highly customizable and extensible using LINQ queries. Authors of [4] found it to be well represented in both the online as well as academic mediums.

2.3   SonarQube

The SonarQube static analysis platform for code quality and security implements the SQALE method. It is currently the most popular such tool in both the industry as well as academia [4]. The base *"Community"* edition is free & open-source and, according to its developers, currently used within more than 200k companies. The current version provides analysis for 17 languages including C#, Java, JavaScript and Python. Subsequent tiers are paid, but provide additional features such as analysis of additional Git

---

[4] https://www.sonarqube.org/.

[5] https://www.vector.com/int/en/products/products-a-z/software/squore/.

[6] https://www.ndepend.com/.

Table 1. Rule severity characterization according to SonarQube [45].

Severity	Impact	Likelihood	Description	Example
Blocker	✔	✔	Bug with a high probability to impact application behavior in production. Code MUST be immediately fixed	Memory leak, unclosed database connection
Critical	✔	✘	Either a bug with a low probability to impact application behavior in production or a security flaw. The code MUST be immediately reviewed	Empty catch block, SQL injection
Major	✘	✔	Quality flaw which can highly impact developer productivity	Duplicated blocks of code, unused parameters
Minor	✘	✘	Quality flaw which can slightly impact developer productivity	Lines should not be too long, "switch" statements should have at least 3 cases
Info	✘	✘	Neither a bug nor a quality flaw, just a finding	TODO's in code

branches, parallel processing and horizontal scalability. SonarQube can be deployed as a stand-alone server that exposes a web front-end and an API for programmatic access. Alternatively, SonarCloud[7] can be used to analyze public and private source code repositories, while SonarLint[8] is available as an IDE plugin able to analyze source code as it is being written.

Source code analysis is implemented in the form of plugins. Support for additional languages, or additional language rules can be added by developing new plugins, which can be deployed in every version of SonarQube. Rules are specific to a programming language and provide constraints to which source code must conform. When a rule violation is discovered during static analysis, an issue is created. Issues represent source code problems. Each issue has a precise location in the source code and is characterized by information it inherits from its generating rule. This includes the *type*, *severity*, *tags* and *remediation time*. Issues have exactly one of the maintainability, (*code smell*), reliability (*bug*) or security (*vulnerability*) types. Their severity is assigned according to the guidelines in Table 1. Each issue is assigned one or more tags, which provide an additional mean of categorizing issues into areas such as *redundant* (unnecessary code is present) or *performance*. Issue remediation time is estimated using a function defined at the rule level. These are either constant time or they also add a linear offset. For instance, Java rule *java:S3776* states that *"Cognitive Complexity of methods should not be too high"*[9], and generates code smells of critical severity with an estimated remediation time of 5 min, to which 1 min is added for each complexity point exceeding a configurable threshold value.

---

[7] SonarCloud - https://sonarcloud.io/.

[8] SonarLint - https://www.sonarlint.org/.

[9] Java rule documentation is available within a deployed SonarQube instance or online at https://rules.sonarsource.com/java.

Rules can be individually (in)activated and added to quality profiles, which are groupings of active rules that are employed when analyzing a project. For each programming language, SonarQube provides the *SonarWay* default quality profile, which aims to strike a balance between the number and importance of discovered issues. In addition to adding new plugins, users can create and edit quality profiles according to their goals and expectations.

SonarQube defines technical debt as the total estimated remediation time to fix all maintainability issues in accordance with the quality profile used. In our work we follow existing research [23,27] and recent standards [17] and extend this definition to include all detected issues. As such, in the remainder of this paper we refer to technical debt as the estimated remediation time for all issues across the maintainability, reliability and security domains. To account for application size, TD is normalized in the form of the *technical debt ratio*: $TDR = \frac{TechnicalDebt}{DevTime}$. $DevTime$ is the total time required to develop the system, with 30 min estimated to develop 1 line of deployment-ready code. The application is assigned a SQALE rating between A (best, requires $TDR < 5\%$) and E (worst, when $TDR \geq 50\%$).

While SonarQube and similar tools provide quantitative models of software quality, existing research also pointed out some existing pitfalls. Authors of a large-scale case study [38] showed that many of the reported issues remained unfixed, which could be the result of these tools reporting many false-positive, or low-importance results. A study of SonarQube's default rules [23] also showed most of them having limited fault-proneness. These findings are also mirrored in our work [33], where we've shown that issue lifetimes were not correlated with severity or associated tags.

3   Related Work

Within the past decade the topic of technical debt has attracted a lot of interest from the research community, but also from practitioners' awareness in adopting TD estimation and management tools and methods. A lot of effort has been dedicated to TD identification and management. Given the topic of interest for this study, we will refer to contributions to long term TD evaluation, respectively to studies targeting open source software. A systematic literature review performed in [13] provides a good perspective on approaches addressing TD. The study concludes that significant empirical evidences in handling TD is needed and that TD prioritization demands a more systematic approach.

Long term evaluation of technical debt includes cross sectional analysis. An evaluation of the fault proneness of SonarQube rules [23] performed on 21 open source Java projects revealed that only relatively few rules were introducing bugs and most of the detected issues that were tagged as bugs did not generate faults. In [1], the relation between several system characteristics and TD was evaluated in the frame of 91 open source Java projects. Application domain, size and number of releases and commits were found as impacting TD, while other characteristics, namely development decisions, branches and number of contributors did not show a significant relation with TD. A study of long term evaluation of SonarQube TD estimations, metric based estimations and Maintainability Index has been reported in [34]. It showed that SonarQube had the highest accuracy in evaluating the overall technical debt, but metric based methods were more precise in detecting debt hotspots.

Longitudinal approaches to TD also included the study described in [7]. It presents an empirical approach based on surveys and interviews that concluded that on average, almost a quarter of development time was wasted to technical debt and that existing debt often introduced additional TD. In [37], authors presented a longitudinal study of architectural technical debt performed in three steps: measuring TD through coupling metrics and architectural flaws, followed by refactoring of the overall software system, and finally performing a follow-up evaluation of the architectural debt.

In [12], an evaluation of 66 open source projects over 5 years investigated the evolution of technical debt on a weekly basis. It concluded that TD normalized to size was decreasing over time. It also explored which types of technical debt were more frequent and time consuming. A similar approach was presented in [11], tracking TD during the lifespan of 47 open source projects. It proved that TD was a temporal phenomenon and that no correlation was detected with developers' experience or with the number of commits. Both [11, 12] addressed similar research objectives as our study. While the aforementioned studies concentrated on the temporality of debt, our focus on its composition, diffusion and evolution therefore adds a distinct perspective on the longitudinal evaluation of debt.

As mentioned, open source projects have been the focus of several empirical studies targeting technical debt, such as [5, 23, 27, 33, 37], due to access to source code and development history. Compared to cross sectional or limited time longitudinal studies, our approach distinguishes itself by covering the entire lifespan of the target applications.

4   Case Study

The study was planned and carried out in accordance with existing best practices defined for case study research [42, 43]. We also observed the standards for empirical research established by the ACM SIGSOFT [41], as well as existing methodological guidelines targeting longitudinal research [20], to which we refer when appropriate.

Our work continues existing research efforts in the area of source code maintainability [19, 31] and in particular, TD [2, 33, 36, 37]. We provide a description and characterization of source code TD over the target applications' entire lifetime. We extend our existing results [36] by carrying out a detailed analysis regarding TD distribution in source code and the effect refactoring has on its prevalence and characteristics. We contextualize our findings by considering and comparing our results with those from existing literature.

4.1   Research Questions

Our study's main objective was defined in accordance with the goal question metric approach [9] as an *"empirical exploration of source code technical debt with the purpose of understanding its composition, diffusion and evolution over the lifetime of open-source software"*. Next, we operationalize the main objective using the following research questions:

Table 2. Details for the earliest and latest studied version of each application.

Application	Version (Released)	LOC	Packages	Issues (SQALE rating)			TD work days
				Bugs	Vulnerab.	Code Smells	
FreeMind	0.0.3 (July 2000)	2,770	5	11	0 Ⓐ	458	9
	1.1.0Beta2 (Feb 2016)	43,269	31	172 Ⓔ	2 Ⓔ	7,882 Ⓒ	174
jEdit	2.3pre2 (Jan 2000)	22,311	10	69	0 Ⓐ	3,480 Ⓑ	82
	5.6.0 (Sep 2020)	96,912	31	399 Ⓔ	4 Ⓔ	19,241 Ⓐ	296
TuxGuitar	0.1pre (June 2006)	8,960	30	34	2	1,809 Ⓐ	27
	1.5.6 (April 2022)	107,650	244	1,563 Ⓔ	13 Ⓔ	17,781	310

RQ_1: *What are the characteristics of source code technical debt?* The main precursors of TD are time and budgetary constraints that affect technical development [24]; existing research has identified that short-term focus on feature development and failing to address existing issues have a more important effect on the prevalence of debt than software size [33,35,36]. For the sake of clarity, we break RQ_1 down into two subquestions. We use $RQ_{1.1}$ to examine how source code TD is diffused across application releases and packages, while we dedicate $RQ_{1.2}$ to continue our work [36] and examine the composition of debt using our extended ruleset.

$RQ_{1.1}$: *How is technical debt diffused in the application source code?* Research targeting several large systems has shown that the majority of defects were located in a relatively small number of source files [49]. We confirmed this finding in our previous research [36], where over 50% of TD was located in fewer than 20% of the studied application's packages. We continue our investigation in order to cover how maintainability, reliability and security issues are diffused at package and source file levels, and investigate the relation between global and local debt composition.

$RQ_{1.2}$: *What is the composition of source code technical debt?* SonarQube remains the most widely used TD assessment tool both in academia, as well as the industry [3]. It produces detailed and comparable results, that have already been used across multiple studies targeting software quality [15,35,47], TD [5,36,44], as well as to study SonarQube itself [23,27]. With regards to debt composition, existing studies revealed that a small number of SonarQube rules aggregated most of the application's debt [5, 27,33]; in our previous research [33], we've discovered that some of these rules were prevalent in generating issues across many target applications. Through $RQ_{1.2}$ we aim to provide a detailed assessment of TD composition and compare our findings with those reported in the literature.

RQ_2: *How does source code technical debt evolve over the long-term?* Most of the empirical research targeting TD are cross-sectional [5]. Among those which considered a longitudinal approach, they either targeted several consecutive application versions [15,47], or recorded source code snapshots at a given interval [27]. In contrast with most existing research, we carried out our evaluation over the target applications' entire lifetime [33,34,36], ensuring a sufficient number of measurement waves [20]. This view allowed us to carry out an initial long-term characterization of TD and its driving factors [33,36]. In addition, as refactoring remains one of the main solutions proposed for TD [2,30], we aimed to study its effects on the long-term evolution of debt. Therefore, we broke RQ_2 down into two sub-questions, each dedicated to one of the aforementioned aspects.

$RQ_{2.1}$: *How do technical debt characteristics change over an application's lifetime?* Existing research has shown initial versions to have greater variability in debt prevalence and characteristics [36] when compared to mature versions of the same application. Changes to application architecture, as well as prioritizing the implementation of new features lead to developers wasting up to 23% of their time to existing TD, in addition to being forced to add additional debt caused by existing issues. This leads to the *"crisis model"* [30], where application development is paralyzed until sufficient of the existing debt is resolved.

$RQ_{2.2}$: *What is the effect of refactoring on the prevalence and characteristics of technical debt?* Refactoring was reported as the main practice for TD repayment [40], ahead of improved testing and design. A comparison of refactoring strategies applicable in the industry [30] has shown *partial refactoring*, which aims to lessen the number of crisis points and delay them beyond key lifecycle moments as the best long term strategy. Through answering $RQ_{2.2}$ we aimed to investigate the source code locations and issue types developers prioritized when refactoring.

For each of the proposed RQs, we carried out a comparative evaluation both across the target applications, as well as across existing literature. Our goal was to separate trends that were specific to a certain application or study from more general findings which might be indicative of more significant trends.

4.2 Data Collection and Analysis

The present work continues our efforts in exploring and characterizing open-source software technical debt over the long term. The goal is to provide a more detailed evaluation starting from our previous results [33,36], upon which we improve by extending our analysis tools and considering the effects of refactoring on debt prevalence and characteristics. As such, we maintained our selection of target applications [33] to *FreeMind*[10], a popular mind mapping application, *jEdit*[11], a text editor geared towards programmers and *TuxGuitar*[12], a multi-track tablature editor.

We briefly present our inclusion and exclusion criteria here, and refer the interested reader to their detailed description in [33]. Our literature survey revealed a gap in the research pertaining to the long-term evaluation of TD in open-source software. We

---

[10] http://freemind.sourceforge.net/wiki/index.php/Main_Page.

[11] http://jedit.org.

[12] http://www.tuxguitar.com.ar.

found this especially true in the case of GUI-driven applications. As such, we decided to include Java applications that had an established user base together with a long and fully open-source development history. We excluded applications that had complex hardware or software dependencies or those which suffered from long development hiatuses.

The **FreeMind** mind-mapper has a history spanning more than 15 years of active development, which resulted in a large user base and the creation of a rich plugin environment. Its first released version was 0.0.3 and comprised 5 packages and 2,770 lines of code[13]. As shown in Table 2, this is the least complex application version in our study, which is reflected in its functionalities and user experience. Subsequent versions have improved these greatly. Milestone versions 0.8.0 and 1.0 both included important upgrades in terms of user interface and functionality. As shown in Fig. 1, development was interrupted for around $2\frac{1}{2}$ years immediately after the release of version 0.8.0, after which it continued at a steady pace until the most recent version, 1.1.0Beta2. The application has remained popular, having over 25 million downloads over its lifetime, over 496k of those within the last year[14].

jEdit is a mature text editor targeting programmers, and backed by a development history of over 20 years. Its initial public version was 2.3pre2, released in January 2000. Consisting of 10 packages and 22k lines of code, it is the most fully-featured initial application version in our study. It established an application architecture that was used in all subsequent versions. Release history has shown good cadence, as we did not encounter development hiatuses or major code rewrites. The application also provides a plugin environment that developers have taken advantage of[15]. jEdit remains a popular text editor, having over 66k downloads within the last year and over 9.2 million over its lifetime.

The third application in our study is the **TuxGuitar** tablature editor. TuxGuitar can be compiled to work with one of several cross-platform GUI toolkits, including SWT and Qt. Its distribution includes plugins for data input/output and processing, others being available online. For each released version, we employed its default code base and considered these plugins to be part of the application itself. Like in the case of jEdit, the application's initial version established an architecture that was employed in all its future releases. These were mostly incremental in nature, but also included additional plugins, important refactorings and functionality updates. We also identified a development hiatus after the release of version 1.2, after which development continued, the latest version at the time of writing being released in April, 2022. As each plugin is shipped in its own package, TuxGuitar releases have the largest number of packages as well as package-level changes among the studied applications. The earliest release comprised 8,960 lines of code organized in 30 packages; we counted over 350 packages used throughout all the application's versions. With regards to popularity, TuxGuitar has been downloaded 7.3 million times overall, with 210k of these downloads taking place within the last year.

Data collection in existing longitudinal studies was usually carried out at release [5, 18] or commit [23, 26, 49] levels of granularity. Authors of [27] studied source code snapshots taken at 180 days in order to allow for more changes to accumulate. We

---

[13] Metrics calculated via SonarQube 9.5.

[14] Data points recorded on August 2, 2022, from SourceForge.

[15] jEdit plugins - http://plugins.jedit.org/list.php.

chose to include all public releases of the target applications. This allowed us to fully answer the proposed RQs and extend our previous investigation [36]. It also ensured that we observed ACM's standards for empirical research [41] and resulted in sufficient measurement waves [20] to alleviate the threats to our study's validity.

We handled the situation of several preview versions being released over the span of a few days by including only the latest of these versions in our study. This helped keep the number of analyzed versions manageable and resulted in 114 releases, comprised of 38 FreeMind, 46 jEdit and 30 TuxGuitar versions.

Next, we prepared each application version by manually examining and compiling its source code at the appropriate Java compiler level. This was important especially for older application versions, which otherwise would trigger both compile warnings as well as SonarQube issues. For instance, Java 1.3 predates generics, so unless the appropriate compiler level is specified it will raise compile warnings and generate SonarQube issues regarding the usage of raw types (e.g., java:S3740). We separated library code that we found packaged together with application sources into external JAR files that we added to the classpath. This was the case in several jEdit versions, which included source code for the *BeanShell* interpreter and *com.microstar.xml* parser. As previous research has shown that up to a third of open-source software required manual fixes to compile and run correctly [6], we tested each released version's functionalities through their user interface, in order to make sure that each release was code complete.

We refer to application releases using the version numbers assigned by developers. Figure 1 data includes version numbers and release dates; all studied releases remain available for download and can be identified by their version number. Our analysis does not factor in version numbers or hiatuses in development, as these fall outside the scope of our research.

Our previous studies [33,36] were carried out using SonarQube's default quality profile, called *SonarWay*. This profile was defined to provide a good balance between the importance of detected issues without overwhelming first-time users [46]. For the present investigation, we curated an extended ruleset. We started from the 471 rules in the *SonarWay* profile, to which we added an additional 99 of the initially inactive Java rules. We installed the *Code Smells and Anti Patterns detection* (CSAP) SonarQube plugin, and activated 13 of its rules to detect Fowler's architectural issues and code smells [14].

We made sure to inactivate rules pertaining to code formatting and indentation standards, as they vary between projects and even within the same project over the long-term. We also ensured there were no rule duplications; for instance, rules for method and class complexity exist both in SonarQube as well as the CSAP plugin. In these cases, we favoured SonarQube's default implementation and thresholds. The resulting quality profile comprises 583 rules for Java and is included in this paper's open data package [32].

We set up a local instance of SonarQube 9.5 configured for historical analysis. We ensured that analysis data for older application versions was not purged. Applications versions were scanned in chronological order, which allowed SonarQube to identify in which release each issue was created and resolved. We used this information to determine how much TD was new to each version, as shown in Fig. 1. Light-gray vertical bars illustrate the technical debt ratio for each application version, while the darker

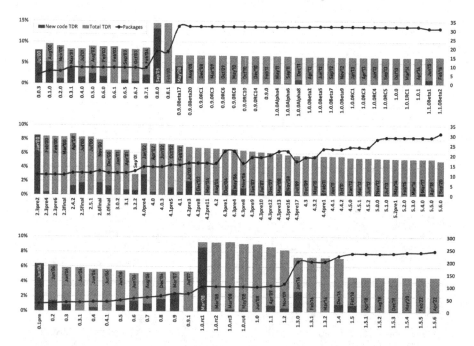

Fig. 1. FreeMind (top), jEdit (middle) and TuxGuitar (bottom) versions. Bars represent each version's technical debt ratio (TDR); darker segment shows the newly added debt to each version (left-side scale). The dotted line represents the number of packages (right-side scale).

shade indicates the debt ratio corresponding to the newly added debt in that version. For each application, all debt was considered new in the first analyzed version. As the debt ratio is normalized for application size, Fig. 1 provides a high-level view of application-level debt across all versions, independent of any application size metrics. We also included the number of application packages, in order to answer $RQ_{1.2}$. More detailed information regarding target application sizes is available in Table 2.

Scanning all application versions using our extended ruleset for Java resulted in 126,895 issues, of which 9,647 were bugs, 117,218 code smells and 30 vulnerabilities. In total, these were estimated to 2,435 work-days of TD. Within our analysis window, 79,928 of these issues were resolved or no longer appeared in newer releases.

Data analysis was carried out in two phases. First, we set up the SonarQube server and scanned each target application version using our curated ruleset. Then, we used a number of Python scripts to extract analysis results using SonarQube's API, which we then further processed. We created an open data package [32] that includes the database files for SonarQube, the rule configuration we employed, the analysis script source code as well as their output.

4.3 Results and Discussion

In this section we detail and discuss our results, organized according to the previously defined research questions.

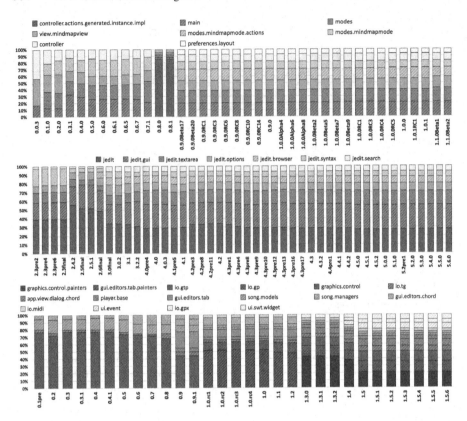

Fig. 2. Per package TD for FreeMind (top), jEdit (middle) and TuxGuitar (bottom). Illustrated values represent 75% of overall debt for FreeMind and jEdit, and 50% for TuxGuitar. Package names shortened for legibility.

RQ_1: *What Are the Characteristics of Source Code Technical Debt?*

We first present our findings regarding the diffusion of TD across application versions and their packages, followed by our analysis of its composition.

$RQ_{1.1}$: *How is technical debt diffused in the application source code?* We use Fig. 1 to illustrate the presence of debt in each application release. We employ the TDR in order to normalize for changes in application size. We observed most application versions received a B rating according to SQALE, which corresponds to a TDR between 5% and 10%. Notable exceptions were the two 0.8.* FreeMind versions, as they accrued significant additional debt, leading to a C rating. In the case of the remaining applications, we identified jEdit 4.0pre4 and TuxGuitar 1.0rc1; both versions accumulated significant additional debt, but remained under 10% debt ratio. While we did not ascribe significance to version numbers, all these versions had in common more complex user interfaces and several new functionalities, which can explain the presence of additional issues.

Next, we examined debt diffusion at package-level in each studied version. Given the large total number of packages, in Fig. 2 we illustrated a representative selection. The full data set is available in our open data package [32]. In the case of FreeMind and jEdit, over 75% of total debt was shared between 8 and 7 packages, respectively. We used Spearman's rank correlation to study the relation between package lines of code and debt. For both FreeMind and jEdit, we confirmed very tight correlation, with $\rho > 0.9, \sigma < 0.1$; detailed data points are available in our open data package [32]. For TuxGuitar, each plugin was deployed in its separate package, which led to a large overall number of packages, as well as package-level changes. As such, the 16 packages represented in Fig. 2 only cover half the total debt in TuxGuitar. Furthermore, in this case we found a more limited, and varying correlation between package lines of code and debt ($\rho \approx 0.68, \sigma \approx 0.21$).

In comparison with our previous work [36], we observed that using a more extensive ruleset revealed additional debt, with most studied versions regressing from an A rating [36] to B. However, the initially identified trends [33,36] have not changed as a result of employing an extended set of rules. This includes the observation that mature application versions tended to have improved TDRs when compared with their earlier counterparts. We also discovered that correlation between package lines of code and TD was maintained in the case of FreeMind and jEdit. In TuxGuitar, extending the ruleset further lowered the reported correlation from its previous value of $\rho \approx 0.835$ [36].

$RQ_{1.2}$: *What is the composition of source code technical debt?* To determine the composition of debt, we examined the reported issues in terms of the rules that generated them. We confirmed the finding of previous studies [23,27,36] that most debt was generated by a small number of rules. For each application, we considered the 10 most prevalent rules according to the remediation time of the generated issues. We illustrate this in Table 3. We first note the degree of overlap, as the 19 rules presented generated more than 50% of each application's overall debt. Three of the rules belong to the CSAP plugin used to identify the "traditional" code smells discussed by Fowler [14].

Regarding their prevalence, each application appeared to have its own "debt profile". For instance, rule *java:S2164* was prevalent in TuxGuitar, but much less so in the other two applications. However, issues such as the use of magic numbers (*java:S109*), redefining polymorphic code using empty methods or classes coupled to many other entities (*java:S1200*) remained prevalent. We took special interest in FreeMind versions 0.8.* due to the sudden spike in TD reported. We discovered it was due to generated code residing in the *freemind.controller.actions.generated.instance.impl* package, and included the use of non-standard variable names, duplicated code, the usage of vendor specific implementations (*sun.** packages in particular) and other issues.

We carried out a comparison with recent empirical results from the literature. A case study targeting 33 projects from the Apache Foundations revealed the 10 most often encountered code smells and bugs [27]. Code duplication, exception handling issues (*java:S1166*) and the presence of non-transient and non-serializable fields in *Serializable* classes (*java:S1948*) are also represented in our results.

Authors of [5] provide the rules that were violated more than 150 times in a selection of open-source projects, of which 6 are also represented in our own study's top 10. These are code duplication (*common-java:DuplicatedBlocks*), higher than allowed

Table 3. Proportion of TD generated by the top 10 rules in each application. Descriptions from SonarQube 9.5.

Rule ID	FreeMind	jEdit	TuxGuitar	Description (area, severity)
java:S2164	0.83%	0.61%	26.14%	Math should not be performed on floats (bug, minor)
java:S109	4.24%	4.35%	16.99%	Magic numbers should not be used (code smell, major)
java:S125	2.22%	15.89%	0.37%	Sections of code should not be commented out (code smell, major)
cs:rpb[a]	5.39%	6.70%	5.05%	A class that redefines inherited method using empty bodies, thus breaking polymorphism (code smell, major)
cj:db[b]	5.97%	1.01%	5.36%	Source files should not have any duplicated blocks (code smell, major)
java:S1200	3.66%	2.97%	4.12%	Classes should not be coupled to too many other classes (code smell, major)
java:S3740	5.21%	1.64%	1.76%	Raw types should not be used (code smell, major)
java:S1948	5.75%	2.52%	0.08%	Fields in a "Serializable" class should either be transient or serializable (code smell, critical)
java:S1213	1.95%	6.32%	0.03%	The members of an interface or class declaration should appear in a predefined order (code smell, minor)
java:S1699	2.60%	3.41%	1.03%	Constructors should only call non-overridable methods (code smell, critical)
java:S3776	1.56%	2.84%	2.24%	Cognitive Complexity of methods should not be too high (code smell, critical)
java:S1149	3.81%	2.54%	0.15%	Synchronized classes Vector, Hashtable, Stack and StringBuffer should not be used (code smell, major)
java:S818	0.09%	0.07%	5.79%	Literal suffixes should be upper case (code smell, minor)
java:S1874	2.26%	2.49%	0.43%	"@Deprecated" code should not be used (code smell, minor)
cs:a[c]	3.29%	1.24%	0.37%	A class that provides mutable class variables, which consequently could be used as global variables (code smell, major)
java:S134	1.02%	1.69%	1.62%	Control flow statements "if", "for", "while", "switch" and "try" should not be nested too deeply (code smell, critical)
java:S2972	1.20%	2.71%	0.40%	Inner classes should not have too many lines of code (code smell, major)
java:S1166	0.93%	0.76%	1.58%	Exception handlers should preserve the original exceptions (code smell, major)
java:S2208	0.09%	2.81%	0%	Wildcard imports should not be used (code smell, critical)
TOTAL	**52.09%**	**62.57%**	**74%**	

[a] code_smells:refused_parent_bequest
[b] common-java:DuplicatedBlocks
[c] code_smells:antisingleton

cognitive complexity (*java:S3776*), the usage of non-transient, non-serializable fields in serializable classes (*java:S1948*), sections of commented code (*java:S125*), the use of synchronized data structures (*java:S1149*) or deprecated code (*java:S1874*). In [23], authors investigated the predictive power of SonarQube issues. While a relation between reported issues and detectable faults could not be ascertained, authors found certain rules to have some predictive power. Among them, *java:S125* appears in Table 3, while *java:S1117* and *java:S1192* generated many issues in our studied applications but were outside the reported top 10.

Ensuring a sound comparison between empirical research efforts is in many cases complex at best. While we found significant overlap between the detected issues across studies, we have to acknowledge that they were carried out on different target applications and used different versions and configurations of SonarQube. For instance, the default SonarWay Java profile includes 471 rules in SonarQube 9.5, while our extended ruleset covers 583 rules. Furthermore, older Sonar versions include fewer rules and it is our experience that analyzing the same project with a newer version will lead to differences in reported results [36]. In addition, we must account for the way debt is reported across different studies. While we measured debt in terms of remediation time, other works [5] relied on counting generated issues. When comparing the results obtained using our extended ruleset with those of the default quality profile [36], we observed a more varied composition of debt; this was especially true when considering the issues generated by the CSAP plugin. As such, we believe that experienced practitioners could start with using an extended SonarQube ruleset, which can then be fine-tuned to keep and further configure those rules that are considered to be fault-prone.

RQ_2: How Does Source Code Technical Debt Evolve over the Long-term?

We first discuss the evolution of TD characteristics over the lifetime of the studied applications, after which we discuss the impact of refactoring on its prevalence and characteristics.

$RQ_{2.1}$: *How do technical debt characteristics change over an application's lifetime?*
In our answer to RQ_1 we analyzed overall application debt. The next step was to study the long-term evolution and characterization of debt across target application releases. We will focus our examination on source code packages and SonarQube rules to describe debt items. The first step was to investigate the existence of a relation between packages lines of code and the presence of debt - do 'large' code packages incur the most debt? We calculated the Spearman rank correlation between debt and package lines of code for each individual package of each application release. We discovered very high correlation in FreeMind ($\rho \approx 0.97, \sigma \approx 0.01$) and jEdit ($\rho \approx 0.96, \sigma \approx 0.08$) and a weaker, and more varying one in TuxGuitar ($\rho \approx 0.68, \sigma \approx 0.21$). These findings remained consistent with those of our previous study [36], where the default Sonar-Way ruleset was employed. It also confirmed previous results showing that code-heavy packages also incurred the majority of an application's debt [35, 49].

We investigated the overall debt composition of each target application within our answer to RQ_1. The next step was to determine whether the observed characteristics were consistent across multiple application releases. To achieve this, for each application release we calculated each source code package's contribution to overall debt.

Then, for each pair of consecutive application releases (e.g., jEdit 5.2.0 and jEdit 5.3.0) we applied Spearman's rank correlation for TD levels across all packages. High correlation shows that the hierarchy of debt-carrying packages was maintained across versions, even when the amount of debt was changed. We obtained high correlation ($\rho > 0.9$) across all consecutive releases, except FreeMind 0.3.1, which was an early application version subject to many code-level changes and TuxGuitar 1.0rc1, where the introduction of new functionalities was mirrored in the additional debt accrued. Both these versions are among those that incurred significant additional debt, as shown in Fig. 1. In contrast, debt diffusion across jEdit packages remained very consistent across all its versions. We ascribe this consistency to the creation of a sound application architecture before its first release, which remained largely unmodified within the application's lifetime.

Figure 1 revealed the existence of several versions that accrued significant additional debt, as well as versions where large swaths of TD were resolved. We note FreeMind version 0.9.0Beta17, where we observed most of the debt originally incurred in version 0.8.0 being resolved, while additional debt was simultaneously added as a result of implementing new application functionalities. In the case of jEdit, we considered version 4.0pre4 to be of interest, as the only jEdit version to incur significant debt. Our manual examination, coupled with running the application revealed it to be an important release that updated the user interface and included additional functionalities related to the management of the text area, buffering and improvements to the document model. This version's increased TDR was heavily influenced by the inclusion of commented code (*java:S125*), an issue that made its appearance in this version and remained prevalent throughout all subsequent ones. Manual code examination revealed the majority of the issues were caused by a jEdit-specific annotation allowing users to group blocks of code, which SonarQube registered as deprecated code. This again shows the importance of examining analysis outputs in detail, as addressing such issues is possible by either updating SonarQube's rule configuration or assigning them a lower severity.

The final step was to drill down to rule level within each package and investigate whether the composition of TD varied within the same package across application releases. We found that in the most part, TD composition remained consistent across multiple application releases. We found such analyses to be difficult to undertake and very effort-consuming, as package deletions and refactoring had to be manually identified. One such example was TuxGuitar package *org.herac.tuxguitar.io.gp*, which carried an important TD load up to version 1.0rc1. At this point, it was refactored into *org.herac.tuxguitar.io.gtp*, as shown in Fig. 2. The new package carried the same amount of debt, but the normalized debt ratio was lower due to additional debt incurred in that version.

To conclude, we observed that debt composition remained stable across most consecutive releases, as well as across these releases' packages. However, we identified versions where significant development efforts, sometimes combined with refactoring led to important changes such as the appearance of a new issue type generating important remediation effort. As such, we believe it is advisable for practitioners to study analysis tool outputs in detail, in order to ensure that the effect of development work remains measurable and that multiple changes do not shadow one another.

$RQ_{2.2}$: *What is the effect of refactoring on the prevalence and characteristics of technical debt?* We aimed to identify which of the versions included in our study were impacted by significant refactoring efforts. We observed that the value of the TDR could be misleading when searching for these versions. For instance, jEdit version 3.2.2 and TuxGuitar 1.3.0 both showed a decreased value for this indicator. However, detailed examination revealed the change was caused by the introduction of additional code; while this code did not contribute additional debt, it skewed the TDR measurement as the same amount of debt was spread out across a larger codebase. Therefore, we used manual source code examination guided by the source code metrics provided by Sonar-Qube to identify versions where refactoring had taken place. We earmarked FreeMind 0.9.0Beta17 and TuxGuitar 1.0rc1 for a more detailed discussion.

In the case of FreeMind 0.9.0Beta17, the refactoring of an entire package of generated code was the main reason for the significant improvement of the TDR. Technical debt decreased from 582 days in FreeMind 0.8.1 to 159 days in version 0.9.0Beta17. However, as shown in Fig. 1, the newer version also introduced its own share of TD. A detailed examination revealed this to be mostly caused by code in packages under *freemind.modes.**, where the new refactored code was introduced. An examination of version 0.9.0Beta17 did not reveal any regression in term of functionalities. Furthermore, our analysis of subsequent versions revealed that 0.9.0Beta17 was the final version to include changes of this scale to the structure of the application.

In the case of TuxGuitar, version 1.3.0 increased application size from 70k to 87k lines of code, with a corresponding increase in TD from 351 days to 386 days. We noted that TuxGuitar versions showed rather good debt management from their earliest versions, with the introduction of additional source code reflected by an increase in TD only for version 1.0rc1. We examined the distribution of debt across application packages in versions 1.2 and 1.3.0. We noted that in both versions, the correlation between package lines of code and the presence of debt was rather weak, with a Spearman rank correlation of $\rho \approx 0.4$. We identified the cause of the change to be refactoring carried out at package level, which resulted in sections of source code being moved across packages. Our answer for $RQ_{2.1}$ described the most important of these updates, which combined moving and refactoring code between two packages. This illustrates one limitation of our analysis tooling, as accurate detection of refactorings that change source code location is a non-trivial issue.

Overall, our analysis confirmed that refactoring remains a successful tool in TD management. It enables not only controlling the amount of technical debt present, but can also assist with controlling the prevalent issue types and their distribution, as long as adequate monitoring tools are in place. We also showed that over-reliance on aggregate measures such as the TDR can be misleading, as a detailed analysis should be carried out regarding the issue types and locations before taking remedial action.

4.4 Threats to Validity

We designed and carried out our study with consideration to the existence of validity threats. As such, we consulted and observed existing best practices for empirical [39] and case study research [20,42]. We repeated the design and planning steps first undertaken in the precursor study: we refined the main objective, we established the extended research questions, we collected, processed and analyzed the application data. In order to encourage extending our study or verifying its conclusions we curated a comprehensive open data package [32].

We addressed *internal threats* by carrying out a manual code examination of all studied versions [36], as well as publishing our analysis code. At each step, we verified our results using SonarQube's web query capabilities. It is our reliance on SonarQube which represents a potential threat, as existing research have pointed out differences between the results obtained when using different tools [18,47]. We corroborated these finding in our own work, as using different SonarQube versions (7.9 [34], 8.2 [35], 9.0.1 [36]) resulted in different debt levels being reported, due to improvements in analysis precision, improved taint as well as improved estimations of remediation time.

In our study, the selection of GUI-driven Java applications, SonarQube and its configuration as analysis tool must be taken into account in order to mitigate *external threats*. Our choice of target applications improves data triangulation as defined in [42] and facilitates cross-application analysis. At the same time, it limits the generalizability of obtained results, as they might not be representative for other system types. We addressed this by placing our work in the context of empirical research results studying various system types.

We mitigated *construct threats* by using the latest version of SonarQube, the most widely used static analysis platform for software quality and security [3]. We used an extended ruleset together with an external plugin and validated that rules did not overlap in scope. One of our study's limitations stems from most release versions being Java 1.8 compliant, which excluded the application of SonarQube rules specifically targeting Java 9 or newer code from our analysis. In addition, several rules showed a partial overlap in scope, such as those measuring cyclomatic and cognitive complexity (*java:S1541* and *java:S3776*, respectively).

Existing research has shown individual rules to lack fault-predicting power, with some rule combinations being more successful in predicting actual software issues [23]. For instance, while rule *java:S2164* generates the most prevalent issue in TuxGuitar, its fault-proneness remains context-dependant. Likewise, we do not expect the use of magic numbers (*java:S109*) or commented-out code (*java:S125*) to be directly linked to software faults.

Finally, restricting our analysis to released versions meant that source code which was not included in release versions remained unrepresented in our study. Other research alleviated this risk using denser measurement waves [23,27,49] that were focused on a shorter time window. As our focus remained long-term debt characterization, we prioritized examining the entire development history over a denser sampling strategy.

5 Conclusions and Future Work

We extended our previous investigation [36] regarding the long-term characterization of TD in three open-source applications. In contrast to our previous work, where we employed the default SonarWay profile, we curated an extended ruleset and included an external plugin for detecting additional code smells. Our current study includes both minimally-viable application versions, as well as fully-developed releases with a significant user base. This allowed us to comprehensively evaluate our results and compare them against those obtained using SonarQube's default rule configuration [5,23,27,33].

We confirmed our previous conclusion that a small number of rules remained responsible for most of the estimated remediation time. Table 3 also showed that some of the rules in the extended configuration were the source of newly added debt. This was the case of the *refused parent bequest* rule, which generated consistent debt across the three studied applications. Other rules that generated significant debt and which deserve additional scrutiny relate to the use of floating point numbers (*java:S2164*), magic numbers (*java:S109*) and tight coupling between a large number of classes (*java:S1200*).

Technical debt levels appeared to fluctuate most in early application versions, which we found to be affected by changes in architecture, source code organization and refactoring. Later application versions showed very good stability, even when analyzed using our extended ruleset. We also noted that the inclusion of more than 100 additional rules in our analysis deteriorated the evaluation of most releases by one step on the SQALE rating, which was most often from *A* [36] to *B*.

We believe that using an extended ruleset augmented with additional plugins can provide further benefits to practitioners. In our case, it revealed issues such as the use of possibly error-prone floating point mathematical operations in TuxGuitar, excessive class coupling and the use of magic number across all three applications. We believe that starting out with an extended ruleset, then subsequently restraining it to focus analysis on those aspects that stakeholders deem important could represent a sound approach when integrating tools such as SonarQube into the development process.

As future plans, we aim to further extend our analysis toolbox to include additional tools and extended configurations. Our goal is to expand our investigation to cover additional systems and system types, in order to enable a more comprehensive study of source code technical debt. We aim to go beyond providing a characterization and attempt to identify the causes behind specific issues as well as discover the existence of a relation between static analysis results and documented software faults.

References

1. Alfayez, R., Alwehaibi, W., Winn, R., Venson, E., Boehm, B.: A systematic literature review of technical debt prioritization. In: Proceedings of the 3rd International Conference on Technical Debt, p. 1–10. Association for Computing Machinery, New York (2020). https://doi.org/10.1145/3387906.3388630
2. Arif, A., Rana, Z.A.: Refactoring of code to remove technical debt and reduce maintenance effort. In: 2020 14th International Conference on Open Source Systems and Technologies (ICOSST), pp. 1–7 (2020). https://doi.org/10.1109/ICOSST51357.2020.9332917
3. Avgeriou, P., et al.: An overview and comparison of technical debt measurement tools. IEEE Softw. **38**, 61–71 (2021). https://doi.org/10.1109/MS.2020.3024958
4. Avgeriou, P.C., et al.: An overview and comparison of technical debt measurement tools. IEEE Softw. **38**(3), 61–71 (2021). https://doi.org/10.1109/MS.2020.3024958
5. Baldassarre, M.T., Lenarduzzi, V., Romano, S., Saarimäki, N.: On the diffuseness of technical debt items and accuracy of remediation time when using SonarQube. Inf. Softw. Technol. **128**, 106377 (2020). https://doi.org/10.1016/j.infsof.2020.106377. https://www.sciencedirect.com/science/article/pii/S0950584919302113

6. Barkmann, H., Lincke, R., Löwe, W.: Quantitative evaluation of software quality metrics in open-source projects. In: 2009 International Conference on Advanced Information Networking and Applications Workshops, pp. 1067–1072, May 2009. https://doi.org/10.1109/WAINA.2009.190

7. Besker, T., Martini, A., Bosch, J.: Technical debt cripples software developer productivity: a longitudinal study on developers' daily software development work. In: Proceedings of the 2018 International Conference on Technical Debt, TechDebt 2018, pp. 105–114. Association for Computing Machinery, New York (2018). https://doi.org/10.1145/3194164.3194178

8. Besker, T., Martini, A., Bosch, J.: Carrot and stick approaches when managing technical debt. In: Proceedings of the 3rd International Conference on Technical Debt, TechDebt 2020, pp. 21–30. Association for Computing Machinery, New York (2020). https://doi.org/10.1145/3387906.3388619

9. Basili, R., Caldiera, G., Rombach, H.D.: The Goal Question Metric approach. In: Encyclopedia of Software Engineering, pp. 528–532 (1994)

10. Curtis, B., Sappidi, J., Szynkarski, A.: Estimating the size, cost, and types of technical debt. In: 2012 3rd International Workshop on Managing Technical Debt (MTD), pp. 49–53 (2012)

11. Digkas, G., Ampatzoglou, A., Chatzigeorgiou, A., Avgeriou, P.: The temporality of technical debt introduction on new code and confounding factors. Softw. Qual. J. **30**(2), 283–305 (2022). https://doi.org/10.1007/s11219-021-09569-8

12. Digkas, G., Lungu, M., Chatzigeorgiou, A., Avgeriou, P.: The evolution of technical debt in the apache ecosystem. In: Lopes, A., de Lemos, R. (eds.) ECSA 2017. LNCS, vol. 10475, pp. 51–66. Springer, Cham (2017). https://doi.org/10.1007/978-3-319-65831-5_4

13. Döhmen, T., Bruntink, M., Ceolin, D., Visser, J.: Towards a benchmark for the maintainability evolution of industrial software systems. In: 2016 Joint Conference of the International Workshop on Software Measurement and the International Conference on Software Process and Product Measurement (IWSM-MENSURA), pp. 11–21 (2016)

14. Fowler, M.: Refactoring: Improving the Design of Existing Code. Addison-Wesley, Boston (1999)

15. Griffith, I., Reimanis, D., Izurieta, C., Codabux, Z., Deo, A., Williams, B.: The correspondence between software quality models and technical debt estimation approaches. In: 2014 6th International Workshop on Managing Technical Debt, pp. 19–26 (2014)

16. Griffith, I., Reimanis, D., Izurieta, C., Codabux, Z., Deo, A., Williams, B.: The correspondence between software quality models and technical debt estimation approaches. In: 2014 6th International Workshop on Managing Technical Debt, pp. 19–26 (2014). https://doi.org/10.1109/MTD.2014.13

17. ISO: ISO/IEC 5055:2021 standard for automated source code quality measures (2021). https://www.iso.org/standard/80623.html

18. Izurieta, C., Griffith, I., Huvaere, C.: An industry perspective to comparing the SQALE and Quamoco software quality models. In: 2017 ACM/IEEE International Symposium on Empirical Software Engineering and Measurement (ESEM), pp. 287–296 (2017)

19. Kapllani, G., Khomyakov, I., Mirgalimova, R., Sillitti, A.: An empirical analysis of the maintainability evolution of open source systems. In: Ivanov, V., Kruglov, A., Masyagin, S., Sillitti, A., Succi, G. (eds.) OSS 2020. IAICT, vol. 582, pp. 78–86. Springer, Cham (2020). https://doi.org/10.1007/978-3-030-47240-5_8

20. Kehr, F., Kowatsch, T.: Quantitative longitudinal research: a review of is literature, and a set of methodological guidelines. In: ECIS 2015 Completed Research Papers (2015). https://aisel.aisnet.org/ecis2015_cr/94

21. Kiuwan. https://www.kiuwan.com/

22. Lefever, J., Cai, Y., Cervantes, H., Kazman, R., Fang, H.: On the lack of consensus among technical debt detection tools, pp. 121–130. IEEE Press (2021). https://doi.org/10.1109/ICSE-SEIP52600.2021.00021

23. Lenarduzzi, V., Lomio, F., Huttunen, H., Taibi, D.: Are SonarQube rules inducing bugs? In: 2020 IEEE 27th International Conference on Software Analysis, Evolution and Reengineering (SANER), pp. 501–511 (2020). https://arxiv.org/abs/1907.00376

24. Lenarduzzi, V., Orava, T., Saarimaki, N., Systa, K., Taibi, D.: An empirical study on technical debt in a Finnish SME. In: 2019 ACM/IEEE International Symposium on Empirical Software Engineering and Measurement (ESEM), pp. 1–6. IEEE Computer Society, Los Alamitos, September 2019. https://doi.ieeecomputersociety.org/10.1109/ESEM.2019.8870169

25. Lenarduzzi, V., Besker, T., Taibi, D., Martini, A., Arcelli Fontana, F.: A systematic literature review on technical debt prioritization: strategies, processes, factors, and tools. J. Syst. Softw. **171**, 110827 (2021). https://doi.org/10.1016/j.jss.2020.110827. https://www.sciencedirect.com/science/article/pii/S016412122030220X

26. Lenarduzzi, V., Saarimäki, N., Taibi, D.: The technical debt dataset. In: 15th Conference on Predictive Models and Data Analytics in Software Engineering, January 2019

27. Lenarduzzi, V., Saarimäki, N., Taibi, D.: Some SonarQube issues have a significant but small effect on faults and changes. A large-scale empirical study. J. Syst. Softw. **170**, 110750 (2020). https://doi.org/10.1016/j.jss.2020.110750. https://www.sciencedirect.com/science/article/pii/S0164121220301734

28. Letouzey, J.L.: The SQALE method for evaluating technical debt. In: Proceedings of the 3rd International Workshop on Managing Technical Debt, MTD 2012, pp. 31–36. IEEE Press (2012). http://dl.acm.org/citation.cfm?id=2666036.2666042

29. Marinescu, R.: Measurement and quality in object oriented design. Ph.D. thesis, Faculty of Automatics and Computer Science, University of Timisoara (2002)

30. Martini, A., Bosch, J., Chaudron, M.: Investigating architectural technical debt accumulation and refactoring over time. Inf. Softw. Technol. **67**(C), 237–253 (2015). https://doi.org/10.1016/j.infsof.2015.07.005

31. Molnar, A., Motogna, S.: Discovering maintainability changes in large software systems. In: Proceedings of the 27th International Workshop on Software Measurement and 12th International Conference on Software Process and Product Measurement, IWSM Mensura 2017, pp. 88–93. ACM, New York (2017). https://doi.org/10.1145/3143434.3143447. http://doi.acm.org/10.1145/3143434.3143447

32. Molnar, A.J.: Open Data Package for Chapter "An Exploration of Technical Debt Over the Lifetime of Open-Source Software", August 2022. https://doi.org/10.6084/m9.figshare.20553186.v2

33. Molnar, A.J., Motogna, S.: Long-term evaluation of technical debt in open-source software. In: Proceedings of the 14th ACM/IEEE International Symposium on Empirical Software Engineering and Measurement (ESEM), ESEM 2020. Association for Computing Machinery, New York (2020). https://doi.org/10.1145/3382494.3410673

34. Molnar, A., Motogna, S.: Longitudinal evaluation of open-source software maintainability. In: Proceedings of the 15th International Conference on Evaluation of Novel Approaches to Software Engineering (ENASE), pp. 120–131. INSTICC, SciTePress (2020)

35. Molnar, A.-J., Motogna, S.: A study of maintainability in evolving open-source software. In: Ali, R., Kaindl, H., Maciaszek, L.A. (eds.) ENASE 2020. CCIS, vol. 1375, pp. 261–282. Springer, Cham (2021). https://doi.org/10.1007/978-3-030-70006-5_11

36. Molnar., A., Motogna., S.: Characterizing technical debt in evolving open-source software. In: Proceedings of the 17th International Conference on Evaluation of Novel Approaches to Software Engineering - ENASE, pp. 174–185. INSTICC, SciTePress (2022). https://doi.org/10.5220/0011073600003176

37. Nayebi, M., et al.: A longitudinal study of identifying and paying down architecture debt. In: Proceedings of the 41st International Conference on Software Engineering: Software Engineering in Practice, ICSE-SEIP 2019, pp. 171–180. IEEE Press (2019). https://doi.org/10.1109/ICSE-SEIP.2019.00026

38. Nugroho, A., Visser, J., Kuipers, T.: An empirical model of technical debt and interest. In: Proceedings of the 2nd Workshop on Managing Technical Debt, MTD 2011, pp. 1–8 (2011)

39. Ralph, P. (ed.): ACM SIGSOFT empirical standards for software engineering research, version 0.2.0 (2021). https://github.com/acmsigsoft/EmpiricalStandards

40. Pérez, B., et al.: What are the practices used by software practitioners on technical debt payment: results from an international family of surveys. In: Proceedings of the 3rd International Conference on Technical Debt, TechDebt 2020, pp. 103–112. Association for Computing Machinery, New York (2020). https://doi.org/10.1145/3387906.3388632

41. Ralph, P.: ACM SIGSOFT empirical standards released. SIGSOFT Softw. Eng. Notes **46**(1), 19 (2021). https://doi.org/10.1145/3437479.3437483

42. Runeson, P., Höst, M.: Guidelines for conducting and reporting case study research in software engineering. Empir. Softw. Eng. **14**, 131–164 (2008)

43. Runeson, P., Host, M., Rainer, A., Regnell, B.: Case Study Research in Software Engineering: Guidelines and Examples, 1st edn. Wiley (2012)

44. Sjøberg, D.I., Anda, B., Mockus, A.: Questioning software maintenance metrics: a comparative case study. In: Proceedings of the ACM-IEEE International Symposium on Empirical Software Engineering and Measurement, ESEM 2012, pp. 107–110. ACM (2012). http://doi.acm.org/10.1145/2372251.2372269

45. SonarSource: SonarQube platform user guide (2020). https://docs.sonarqube.org/latest/user-guide/issues

46. SonarSource discussion forum: Why are so many rules inactive by default? (2019). https://community.sonarsource.com/t/why-are-so-many-rules-inactive-by-default/12957/2

47. Strečanský, P., Chren, S., Rossi, B.: Comparing maintainability index, SIG method, and SQALE for technical debt identification. In: Proceedings of the 35th Annual ACM Symposium on Applied Computing. p. 121–124, SAC 2020. Association for Computing Machinery, New York (2020). https://doi.org/10.1145/3341105.3374079

48. Verdecchia, R., Malavolta, I., Lago, P.: Architectural technical debt identification: the research landscape. In: Proceedings of the 2018 International Conference on Technical Debt TechDebt 2018, pp. 11–20. Association for Computing Machinery, New York (2018). https://doi.org/10.1145/3194164.3194176

49. Walkinshaw, N., Minku, L.: Are 20% of files responsible for 80% of defects? In: Proceedings of the 12th ACM/IEEE International Symposium on Empirical Software Engineering and Measurement, ESEM 2018, pp. 1–10. Association for Computing Machinery, New York (2018). https://doi.org/10.1145/3239235.3239244

50. Ward, C.: The WyCash portfolio management system. SIGPLAN OOPS Mess. **4**(2), 29–30 (1992)

A New Metric for Multithreaded Parallel Programs Overhead Time Prediction

Virginia Niculescu$^{(\boxtimes)}$ ⓘ, Camelia Şerban ⓘ, and Andreea Vescan ⓘ

Faculty of Mathematics and Computer Science, Babeş -Bolyai University,
Cluj-Napoca, Romania
{virginia.niculescu,camelia.serban,andreea.vescan}@ubbcluj.ro
https://www.cs.ubbcluj.ro/

Abstract. The paper proposes a metric that evaluates the overhead introduced into parallel programs by the additional operations that parallelism implicitly imposes. We consider the case of multithreaded parallel programs that follows SPMD (Single Program Multiple Data) model. Java programs were considered for this proposal, but the metric could be easily adapted for any multithreading supporting imperative language. The metric is defined as a combination of several atomic metrics considering various synchronisation mechanisms that could be discovered using the source code analysis. A theoretical validation of this metric is presented, and an empirical evaluation of several use cases. Additionally, we propose an Artificial Intelligence based strategy to refine the evaluation of the metric by obtaining approximation for the weights that are used in combining the considered atomic metrics. The methodology of the approach is statistical using the multiple linear regression, which considers as dependent variable the execution times of different concrete use-cases, and as independent variables the corresponding overhead times introduced by the considered synchronization mechanisms, which are approximated through the atomic metrics. The results indicated a high degree of correlation between the dependent and independent variables. The Root Mean Square Error obtained is 0.155186, thus being very small, the predicted and observed values are very close.

Keywords: Parallel programming · Metrics · Overhead · Multithreading · Synchronization · Estimation · Multiple linear regression

1 Introduction

When we refer to parallel programming, we could think that by doubling the hardware resources, the execution time would be reduced to the half. Usually this doesn't happen because parallelism also involves some additional costs, that are in general refer to as the overhead time. In addition to the inherent serial part problem pointed out by Amdahl's Law [1], parallel computing is also limited by the overhead costs such as: starting threads/processes, handling and termination costs, synchronization problems – task coordination, cost of communication between multiple tasks (threads/processes), overhead cost of some software libraries , parallel compilers or interpreters and supporting OS. In order to improve the parallel programs performance, an accurate quantification of these overheads is needed.

© The Author(s), under exclusive license to Springer Nature Switzerland AG 2023
H. Kaindl et al. (Eds.): ENASE 2022, CCIS 1829, pp. 315–336, 2023.
https://doi.org/10.1007/978-3-031-36597-3_15

For multithreaded parallel programs the communication costs between the threads are eliminated but they are compensated by the additional synchronization costs.

One of the models that are widely used in parallel programming is the SPMD (Single Program, Multiple Data) model. SPMD programming model [8] is characterized by the fact that all the processes/threads execute a copy of the same program on different data. The differentiation between the execution on each processing element (thread/process) can be done based on the ID of each process/thread. This facilitates the design and the construction of a parallel program that consists, in this case, of a single code running on all processing elements. It can also be used for module/component development not only for an entire application.

The overhead time (T_O) is estimated, in general, as being the difference between the product of the parallel time (T_p) with the number of processing elements (p), and the sequential time (T_s):

$$T_O = p * T_p - T_s \tag{1}$$

This is a very general evaluation and it is difficult to be used in the design stage of the development.

For a certain class of parallel programs – as SPMD on shared memory platforms – written in a particular language (as Java) – where we know the specific synchronization mechanisms that could be used, we may estimate more accurately the overhead time. We propose in this paper such a model for SPMD multithreaded Java programs, based on a synchronization overhead metric. Programs written in Java language are considered for this proposal, but because synchronization mechanisms are similar no matter what language is used for their implementation, it could be easily adapted for any multithreading supporting imperative language.

This paper represents an extension of a preliminary study published in a research paper [14] presented at the conference ENASE'2022, where we proposed a model for overhead evaluation based on a metric defined as an aggregation of several atomic metrics related to various synchronization mechanisms. For the proposed metric a theoretic validation by using Weyuker's metric properties [13, 18] has been proven. Initially, an empirical approach for weights approximation was performed. That approach for weights determination came up with some shortcomings that we aim to address here by offering a new method based on statistical analysis applied on performance evaluation on a series of executions.

Thus, the new contributions of this paper are the following:

– an new improved definition of the metric, which is a combined metric constructed based on several atomic metrics that are related to various synchronization mechanisms.
– an empirical evaluation of the metric, based on concrete experiments executed on different machines and with different Java versions for several implementation variants of the same problem,
– a statistical evaluation of the weights used for aggregating the specific atomic metrics; this is based on using the multiple linear regression that considers as dependent variable the execution times of six implementation variants of the same problem

(the *reduce* operation) for different values of the input size, and as independent variables the corresponding overhead times introduced by the considered synchronization mechanisms, which are approximated through the atomic metrics.

Regarding the usability of the proposed metric we could mention the possibility to estimate the overhead time at the design stage, compare different design solutions for a given problem, or estimate the need for refactorization.

The paper is structured as follows. Section 2 discusses related work regarding theoretical validation of software metrics, and also existing tools proposed for performance assessment in concurrent programs. Section 3 describes the main synchronization mechanisms in Java, while the definition of the new metric is given in Sect. 4, together with its theoretical validation. The empirical analysis of the metric for several use-cases is presented in Section 5. Section 6 describes the process of weights evaluation using the statistical approach. The conclusions and further work are emphasized in the last section.

2   Related Work

This section briefly describes, on one hand, existing approaches regarding both theoretical and empirical validation of software metrics and, on the other, different existing tools for performance evaluation in multithreaded programs.

Evaluation of Software Metrics - Various Criteria. Measures and ways of measuring in Software Engineering (SE) domain are different from that of other engineering domains. In comparison with measuring the length of an engineering product, measuring the size of a software, such as program length, is not so easy and there are few formal approaches that rigorously apply software measures. Thus, only describing in natural language what a code line means, it is not clear, whether blank lines, irrelevant lines, comment lines etc., should be considered or not. Thus, a formal definition and validation is needed.

Formal approaches in SE are usually based on different types of metrics that are used in order to quantify those aspects that are considered important for the assessment. Many researchers [2, 3, 18, 19] contributed to lay a foundation for measuring software, both for metrics definition and metrics validation. There are basically two categories of techniques for metrics' validation: *the empirical validation* which confirms the metrics actual applicability, and *the analytical evaluation* defined based on definite measurement theories.

Even if the empirical validation is the most dominant of these two techniques, prior to the empirical validation (i.e., applying to industry), every metric has to be analytically evaluated to confirm that it has scientific foundation, and it was defined based on definite measurement theories.

Tools for Performance Evaluation. Software performance is in many cases increased by implying parallel and concurrent computation. In order to make effective the development of such programs, the developers have come to expect tools that are able to augment the design and execution infrastructure with different capabilities such as design assistance, performance evaluation, debugging or execution control. There is quite a large set of tools like these, and further on we will mention just a few that were proposed for multithreaded programming, and which are related to the overhead time.

Tmon, a tool for monitoring, analyzing and tuning the performance of multithreaded programs was proposed by Minwen, Ji et al. in [11]. The tool relies on two measures performed at the run-time of the program; it uses thread waiting time and constructs thread waiting graphs to show thread dependencies and thus performance bottlenecks, and it identifies semi-busy-waiting points where CPU cycles are wasted in condition checking and context switching. The evaluation is based on measurements performed at the run-time of the program.

A static analysis tool called *Iceberg* [16] was proposed in order to identify performance bugs in concurrent Java programs. Detecting a performance bugs is not an easy task because of its nature of being infrequent, transient, and hard to reproduce. The focus of this tool is on identifying critical sections with high variability in their latency: in most cases they execute fast, but occasionally they stall, holding a lock for an unusually long time, and preventing other threads from making progress. Iceberg tool was improved in order to perform a dynamic analysis of Java programs [17], too. This new feature could help for gathering data about the variability of the performance of critical sections in code.

A tool that automatically detects the inefficiency intervals representing time periods when a concurrent application is not using all its capabilities of the parallel system was proposed in [6]. The tool uses a monitorization scheme and aims to release users from analyzing the huge quantity of performance information generated for the execution of an application. The automatic tool analyses in the trace files the inefficiency intervals found that represent time periods when the application is not using all the capabilities of the parallel system.

Another lock profiler designed in the context of a new metric, critical section pressure, is proposed in paper [5]. There are several applications serving as testing environment for this tool, the results showing that it can detect phases where a lock hinders the threads process with scenarios that would otherwise not necessarily be tested by developers.

In relation to the existing approaches our proposed metric can be used early in the development life-cycle, when the system design is known, to predict the overhead added by the parallelism. In this way, the design could be improved by choosing the most appropriate synchronization mechanisms. As far as we know there are no references in literature regarding such a metric.

3   Synchronization Mechanisms in Java

In order to evaluate the overhead brought through synchronization we will consider the following synchronization mechanisms:

- critical sections
  - using `Locks`
  - using `synchronized` methods and blocks
- conditional waiting

- using `wait`/`notify` calls
- using `Condition` variables and the corresponding `await`/`signal` calls
- barriers - using `CyclicBarrier`
- 'rendez-vous' mechanisms using `Exchanger`

A *lock* is a synchronization mechanism for enforcing the access limitation to a resource in an execution environment where there are many threads of execution. A lock is designed to enforce a mutual exclusion concurrency control policy [7,15]. In Java, `Lock` class provides implementation for this mechanism [9].

Synchronized methods and blocks in Java are implemented based on the association of each object to a monitor [9], and they are mechanisms for defining critical sections. A *monitor* is an abstract concept (data structure) construct that controls access to shared data. A monitor encapsulates: shared data structures, procedures that operate on the shared data structures, and synchronization between concurrent procedure invocations. In case of Java we may consider that the encapsulated data are the object attributes, and by defining `synchronized` methods we may define the procedures (methods) that should be called based on mutual exclusion [7,9,15]. Monitors could also include conditional synchronization; Java provides only one condition queue per monitor using the corresponding `wait`/`notify` methods.

Mutual exclusion could be enforced in Java parallel programs also by using synchronized methods or blocks, which define procedures of the monitor associated to each Java object.

Synchronization conditions (also known as condition queues or condition variables) provide a means for one thread to suspend execution (to "wait") until notified by another thread when some state condition arrives to be true. Because access to the shared state information occurs in different threads, it must be protected, and so introduced into a critical section. The correspondent Java implementation is the class `Condition`, and its instances should always be associated with a lock [9].

A *barrier* is a synchronization method that forces a group of threads or processes to stop at the point of the barrier, and not proceed until all other threads/processes reach this barrier. A Java `CyclicBarrier` object is an object that implements a barrier, which can be used (reused) cyclically - in multiple points of the program execution. The method `await` is used to specify the synchronization points [7,9,15].

The Java `Exchanger` [9] class implements the "rendez-vous" concept, which specifies a two-way synchronization and communication between two threads or processes: if one thread arrives to the rendez-vous point it waits for the other to arrive and then they exchange information [7,15].

There are also many other synchronization mechanisms and an example worth to be mentioned is the semaphore. A *semaphore* [7,15] is a synchronization construct that is typically used to coordinate the access of multiple threads/processes to resources. It also has a Java implementation – class *Semaphore* [9]. We don't consider them in this paper because usually they are not used in SPMD type of programs. Also, working with atomic variable is very fast but there are important constraints related to what operations we can do with them.

Details about other synchronization mechanisms could be found in [7,9,15].

As noticed, critical sections could be obtained through multiple mechanisms: - e.g. locks, synchronized blocks.

Synchronization mechanisms are obviously necessary in order to write correct mutithreading programs. But, in general, a problem could have different solutions based on different synchronisation mechanisms. So, an important question is: Do their choice influence the program performance? Theoretically, we may assume that the answer is affirmative, and also from some simple experiments we noticed that there are some differences.

4 Overhead Metric

As we specified in the Introduction, the overhead time is usually estimated using the formula given in Eq. 1. This formula treats the overhead globally, without emphasizing details about the mechanisms (synchronization, communications, etc.) that determine this overhead.

We propose a model to approximate the overhead of SPMD Java programs by using a metric defined based on the different characteristics of the synchronization mechanisms.

4.1 Java SPMD Programs

In order to evaluate the overhead brought by the synchronization we will consider the synchronization mechanisms:

  i) *barriers* - using `CyclicBarrier`;
 ii) *conditional waiting* - using `wait`/`notify` calls or using `Condition` variables and the corresponding `await`/`signal` calls;
iii) *rendez-vous* mechanisms using `Exchanger`;
 iv) *critical sections* – using `synchronized` methods and blocks, or using `Locks` together with their methods `lock` and `unlock`.

We consider SPMD programs formed of three parts: threads creation, starting all the threads using the same code/program (in Java the function `run()`), and joining all threads.

Combining two such programs P1 and P2 into a new program

$$P3 = P1 + P2$$

means that the P3 program is obtained by sequentially combing the two running functions

$$run_{P3} = run_{P1} \; ; \; run_{P2}$$

In addition, we also consider that into a program we don't have adjacent critical sections – if they are then they will be merged into one. This is considered an implicit preprocessing optimisation operation of the source code.

4.2 Metric Definition

The proposed overhead metric is an aggregated metric, which is based on atomic metrics that corresponds to the synchronization mechanisms described in Sect. 3.

In a multithreaded Java program of SPMD type, all the threads execute the same program – specified by the run() function. The differentiation between the threads execution is specified using conditional instructions that that are based on the ID of the threads.

The overhead time T_O can be estimated based on a synchronization metric O by using the following definitions:

$$O : \mathbb{P} \to \mathbb{R}, \quad T_O : \mathbb{P} \times \mathbb{S} \to \mathbb{R},$$

$\mathbb{P}$ is the set of all SPMD Java programs and
$\mathbb{S}$ is the set of all execution systems $\qquad$ (2)

$$T_O(P, S) = t_S * [w_{th\_manag} * p + O(P)], P \in \mathbb{P}, S \in \mathbb{S}$$

where

- $P = (P_1, P_2, ..., P_p)$, $P_i : 0 \le i < p$ represents the finite set of threads defined inside a SPMD program;
- t_S represents a time that depends on the performance of the execution system, the number of processors of the system (c_{proc}), and on the threads per cores ratio ($c_{load} = \frac{\#threads}{\#cores}$));
- w_{th_manag} = the weight for managing the threads.

The threads management time includes the time for creating and destroying the threads, but also the time for scheduling the threads for execution on the hardware components (cores). This cannot be ignored even if the main intended purpose of calculating the metric is to optimize the program by using different synchronisation mechanisms.

We have

$$
\begin{aligned}
O(P) = \\
w_{bar} * p * (\#bar) & * f(dis) + \\
w_{wait} * (\#wait) & / f(dis) + \\
w_{cond} * (\#await) & / f(dis) + \\
w_{ex} * (\#ex) & / f(dis) + \\
w_{sync} * \delta(p) * \left(\sum_{i=1}^{\#sync} cs_i \right) & / f(dis) + \\
w_{lock} * \delta(p) * \left(\sum_{i=1}^{\#lock} cs_i \right) & / f(dis)
\end{aligned}
\tag{3}
$$

where:

- $\#bar$ and w_{bar} – the number of synchronization barriers based on the calls of await through CyclicBarriers, and the corresponding weight.
- $\#wait$ and w_{wait} – the total number of calls of wait method of Object, and the corresponding weight.
- $\#await$ and w_{cond} – the total number of await operations called through a Condition variable, and the corresponding weight.
- $\#ex$ and w_{ex} – the total number of exchange operations executed through an Exchanger, and the corresponding weight.

- #*sync* and w_{sync} – the number of critical sections specified with synchronized blocks or methods, and the corresponding weight.
- #*lock* and w_{lock} – the number of critical sections specified with Lock objects and lock, and unlock methods, and the corresponding weight.
- cs_i – the size of a critical section (#i) – this is expressed in number of statements.
- $\delta(p)$ – a function that evaluates the delay introduced by a critical section: since only one thread could execute such a section, all the others have to wait; still the number of threads that could really be executed in parallel depends on the hardware and operating system characteristics.
- dis – a measure of the dissimilarity between the threads estimated as:

$$dis = \frac{\#conditional\_statements}{\#total\_statements}$$

- $f(dis) = (1 + dis)$ – a calibration function; a barrier is delayed when dis is increasing, but all the other synchronization mechanisms are favored in this case.

In general, a high level of loading (c_{load}) increases the execution time, and this is why the entire overhead time depends on this. If the system has a certain number of cores – #*cores* – the operating system should use them to allow all the p threads to be executed using in general a round robin scheduling policy. This general dependency and delay is included into the t_s time.

For the barrier execution if the level of loading is low, the probability that all the threads arrive at almost the same time at the barrier point is very high, and vice-versa if the loading is high it is very probable there are differences between the moments of time when the threads arrive at the barrier point. Also, if the dissimilarity between the threads is high, then the probability of threads arriving at the barrier at different moments in time is also higher. This is why in the overhead metric formula the atomic metric of the barriers' synchronization overhead should be multiplied by the calibration function.

For the critical sections we have the opposite situation: it is desirable that the threads arrive to critical sections at different times, and high level of dissimilarity increase this probability. So, this atomic metric is divided by the calibration function. In addition, the function δ evaluates the delay introduced by a critical section. Theoretically if all the threads would be executed in parallel the value of the function δ should be equal to the number of threads (p). Still, usually the system has a number of cores lower that the number of threads, then the number of threads that could really be executed in parallel depends in a much higher degree on the number of cores.

For the conditional waiting, the dissimilarity should be present in order to assure that a thread satisfies the condition expected by other(s). When we use Condition and wait-notify for conditional synchronization, we need to use them inside the critical sections; the overhead due to these critical sections is included into the corresponding weights w_{wait} and w_{cond}.

4.3 Theoretical Validation of the Metric

Among numerous metric validation criteria that exist in the literature, as we have mentioned them in the Sect. 2, Weyuker's properties are most extensively used for evaluating software metrics; they are guiding tools for identifying good and complete metrics [18].

Property 1: Non-coarseness. $(\exists)$ $(P1)$, $(P2)$ two distinct programs from $\mathbb{P}$ such that $O(P1) \neq O(P2)$.

This is trivially fulfilled by O metric due to the fact that is not defined as a constant map.

Property 2: Granularity. It states that there will be a finite number of cases for which the metric value will be the same.

It is considered that this property is met by any metric measured at the program level, because the universe deals with at most a finite set of programs and so the set of those programs having the same value for the proposed metric is also finite [4].

Property3: Non-uniqueness (Notion of Equivalence). $(\exists)$ $(P1)$, $(P2)$ two distinct programs from $\mathbb{P}$ such that $O(P1) = O(P2)$.

We may consider two programs that each update a variable (based on some formulas) inside a critical section; for the first program we may use with `synchronized` and for the second `Lock`. The values for w_{sync} and w_{lock} could be different but by chosen the sizes m and n of the two critical sections correspondingly, we arrive to the same value for the metric. It is possible to find n and m such that

$$m * w_{sync} = n * w_{lock}, \left(\frac{n}{m} = \frac{w_{sync}}{w_{lock}} \right).$$

Property 4: Design Details Are Important. This property states that, in determining the metric for an artifact, its design details also matters. When we consider the designs of two programs $P1$ and $P2$, which are the same in functionality, does not imply that $O(P1) = O(P2)$.

In our case, we have different means to achieve similar things; for example we have `synchronized` and `locks` for critical sections, and `Object:wait-notify` and `Condition:await-signal` for conditional synchronization.

Property 5: Monotonicity. It states that a component of a program is always simpler than the whole program. For all $(P1)$, $(P2) \in \mathbb{P}$ either $O(P1) \leq O(P1 + P2)$ or $O(P2) \leq O(P1 + P2)$ should hold.

Our metric is defined as a summation of atomic metrics and based on the combing operation we have $O(P1 + P2)$ is bigger or equal than $O(P1)$ or $O(P2)$.

Property 6: Non-Equivalence of Interaction. If $P1$, $P2$ and $P3$ are three programs having the property that $O(P1) = O(P2)$ does not imply that $O(P1 + P3) = O(P2 + P3)$. This suggests that the interaction between $P1$ and $P3$ may differ from that of $P2$ and $P3$.

If the P1 program ends with a critical section, and P2 doesn't end with a critical section, while P3 starts with a critical section, then for $P1 + P3$ the two corresponding critical sections will be implicitly merged, and this reduces the overhead. Then $O(P1 + P3) < O(P2 + P3)$.

Property 7: Permutation. It states that permutation of elements within the program being measured may change the metric value. Being given a program $P1$ that is transformed into a program $P2$ by permuting the order of the statements such that the provided functionalities are preserved, the property states that $O(P1) \neq O(P2)$.

Considering a parallel program $P1$ that defines a critical section (defined through synchronized) that contains n statements, but not all the n statements need mutual exclusion, we can transformed it to obtain $P2$ by moving one of these statements out of the critical section; this way the functionality is preserved and the overhead metric is reduced because the size of the critical section is reduced. For the initial variant we have $O(P1) = w_{sync} * n$ and for the second we have $O(P2) = w_{sync} * (n - 1)$

Property 8: Renaming Property. When the name of the measured artifact changes, the metric should not change. That is, if program $P2$ is obtained by renaming program $P1$ then $O(P1) = O(P2)$.

As the proposed metric is measured at the program level and, it does not depend on the name of the program nor on the name of its classes, methods and instance variables (through which the synchronization mechanisms are implemented) it also satisfies this property.

Property 9: Interaction Increases Complexity. It states that when two programs are combined, interaction between them can increase the metric value. When two programs $P1$ and $P2$ are considered $O(P1) + O(P2) \leq O(P1 + P2)$.

In general for the proposed metric we have that $O(P1) + O(P3) = O(P2 + P3)$ (based on the combining operations).

Hence, the proposed metric has a solid theoretical foundation and can be utilized for the purpose of overhead estimation of SPMD programs.

5 Applications and Experiments

In order to arrive to an empirical validation and to emphasize how the metric could be used we have considered as a use-case a problem that could be solved using several variants, each of these using different synchronization mechanisms.

5.1 The *reduce* Problem with Its Different Solutions

The considered problem is the so called *reduce* operation:

– for a given list of elements and an associative operator defined on the type of the elements we have:

$$reduce(\oplus)[a_0, a_1, \ldots, a_{n-1}] = e_0 \oplus a_1 \oplus \cdots \oplus a_{n-1}$$

If the elements are real numbers and the operator is the addition operator, *reduce* operation computes the sum of all given real numbers. The sequential computation requires n operations when applied on a list of n numbers.

An efficient parallel computation is based on a "tree-like" computation that is derived from the recursive definition of the *reduce* function:

$$reduce(\oplus)[e] = e$$
$$reduce(\oplus)[p|q] = reduce(\oplus)[p] \oplus reduce(\oplus)[q]$$

where | is the concatenation operator.

An example is illustrated in the Fig. 1[1].

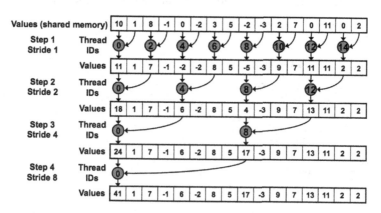

Fig. 1. The computation of the sum by using tree-like computation [10].

As it can be seen in the Fig. 1 the program creates a number of threads equal to the number of elements – n, and the computation is done in $k = \log_2 n$ steps. At each step the threads with an ID divisible with the *stride* $*$ 2 will add to its corresponding element $a[ID]$ the value on the position equal to $ID - stride$. In order to obtain the correct answer is mandatory that this operation to be executed only after the value on the position $ID - stride$ was already updated in the previous step. The threads' execution is done theoretically completely in parallel but the execution of operations executed by different threads is non deterministic (i.e. implicitly not all the threads execute the operations on one level in the same time). In order to impose this synchronization different mechanisms could be used and they lead to 4 variants: with a `barrier` after each level, or with synchronization between pairs that need to exchange information using `wait-notify`, `Condition`, or `Exchange`. For these variants we present some code snippet just to facilitate their understanding[2]. Each of these 4 variants uses a `for` loop with $k = log(n)$ iterations, that represent the levels into the tree computation.

V1 `Barrier`

A barrier is used after iteration in the `for` lop which represents a level in the tree of execution. The associated code snippet if shown in Listing 1.

---

[1] source https://docs.nvidia.com/cuda/samples/6_Advanced/reduction/doc/reduction.pdf.

[2] The complete code could be accessed at the following URL: "shorturl.at/bjlmT".

```
1  for(int j=0;j<k;j++){
2      p*=2;
3      if ((i%p  == 0)&& (i+p/2 < n)){ a[i].add(a[i+p/2]);}
4      barrier.await();
5  }
```

Listing 1. Code snippet for V1.

V2 `synchronized + wait`

At each level there are pairs of threads: thread i and thread $i - p$ (p represents here the stride) that needs to synchronize one to another through `wait-notify` mechanism.

```
1   for(int j=0;j<k;j++){
2       p*=2;
3       if (i%p == 0){
4           synchronized(a[i]){
5               if (i+p/2<n){
6                   while (cond[i+p/2]<j)
7                       try {   a[i].wait();}
8                       catch [...]
9                   a[i].add(a[i+p/2]);
10              }
11              cond[i]++;
12          }
13      if(i>=p )
14          synchronized(a[i-p]){   a[i-p].notify();}
15      }
16  }
```

Listing 2. Code snippet for V2.

The thread i should use the value of thread $i - p$ only after this one finished previous update. All these pairs are disjunctive, and at each step the number of pairs that need to synchronize in pairs decreases by 2. The associated code snippet if shown in Listing 2.

V3 `locks + await from Condition`

This variant is very similar to the variant V2, but instead of `synchronized` and the methods `wait` and `notify`, n variables of type `Condition` are used together with their methods `await` and `signal`.

V4 `Exchanger`

At each level there are pairs of threads that needs to synchronize one to another and this could also be done through an `Exchanger`. All these pairs are disjunctive, and the stride between them is doubled at each iteration. The associated code snippet if shown in Listing 3.

We consider also the multithreaded variants that are directly derived from the sequential algorithm; in this case the numbers are distributed through the threads and each updates of the sum variable with its own value inside a critical section. Obviously, it is not an efficient approach since the computations is still done sequentially due to the critical sections. These variants are considered in order to allow the evaluation of the critical sections overhead, too.

```
1   for(int j=0;j<k;j++){
2       if (i% p2 == 0 && i+p < n)   {
3               ANumber tmp = ex[i+p].exchange(a);
4               a.add(tmp);
5           }
6       else if   ( i% p2 != 0 && i% p == 0 && i-p >= 0)
7                           ex[i].exchange(a);
8       p = p2; p2 = p2*2;
9   }
```

Listing 3. Code snippet for V4.

V5 Critical sections with `synchronized`
Each thread with an ID greater than 0 will add its value to the value stored into the thread with the ID=0.

```
1       synchronized (a[0]){
2           a[0].add(a[i]);
3       }
```

Listing 4. Code snippet for V5.

V6 Critical sections with `Lock`
This variant is similar to the previous one, but instead of using `synchronized`, a variable of type `Lock` is used and the methods `lock` and `unlock`.

5.2   Experiments Execution

Our replication strategy considers experiments with the presented implementation variants of reduction operation executed on different computation systems and with different Java versions.

Experiments on Systems with Different Computation Power. For the first experiments we have considered two systems – (**C1, C2**) – the first is a powerful system that have 4 processors each with 8 logical core, and the second is a system with only one processor with 4 cores, both running Java 8. These first set of experiments were reported also in the previous paper [14].

The detailed characteristics of two systems are the following :

C1 – an x3750 M4 machine, with 4 processors Intel Xeon E5-4610 v2 @ 2.30 GHz CPUs, 8 cores per CPU with hyperthreading, running Java 8 (CentOS 7).
C2 – a computer with 1 processor Intel(R) Core(TM) i7-7500U CPU @ 2.50 GHz, 4 Core(s) with hyperthreading, running Java 8 (macOS).

Due to stochastic nature of the programs' execution, they must be repeated several times in order to mitigate against the effect of random variation. We have used in our evaluation 10 executions and we took their average.

In order to analysis the execution time and emphasizes the differences obtained on the two computation systems we plot the execution times for $n = 32$ on each of the two

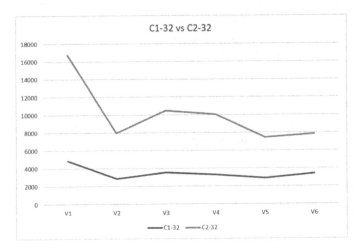

Fig. 2. The execution time for n = 32 on both C1 and C2 machines (from [14]).

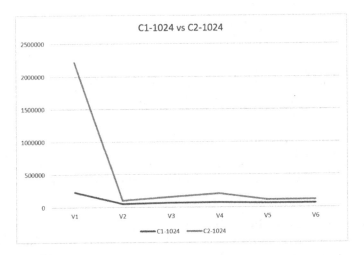

Fig. 3. The execution time for n = 1024 on both C1 and C2 machines (from [14]).

systems in Fig. 2, and separately, for the case when $n = 1024$, in Fig. 3. The execution time is expressed in microseconds.

It can be noticed that the barrier variants for all the cases lead to the highest values of the execution times.

From the general analysis of the results we may conclude that the performance of the variants follow in general the same curve but the system loading given by the number of threads over the number of cores ratio influences the differences between them.

The execution time depends on the effective computation and on the total overhead. The time corresponding to the addition of the numbers is very small in comparison with the total execution time, since additions could be executed very fast (the parallelization of the reduction operation is very efficient when the associative operator is a more computationally costly operator). In these condition it is correct to say that a

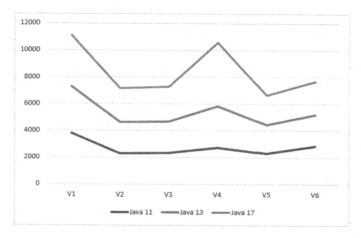

Fig. 4. The execution time for n = 32 on C3 machine with different Java versions.

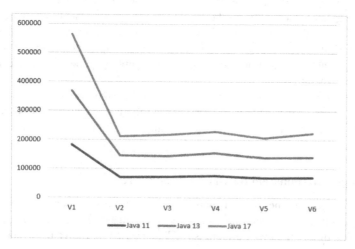

Fig. 5. The execution time for n = 1024 on C3 machine with different Java versions.

comparison of the execution times gives us comparison of the impact of using different synchronisation mechanisms.

Experiments with Different Versions of Java JDK. In order to see if the impact of the overhead introduced by different synchronization mechanisms depends on the Java version, we have conducted also some experiments for the same use case of the *reduce* problem on the following variants of Java JDK: 11, 13 and 17. For this evaluation we have used another computation system [**C3**] with the following characteristics: processor: Intel(R) Core(TM) i7-10510U CPU @2.30 GHz RAM: 16.0 GB, OS: Win10 64-bit operating system, disk: SSD 500 GB.

For each of these three Java versions we tested the six implementation variants of the *reduce* problem for two size of the input: $n = 32$ and $n = 1024$. The obtained execution times are plotted in Fig. 4 for $n = 32$ and in Figure 5 for $n = 1024$. The execution time is expressed in microseconds.

Analysing the results we can conclude that although there are differences in the range of the execution times for the three considered versions of Java, the graphs of these execution times follows approximately the same curve, translated on the vertical axis.

Also, it can be noticed that for $n = 32$ the differences between the different variants $(V1 - V6)$ are greater than for $n = 1024$; the differences are fading as the number of threads and the system loading are increasing.

6   Overhead Metric's Weights Evaluation

The evaluation of the weights is not an easy task, but it is important since depending on the value of the weights we may estimate which variant could be better, depending on the number of threads and the system loading.

In our previous work [14] we proposed an empirical approach in order to determine the weights coefficients from the Eq. 3. This empirical strategy was based on the execution time for all previously specified variants of the *reduce* problem, on different arrays' size. That approach came up with some shortcomings that we aim to address by offering a new method based on statistical analysis applied on performance evaluation on a series of executions.

The strategy that we followed in order to approximate the weights is based on linear regression analysis. This method fits very well in the context of the proposed metric because the equation itself that defines it is a linear combination of weights and variables.

6.1   Weights Determination Based on Linear Regression

This section describes the applied method that we have used for Overhead Metric weights determination, i.e. the linear regression statistical method. In regression analysis, the value of an unknown variable is predicted based on the value of one or more known variables.

Linear regression (LG) [12] is a statistical technique and establishes a linear (i.e., straight-line) relationship between variables.

In case of multivariate linear regression, the linear regression is based on an equation with the following form:

$$Y = \beta_0 + \beta_1 X_1 + \beta_2 X_2 + \dots + \beta_m X_m \tag{4}$$

where $X_i, 0 < i < m$ are the independent variable, $\beta_i, 0 \leq i < m$ are coefficients, and Y is the dependent variable.

Having this into account we formalize out the problem of weights determination for the proposed metric as a linear regression problem:

$$\begin{aligned} T = c_0 &+ w_{th\_manag} X_{th\_manag} + \\ &w_{bar} X_{bar} + w_{wait} X_{wait} + w_{cond} X_{cond} + w_{ex} X_{ex} + \\ &w_{synch} X_{synch} + w_{lock} X_{lock} \end{aligned} \tag{5}$$

where T is the dependent variable obtained from the running time execution as $T = T_{execution}/t_s$, and the independent variables, X_{th_manag}, X_{bar}, X_{wait}, X_{cond}, X_{ex}, X_{synch}, X_{lock}, are defined based on the overhead metric formula:

- $X_{th\_manag} = p$
- $X_{bar} = p * (\#bar) * f(dis)$
- $X_{wait} = \#wait/f(dis)$
- $X_{cond} = \#await/f(dis)$
- $X_{ex} = \#ex/f(dis)$
- $X_{synch} = \delta(p) * \left(\sum_{i=1}^{\#sync} cs_i \right) / f(dis)$
- $X_{lock} = \delta(p) * \left(\sum_{i=1}^{\#lock} cs_i \right) / f(dis)$

The coefficients of the independent variables are the weights of our proposed metric.

6.2 Dataset Construction

In order to arrive to a reasonable number of observations from which to obtain a data sets for applying the linear regression, we have conducted several concrete experiments using all the six variants of the *reduce* problem presented in the previous section.

Table 1. The execution time of all 6 variants for different values for n. The execution time was computed in nanoseconds.

	32	64	128	256	512	1024	2048	4096	8192
Barrier	1869749	3485860	7029780	13687530	31982910	71170929	187189410	554105110	2549920870
Wait-Notify	1173699	2348630	4259560	8852670	17674430	36092540	75535010	143362280	285114950
Condition	1367780	2350329	4423790	9503150	18825850	37256720	72437890	145124620	287862170
Exchanger	1598130	3113500	5475450	11298870	21505350	38788390	78376940	149477620	304151610
Critical - Synchronized	1182140	2146350	4259550	8805520	17327649	38113190	68676240	140794870	280081110
Critical Lock	1709660	2371529	4214850	8810649	17519199	35372750	70773870	138860980	279472690

The executions were done for different values of n – the number to be added (which for these cases it is also equal to the number of the created threads $n = p$); nine values for n were considered: $n = 2^4, 2^5, 2^6, 2^7, 2^8, 2^9, 2^{10}, 2^{11}, 2^{12}$. All these experiments were done on the same system – C3 machine.

In this way we obtain $6 \times 9 = 54$ records for which we have the concrete execution times.

All the executions were done on the system C3, and the results in execution time terms are specified in Table 1.

In addition, for each variant of the *reduce* problem, we have computed the dependent variables, from their formulas and based on a source code analysis.

V1 Barrier

– a barrier is used after each level in the tree execution;

$$\begin{aligned} \#bar &= \log_2 n = k \\ DIS &= k/(3k) = 0.33 \\ \Rightarrow X_{bar} &= n * log(n) * 1.33 \end{aligned}$$

V2 `synchronized + wait`
At each level there are pairs of threads that need to synchronize one to another through `wait-notify` mechanism. All these pairs are disjunctive, and at each step the number of pairs that need to synchronize in pairs decreases by 2.

$$
\begin{aligned}
\#wait &= \textstyle\sum_{i=1}^{\log_2 n} n/2^i = n \\
DIS &= 2k/(5k) = 0.4 \\
\Rightarrow X_{wait} &= n/1.4
\end{aligned}
$$

V3 `locks + await from Condition`
At each level there are pairs of threads that needs to synchronize one to another through conditional variables. (Similar to variant V2.)

$$
\begin{aligned}
\#cond &= \textstyle\sum_{i=1}^{\log_2 n} n/2^i = n \\
DIS &= 2k/5k = 0.4 \\
\Rightarrow X_{cond} &= n/1.4
\end{aligned}
$$

V4 `Exchanger`
At each level there are pairs of threads that need to synchronize one to another through an `Exchanger`. All these pairs are disjunctive.

$$
\begin{aligned}
\#ex &= \textstyle\sum_{i=1}^{\log_2 n} n/2^i = n \\
DIS &= 2k/(5k) = 0.4 \\
\Rightarrow X_{ex} &= n/1.4
\end{aligned}
$$

V5 Critical section with `synchronized`
There is one critical section of size 1.

$$
\begin{aligned}
\#sync &= 1;\ cs_i = 1 \\
DIS &= 0 \\
\Rightarrow X_{sync} &= \delta(p)
\end{aligned}
$$

V6 Critical section with `Lock`
There is one critical section of size 1.

$$
\begin{aligned}
\#lock &= 1;\ cs_i = 1 \\
DIS &= 0 \\
\Rightarrow X_{lock} &= \delta(p)
\end{aligned}
$$

For the thread management, the variable X_{th_manag} is equal to p – the number of threads, and for our implementation variants $n = p$.

As a result, we were able to obtain concrete values for the independent variables for each of the concrete values of n.

To estimate the value of the dependent variable T for each of the considered cases, we have used $t_s = c_{load}/log(c_{load})$; the reason for this choice was given by the fact that the system is slow-down by the threads per cores ratio but still not in a direct linear dependency, but based on a function with lower slope.

Similarly, the function δ was approximated to $\delta(p) = (n/c_{load})log(n)$. In this case the number of cores ($\#cores = n/c_{load}$) specifies the maximum level of real parallelism (that for critical section should be reduced to 1) but this is still influenced, even in a low measure, by the number of threads – $p = n$.

These choices were based on a detailed empirical analysis of the execution behavior, but they represents just an approximation of it.

6.3   Results of Linear Regression Analysis

This section outlines the obtained results by applying linear regression to estimate the coefficient values of X_{thread}, X_{lock}, X_{synch}, X_{bar}, X_{ex}, X_{cond}, and X_{wait} from by Eq. 5.

The obtained model has the correlation between the dependent and independent variables provided by R value, 0.988, indicating a high degree of correlation. R-square shows the total variation for the dependent variable that could be explained by the independent variables. A value greater than 0.5 shows that the model is effective enough to determine the relationship. In our case, the value 0.97528 is very good. This R-square value indicates that 97.51% of the variance in time execution scores can be predicted from the independent variables.

The Adjusted R-square shows the generalization of the results i.e. the variation of the sample results from the population in multiple regression. The obtained Adjust R^2 for our model is 0.975281, indicating that how much of the total variation in the dependent variable can be explained by the independent variables. In this case, 97.52% can be explained, which is very large. The Standard Error of the Estimate, also called the Root Mean Square Error (RMSE), is the standard deviation of the error term, and is the square root of the Mean Square Residual. RMSE is a quadratic scoring rule that also measures the average magnitude of the error. The lower this RMSE value is, the better the model is in its predictions. If you have a smaller value, this means that predicted values are close to observed values. In our case, the value is 0.155186, thus being very small, the predicted and observed values are very close.

The ANOVA analysis determines whether the model is significant enough to determine the outcome. Analyzing how well the regression equation fits the data (i.e., predicts the dependent variable), it is detected that the obtained p value (0.000) is less than 0.05. Thus, overall, the regression model statistically significantly predicts the outcome variable (i.e., it is a good fit for the data).

Finally, the obtained multiple regression equation is as stated in Eq. 6.

$$T = -0.038 + 0.135 * X_{thread} + 0.854 * X_{bar} + 0.022 * X_{wait} +$$
$$0.023 * X_{cond} + 0.032 * X_{ex} + 0.022 * X_{synch} + 0.022 * X_{lock} \tag{6}$$

From these we may extract a general approximation of the overhead metric as being:

$$
\begin{aligned}
O(P) = \\
0.854 * p * (\#bar) \qquad & * f(dis) + \\
0.022 * (\#wait) \qquad & / f(dis) + \\
0.023 * (\#await) \qquad & / f(dis) + \\
0.032 * (\#ex) \qquad & / f(dis) + \\
0.022 * \delta(p) * \left(\sum_{i=1}^{\#sync} cs_i \right) & / f(dis) + \\
0.022 * \delta(p) * \left(\sum_{i=1}^{\#lock} cs_i \right) & / f(dis)
\end{aligned}
\tag{7}
$$

where the notations are those used in Eq. 3.

This result confirms the estimation performed through the empirical analysis that emphasized that using conditional synchronization using the `Object` methods `wait` and `notify` inside critical section defined based on each object monitor (that is, with `synchronised`) is more efficient than using `Condition` variables, and the fact that `Exchange` is a more costing alternative for conditional synchronization. As expected, the barriers are very expensive and for critical sections the difference between using `synchronized` or `Lock` is not so important.

In addition, from Eq. 7 we may conclude that the overhead due to thread management cannot be neglected, but at the same time it cannot be avoided.

7   Conclusions

When writing parallel programs, an important goal is to reduce the overhead time, which in many cases is responsible for reducing the advantage of parallel computation.

In order to balance the advantages and disadvantages of writing parallel programs, we proposed a metric that estimates the overhead time for multithreaded Java SPMD parallel programs; the Java programming language was considered here, but the metric can be easily adapted for other languages as the synchronization mechanisms are similar in most of the implementation languages.

The proposed metric corresponds to a proper definition of a software metric, and we provided a theoretical validation using Weyuker's properties.

The proposed metric is an aggregated one, composed of atomic metrics that correspond to several synchronization mechanisms. In order to have an accurate evaluation of the overhead, it is very important to estimate very well the weights included into the metric.

A first evaluation of the aggregated metric was performed based on different implementation variants of the *reduce* operation; the results proved to be promising since their empirical validation experiments on different systems provide similar results. For a proper empirical validation, this should be improved, and so, we conducted a statistical evaluation of the weights used in the aggregation of the specific atomic metrics. This approach was based on a multiple linear regression that considers as the dependent variable the execution time of different implementation variants of the *reduce* operation, and as independent variables the overhead times introduced by the considered synchronization mechanisms, which are approximated through the atomic metrics.

There are several usability cases that could be emphasized for the proposed metric:

- estimate the overhead time at the development stage;
- compare different design solutions for a given problem, and choose the most optimal from the overhead point of view;
- estimate the need for refactorization of a given program by evaluating the improvements that could be achieved by changing the design method or only by changing the synchronization mechanisms.

References

1. Amdahl, G.M.: Validity of the single processor approach to achieving large scale computing capabilities. In: AFIPS Computer Conference, pp. 483–485 (1967)
2. Kitchenham, B., Fenton, N.: Towards a framework for software measurement validation. IEEE Trans. Softw. Eng. **21**(12), 929–943 (1995)
3. Briand, L.C., EK, S.M.: On the application of measurement theory in software engineering. Tech. rep., ISER Technical Report (1995)
4. Chidamber, S., Kemerer, C.: A metric suite for object- oriented design. IEEE Trans. Softw. Eng. **20**(6), 476–493 (1994)
5. David, F., Thomas, G., Lawall, J., Muller, G.: Continuously measuring critical section pressure with the free-lunch profiler. SIGPLAN Not. **49**(10), 291–307 (2014)
6. Espinosa, A., Margalef, T., Luque, E.: Automatic performance evaluation of parallel programs. In: Euromicro Workshop on Parallel and Distributed Processing, pp. 43–49 (1998)
7. Garg, V.K.: Concurrent and Distributed Computing in Java. John Wiley fsSons Inc, USA (2004)
8. Grama, A., Gupta, A., Karypis, G., Kumar, V.: Introduction to Parallel Computing, Second Edition. Addison-Wesley (2003)
9. Göetz, B., Peierls, T., Bloch, J., Bowbeer, J., Holmes, D., Lea, D.: Task execution. Java Concurr. Pract, 113–134. Addison Wesley Professional (2006)
10. Harris, M.: Optimizing Parallel Reduction in CUDA. https://docs.nvidia.com/cuda/. Accessed 25 Jan 2022
11. Ji, M., Felten, E.W., Li, K.: Performance measurements for multithreaded programs. In: ACM SIGMETRICS Joint IC on Measurement and Modeling of Computer Systems, pp. 161–170. ACM (1998)
12. Lederer, J.: Tuning-Parameter calibration. In: Fundamentals of High-Dimensional Statistics. STS, pp. 109–137. Springer, Cham (2022). https://doi.org/10.1007/978-3-030-73792-4_4
13. Misra, S., Akman, I.: Applicability of Weyuker's properties on OO metrics: some misunderstandings. Comput. Sci. Inf. Syst. **5**(1), 17–23 (2008)
14. Niculescu., V., Şerban., C., Vescan., A.: Towards an overhead estimation model for multithreaded parallel programs. In: Proceedings of the 17th International Conference on Evaluation of Novel Approaches to Software Engineering - ENASE, pp. 502–509. INSTICC, SciTePress (2022). https://doi.org/10.5220/0011083400003176
15. Raynal, M.: Concurrent Programming: Algorithms, Principles, and Foundations. Springer-Verlag, Berlin Heidelberg (2013)
16. Shah, M.D., Guyer, S.Z.: Iceberg: a tool for static analysis of java critical sections. In: ACM SIGPLAN International Workshop on State Of the Art in Program Analysis, pp. 7–12. ACM (2016)
17. Shah, M.D., Guyer, S.Z.: Iceberg: Dynamic analysis of java synchronized methods for investigating runtime performance variability. In: ISSTA/ECOOP Workshops, pp. 119–124. ACM (2018)

18. Weyuker, E.: Evaluating software complexity measure. IEEE Trans. Softw. Eng. **14**(9), 1357–1365 (1988)
19. Zuse, H.: On Weyuker's axioms for software complexity measures. Softw. Qual. J. **1**(4), 225–260 (1992)

Author Index

H. Kaindl et al. (Eds.): ENASE 2022, CCIS 1829, pp. 337–338, 2023.
https://doi.org/10.1007/978-3-031-36597-3

Printed in the United States
by Baker & Taylor Publisher Services